Remind
Me to
Tell You

Dear Dan —

Thank you for your
friendship and kindness
in 2012.

I hope my book proves
to be a valuable read.

John

Xmas 12

"Remind Me to Tell You"

*A History of
Major Harry J. Fleeger
& His Friends, POWs
of the Japanese*

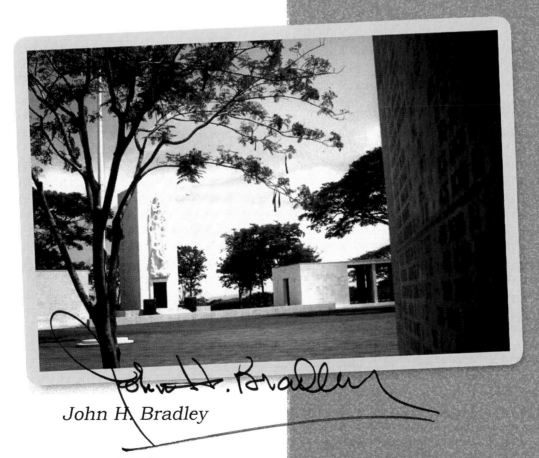

John H. Bradley

Ω Ω Ω
ReutelPress
Houston

First published in December 2010.

Other publications

Bradley, John H. (Jack A. Dice, Contributing Author). *The Second World War, Asia and the Pacific.*

Krasnaborski, Edward (John H. Bradley, Contributing Author). *Atlas for The Second World War, Asia and the Pacific.*

Bradley, John H. *West Point and the Hudson Highland during the American Revolution.*

Sanders, Harry C., Jr. and John H. Bradley. *Pearl Harbor Changed My Life, A Memoir.*

Cover and interior design: Desiree Terry, 3inonedesign

Production assistant: Penny Leas

Printed in Texas by Americas-Press.

Published by **Reutel Press**
14027 Memorial Drive, Box 189
Houston, TX 77079
713-827-0504

Email:
reutelpress@aol.com
outpro@aol.com

ISBN Number: 978-0-578-07176-3

1. POWs of the Japanese 2. Luzon and Bataan Campaigns 3. POW Ships 4. 26th Cavalry Regiment (Philippine Scouts)

The Last Stand

I was with the Filipinos
And we had backed into Bataan.
Came the last day of fighting,
And a shell had laid me low;
Then I heard the lines were breaking.
So I waited for the blow.

While bleeding in the bamboo
With my fever running high.
A horse pulled up from nowhere
With a funny-looking guy
That swung from off his saddle,
Then dropped the bridle down,
And walked into the thicket
Where I was tossing on the ground.

The horseman was a picture,
With long and golden hair,
Tall and blond complexioned,
He bore a martial air.
His boots were high and heavy-spurred;
His gauntlets full and wide;
Two pistols and a cavalry sword
Hung loosely by his side.

"Ah, the Twenty-Sixth!" I shouted.
"Is the cavalry up the way?"
The horseman smiled and shook his head,
And then I heard him say:
"The Little Big Horn, Corregidor, Dunkirk or Bataan —
Garry and I will forever ride
Where brave men make their stand.

Charles Brown (POW), *Bars from Bilibid Prison*, 1947

9 Jan 45
Enoura Maru
In Takao Harbor

24 Oct 44
Arisan Maru
At sea nearing
Formosa

15 Dec 44
Oryoku Maru
In Subic Bay

17 Sep 44
Shinyo Maru
Off Mindanao coast

POW Ship Sinkings

DEDICATED TO JIM FLEEGER

&

MY CLASSMATES
BOB JULIAN
ROY KIRKPATRICK (DECEASED)
BUTCH SAINT
GERRY SCHURTZ

&

JAMES WILLIAM DUNMYER, USMA 1962
JOHN BROADUS LEWIS, USMA 1951

WHO LOST THEIR FATHERS ON POW SHIPS

AND

FOLLOWED THEM INTO THE UNITED STATES ARMY
AND HAD DISTINGUISHED CAREERS
IN PEACE AND WAR

Acknowledgments

Many friends and associates helped make this book possible.

My wife Ann helped me the most by reading and proofing the manuscript and making many suggestions to improve it, especially when I dealt with organization and numbers. She said this was an important story that should be published.

Two new friends contributed unsparingly to the publication of this book. Penny Leas read and proof read the manuscript, provided many valuable editing suggestions, and ensured that the final manuscript was ready for printing. Desiree Terry volunteered her time to prepare the covers and the introductory pages for each chapter. She also suggested innovative ways to improve the format. In addition, Desiree worked to make the maps and illustrations more attractive and then worked with Penny Leas to prepare the final manuscript for printing. Both believed that the story needed to be told, and for that I am deeply grateful.

Tom McCann of Commonwealth Films in Boston, an inspiring author, film writer, and producer, reviewed the manuscript and encouraged me to go forward and publish it. His wife, Joan, said the story reminded her of "walking through the Vietnam Memorial."[1]

Professor Ralph Weber, a distinguished historian with family connections to this era - his wife and her mother were civilian POWs of the Japanese and his wife's father died on a POW ship - also reviewed the manuscript and provided many valuable suggestions.

World War II infantry officer, Herbert Goodman, and his wife, Mary, gave unstinting support. Herb went out of his way to send copies of the manuscript to people he thought would support its publication.

My friend, the late Captain Bob Morrison, USN-Retired, a submariner with deep interest in the Pacific War, added useful comments. So did his wife, author Susan Keyes Morrison, a classmate at the American School in Manila and at La Jolla High School in California.

Two other friends – Nina Alford, an award-winning American History teacher, and Nancy Huebsch Rosasco, another respected classmate from La Jolla High School - read the manuscript and provided many useful suggestions.

Retired Army Lieutenant Colonel John Lewis gave me a copy of an unpublished manuscript that covered some of the actions of 26th Cavalry officers who fought in the Visayas and on Mindanao. He also loaned me an invaluable book about U. S. chaplains who served in the Philippines and in the POW camps. These sources provided vital information for the book.

Dwight Beach, another friend, gave me access to his family's papers concerning his uncle who died on a POW ship. Moreover, he promised to buy many books to give to his family in remembrance of his uncle. My kind of guy.

Lastly, my thanks to Jim Fleeger for providing me with his dad's diaries and letters and associated family papers and photographs.

I deeply appreciate all the comments made to improve the manuscript and all the assistance given to get this book published.

Contents

Appendices

Note

_____

[1] Telephone conversation with Thomas McCann, 6 August 2008.

Prologue

Captain Fleeger near his quarters at Ft. Stotsenburg on Luzon

Jim Fleeger has been a friend for many years in Houston. Early in our friendship, Jim told me that his father, Major Harry Fleeger, had served with the 26th Cavalry on Bataan, had survived the Bataan Death March, had been imprisoned in Camp O'Donnell and Cabanatuan, and had been lost on a Prisoner of War (POW) ship. I was interested because my dad had been killed in a civilian POW camp and several of my friends had lost their fathers or other male relatives while they were POWs. Also, over the years I had met some of the survivors: General Harold K. Johnson, Colonel Melvin Rosen, and Colonel Morris Shoss, and had the privilege of serving under and becoming a lifelong friend of Lt. General Thomas J. H. Trapnell.

A few years ago, Jim mentioned that he had his dad's diaries from Cabanatuan and asked if I would like to see them. I jumped at the chance. Jim said that someone had looked at the diaries years ago and planned to write a book, but nothing ever materialized. After I had a chance to read them, I thought that something could be done with the diaries even though there was no real narrative in them because Major Fleeger had just written brief notes about events and people. When Jim gave me some remaining letters from his dad, and some other materials, I found more information that enhanced the story embedded in the diaries.

ΩΩΩ

Jim's dad and his comrades experienced cruelties and depravations that most Americans cannot imagine. They saw the Japanese decimate their units and groups in combat. They saw the Japanese beat, kill, murder, and execute POWs. They watched comrades starve to death in prison camps, as they also starved. They saw sick men die in "zero wards" because of Japanese indifference and the lack of food, water, and rudimentary medicine. They saw the Japanese bury wounded and sick prisoners of war alive. They saw the Japanese deliberately let wounded soldiers die on POW ships because they would not provide any medical help and saw the Japanese let wounded and sick prisoners freeze to death on them. Moreover, those who survived often suffered many of the atrocities that killed their friends. And many who survived faced their greatest shock after they returned to the United States and discovered that their families and friends did not believe their stories about life as POWs.

NEARLY ALL THE SURVIVORS ARE GONE NOW, SO OTHERS MUST TELL THEIR STORIES.

Nearly all the survivors are gone now, so others must tell their stories. Only two people Harry Fleeger mentioned in his letters and diaries still live - his wife, over 100 years of age, and his son, Jim, now in his seventies.

Fleeger's beloved Louise remarried, has been widowed a second time, and now lives [2010] in an assisted living facility in Houston, Texas under the watchful eyes of her son and his wife.

Research and Writing

Writing this story has taken over three years. At first, I expected to finish in about a year, but then the detective work grew as I tried to identify and learn something about the cavalry officers and Fleeger's friends. I used the website of the American Battle Monuments Commission (ABMC), an invaluable source, to identify the cavalry officers and the other POWs who perished in the war, and to find out whether the U. S. Government recovered their remains and buried them in the American Military Cemetery in Manila, or just memorialized them there on the Tablets of the Missing. With one or two exceptions, the Battle Monuments Commission identified all the dead among the officers and soldiers mentioned in this book. The ABMC also has listed the casualties by units, and in many cases that information proved useful.

I found the National Archives (NARA) Website to be an invaluable source to identify POWs who survived, to find additional information about many POWs, and to discover information about those POWs who perished but are not buried in Manila or identified on the Tablets of the Missing. The NARA Website also provided information about POWs held in different POW camps in the Philippines, Formosa, Japan, Korea, and Manchuria, but listed the names randomly, making it more difficult to find specific individuals.

I examined the available POW rosters for five Japanese POW ships, the *Shinyo Maru, Arisan Maru, Oryoku Maru, Enoura Maru,* and *Brazil Maru,* and the camp rosters for Cabanatuan, Bilibid, Davao, Formosa, Jinsen, Mukden, and other Japanese camps to find or confirm POW survivors and to discover any unidentified casualties.

At this time, I cannot confirm the death of one cavalry officer or determine what happened to two POW-soldiers Major Fleeger mentioned in his Diaries.

To gain information about the actions of the cavalry officers and the soldiers, I checked numerous POW histories, autobiographies, biographies, articles, and web sites. I also gained access to three unpublished POW diaries and extracts of two more, obtained a copy of an unpublished memoir by a veteran of the fighting on Mindanao, and have an original manuscript for a published memoir. I found important details about West Point graduates whom Fleeger mentioned in his letters and diaries in the *Cullum Files* of the Association of Graduates of the United States Military Academy. They often added important details that are not found elsewhere.

I annotated some key publications in the Selected Bibliography.

Unfortunately, I missed opportunities to gain more insightful information because I did not begin my research many years ago when key people were alive and alert. Mrs. Fleeger is now infirm. General Trapnell never talked much about his experiences before his death. Brigadier General Bradford Chynoweth focused on current military matters rather than World War II when I corresponded with him years ago. I never pursued interviews with Colonel Rosen and Colonel Shoss, both of whom could have added to the general POW story, if not the Fleeger story. Consequently, I have relied on the published oral histories of many of the veterans for some of the more unique commentaries.

I HAVE ADDED MYRIAD FOOTNOTES, INCLUDING ONES REFERRING TO FLEEGER'S TYPED DIARY.

I have done several things to enhance the story. To maintain historical accuracy, I have not manufactured dialogue as I believe it a disingenuous way to make a book more modern or readable and doing so warps history. Also, to maintain historical accuracy and in many cases to add information about people and events, I have added myriad footnotes, including ones referring to Fleeger's typed diary. To clarify, codify, and present special information, I have added several appendices that deal with the officers and soldiers mentioned in the book. To emphasize parts of the story, I have used photographs and newspaper clippings to highlight chapters because they add to the story in each chapter. I have included selected photographs of Harry Fleeger and his family in order to enhance the historical record for the day. There are photos of the American Cemetery in Manila where so many of the soldiers in this story are memorialized and where some are buried. One photo shows a panel of the Tablets of the Missing; another shows one of the many rows of the missing that exist in the cemetery; and another shows a large white cross that marks each grave of the fallen soldiers. Most likely, some of the soldiers and POWs killed on Luzon and Bataan found their final resting place under one of the white crosses marked "unknown."

Take-Aways

A highly successful and insightful business friend always asked at the end of a meeting or after reading a book, "What are the take-aways?"

One certain take-away from this book is that human nature has not changed. Man's constant inhumanity to man flourished during the war as the Japanese brutalized their POWs.

Another clear take-away is that the "fog of peace" leads to terrible war. In the fog of peace during the 1930s, American and British failure to confront Japan in Manchuria

One certain take-away from this book is that human nature has not changed. Man's constant inhumanity to man flourished during the war as the Japanese brutalized their POWs.

MAN'S CONSTANT INHUMANITY TO MAN FLOURISHED DURING THE WAR AS THE JAPANESE BRUTALIZED THEIR POWs.

Another clear take-away is that the "fog of peace" leads to terrible war. In the fog of peace during the 1930s, American and British failure to confront Japan in Manchuria and China led to the Pacific War. Coincidently, the blindness of top political leaders to military preparedness in the 1930s led to the defeat and the unnecessary deaths of thousands of American and Filipino soldiers and airmen and of American sailors and marines in the Philippines, and of thousands of their Allied comrades across Asia, the Netherlands East Indies, and the Pacific by mid 1942.

A third take-away is that Carl Clausewitz's dictum, "War is the continuation of politics by other means," definitely applied to Japan's actions. Other famous comments about war also applied to the war against Japan. Attributed to Plato, the Greek philosopher, the often reported comment, "Only the dead have seen the end of war," rang true. So did Sherman's comment that "War is Hell," and MacArthur's assertion that "There is no substitute for Victory."

A troubling take-away is that political and military leaders often make decisions in war, as in peace, on the basis of a "cost-benefit analysis." President Franklin Roosevelt's decision to fight Germany first and assume the strategic defensive in the Philippines benefited Great Britain and ultimately France, Belgium, the Netherlands, and the Soviet Union, but key American leaders knew that Roosevelt's decision would cost the lives of thousands of American and Filipino soldiers because they would have to fight for the United States without adequate training, guns, tanks, ammunition and without substantial air and naval support in 1941 and 1942.

Even though from an American perspective the decision to fight Germany first seemed logical and sensible in 1942, President Manuel Quezon of the Philippines saw it much differently. According to an American colonel, Quezon expressed "considerable bitterness towards the Administration for its failure to support the Philippine Government, while sending troops and great quantities of war material to Europe. He said that since the Philippine Islands were American territory that the first consideration of the Government should be towards its own, and only <u>PART</u> of the force sent to Europe would be sufficient to hold the Japanese at bay, but due to the influence of Churchill the government concluded to abandon the Islands."[1]

tions, viz., the Netherlands East Indies, Australia, Ireland, England, Russia…however, not only has nothing arrived here but seemingly no attempt has been made to transport anything here. The British and American navies, the two strongest fleets in existence, have seemingly pursued a strategy that excludes any attempt to bring aid to the Philippines. Consequently, while perfectly safe itself, the United States has practically doomed the Philippines to almost total extinction to secure a breathing space. You have assured us eventual liberation, but what is needed is present help and preservation.[2]

Roosevelt replied to MacArthur: "My reply must emphatically deny the possibility of this government's agreement to the political aspects of President Quezon's proposal… The duty and necessity of resisting Japanese aggression to the last transcends in importance any other obligation now facing us in the Philippines." The Philippine President nailed the American President for his strategic decision and the resultant sacrifice of the Filipinos; the American President stood firm: it would be Europe First. Consequently, the Filipinos would pay a great price for Roosevelt's decision and the benefit of the United States.

Later, Roosevelt did not waver from his decision even when he learned about the Bataan Death March after Lt. Colonel Ed Dyess and others had escaped from the Davao POW Camp on Mindanao and had been evacuated to Australia. The President suppressed the information because many Americans believed that he feared that irate Americans would demand more aggressive action against Japan to the detriment of the war against Germany. In fact, he told General MacArthur and other military leaders that he alone would make the decision to release the information. The U. S. Government eventually permitted the publication of Dyess' story about the Bataan Death March in January 1944, months after Dyess had returned to the United States, and just after he died in an air accident.[3]

BY SUPPRESSING THE TERRIBLE NEWS, ROOSEVELT MAINTAINED HIS STRATEGIC FOCUS, BUT MORE POWS DIED BECAUSE HE DID NOT SPEED UP OPERATIONS IN THE PACIFIC…

By suppressing the terrible news, Roosevelt maintained his strategic focus, but more POWs suffered and died because he did not speed up operations in the Pacific that may have rescued them before 1945; and the President did not personally demand that Japan properly care for and safeguard the POWs.

Naval leaders in the Pacific also utilized a cost-benefit program. Admiral Chester Nimitz decided to conduct "unrestricted submarine warfare" immediately after Pearl Harbor, and American submariners then aggressively sought to sink all Japanese ships. Their policies led to the torpedoing and bombing of many unmarked POW ships throughout the war when air, military, and naval commanders in the Pacific must have known that many POW ships sailed inside Japanese convoys. In these cases, the benefit – the destruction of Japanese resupply and troop ships - apparently outweighed any potential costs to the Allies: the deaths of hundreds of POWs.

A sad, but constant take-away from the war against Japan and wars since World War II is that political leaders have paid little attention to the rescue of POWs. They seemed to accept that POWs were a normal result of war – and they are - but they did not take vigorous action to rescue them, demand that the capturing powers properly account for them and treat them properly, or threaten severe consequences for improper treatment. That policy was clear in the Pacific War.[4] After the war ended in 1945, the U. S. Government arrested, tried, and imprisoned or executed many Japanese who savaged POWs, but it could not do so against the countries which brutalized American POWs in other wars.

A dishonorable take-away is that governments seldom take good care of POWs after they return home. The POWs become forgotten people in the wake of joyous victory or unpopular war. In the case of the Americans held by the Japanese, many of the returnees complained about the lack of medical treatment in the United States. One former POW of the Japanese wrote:

> *"The guys have problems. I can't sleep at night. My feet burn. They drive me crazy. I got hit by a rifle butt back here on my shoulder. My whole neck is sore up to my ears. Sometimes I pop aspirin or Tylenol all day long. Don't do a damn bit of good. We go to the VA and they won't do a thing damn thing for us... They tell us we have to prove that our ailments are service connected. Why should I have to prove it? Think the Japs kept records of the beatings given us in Cabanatuan."[5]*

In addition, many – if not most – American POWs of the Japanese remain irate that their Government paid

THE DYESS STORY

THE EDITOR COMMENTED ABOUT THE DELAY IN RELEASING THE STORY AFTER DYESS IN SEPTEMBER CHOSE TO PUBLISH HIS STORY IN THE CHICAGO TRIBUNE:

"THE TRIBUNE OBTAINED THE WAR DEPARTMENT'S PERMISSION FOR COLONEL DYESS TO TELL HIS STORY. ONLY THREE DAYS LATER THE SECRETARY OF WAR WITHDREW THE PERMISSION AND FORBADE DYESS TO DIVULGE ANY FURTHER DETAILS OF HIS PRISON CAMP EXPERIENCES OR ESCAPE FROM THE JAPS.

THE TRIBUNE HAD THE STORY, BUT IT FACED A FOUR-AND-A HALF MONTH BATTLE FOR ITS RELEASE. OFFICIAL RELUCTANCE, INDECISION, RESISTANCE, AND ACTUAL HOSTILITY CONTRIBUTED TO THE LENGTHENING OF THE FIGHT."

HE ADDED, "THAT THE DYESS STORY STIRRED THE NATION MORE DEEPLY PROBABLY THAN ANY EVENT SINCE PEARL HARBOR, THERE CAN BE NO DOUBT. THIS WAS EVIDENCED BY TREMENDOUS READER RESPONSE RECORDED IN HUNDREDS OF NEWSPAPERS THAT GAVE IT TO THE PEOPLE AND BY THE CONCERTED DEMAND ON CONGRESS TO STRENGTHEN OUR FORCES IN THE PACIFIC."

CHARLES LEAVELLE
THE DYESS STORY, 11, 20

them one-dollar-a-day for "missed meals" (a maximum of $1,300) and one-dollar-and-fifty-cents-a-day for forced labor and or "inhumane treatment" (a maximum of $1,800) for their time as POWs, but paid $20,000 to the loyal and disloyal Japanese-American and Japanese civilians detained by the United States in American camps.[6]

But perhaps the most important take-away from this book is gaining an understanding of the impact of prisoner-of-war life on one typical American soldier. Faced with the results of battle, the deaths of friends, grim atrocities, and terrible living conditions, Harry Fleeger reduced his life to his simplest needs – food to survive, clothes to cover his nakedness, rudimentary shelter, love of his wife, and eventual freedom.

If Fleeger had survived, he most likely would have acted similarly to other freed POWs who could not throw food away, who placed health above nearly everything else, and who could not talk about their imprisonment. And as many combat veterans do, he probably would have ignored seemingly important matters in his recovered life because he considered them trivial compared to the life-and-death situations he had just survived. In addition, Fleeger may have returned a different person – as he feared - with strange habits, new fears, nightmares, different needs and values, and an intolerance for issues not related to survival. Consequently, he would have had a tough time adjusting to his wife and sons, and they, in turn, would have had a tough time adjusting to him because they may not have understood him or cared for the person he had become.

...THE MOST IMPORTANT TAKE-AWAY – GAINING AN UNDERSTANDING OF THE IMPACT OF PRISONER-OF-WAR LIFE ON ONE TYPICAL AMERICAN SOLDIER.

I suspect that Fleeger would have clearly understood the importance and validity of the comment that "Freedom Is Not Free" and would be confused when other Americans did not grasp the profundity of the concept. And I suspect that he would be horrified by those Americans who live blissfully under the protection of the American Flag, but who never understand how privileged they are to do so, and who never think that some day they might not be so fortunate because, in contrast to the Roman Empire and British Empire, they believe that the United States are forever.

Harry Fleeger

Major Harry Fleeger did not survive the war, but he left behind three diaries which someone buried in Cabanatuan POW Camp after he left the camp. The first of these was a small four by six and one-half inches, brown "Lecture Note Book." On the cover the major wrote:

JUNE 2, 1942
MAJOR H. J. FLEEGER
BAHAY #8
PRISON CAMP
CABANATUAN, P. I.

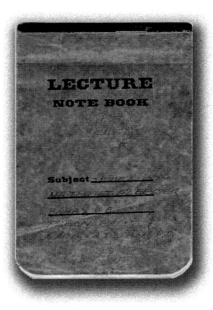

One the first page of the note book, Fleeger inscribed:

APRIL 9, 1942
MAJOR H. J. FLEEGER
PRISON CAMP
CABANATUAN, P. I.
LETTERS FOR
MRS. H. J. FLEEGER
PARKER
SOUTH DAKOTA
U. S. A.
AFTER WAR II

Fleeger dated his first entry "June 3, 1943" and wrote: "We have rats in the rafters..." He wrote about people and many subjects, but did not maintain any chronology in this tightly written book. The major wrote several entries in 1942 and 1944 as well as in 1943, and scattered them around. For example, he dated his entry on the second to the last page in the notebook, "April 12, 1943," which pre-dated his first entry. The April entry was a letter which read: "Dearest Lou, Just back to our bahay after four weeks in the hospital." On the last page of the handwritten diary, page 112, which he did not date, Fleeger drew four sketches of the wooden shoes – "Skivvies" - he wore.

Toward the end of the notebook, Major Bill Chandler,[7] Fleeger's comrade from the 26th Cavalry, wrote the following on the day Fleeger departed for Japan:

Major Fleeger left on detail, probably to Japan, at 9:00 A.M., to-day, October 9, 1944, with only a few hours notice. He was in good health and spirits. – He left me with me 3 notebooks, this one, a Blue Bureau of Education Commonwealth Notebook and a homemade notebook, to be transmitted to Mrs. H. J. Fleeger, Parker, So. Dakota at earliest possible date. Should I be sent out, I will pass them on to another.[8]

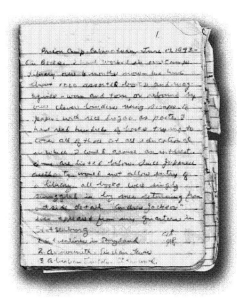

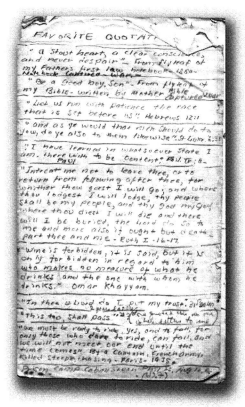

Chandler did that.

Fleeger inscribed a second diary as follows.

**MAJOR H. J. FLEEGER
PRISON CAMP
CABANATUAN, P. I.
1942-43
FOR
MRS. H. J. FLEEGER
PARKER
SOUTH DAKOTA
U. S. A.**

The tattered six by eight inch notebook originally had a blue cover. The major wrote his first entry on 17 June 1943. He dealt with his work in the camp library. He did not fill this book, writing on only forty-one pages. Fleeger wrote down some reminiscences, many names and addresses, several poems, and summarized some of his pay data. His last entry concerned a poem: "Above poem was written by 1st Lt. Fred Koenig, U.S. Army, in Prison Camp at O'Donnell, Phil. Is, and dedicated to those prisoners who died there. I will write the agonies of 'Boot Hill' – as part of my post-war notes." This diary had the least amount of information in it.

The third diary had no inscription, but Fleeger packed it with information about his favorite foods, included many quotations, provided an invaluable list of all the officers of the 26th Cavalry, and wrote his history of his regiment on Luzon and Bataan. Fleeger made the nine by five and one half inch diary from pages of scrap paper such as relatively blank pages from AR 35-5020, "Vouchers for Travel of Military Personnel," AR 35-5320 and "Money Allowance, Transportation of Dependents, Regular Army," and he bound the paper together with string at the top of the pages. He wrote on the front and back of most of the forty-six pages. For his first entry, he wrote a quotation – "A stout heart, a clear conscience, and never despair." He added, "From flyleaf of my father's first law book – 1880." On one page where he listed the medical officers of the regiment, Fleeger wrote in ink. He wrote all other entries in his diaries in pencil. On the last page, he wrote down the nicknames of his *bahay* mates and included his own: "Pot Got, Pinky, Smooth Bore, and Pot Belly." Fleeger apparently used the third book as his "think book."

Periodically, it seemed, Fleeger wrote new information in available empty spaces because often the information did not fit the subject or subjects about which he previously had written.

After the war, Chandler sent the diaries to Louise Fleeger, who, in turn, sent one book to the War Department. She also loaned the diaries to *The Cavalry Journal* which printed Major Fleeger's combat entries *in toto* in the November-December edition of the journal[9]. Later, Mrs. Fleeger loaned all of them to a writer who planned to prepare a manuscript about her husband's actions in the Philippines. The writer never completed a manuscript but did have the surviving diaries typed into a single document and returned all the documents to Mrs. Fleeger. The typed diary has proved invaluable because the researcher arranged Fleeger's dated comments chronologically.

Jim Fleeger now safeguards the originals and the typescript. This book is based on the typescript copy, but I have verified the information quoted in the original diaries.

Typed Diary

The first entry in the typed diary described Harry Fleeger's condition on his birthday, 27 June 1942, and it set up the story of his imprisonment: "In prison camp at Cabanatuan, P. I. I was very weak and ill, two month illness following the move June 1 from O'Donnell prison camp. Damned near died in fact. Weather very hot. Day spent resting and had supper with Harry Fischer.[10] Pryor

"IN PRISON CAMP AT CABANATUAN, P. I. I WAS VERY WEAK AND ILL ..."

Thwaits[11] gave us a can of Libby's Pork and Beans, so we had some on our rice for supper. Bill [Chandler] arrived in camp from Bilibid Prison.[12] So to bed – (Bill's wound healed)."[13]

In 1942, he wrote twenty-two dated entries, in 1943, he wrote forty-seven, and in 1944, he wrote forty-four entries. Most were not long and detailed as his prewar letters were. He did not date most of his long lists of things to do and think about, of library books, or people, and Fleeger did not date his summary of the Philippine Campaign. He ended the diary on 8 October 1944 talking about food and his wife.

Received 4 more short letters. Helps to know how you think of me too – No tobacco till Morris [Cummings] came over. He always does. I'm reminded to remember him at home – and if we don't write or visit at least to remember birthdays – he proves a real friend and is a fine person to know. Very hungry. Weigh 119 – want to recall these days when I have food again – Want Klim [powdered milk used extensively in the Philippines] – Peanut butter – Ovaltine on the table – gifts of food – etc – and want to feed someone who is hungry someday at home – still think Boxing Day a good day for that each year. I hope to learn to give. Farming every day – over two weeks since the air attack Sept 21st. We wait and hope – 63 British and Dutch arrived – of 1200 – we fear a trip north now with real reason. The month will tell – 2½ years a prisoner tomorrow – My love is more each day of Lou – will it ever end.

A few days later, the Japanese loaded Fleeger and another 1,782 POWs on the *Arisan Maru* in Manila.[14] The Japanese did not identify the ship as a POW ship, and on 24 October, four days after the *Arisan Maru* sailed from Manila, an American submarine torpedoed the Japanese freighter in the East China Sea. Nine POWs survived the sinking. Harry Fleeger did not.

Letters

After I had worked with the diaries for some months, Jim Fleeger provided me with several letters that his father had written before war began. These long epistles proved to be a treasure trove because Harry Fleeger wrote in great detail about his many concerns, expressed his deep love of his wife, and set the stage for many of the brief comments he wrote in his diaries. I have extracted passages from the letters and did not reproduce them *in toto*.

Result

As I worked with the material, I found that there were many stories in the diaries – stories which really told more about Jim's dad than they did about his imprisonment.

Additionally, Jim's dad mentioned many other soldiers – his *bahay* mates, his "blood brothers," his acquaintances, and some of the young soldiers he dealt with – who piqued my interest.

What I have developed in this narrative, I would classify as a "personal history" of Major Harry Fleeger during World War II and a "memorial" to his comrades in the 26th Cavalry and in Cabanatuan. For the most part, I have used direct quotations from his letters and diaries to tell his story. I have added information from many other sources to tell brief stories about events and his friends and comrades. My overall goal was to highlight the experiences of Fleeger and many of the soldiers who never made the history books as individuals, but only made them as part of a group: the 26th Cavalry, the Bataan Death March, POWs of the Japanese, or Hell Ship victims.

ΩΩΩ

I have made no attempt to fill in the parts that Jim's dad labeled "Reutel" – "Remind me to tell you later" -- because I can only guess at them. In the diaries, "Reutel" seemed to presage something unpleasant or damning. In some cases, however, I have added unpleasant information to emphasize some of the problems that POWs faced and have suggested that information might fall under the title of Reutel.

This is a small attempt to add to the history of the American POWs of the Japanese in World War II – many of whom have no final resting place - and who in Abraham Lincoln's words "gave the last full measure of devotion" so that this "nation might live" and "that government of the people, by the people, for the people, shall not perish from the earth."

JOHN H. BRADLEY
14 June 2010

Notes

---

[1] Colonel H. W. Tarkington, *There Were Others* (unpublished manuscript, n.d.), 258. Copy in Possession of author. Tarkington summarized Quezon's conclusions when "he discussed the Philippine situation with the Commanding General and other officers of the Mindanao Force."

---

2 Quoted in Douglas MacArthur, *Reminiscences* (NY: McGraw Hill, 1964). 138. Roosevelt's answer is at 139.

3 Katherine Clark, "Prisoners of War and the Bataan Relief Organization," a pamphlet, n.d., 62-3. Pamphlet in possession of the author. See also Lt. Col. Wm. E. Dyess, *The Dyess Story, The Eye-Witness Account of the DEATH MARCH FROM BATAAN and the Narrative of Experiences in Japanese Prison Camps and of Eventual Escape* (NY: GP Putnam's Sons, 1944), 11 and 20.

4 The North Koreans proved as brutal and murderous as the Japanese; the North Vietnamese proved more vicious and cruel. The Communists massacred POWs, killed the wounded and stragglers, randomly shot POWs for non-capital reasons, and conducted many death marches. See Rudy Tomedi, *No Drums, No Bugles* (NY: John Wiley & Sons, 1993), 48-49 (death marches, executions), 57 (death marches), and 59 (tunnel massacre). See also Donald Knox, *The Korean War, Uncertain Victory* (San Diego: Harcourt, Brace Jovanovich, 1988), 332-3. Corporal Jack Browning, M Company, 34th Infantry, reported: "...our Korean officer was so mean, he was called the Tiger...[and] one morning he decided to give us a lesson in Communist discipline. He picked out one of our officers, Lieutenant Thornton, put a blindfold on him, and just shot him through the head as an example." Browning also reported that "one of our sergeants had been on the Bataan Death March in the Philippines. He said that our march was tougher and that we lost more men per mile that the people in the Philippines did." Terrible treatment continued during the Vietnamese War. The enemy shackled POWs in prison cells for weeks at a time, kept them locked in small cages (as the Japanese did in Cabanatuan), tortured them, starved them, threatened to kill them for being "war criminals," and killed and executed some POWs. See Robinson Reiser, *The Passing of the Night, My Seven Years as a Prisoner of the North Vietnamese* (Old Saybrook, CT: Konecky & Konecky, 1973). Reiser recounted all of the listed incidents in his memoir.

5 Donald Knox, *Death March* (San Diego: Harcourt Brace Jovanovich, 1981). See comments about medical treatment, 476-7 (PFC Robert Brown), 477 (SSG Harold Feiner), and 479 and 482 (SGT Forrest Knox).

6 Linda Goetz Holmes, *Unjust Enrichment, How Japan's Companies Built Postwar Fortunes Using American POWs* (Mechanicsburg, PA: Stackpole Books, 2001), 138.

7 William Chandler, Class of 1931, *Register of Graduates and Former Cadets, United States Military Academy, 1989* (hereafter, *USMA Register* with designated year, i.e., *1989 USMA Register*), #9124, 373. Chandler served first as the S-3 and then as the S-2 and S-3 of the 26th Cavalry while Fleeger was in the regiment. Chandler wrote Fleeger's obituary years later.

8 From the typed *Diaries of Major H. J. Fleeger* (hereafter, *Diaries*), 169.

9 *Diaries* and Major Harry J. Fleeger, "Brief Regimental History 26th Cavalry World War II – Bataan," *The Cavalry Journal*, November – December 1945, 6-9.

10 Major Harry O. Fischer, 803rd Engineers.

11 2nd Lieutenant Prior Thwaits, Coast Artillery Officer, New Mexico National Guard.

12 Bilibid was an old civil prison located just north of the main business district of Manila. During the war, the Japanese kept American and Filipino military and civilian POWs there. The US 37th Infantry Division rescued the survivors of Bilibid in February 1945. General Douglas MacArthur visited the survivors soon afterwards.

13 *Diary,* 6.

14 I have used 1,783 as the number on the *Arisan Maru, Number* taken from Lee A. Gladwin, "American POWs on Japanese Ships Take a Voyage into Hell," *The U. S. National Archives & Records Administration*, Winter 2004, Vol. 35, No. 4, two parts. See http://www.archives.gov/ publications/prologue/2003/winter/hell-ships-1html?template=pr, 5. Gladwin said that the Japanese reported that number in one of their messages about the ship. Gregory F. Michno, *Death on the Hellships* (Annapolis: Naval Institute Press, 2001), 249 (hereafter, *Hellships*) reported that there were 1,782 POWs on the ship. Later, he listed 1,800 POWs, 316.

Maps

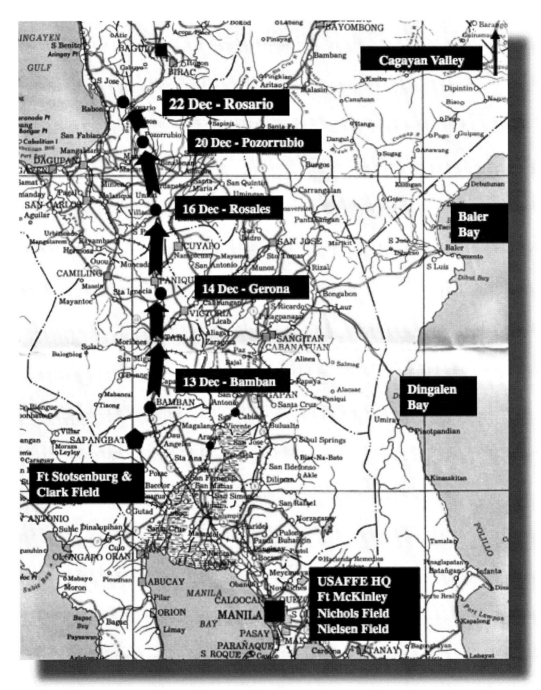

Map 1 - 26th Cavalry Movement to Contact

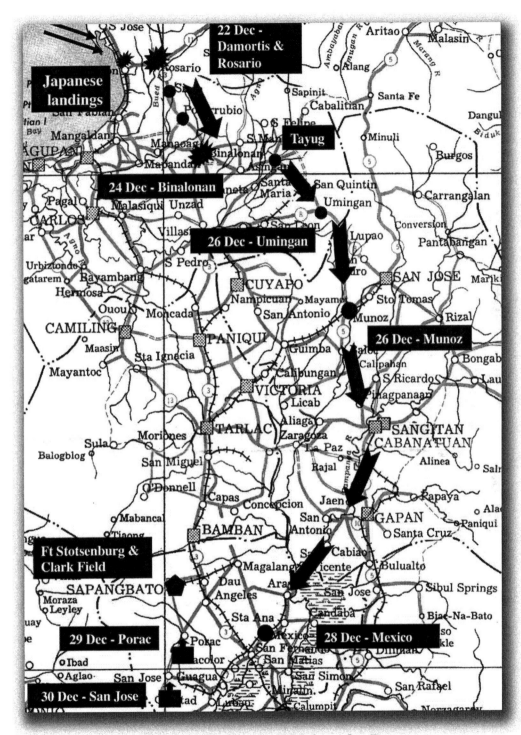

Map 2 - 26th Cavalry Withdrawal to Bataan

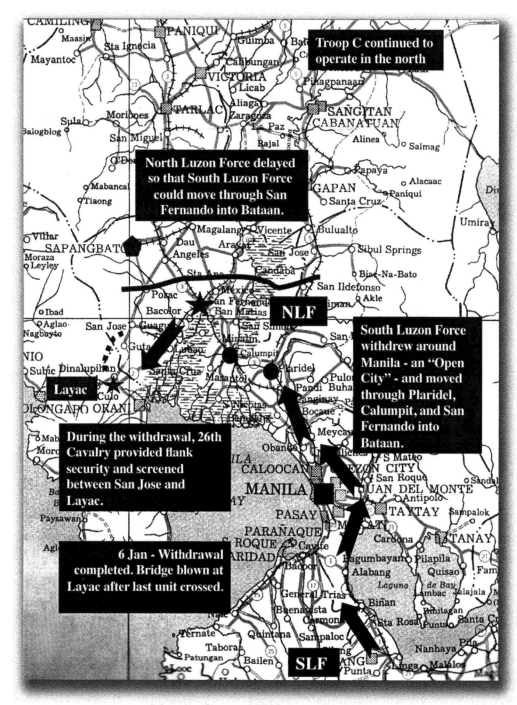

Map 3 - General Withdrawal into Bataan

Map 4 - Bataan 1942

6 January
Fil-American troops occupied the new Main Battle Position - which stretched from just north of Moron to just north of Abucay- to allow time to strengthen the Reserve Battle Position.

26 January
Fil-American troops withdrew to the Reserve Battle Position (originally planned to be the Main Battle Position) - which stretched from Bagac to just below Orion - and stopped the Japanese advance.

8 February
Lt. Gen. Masaharu Homma called off all attacks in order to reorganize, refit, and reinforce.

3 April
Homma launched heavy attacks.

9 April
Maj. Gen. Edward King surrendered all Bataan forces.

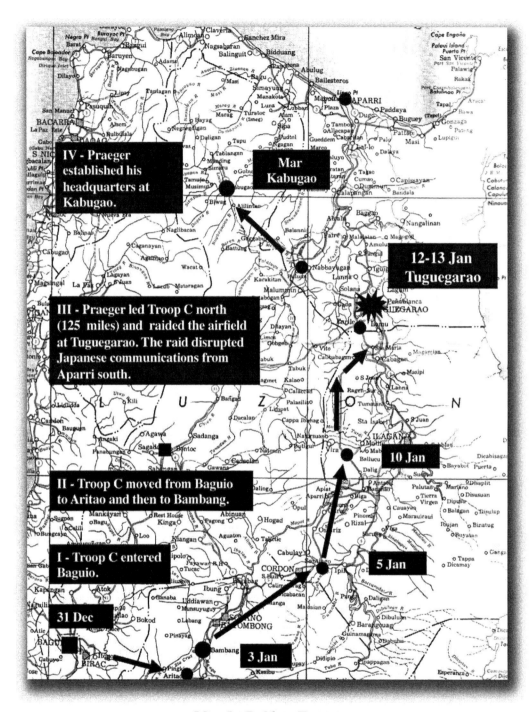

IV - Praeger established his headquarters at Kabugao.

Mar Kabugao

12-13 Jan Tuguegarao

III - Praeger led Troop C north (125 miles) and raided the airfield at Tuguegarao. The raid disrupted Japanese communications from Aparri south.

10 Jan

II - Troop C moved from Baguio to Aritao and then to Bambang.

5 Jan

I - Troop C entered Baguio.

31 Dec

3 Jan

Map 5 - Raid on Tuguegarao

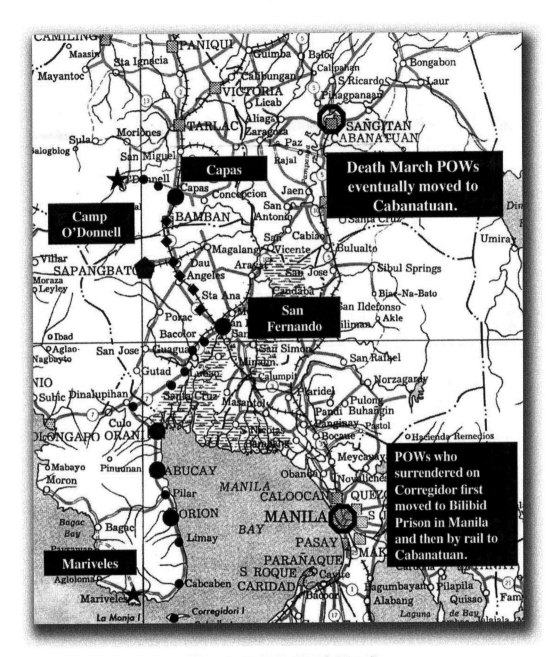

Map 6 - Bataan Death March

The Death March began after Maj Gen King surrendered the Fil-American forces on Bataan and ended at Camp O'Donnell.

The starting point for most POWs was Mariveles.

Most POWs marched from Mariveles to San Fernando where they boarded trains to Capas. From Capas they marched to Camp O'Donnell.

One

"Hi! I'm Fleeger"

Cadet Fleeger

Harry Fleeger fought his only war with the 26th United States Cavalry (Philippine Scouts) on Luzon and Bataan in 1941 and 1942. Captured by the Japanese after the American and Filipino forces surrendered on Bataan, he survived the Bataan Death March, imprisonment in pestilent Camp O'Donnell north of Bataan, initial illness, and imprisonment in the new camp called Cabanatuan which was north and slightly east of Manila.

Cliffie's Son

Fleeger was born in Parker, South Dakota on 27 June 1908. The second son of Judge Louis L. Fleeger and Mrs. "Cliffie" Fleeger, young Fleeger was short, slightly built, and red-headed. Bright and athletic, he graduated as the valedictorian of his Parker High School Class of 1926 and played two years of football as an end. After attending Iowa State Teachers' College for a year, he entered the U. S. Military Academy at West Point, New York on 1 July 1927.

World War I veterans – all West Pointers -- controlled the Military Academy that Fleeger entered. One wonders whether Fleeger knew much about them or how they impressed him. Brigadier General Merch B. Stewart was the Superintendent in July 1927. He had served as the Commandant of Cadets for four years before becoming the Superintendent and had an extended combat record. Infantryman Stewart had earned a Silver Star Citation in Cuba, served in the Philippine Insurrection, and commanded a brigade in Europe during World War I. Another distinguished veteran of Cuba, the Philippine Insurrection, and World War I, and formerly a cavalry officer, Major General Edwin B. Winans, succeeded Stewart. He also had served in the China Relief Expedition and the Punitive Expedition into Mexico. Major General William R. Smith, formerly an artilleryman and coast artilleryman and the commander of an infantry division in France, followed Winans. Fleeger served under two Commandants: Lt. Colonel Campbell B. Hodges, an infantryman from Louisiana and a classmate of General Douglas MacArthur, and Lt. Colonel Robert C. Richardson, Jr., a cavalryman from South Carolina. Hodges had served in the Vera Cruz Expedition and with the 31st Infantry Division in France, and Richardson had served in the Moro Expedition in the Philippines where he earned a Silver Star and a Purple Heart in combat and then had served in the General Headquarters of the Allied Expeditionary Force in France. After leaving the position as Commandant, Lt. Colonel Richardson assumed the post as Commandant of the

WORLD WAR I VETERANS – ALL WEST POINTERS - CONTROLLED THE MILITARY ACADEMY THAT FLEEGER ENTERED.

Cavalry School. He would be the only one of these distinguished World War I veterans to serve in World War II.[1]

Fleeger entered a small, isolated environment on the Hudson River with 259 other new cadets. The maximum strength for the Corps of Cadets was 1,334, including four Filipinos. At the time of his entry only 8,477 cadets had graduated from West Point and a surprising number, 3,000, had served in World War I.[2]

FLEEGER ENTERED A SMALL, ISOLATED ENVIRONMENT ON THE HUDSON RIVER...

The Corps of Cadets was organized into a regiment of several companies. Each company had cadets from four classes. The First Class (seniors or "Firsties") provided the cadet officers and non-commissioned officers for the companies, battalions, and the regiment. The Second Class (juniors or "Cows") provided several "Cow Corporals" for each company. The remainder of the Second Class, the Third Class (sophomores or "Yearlings"), and the Fourth Class (freshmen or "Plebes"), provided the privates in the companies. The Plebes lived in a special, restricted, high-pressure world which began in "Beast Barracks." The *Bugle Notes* for 1928 described the two months of military training before a new Plebe joined the Corps:

> *This period, which is the most rigid and exacting of the entire four years at West Point, is spent under a group of selected instructors from the First Class, known as the "Beast Detail," supervised by officers of the Tactical Department. During this time the new Cadet acquires with amazing rapidity smartness and precision in all his military drills and duties. It is characterized throughout by fair but unfailing demands, on the part of the instructors, that orders and instructions be correctly and promptly executed even to the minutest detail.[3]*

Bugle Notes also carried a message from the First Captain to new Cadets. He wrote: "No fortunes of gold are made in the Army and few gain "far-flung fame" in its ranks. In service to the nation you will find a wealth of happiness to which none other can be compared. Devote your lives to Duty, Honor, and Country and in that devotion you will find your reward." He added:

> *For gold the merchant sails the main,*
> *The farmer plows the manor,*
> *But glory is the soldier's pride,*
> *And the soldier's wealth is honor.[4]*

Plebes had few privileges. They could not use places such as Diagonal Walk, Flirtation Walk, and the club rooms of the upper classes. They could not use Cullum Hall except when dating. They could not use the front doors of barracks or walk across The

STANDING RETREAT
"NOT A VERY GOOD PICTURE. TURNING OUT FOR RETREAT AT 6 P.M. EVERY NIGHT ON [PLEBE] HIKE. DO I LOOK LIKE A SOLDIER? YOU OUGHT TO SEE ME DO THE MANUAL OF ARMS DAD."

BRACING
"IF SOMEBODY WAS CRAWLING ME I COULD PULL MY CHIN IN TWICE AS FAR."

Plain. They could not play golf or tennis unless they played on the tennis or golf teams. They had to be in full uniform when they left their rooms, and they could not wear the capes of their overcoats thrown back unless they were under arms, on leave, or on special occasions. And they could not smoke except in their rooms. As "Mr. Ducrot," "Mr. Dumbflicket," "Mr. Dumbguard," and "Mr. Dumbjohn," the Plebes, as Fleeger learned quickly, had to respond instantly to the queries of the upper classmen. When asked "What time is it," a plebe had to respond:

Sir, I am deeply embarrassed and greatly humiliated that due to the unforeseen circumstances over which I have no control, the inner workings and hidden mechanisms of my chronometer are in such in accord with the great sidereal movement by which time is commonly reckoned, that I cannot with any degree of accuracy state the exact time, Sir; but without fear of being very far off, I will state, that it is ___ minutes, ___ seconds, and ___ ticks after the ___ hour.[5]

Besides learning "Plebe Poop," as above, Fleeger found that Plebes performed special duties. In barracks before every formation, a plebe Minute Caller called out "The Minutes" so that the upperclassmen wore the correct uniform and would not be late for the formation. Minutes went like this:

*Sir, there are five minutes until parade formation!
The uniform is Full Dress Grey over White under arms.
Five minutes sir!*

In the Mess Hall, three plebes normally sat at each table with a First Class Table Commandant and six other upperclassmen. The plebes sat at attention during every meal and performed specific duties. One plebe served as the "Gunner." He sat at the end of the table opposite to the Table Commandant and announced the arrival of food for the table: "Sir, the slum (stew) is on the table. Slum for the Head of the Table!" The Gunner's most challenging duty was handling desserts such as cakes, pies, and ice cream bars. If a Gunner, Mr. Fleeger would ask after announcing the arrival of the dessert, "How many gentlemen would like dessert?" If only nine or seven or five (including the plebes) did, Fleeger faced the problem of cutting nine or seven or five "equal" portions. Rather than risk screwing up, he would wisely decide that he would not eat dessert and then cut an even number of pieces. The Water Corporal handled cold beverages and after announcing the beverage, he would ask who wanted the available cold beverage and then would fill the glasses the upperclassmen sent to him. Once filled, he would announce, "Milk for the Head of the Table" or "Lemonade for Mr. Johnson." If milk were the beverage, the Water Corporal had to be prepared to answer a query of an upperclassman who wanted seconds: "How's the cow, Mr. Coury?" The correct answer would be: "Sir, she walks she talks, she is full of chalk. The lacteal fluid extracted from the female of the bovine specie is highly prolific to the (number of glasses left) degree!" The Coffee Corporal would handle the serving of hot beverages in a similar manner. When the Plebes had completed their initial duties, the Gunner would announce the fact to the Table Commandant and request permission for the plebes to eat. Often, the Plebes did not have many minutes to eat their meals.

> *"**HONOR IS THE MOST CHERISHED PRINCIPLE OF LIFE...**"*

Honor

The First Class introduced Fleeger and his classmates to the concepts of Duty, Honor, Country." *Bugle Notes* stated - "Country" needed no definition: "Our country, right or wrong" is the patriot's slogan throughout the nation" and then emphasized:

> *Performance of one's duty implies far more than mere obedience to the letter of the law. In other walks of life, technicalities and evasive tactics are condoned and even lauded as an indication of cleverness. In the Army, where lives are the price of failure, there are no technicalities, and an order is given, a statement received at its face value. When it becomes a soldier's duty to obey an order it also becomes his duty to look beneath the surface of that order for its spirit, and, in so doing, to put his whole being into its performance. A fearless readiness to assume responsibility and determination to do, not just the job, but the whole and the best job, are what is expected of a West Pointer.*

Bugle Notes continued: "Honor is the most cherished principle of life; it is the beacon which guides everyone during their stay at the Military Academy and during the career of later life..." Then, the book said that "The basic principles of the Honor System are: no lying, no cheating, no half-truths...," and added:

SLUM AND GRAVY

SONS OF SLUM AND GRAVY.
WILL YOU LET THE NAVY,
TAKE FROM US A VICTORY?

HELL NO!

HEAR A WARRIOR'S CHORUS
SWEEP THAT LINE BEFORE US,
CARRY ON THE VICTORY!
ONWARD! ONWARD! CHARGE
AGAINST THE FOE.

FORWARD, FORWARD, THE
ARMY BANNERS GO!
SONS OF MARS AND THUNDER,
RIP THAT LINE ASUNDER,
CARRY ON THE VICTORY.

1. *No intentional dishonesty is excusable, and under no circumstances will it be condoned.*
2. *Everyone is honor bound to report any breach of honor which comes to his attention.*
3. *Offenders of the Code of Honor are never granted immunity.*
4. *Quibbling, evasive statements, or technicalities in order to shield guilt or defeat the ends of justice, will not be tolerated.*
5. *The Code of the Soldier demands courageous and fearless honesty in setting forth the truth, regardless of the consequences.*

In the classroom, the code required that, "No cadet shall impart or receive any unauthorized assistance, either inside or outside the section room or examination room, which would tend to give any Cadet an unfair advantage." [6]

Fleeger learned that cadets had a separate language with which they could communicate with each other without their civilian friends understanding what they meant. They could "bone" (study) for a "board fight" (blackboard recitation in class) or a "writ" (exam). They could have a "boodle fight" (a gathering where cake, candy, or ice cream was served). They could "drag" (date) on weekends, perhaps with their OAO (one and only). They could drag "pro" (pretty girl) or "D" (not so pretty girl). They could be hives (good students) or goats (poor students). They could be "quilled" (given demerits for delinquencies) or "slugged" (awarded a serious punishment for a grave disciplinary offense).[7]

Fleeger also found that he faced a math-heavy curriculum that focused on Civil and Military Engineering, Chemistry and Electricity, Ordnance and Gunnery, Mathematics, and Drawing. His other courses would include Natural and Experimental Philosophy, Modern Languages, English, Economics and Government, Political History, and Military Hygiene. The Military Academy awarded no degree for the successful completion of its stiff academic curriculum.[8]

Intercollegiate athletics – especially football - provided all the cadets, especially the plebes, with a source of common pleasure. Victories over Navy increased morale; defeats added to any existent gloom. Songs such "Slum and Gravy" emphasized the combination of sports and the martial spirit.[9]

ΩΩΩ

One Superintendent summarized the daily cadet life.

> *The cadet day at West Point starts with first call at 5:30 a.m. on weekdays. At 7:55 a.m. academic sessions open and with the exception of an hour's interval for luncheon, continue until 3 p.m. Either military drills or intramural athletics are then held from 3:15 until 4:20 p.m., when the young men are excused until supper at 6:20 p.m. Call to quarters at 7:15 finds each cadet in his room studying where he remains until tattoo at 9:30 p.m., when he may close his books for the day and use the half hour before taps at 10 p.m. as he desires.*

The general added: "The academic curriculum, like all other courses at the military academy, contains no elective subjects. Classes are small, comprising about 14 cadets, so that each man receives a vast amount of instruction. They are required to recite every day in every subject....Each week the academic standings are published...The West Point system keeps both the individual cadet and the authorities fully conversant at all time with the academic progress of each man. Failure to maintain the high standards required, immediately bars a cadet from participation in varsity athletics, as well as a number of privileges."[10]

What the Superintendent did not say, was that West Point had re-trenched after the superintendence of MacArthur. New superintendents had canceled training visits to nearby Camp Dix, NJ and had returned the traditional summer training after Plebe Year to Summer Camp at Ft. Clinton, next to the Plain. The new leaders had revoked the short six-hour leaves that MacArthur had initiated, and pinned the cadets once again to their "rock-bound highland home." However, MacArthur's reforms of the Honor System and his expanded athletic and intramural athletic programs remained. One other tradition remained in place: horsemanship. In 1928, the Academy leaders – apparently ignoring the experience of cavalrymen, machine guns, and tanks during World War I - doubled the number of hours devoted to equitation instruction for First Classmen.[11]

ONE OTHER TRADITION REMAINED IN PLACE – HORSEMANSHIP.

Such was the new world Fleeger lived in until he graduated in 1931. At graduation, his entry in the *Howitzer,* the cadet yearbook, described a cocky young man who had survived all the challenges:

> *Hi! I'm Fleeger! Who are you?" This was the way this pampered pet of Uncle Sam entered our great institution four years ago and addressed the First Sergeant. And the same attitude he has maintained throughout these four years. Simply aggressive and straightforward.*

His anonymous biographer, most likely a "wife" (roommate), continued:

> *Joe, as we all know him, will always be remembered and especially by those who know him intimately, as a real friend and pal. Ready at any time to drive your blues away or to sit up and help you with "descrip," his is a disposition hard to beat – or even tie! As a member of the Honor Committee he has given us much valuable advice and helped to maintain the high standards characteristic of West Point. Going into the air corps, Joe had expressed a weakness for lilies, but will he need them? On considering the level-headedness he has shown when confronted with the perplexities of "Kaydetin" we feel assured that the tides of flying will hardly disconcert him for long."*

In June 1931, a hometown newspaper announced, "Fleeger will graduate a cadet sergeant, having been appointed to that rank last June by Major General William Smith, superintendent. Academically he stands well above the center of his class and for the past year has been a member of the honor committee of the corps of cadets, the most important and influential organization in cadet life." Fleeger graduated 109 in order of merit out of his class of 297.

The paper then reported some of superintendent's remarks.

> *During the past four years this cadet received a comprehensive general education of collegiate grade together with sufficient military training to qualify him for the duties of a second lieutenant in any branch of the regular army to which he may be assigned. During these four years he had been under rigid discipline and has led a Spartan-like life.* [12]

Cavalry Officer

Second Lieutenant Fleeger entered a starved and emaciated army. Administrations after World War I provided meager budgets for the Army as world leaders tried to reduce the size and power of the great navies of the world, stabilize fortifications in the Pacific, and outlaw

FLEEGER ENTERED A STARVED AND EMACIATED ARMY.

war as a means to settle international disagreements. On paper, the Army looked substantial. There were nine Corps Areas in the United States, each of which was supposed to have "one reinforced brigade of the Regular army and not less than one division of the National Guard and one of the Organized Reserve." All told there were forty-seven infantry divisions on the books in the U. S. and three overseas: the Hawaiian Division, the Panama Division, and the Philippine Division. Congress had so reduced the appropriations for the Army that in 1927, there were only 118,000 troops on active duty, 165,000 in the National Guard, and 80,000 officers and 2,000 enlisted soldiers in the Organized Reserves.[13] With the advent of the Crash of 1929 and the resultant Great Depression, Congress would provide less money for soldiers and in March 1932 would reduce the pay of officers and soldiers by ten percent to meet budget shortages.[14] Moreover, Congress and the President refused to deal with the deficiencies in people and material that the Secretaries of the Army and the Chiefs of Staff reported to them each year.

As mentioned, Fleeger wanted to fly, but poor eyesight cancelled his plans, and he chose the cavalry as his branch. At the time and through the 1930s, Army leaders wrestled with the future of cavalry: would the Army keep its horse cavalry units and supplement them with tanks and armored cars or would the Army replace the horses with tanks and armored cars entirely? In 1931, General Douglas MacArthur, Chief of Staff of the U. S. Army, had

MANY CAVALRYMEN BELIEVED THAT THE HORSE COULD NOT BE REPLACED.

abolished the Tank Corps and had given the Infantry and the Cavalry the mission of developing tanks.[15] Split responsibility and lack of money then and in the following years would hinder tank development. So would the opposition of some cavalry leaders. Many cavalrymen believed that the horse could not be replaced.

In 1935, Fortune magazine commented that "U. S. strategists have always emphasized [the cavalry], and even during the lean days of the twenties, when the Army was reduced to three scant infantry divisions, they managed to save from destruction a skeletonized division of cavalry. Critics say that this is because the Army likes to play polo, but on the other hand there are sound arguments for the man on horse when supplemented by machines." The commentators then described the new cavalry, but left out horse-mounted units:

A mechanized cavalry regiment will go into action with about twenty armored cars (they cost $20,000 each, including the necessary maintenance parts); thirty so-called personnel carriers, which are big trucks with tracks for rear wheels, *manned by machine gunners (cost: $9,000 each with parts]; six self-propelled chemical warfare mortars for gas and smoke screens; and fifty-six combat cars (at $26,500 each), which is the cavalry's name for tanks. The fire power of such a mechanized cavalry regiment will be 302 .30 caliber machine guns, 93 anti-tank guns, 127 submachine guns, 798 pistols, and 40 rifles – a formidable combination of power with speed, especially when descending on one's flank.[16]*

In 1941, after two years of tank-driven *blitzkrieg* warfare in Europe, Fleeger's former Commandant of Cadets, Major General Richardson, wrote: "Horse cavalry must be judged today by its perfected organization, by the power of its arms, and by its battlefield mobility. If there is one lesson that the actual battle experiences of the present war [in Europe] has clearly shown, it is the rebirth of the Cavalry as a powerful combat force.[17]

Some cavalry officers, however, saw the tank as the cavalry weapon of the future. But some tank-experienced officers such as Colonel George S. Patton, Jr., remained ambivalent. Patton focused on developing and operating horse cavalry units and developing officers who could excel in the mounted branch until he absorbed the lessons of the German *blitzkrieg* victory in France in 1940. Because the Army did not organize an armored force until World War II, Fleeger's career would focus primarily on horse cavalry, but he would see new armored cars in action.[18]

ΩΩΩ

After graduation, Fleeger married Susan Louise Morgan, his childhood sweetheart. The young couple moved to their first post, Ft. Des Moines, IA, not far away from Parker, where Fleeger served as a cavalry platoon leader and a troop commander with the 14th U. S. Cavalry. He later was detached for six months to serve with the Civilian Construction Corps, as many officers did during the Depression.[19] Fleeger spent his CCC time in Northern Iowa and Minnesota. While at Ft. Des Moines, the couple welcomed the arrival of their first-born, James Elliott Fleeger. Also during this time, the young couple provided a home for Louise's younger sister, Virginia, while she awaited the birth of her first child.[20]

FLEEGER SERVED IN A GRAYING OFFICER CORPS.

In 1935, he attended the Troop Officers' Course at the Cavalry School at Ft. Riley, KS. There "he once more distinguished himself as a serious student, a dedicated soldier, and an accomplished horseman and a friend to be depended upon in all seasons."[21] That year, Fleeger served in a graying officer corps. The average age of the 1,571 active second lieutenants was about twenty-six and that of the 2,667 first lieutenants was thirty-four. One first lieutenant was fifty-seven. Based on those ages, young Fleeger could look forward to becoming a captain at about forty-three, the average of the 3,450 serving captains, a major at forty-five, and a lieutenant colonel at fifty-two. And if he aspired to be a general officer, he would have to wait until his late fifties or early sixties.[22]

After graduating from the course, Fleeger joined the 13th U. S. Cavalry at Ft. Knox, KY where he worked on the development and experimentation of early mechanized cavalry organizations. At Ft. Knox, the Fleeger's second son, Larry, was born.[23]

In 1937, Fleeger returned to Ft. Riley to attend the advanced equitation course. From horses to mechanization and back to horses, it was transitional time for the U. S. Cavalry. The next year, the Army sent Fleeger to the Infantry School at Ft. Benning, GA to attend the Infantry Regular Course.

While serving in the United States, Fleeger gained considerable publicity as a member of the Ft. Des Moines polo team. A photo caption in the *Minneapolis Star* on Thursday, 16 February 1933, read: "Once more the Fort Des Moines polo team, perennial winner in Twin City and Northwest outdoor competition, is back, but this time as indoor performers. Friday night they will face off against the Fort Snelling trio at the reservation riding hall. This is the trio that will attempt to add to its reputation via the indoor route. The men are ... Capt. Glenn S. Finley, Second Lieut. Harry Fleeger and First Lieut. W. H. Nutter, all of the Fourteenth Cavalry."[24] On 11 June 1934, an article in a paper in Omaha, NE reported on "Omaha's first official polo match in many years." between the Army team and the Omaha Polo Club team. It said that, "The crack Des Moines team will have Major W. F. Waddelton at No. 1, Lieutenant Harry Fleeger at No. 2, Glen S. Finley, jr., No 3, and Captain Glen S. Finley of the Fourteenth cavalry at No. 4." It added that, "The army men have won 12 straight matches."[25]

They'll Help Revive Polo Here Today

Des Moines Riders Here

Meet Omaha Club "4" at Ak Field Today; First Match in Years

POLO WAS THE "ARMY'S FAVORITE AND MOST CRITICIZED SPORT." CERTAINLY CAVALRY OFFICERS SUCH AS FLEEGER LOVED IT AND MADE IT PART OF THEIR EXISTENCE.

Polo was the "army's favorite and most criticized sport." Certainly cavalry officers such as Fleeger loved it and made it part of their existence. One major general in 1936 considered polo to be a great asset "and kept crack players around him" wherever he went. Another major general, assigned to Third Army at San Antonio, Texas at the time said that "polo, including grooms, stables, and remount stations cost the taxpayer $1,000,000 a year" and had "no military value."[26]

Philippine Scout

By the time he deployed with his wife and two sons to the Philippines in 1939 and joined the 26th Cavalry Regiment (Philippine Scouts), First Lieutenant Fleeger had gained a reputation as an excellent horseman and a skilled polo player, and comrades – many of whom were West Point classmates - considered him a bright young officer. With eight years service and his exposure to mechanized and infantry operations, he brought valuable experience to his regiment. In the Philippines, he underwent two years of hard training with the 26th Cavalry before war began. He also rode in horse shows, played polo (as did so many cavalry officers there), and participated in gymkhanas. While assigned to the regiment, he wrote an article that was published in the *U. S. Cavalry Journal* after war began.[27] Promoted to temporary captain, Fleeger took command of Troop E and continued in that position until appointed the Regimental Adjutant (S-1) in November 1941. By that time, his family had returned to the United States and he expected to rotate home and join them.

Notes

[1] *1980 USMA Register*, 7 (Superintendents), 8 (Commandants), 278 (#3403, Major General Edward Baruch Winans, Class of 1891), 279 (#3459, Major General William Ruthven Smith, Class of 1892), 284 (#3715, Major General Merch Bradt Stewart, Class of 1896), 293 (#4177, Major General Campbell Blackshear Hodges, Class of 1903), and 294 (#4236, General (posthumous) Robert Charlwood Richardson, Jr., Class of 1904.

[2] *Bugle Notes, The Handbook of the United States Corps of Cadets*, United States Military Academy, West Point, NY, Volume XX, 1928-1929, 145. (hereafter, *Bugle Notes*).

[3] *Ibid*, 80.

[4] *Ibid*, 43.

[5] *Ibid*, 136.

[6] *Ibid*, 45 (country), 45-6 (duty), and 47-49 (honor).

[7] *Ibid*, 127-142.

8 *Ibid*, 143-144. The Bachelor of Science degree was first awarded to graduating cadets in 1933. See Robert Cowley and Thomas Guinzburg (eds.), *West Point, Two Centuries of Honor and Tradition* (Warner Books: West Point Project, LLC, 2002), 173.

9 "Slum and Gravy," *Bugle Notes*, 124.

10 "Harry J. Fleeger, Parker, Will Get Diploma From West Point Thursday." No source. Undated. (James Fleeger's files).

11 Cowley and Guinzburg (eds.), *West Point,* 172-75.

12 "Harry J. Fleeger, Parker, Will Get Diploma From West Point Thursday."

13 *Bugle Notes*, 82-83 (strengths) and 84-85 (corps).

14 Colonel Raymond K. Blum, Jr., (Editor-in-Chief), *U.S. Army, A Complete History* (NY: The Army Historical Foundation, 2004), 445.

15 D. Clayton James, *The Years of MacArthur*, Volume 1, *1880-1941* (Boston: Houghton Mifflin Company, 1970), 358.

16 "Who's in the Army Now?" in *Fortune*, September 1935, 126 and 129.

17 Major General Robert C. Richardson, Jr., "The Wider Role of Cavalry," *The Cavalry Journal,* L (January-February 1941), 8.

18 Dennis Showalter, *Patton and Rommel, Men of War in the Twentieth Century* (NY: Berkley Caliber, 2005), 132-3. See also Roger H. Nye, *The Patton Mind, The Professional Development of an Extraordinary Leader* (Garden Park, NJ: Avery Publishing Group, 1993), 113.

19 In 1935, 600,000 men served in the CCC. General Douglas MacArthur and the Army organized and managed the CCC "without the use of Army discipline." See "Who's in the Army Now?" in *Fortune*, September 1935, 135.

20 Telephone conversation with Jim Fleeger, 12 June 2009.

21 "Obituary for Harry James Fleeger," *Assembly Magazine*, Association of Graduates, U. S. Military Academy, (hereafter, *Assembly Magazine*) July 1989, 175. See also *American Battle Monuments Commission Website* (hereafter, *ABMC Website*).

22 "Who's in the Army Now?" in *Fortune*, September 1935, 39. There were 1,725 majors who averaged forty-three years of age. There were only 450 majors who were not forty. There were 577 lieutenant colonels whose average age was fifty-two and 470 colonels who averaged fifty-eight years of age. The five youngest colonels were fifty-three. The twenty-six brigadiers and twenty-one major generals averaged sixty-one years of age.

23 Telephone conversation with Jim Fleeger, Houston, TX, 12 June 2009.

24 "They'll Show Us Indoors, Fort Des Moines Polo Team Back Again," *Minneapolis Star*, Thursday, 16 February 1933. (James Fleeger's files).

25 "Des Moines Riders Here, Meet Omaha Club "4" at Ak Field Today; First Match in Years." No identified source. Omaha, NE newspaper, 11 June 1934. (James Fleeger's files).

26 "Who's in the Army Now?" in *Fortune*, September 1935, 40.

27 Phone interview with James Fleeger, Houston, TX, 26 December 2005. Some information provided/confirmed by Mrs. H. J. Fleeger during the phone call.

Two

"War seems very remote over here"

Captain Fleeger at Ft. Stotsenburg

Duty in the Philippines was very good duty. General MacArthur, who had served there twice before, returned in 1936 to become a field marshal in the Philippine Army and the Military Advisor to President Manual Quezon of the Philippines after serving for five years as the Chief of Staff of the U. S. Army. Many officers such as Fleeger's classmate, Samuel E. Jones, requested second tours.

The Americans served at excellent posts: Ft. Santiago inside the old Walled City of Manila, Ft. William McKinley and Nichols Field south of Manila, Ft. Stotsenburg and Clark Field about sixty miles north of Manila. They also served on Corregidor and the harbor forts in Manila Bay. Some fortunate ones worked and lived in the temperate mountains near Baguio, at Camp John Hay, the small post named for the Secretary of State who promulgated the Open Door Policy that affected relations with Japan.

A Good Life

Living was easy. Most officers employed Filipino servants to help their families, and most of the officers and their wives had access to good golf and tennis clubs, swimming pools, and other recreational facilities, as well as superb shopping in Manila.

Fleeger served comfortably at Ft. Stotsenburg with the 26th Cavalry (PS). As a captain, he occupied furnished quarters made of wood and plasterboard with a galvanized iron roof and having a living room, dining room, two to three bedrooms, and one or two baths.[1] The Fleegers had at least one Filipino servant, probably a cook-houseboy, and probably a second, a lavendera (washer woman). Pictures of him on horseback in front of what appear to be his quarters show a snappy officer in starched khakis on a fine horse, content with his environment. Other photos of his wife, some on horseback, indicate that her life was good also. A unique benefit made life even more pleasant for the Americans in the Philippines: "Officers, Warrant Officers, and Members of the Army Nurse Corps, are authorized thirty days Detached Service annually at Baguio for health, which is not counted against leave allowances."[2] Thus, officers could save their annual leave until they returned to the United States and could enjoy the wonderfully cool and refreshing mountain city which stood as a gateway to the great valleys to the north. In those valleys, the Igorot tribes had built spectacular, terraced paddies on the steep mountain slopes so they could grow rice. For courageous drivers and intrepid tourists, the drive north to Bontoc along the high ridgelines and on roads cut out of the sides of the mountains was breathtaking. The officers could also enjoy the facilities at Camp John Hay, a place that the U. S. Armed Forces used as a rest and recreational center for their personnel well into the 1980s.

ΩΩΩ

In the earliest surviving letter from the Philippines in 1940, Fleeger wrote to his friend, Keith Selby, the husband of Louise's sister Berta, about life on Luzon. [3]

> *The trip over was entirely worth while. Slightly extended and has to be approached with fixed determination to really vacation. Hawaii is a beautiful place, even more so than we had imagined, and a grand experience. However, after seeing Manila, we feel that Honolulu was quite tourist, for over here, even though Manila is very cosmopolitan, it is still native for the most part. Places to be visited here include Baguio, our very fine mountain resort with very suitable Army accommodations, Manila, and various sightseeing locations on the island of Luzon.* [4]

He sent a copy of the typed letter to his mother with a 9 January postscript.

Encouraging his friend to visit, Fleeger proposed: "Ideal trip from the mainland (I mean the U. S.) would be by clipper from Frisco to Manila, touching Honolulu, Wake Is., and Guam enroute. Here we could go to Baguio, Zamboanga, Manila, etc or just visit and have Celestino bring in more Scotch. From here we could catch small boats to make the Japan – China circle, and from Japan you could go back to the mainland while we cut down to Manila on another small boat...Naturally if Clipper were used either way, it should be coming over in order that you can take back your quota of purchases." [5]

The "Clipper" Fleeger spoke of was a four-engine Pan American Airlines flying boat that would land and take off in Manila Bay. It was a marvel of the day. Manilians often would go down to the seawall on Dewey Boulevard to watch a Clipper land or take-off. [6] As Fleeger reported, "The Clipper price will make you sort of brace your feet and sway," and "The Clipper trip would really be something to hang on your belt though." [7]

Then he talked about shopping, always a highlight for the Army and Navy families in the Philippines: "Lou has no doubt written to you about shopping. Oriental rugs, silver, linens, and what not are cheap and good. We are sorry that being poor folks, we can't have some of the very fine things that are available.

"LOU HAS NO DOUBT WRITTEN TO YOU ABOUT SHOPPING."

In fact it darn near broke Lou's heart. Our purchases are modest and we will probably always regret it." Emphasizing that duty was good in the Philippines, Fleeger reported: "So far we are enjoying ourselves entirely. We will certainly develop a tremendous appreciation for American civilization – cow's milk)* if nothing else, and it should widen our outlook.

---

* Fresh milk was not available during these years and for many years thereafter because there were no dairy cattle on Luzon.

EAST INDIES COLONY GETS MARTIAL LAW

GERMANS INTERNED AND SHIPS SEIZED – TOKYO ANNOUNCES STATUS QUO POLICY

Special Cable to the New York Times

SINGAPORE, MAY 10 – NEWS OF THE GERMAN INVASION OF THE NETHERLANDS REACHED THE NETHERLANDS EAST INDIES BY WIRELESS. THE GOVERNOR GENERAL ISSUED A PROCLAMATION SIMILAR IN TERMS TO THAT OF QUEEN WILHELMINA AND ANNOUNCED THAT ALL GERMANS OF MILITARY AGE, FROM 16 UPWARD, WOULD BE INTERNED IMMEDIATELY.

ALL THE GERMAN MERCHANT SHIPS THAT HAVE BEEN LYING IN NETHERLANDS INDIES HARBORS SINCE THE OUTBREAK OF WAR WERE SEIZED AND OTHER PRECAUTIONS WERE TAKEN.

WITHIN THREE HOURS IT WAS ANNOUNCED THAT THE MAJORITY OF GERMANS IN BATAVIA, SOURABAYA AND OTHER IMPORTANT TOWNS WERE DETAINED.

NEW YORK *TIMES*,
MAY 11, 1940, 1

The beef steak is tough and strong but it still tastes good because we know he was a well-meaning steer sniffing daisies around Cy's [Cyrus Young][8] country someplace....”[9]

At this time, Japan had been at war with China since 1937. Reflecting on the impact of that war, Fleeger told his friend that “At present Army officers can't debark at Shanghai – but the restriction may be lifted by next summer or fall” and then added, “I forgot to mention that the war seems very remote over here. Japan slaughters Chinese in the usual fashion – but there always seem to be more Chinese. And the war in Europe has not affected American shipping in Pacific waters. I'm sure that it is perfectly normal, and since my guess is as good as anyone's, I'd venture that there will be no change for 24 months at least – with possibly no danger of our entering the scra[p] at all. If we do go in I'll be home no doubt – and it will be apparent well in advance.”[10]

The major's guess about twenty-four months elapsing before anything happened in the Philippines was prescient or perhaps just a good guess, but his comment about “not entering the scrap” was not. His comments about the Japanese in China reflected the news about the Japanese atrocities in Nanking and follow-up stories in the press.[11] During the Rape of Nanking in 1937, the Japanese brutally killed between 260,000 and 350,000 non-combatants and raped 20,000-80,000 Chinese women, killing thousands.[12] The report of the Japanese killing Chinese did not seem to trouble him, but it should have as Fleeger and other Americans pondered their future in the Philippines. They soon would learn how the Japanese treated prisoners of war and captured civilians.

Fleeger ended his letter to Keith saying, “I feel sure that T. H. is a push-over for this trip – so pour it on him. He can mortgage the hail business and have a holiday. I will send him a copy of this lengthy survey on conditions on Luzon."[13] At this time, Fleeger did not seem to be thinking about a possible war in the Philippines.

ΩΩΩ

By the end of 1940, however, the situation in the Far East and the Pacific began to deteriorate. Negotiations began in Washington in March 1941 to try to resolve some of the problems between Japan and the United States. In April, Cordell Hull, the American Secretary of State, proposed four principles as the bases for negotiations. They were a restatement of Secretary of State John Hay's Open Door Policy of 1898. That same month, the U. S. Army began repatriating dependents from the Philippines.

On 24 July 1941, the Imperial Japanese Army occupied Southern French Indochina, and President Franklin Roosevelt froze Japanese assets in the United States, embargoed the sale of aviation fuel to Japan, and directed that all Philippine forces would become part of the American armed forces. The action shocked the Japanese leaders and changed the good life in the Philippines.

President Roosevelt signaled the importance of the change when he recalled General MacArthur to active duty and placed him in command of the Philippine Department replacing Major General George Grunert, who returned to the United States. Within a couple of days, the War Department established U. S. Army Forces Far East (USAFFE) which superseded the Philippine Department and appointed MacArthur to be its commander. Following the extraction of the military dependents, clear thinking observers could assume that the President had begun preparing for war with Japan.

"We Few"

Harry Fleeger and his comrades had to have known the status of the forces in the Philippines in early 1941,

FOUR U. S. NEGOTIATING PRINCIPLES

"RESPECT THE TERRITORIAL INTEGRITY AND SOVEREIGNTY OF EACH AND ALL NATIONS.

SUPPORT THE PRINCIPLE OF NON-INTERFERENCE IN THE INTERNAL AFFAIRS OF OTHER COUNTRIES.

SUPPORT THE PRINCIPLE OF EQUALITY, INCLUDING EQUALITY OF COMMERCIAL OPPORTUNITY.

NON-DISTURBANCE OF THE STATUS QUO IN THE PACIFIC EXCEPT AS THE STATUS QUO MAY BE ALTERED BY PACIFIC MEANS."

SMASHING AIR ATTACKS ON SIX RUSSIAN CITIES, CLASHES ON WIDE FRONT, OPEN NAZI-SOVIET WAR. LONDON TO AID MOSCOW, U.S. DELAYS DECISION

New York *Times*
23 June 1941, 1

and they had to have known that the existing small army units could not have stopped any determined modern army from invading and seizing Luzon. They had witnessed modern forces in action when the Germans overwhelmed the Poles with fast moving panzer forces supported by aggressive air forces and large infantry formations, and they had to have known about the Japanese successes in China where the Japanese Army had overrun the Chinese and Japanese air forces had contributed to its successes. The Americans should have concluded that their small ground forces with old weapons and their small air forces with obsolete aircraft would not be able to stand up well against combat-experienced Japanese forces.

On 31 July 1941, when MacArthur began to organize the defense of the islands, he only had 22,532 American and Filipino troops under his command, too few to repel a determined Japanese invasion. Moreover, Philippine Scouts – as in Fleeger's regiment -- outnumbered the Americans in the fighting units. The Scout Regiments had many long service soldiers, especially the NCOs, and when tested, they would fight determinedly against the Japanese.[14] In one Scout regiment that eventually fought beside Fleeger's regiment, fourteen Filipino Scouts earned Distinguished Service Crosses and well over fifty earned Silver Stars for gallantry in action.[15]

With MacArthur, the combat-experienced, highly decorated, and magnetic general in command, Fleeger and other army officers must have been inspired. One senior officer who was not a fan of MacArthur – he said the general was like a great piece of art, once you got close you to him you could see all the warts – recalled MacArthur's impact on him in 1941. After meeting MacArthur, the colonel said: "I felt that under such a Leader, we should accomplish miracles."[16]

Moreover, the officers must have believed that the United States Government would rectify the military weaknesses in the Philippines if the leaders really wanted to defend the islands while they focused on the growing war in Europe. Fortunately, they tried. The Army began sending additional personnel, new units, modern aircraft, and much needed arms and equipment to reinforce the Philippines. Consequently, by 30 November 1941, MacArthur had 31,095 officers and men in the ground and air corps units. They included 2,473 American officers, thirty-one Philippine Scout officers, 16,643 American enlisted men, and 11,957 Philippine Scouts. Among the new arrivals who bolstered MacArthur's forces were reserve officers such as Lieutenant Kenneth Otto Beach from Michigan, an infantry officer who joined the 31st Infantry Regiment at Nichols Field in June. Beach had volunteered for duty in the Philippines at the advice of his older brother, Captain Dwight Beach, who also had volunteered to serve in the islands. The Army did not send the elder Beach westward, but selected another artilleryman in his place, Captain Alva Fitch. The Army, however, sent Kenneth Otto Beach to the Philippines. Young Beach, who looked like a modern movie star, who had earned a law degree after graduating from the University of Michigan, and who like so many of the newly-arrived officers seemed so full of promise, would not survive the war. Fitch would. And Dwight Beach would never volunteer for an assignment again.[17] Decades later, Kenneth Beach's nephew and Harry Fleeger's son would become good friends.

Many other officers deployed to the islands. Twelve Veterinary Corps Officers, some volunteers, had arrived before Beach. They included Captain William Gochenour and Lieutenant Clayton Mickelsen who joined Fleeger's regiment.[18]

The officers who remained in Manila experienced a "great life" there.

Field officers such as Major John Ward, whom Fleeger would write about,[19] Chaplain Mathias Zerfas who joined the 26th Cavalry, and Chaplain Richard Carberry who befriended a cavalry officer, arrived and took on new assignments in the middle of 1941.[20] Experienced regular officers such as Colonels Bradford Chynoweth, Max Lough, William Morse, and Peter Vachon arrived much later to take senior positions in the Philippine Army. The senior officers "were rather grim." Chynoweth commented: "They knew what they were facing. They were headed for trouble, if not disaster."[21]

With all the new people, new forces, and new equipment, MacArthur still did not have a stout force capable of overwhelming a potential Japanese invasion force.

Many of the American officers, if not most of them, would serve with new Philippine Army units as instructors or commanders. Many of the American soldiers deployed on

THE OFFICERS WHO REMAINED IN MANILA EXPERIENCED A "GREAT LIFE" THERE.

THE PHILIPPINE DIVISION

- 31ST INFANTRY REGIMENT (US)

- 45TH INFANTRY REGIMENT (PS)

- 57TH INFANTRY REGIMENT (PS)

- 26TH CAVALRY REGIMENT (PS)

- 86TH FIELD ARTILLERY REGIMENT (PS)

- 88TH FIELD ARTILLERY REGIMENT (PS)

- 43RD INFANTRY REGIMENT (PS) (MINUS)

Luzon served in the Philippine Division, a Regular Army division, and the only division-sized U. S. Army unit in the islands. When its commander, Major General Jonathan M. Wainwright, looked at his lineup, he found that he had 517 American officers, 1,806 American soldiers, 7,909 enlisted Philippine Scouts (PS), and three infantry regiments that he could lead into combat. He realized that would he have to depend on his Filipino Scouts to provide the bulk of his combat force when the Japanese invaded and he would have to depend on their loyalty to fight a war for the United States on their home ground. The experienced and well-respected cavalry officer also found his regiments scattered around Manila with some elements like the 26th Cavalry (PS) stationed at far-away Ft. Stotsenburg. For years, the division's all-American 31st Infantry Regiment had been billeted in Post Manila and lived a fairly easy life in the old Walled City of the Philippine Capital. Its other two other regiments, the 45th Infantry (PS) and 57th Infantry (PS), staffed with American officers and manned by Scouts, called Ft. McKinley on the south side of Manila their home base.

According to Kenneth F. Zitzman, a Signal Corps officer and a 1935-36 veteran of the division, "The Philippine division was a well trained unit, and in each of my two years we did a lengthy maneuver during which we tried to fight off a Japanese landing at Linguayan Gulf, then slowly, and methodically, fought as we were pushed back over 100 miles to the tip of Bataan where the guns of Corregidor boomed in our support. At that point, the maneuver ended and we all went home."[22] Lieutenant James Gavin, an infantryman, reported similar training on Luzon during his service there from 1936 to 1938. He wrote, "Several times we rehearsed the withdrawal into the Bataan Peninsula. We then maneuvered, falling back as we anticipated the World War II pattern of fighting on the peninsula. The situation was far from good. There were wide gaps in the center of our defenses, and obviously inadequate food and water for the thousands of soldiers and civilians that would crowd into the place."[23] Gavin went on to report the use of pack mules in his Philippine Scout regiment. He explained that a friend's job on Bataan was "to deliver rations and ammunition by pack train at night." Gavin added that "Handling a string of mules at night on a dark jungle trail is a difficult job," and that his friend got lost.[24] Apparently, the Philippine Division or many elements of the division spent ten weeks on maneuvers between June and December 1941.[25]

Regardless of its training status, the division lacked manpower – thus combat power - compared to large World War I divisions and to the later standard 15,000 man World War II infantry divisions.

American officers commanded the division's remaining maneuver units, the 26th Cavalry Regiment (PS), the 43rd Infantry Regiment (PS), and the 86th and 88th Field Artillery Regiments (PS). Few, if any, American enlisted soldiers served in these units. Moreover, these units did not compare to similar units in the United States: the 26th Cavalry had only two squadrons of three troops each rather than the three squadrons of three troops each found in stateside cavalry regiments; the tiny 43rd Regiment had only 328 men assigned instead of about 3,600; and the field artillery regiments approximated battalions. These small ground units on Luzon also lacked the combat power that they would need to deal with invading Japanese divisions. The horse-mounted 26th Cavalry with only a few scout cars, no tanks, and no artillery would fight valiantly but would be vulnerable to enemy air and tank forces. The small artillery units needed more modern equipment and heavier firepower. A young artillery officer commented, "When I got to the PI in 1941, the artillery vehicles were vintage 1923," and the "Artillery issued even to the expanding Philippine Scouts were the American 75mm model 1916, - the first ever manufactured in the US – and had many faults" and "the 24th FA (PS) was armed with the British 75."[26] During the fight on Mindanao, he reported that "there were only 3 artillery pieces for all the southern islands – 2.95 [inch] pack howitzers model 1898 Maxim-Vickers with a muzzle velocity of [800 feet per second]" and which "had only a large spring as a recoil mechanism and the crew had to pull them back into battery with ropes attached to rings on the hubs of the wheels because they jumped back about 4-5 [feet] after each round."[27]

The 192nd and 194th Tank Battalions arrived in September to bolster the American forces. The two maneuver units may have been the most valuable reinforcements for the

THESE SMALL GROUND UNITS ON LUZON ALSO LACKED THE COMBAT POWER THAT THEY WOULD NEED TO DEAL WITH INVADING JAPANESE DIVISIONS.

HARBOR DEFENSE FORCES

- HQ & HQ BATTERY

- 59TH COAST ARTILLERY REGIMENT

- 60TH COAST ARTILLERY REGIMENT

- 91ST COAST ARTILLERY REGIMENT (PS)

- 92ND COAST ARTILLERY REGIMENT (PS)

- USAMP HARRISON

- STATION HOSPITAL (CORREGIDOR)

- CHEMICAL WARFARE DETACHMENT

ground forces. Each battalion had fifty-four (54) light tanks. Purely American, the battalions contained disparate National Guard companies. The 192nd Battalion included companies from Harrodsburg, KY, Janesville, WI, Maygood, IL, and Port Clinton, OH. The 194th had companies from Brainerd, MN, St. Joseph, MO, and Salinas, CA.

On 21 November 1941, only days before war broke out, USAFFE assigned the tank battalions and an independent ordnance company to a Provisional Tank Group, and appointed Colonel James R. N. Weaver to command of the provisional unit. The National Guard tankers would work closely with the 26th Cavalry. But USAFFE and Weaver would need more tanks with larger guns.

The 200th Coast Artillery Regiment (Anti-Aircraft) with 1,809 Americans from New Mexico also arrived in September. The largest of the American ground unit besides the 31st Infantry Regiment of the Philippine Division, the 200th had been organized from former cavalry units of the New Mexico National Guard, and it had a large number of Mexican-American soldiers. [28]

Two chaplains, Albert Braun and Frederick Howden, accompanied the New Mexico troops. Fleeger would live with Braun and would talk about Howden in his diary, and he would meet and work with many of these Coast Artillery soldiers in the months to come.

The newly arrived National Guard tank and coast artillery units were not regular units and as such needed additional training to acclimatize them to Luzon and bring them up to combat standards. They would have fewer than ninety days to prepare for war.

MacArthur also had the small all-American 808th Military Police Company, a stout Harbor Defense Force, and various Service Detachments (Quartermaster Corps, Engineer Corps, Medical Department, etc.) in his command. The Harbor Defense Force totaled 5,225 officers and men, and the service troops totaled 4,268 officers and men, Americans as well as Philippine Scouts.

After reinforcement, the newly formed Far East Air Force had 669 officers and 4,940 enlisted men on station, all Americans. Major General Lewis Brereton, a Naval Academy graduate and an aviation pioneer, commanded the air units which included the large 24th Pursuit Group and the large 19th Bomb Group. One hundred and seven modern P-40E fighters formed the backbone of the fighter force on Luzon. Although new, the P-40s generally could not outperform the Japanese Zero, and their pilots would have a hard time fighting the combat-experienced Japanese pilots. A few fighter pilots who survived the initial Japanese attacks would fight courageously during the first days of war. Filipino Captain Jesus Villamor would earn two Distinguished Services Crosses for his exploits. The Air Corps, however, lacked a sufficient number of modern fighters to challenge the Japanese who had over 500 combat aircraft stationed on Formosa at this time, and who also could deploy carrier aircraft against the Americans in the Philippines. The U. S. Army Air Forces deployed thirty-five modern B-17s to the Philippines with the hope that they could serve as primary strike force and could hinder or deter any Japanese attack. The excellent four-engine bombers had great promise, but they had never been tested in combat. American air leaders should have realized how pitifully small the bomber force was because they knew what had been going on in Europe. In September 1940, the German *Luftwaffe* had launched a "blitz" on London with 500 bombers and 600 fighters, and the British Royal Air Force had launched a 134-bomber- raid on Mannheim on 12 December 1940. These and other German and British air raids against land and sea targets before December 1941 did not accomplish anything of military significance, although they caused high civilian casualties. They, however, were more powerful strikes than thirty-five B-17s could have delivered.[29]

...MACARTHUR DID NOT HAVE SUFFICIENT AIR AND LAND FORCES ON LUZON TO DEFEAT A PROBABLE JAPANESE INVASION.

As the War Department reinforced the Philippines, the Navy added submarines to the Asiatic Fleet but no modern surface ships. Fortunately, the Navy had sent some small, fast, and highly mobile PT boats to the islands. The boats and one other addition –at the last minute, the Navy transferred the 4th Marine Regiment from Shanghai to Manila – would benefit MacArthur. The PT Boats and the small 750- man-regiment would join MacArthur's command after the Asiatic Squadron left Philippine waters.

By 8 December 1941, MacArthur did not have sufficient air and land forces on Luzon to defeat a probable Japanese invasion. In hindsight, MacArthur had sufficient forces to hurt the Japanese if they blundered their operations, but to defend Manila, Manila Bay, and most of Luzon in 1941 and early 1942, he needed a much stouter force – at least two more well-trained and well-equipped American divisions with more artillery and tanks, supported by additional modern fighters. But the Army had no new, well-equipped, and trained divisions or additional fighters to deploy to the Philippines as the United States mobilized for war, and most Army planners as well as Navy planners were prepared to write off the islands if Japan invaded them. Moreover, MacArthur did not ask for any more reinforcements. Therefore, he would have to depend on Filipino divisions which he would have to mobilize, equip, and train. Mobilization would begin on 1 September 1941 (two years after the German invasion of Poland), but it would be many months – perhaps a year - before these units could be expected to be combat worthy. MacArthur would not have that time. He realized his position. An incoming senior American officer slated to command the 61st Philippine Army Division, commented after an interview with MacArthur, "The General had little to offer in way of encouragement. He told me that when I went to my division I would find serious shortages of equipment, but that I must make it do because I could not expect to get more. He said that the officers and non-commissioned officers in the Philippine Army were not all that one could wish for but that for political reasons I must give them every chance."[30]

Harry Fleeger and his comrades, even though reinforced from the United States by December 1941 and apparently strengthened by recently mobilized Philippine Army divisions, faced their impending job with too few first-class troops, too few tanks, too few air squadrons, and too few warships, but they would fight longer than the Danes, the Norwegians, the Dutch, the Belgians, the French, and the British in Europe in 1941, and the British in Hong Kong in 1941 and Malaya in 1941 and 1942.

Separation

After being repatriated to the United States, Louise Fleeger returned to Parker, SD, with her two boys. There, she began to reconstruct her life while her husband struggled to deal with their separation. Very lonely and somewhat adrift, Fleeger wrote a number of

"IT'S HELL WITHOUT WORD FROM YOU LOU."

letters to her that provide a fascinating look at life during the pre-war months in the Philippines and at how the separation from his wife tore at him.

His first letter home, dated 20 August 1941, was a combination news report and love letter and set the tone for all of his letters. [31] He wrote; "Mail has been awfully scarce honey – but we think a clipper got in today so I should have a letter from you tomorrow. And the next one leaving in 3 days so I can answer your last letter tomorrow night." Continuing, "It's hell without word from you Lou. Pouring rain today – Wed – so I came over to work awhile rather than loaf around the house. Good movie tonite, so John [Captain John Wheeler] and I may go to the first show. Everything very quiet Lou – and very dull. Just sort of drag along another day without you – thinking of coming home and wishing it were over. I'm afraid the last half of the drag will be the worst although when I get orders, if I do, it should make the last few weeks easier to stand." Then he talked about the situation in the Philippines. "News over here rather alarming but probably not as much so as pictured at home. Can't tell yet – but I hope and rather expect it to remain as is more or less until next Spring 1942 – when I should be home. (I mean I should be home before then)!" He ended his letter with "I'll be home before long so hang on."

Fleeger covered many subjects in the next surviving letter, dated Saturday 26 September with additional entries on 27, 28, 29 September and 1 October.[32] He talked about the regimental review held that morning ("very good"), said that heavy rain came in during the afternoon and prevented him from playing golf, and that he had left a lot of work at the office.   Then he wrote: ting ready to start polo – (as manager Lou – I won't play again here – that's my promise). I'll have over 20 players and I should have at

"RATHER INDICATED MY RETURN BY XMAS FOR SURE LOU – PROBABLY ORDERS IN NOVEMBER – PROVIDING WE HAVE NO EMERGENCY – AND THAT SEEMS VERY REMOTE NOW..."

least a sort of season in spite of the work." Then he turned to what became his most pervasive subject: going home. "Had a letter from [Philippine] Dept this morning. Dept C.O. finally announced a written policy about return of officers – more or less as Big George [probably Major General Grunert] told Col. Fields [probably Lt. Colonel Albert Fields, Dental Corps]*. Return to be based on replacements but that it was expected that a two year tour could be established in near future. Rather indicated my return by Xmas for sure Lou – probably orders in November – providing we have no emergency – and that seems very remote now – and will continue so through the winter months. I'll send a letter to Harry Stadler [possibly Colonel John H. Stadler, Cavalry][33] – and we rather expect quite a group of cavalry replacements in October. That should release everyone of July & October boats. – So it looks a lot clearer now. The worst seems to be over." He closed with "...very lonely this afternoon – and another Sunday to live through tomorrow. Wish it could be with you...I love you Louise – so hard – this is becoming very hard to take..."

---

* The *1943 Army Directory* lists a Lt. Colonel Albert Fields, DC as missing in action. No other regular army officer named Fields was in the Philippines.

On Sunday, he rode up to the Bamban River, north of Ft. Stotsenburg and reminisced about previously riding there with his wife. He implied that an improved "two-way graded highway" was related to new activity in the area. He worked on polo plans, said the season would begin soon, and that "I'll act as manager until I leave." He continued, "Glad to be because it will keep me that much busier although I'm more or less swamped already. I'll stick and ball and run the string etc. but not play." Then he returned to returning home. "I hope to have orders any way by the time play starts in mid-Nov." He added, "Had a beer at the club at noon – and played golf this afternoon. – Sat around the house an hour before golf and almost went crazy Lou thinking of you. It's awful. Tonite will have a wimpy [hamburger] at the club and I may go to a movie – or just read awhile." Next he spoke about his friends. "John [Wheeler] is in Manila – and Gordon asleep – he took on a snoot full last nite... Both he and I are a bit done up by this wait but manage to do well – and not show it. – Everyone feels a little better about things now that Dept has announced a plan. – Clinty [Regimental Commander, Colonel Clinton Pierce] plans on July and Oct boats leaving before Xmas and we will re-arrange our officers accordingly."

"...HOPE WE CAN GET QUARTERS AT RILEY LOU – I'LL BE PRETTY HIGH RANKING WITH ALL THE RESERVES THERE – IF ANY HAPPEN TO BE EMPTY."

Fleeger then discussed selling some of his things while at the same time he discussed what he was going to do about his saddles and his equipment and what he would need when he returned to Ft. Riley, the historic cavalry post in Kansas. Then, he went back to returning home, writing: "I wrote a letter regular mail to you about our Frisco Trip Lou – and I still plan on your meeting me there unless some real emergency prevents it...Hope we can get quarters at Riley Lou – I'll be pretty high ranking with all the reserves there – if any happen to be empty." He ended the entry with "All for now...so lonely for you – will the next two months ever pass by."

On Monday, he wrote about getting a saddle carrier made and reported that a wealthy reserve cavalry officer [assigned to Headquarters, Ft. Stotsenburg], George Kaufman,[34] told him about the special carrier. He told Lou that "I have a very good field set complete now – was Col. Blaine's, English saddle with all the gadgets. If I go to Riley I will need it with me so can take this and keep it in the stateroom." Continuing, Fleeger wrote: "Saw Dutch this morning for a while – he says Connie is fine – and he hasn't been able to get Soo Falls yet. He too thinks we will surely be out soon, and it helps to have something to look forward too." *

_____

* No biographical information available about Steve, Gordon, Colonel Blaine, Dutch, Connie.

ΩΩΩ

On 1 October, Fleeger recorded: "Organization day – my 3rd Lou – so we have another holiday - Raining hard – typhoon – no doubt several days of it – so I'm home at 11:30 writing some letters – want Steve to send dope from Riley about quarters so will write to him. Got Mird's [Mildred Morgan Young][35] ring today. Very pretty. Sammy[*] delayed awhile leaving so I may send in regular mail. If it is inspected for duty it is still worth it. -- Sold the radio today honey 17 pesos (cost 22) so didn't lose on it. Gordon is having his repaired and we will use it the rest of the time... All 3 clippers now held up – no air mail has arrived for 2 weeks...Very wet lonely day Darling ... I need a letter – it has been so long – will be several days yet ... don't give up Louise – I feel that I will surely be with you by Xmas – and the time will pass in some way."[36]

What is interesting in these early letters is what Fleeger does not say. As a temporary captain[37] commanding Troop E of the 26th Cavalry, he wrote nothing about his troop, his officers, field training, or anything related to the troop's war preparations. Fleeger's comments about working in the office, being bored, the coming polo season, and especially about reassignment indicated a sense of unreality at the fighting level of the command as the threat of war continued to grow, possibly

FLEEGER'S COMMENTS ...INDICATED A SENSE OF UNREALITY AT THE FIGHTING LEVEL OF THE COMMAND AS THE THREAT OF WAR CONTINUED TO GROW...

exacerbated by Fleeger's desire to get home regardless of the reality around him. Was Fleeger alone in blocking out developments, or was everyone that way? At this time, General MacArthur was working furiously to mobilize, train, and equip new Philippine Army Divisions to defend the Philippines, and he needed experienced and able-bodied American officers to advise and train the new Filipino drafts. While he was requesting and getting officers and units assigned to Manila, it would have been unreal for MacArthur to let experienced officers rotate home. The fog of peace seemed to blanket war preparations.

ΩΩΩ

In contrast to Fleeger's comments, Captain Harry Packard, a field artillery officer, had written to his friends much earlier in the year, 12 March 1941, about service in the Philippines.[38] Packard said: "...the defense forces here have finally awakened to the fact that the war is in the air. I am not sure that we would have discovered that fact if we had not received a new influx of officers who had recently been through maneuvers in the

[*] No biographical information available about Sammy.

States. They came over apprehensive and filled with all sorts of screwy ideas about national defense, and jarred us out of our-polo-playing-golf addict attitude that was so pleasant and relaxing."

"THEY ... JARRED US OUT OF OUR-POLO-PLAYING-GOLF ADDICT ATTITUDE THAT WAS SO PLEASANT AND RELAXING."

CAPTAIN HARRY PACKARD

Packard went on to describe his recruiting trip to the central islands and reported that his wife would sail for the United States on 16 April, and he expected many other wives to do so with life changing so much at the fort. He went on to report that "Stotsenburg is turning flip-flops daily" and wrote about dealing with the new Filipino recruits. He spoke about the reorganization of the artillery, saying it "is still in the throes of indecision," and he added, "I daresay we'll stop fighting Indians someday and get organized." And yet, contemplating the future, Packard told his friends:

> As to the Japs, I'm still willing to bet a bottle of good whiskey that we'll have no war here in the Philippines. When I first arrived I thot [sic] the defense of these islands was a joke. I'm getting more confidence – perhaps I've missed too many boats [home]. There's a big change of course in the equipment and men that we now have. Seeing a few planes in the air – knowing that there are a few rounds of ammunition left for the second day of fire – all helps a lot. Six months ago the squadron of bombers at Clark Field had 17 planes and five pilots available to fly them! Leaving one man as OD at the field I think they could put three planes in the air!"

Looking at the world, the artillery officer added: "It all depends on what happens in Europe – if Britain holds out there'll be no trouble here. If Germany gets the upper hand I still am doubtful if Japan will strike here.

Reinforcing Packard's comments about an easygoing life on the island, newly arrived Catholic Chaplain Robert Carberry, who joined the 45th Infantry (PS) at Ft. McKinley in June 1941, wrote home to two of his religious associates and said: "It isn't that I haven't had time to write to both, but in the islands, we try to do only what we have to, we seem to save our strength daily for something that we want to do tomorrow and if it is work or play tomorrow never really comes ... It has been very pleasant, you go to work early, you sign your name at eleven in the morning, to show that you are at work and not in jail or the hospital, and they ask that you do the same on the morrow. I play golf every afternoon that the weather is OK, and in the evening it's either to the show at the Post or to the city of Manila, which is only five miles away."[39]

ΩΩΩ

While Father Carberry visited religious friends and churches in the city, another June arrival, First Lieutenant Edwin Ramsey who joined the 26th Cavalry (PS) at Ft. Stotsenburg, found nightlife there to be dull and unexciting with all the families gone. Consequently, he sought different entertainment in Manila. He remembered that, "On our weekends, which were free, we drove down to Manila. Three hundred years of Spanish influence and forty of American had made it an eclectic and exciting metropolis." He added, "Being cavalrymen, we sought out the sin, and there was no shortage of it. Gambling houses abounded...There were bars of every kind and class, and bordellos warmed the side streets...Our favorite haunt was the La Playa, a bar and restaurant run by a syndicate of American gamblers from Shanghai..."

Ramsey then reported some of the excitement he found: "My squadron commander, Major Jim Blanning,* was chatting at the bar with several Filipinos in stylish white tropical suits and white oxfords with spats. Instinctively I headed for the dance floor, but no sooner had I

> **".. WE SOUGHT OUT THE SIN, AND THERE WAS NO SHORTAGE OF IT."**
>
> LT. EDWIN RAMSEY

reached it than I heard Blanning and the Filipinos arguing. Suddenly one of them hefted his glass and smashed it into Blanning's face. The glass shattered, and the shards splayed across his head and shoulders. I was the nearest American and so I leapt in, grabbed the Filipino, and swung at his jaw. He dropped with a grunt. I seized Blanning's shirtfront, which was soaked with blood, and shoved him toward a group of Americans at the end of the bar." Ramsey then got bloodied and the fight ended when a Filipino drew a revolver. Later, he learned that Blanning had been taken to a hospital and that the glass had just missed his eye. Ramsey, still partying in Manila, soon got involved with a Russian dancer who turned out to be a Japanese spy. More was going on than was seen at Ft. Stotsenburg. [40]

Life in the Philippines for soldiers obviously was schizophrenic. Impressions varied widely. Packard found life more electric as war approached, Carberry found it languid, and Ramsey and Blanning found life full of fun and danger. At the same time, Fleeger, considered his life placid, boring, and most of all lonely. Life, however, was about to change for Fleeger and his comrades. In October 1941, General Hideki Tojo became the

---

* Ramsey seems to have post-dated Blanning's position. Before war began, Major T. J. H. Trapnell commanded the 2nd Squadron, and for a time after war started, Blanning was the Headquarters Commandant of North Luzon Force. After Trapnell became the Regimental Executive Officer on Bataan, Blanning took over the squadron on 2 February 1942. Ramsey served under Blanning on Bataan.

Prime Minister as well as the War Minister in Japan, and he formed a cabinet that "reeked of gunpowder." The Tojo Government would soon decide to go to war.

ΩΩΩ

Fleeger's November letters continued to cover his earlier themes, but he added some new ones that indicated that war was approaching. He started a sixteen-page letter on the 14th with news about polo. "I've had a busy day - worked hard until 4 and then umpired polo – I still run – and <u>umpire</u> polo waiting for Joe Cleary[41] to come in from Phil. Army mobilization - A few periods – not much like the old days. But I'm still firm in my

"I'VE HAD A BUSY DAY - WORKED HARD UNTIL 4 AND THEN UMPIRED POLO..."

promise Lou – not to play until you and I are on the sidelines again. So I umpire - coach - and manage. I do it up brown – as much as it is – So all seem to be satisfied. Nearly all new officers you wouldn't know. It keeps me busy those deadly hours 4 to 6 – so I guess it is alright and I end each day exhausted." [42]

Then he turned to military subjects. "Not much news Lou. John [Wheeler] is on a march and problem so gone tonight... Things happening very fast now Dear – but in spite of it all I still believe my dope of last letter (read it again) is best judgement at this time. However it appears that assistance from States is almost here – in tremendous strength – all secret – and to make room we may not return here after our December maneuvers – but remain permanently in the field. Don't talk about it – as usual – but that's the score more or less – all proceeded by Life [Magazine] reporters, etc. giving it very much the aspect of a show-down. No way to know Lou – may be the day, but as I've said in my last letter – I don't think so. We are all guessing of course. The floods from the main land sort of make us wonder. Don't know yet how it will affect release of officers – but as I told Bill [Captain William Chandler, S-3, 26th Cavalry] today – the important thing may be to remain alive – It is all rather a staggering picture and our life after another week may be one of confusion and work – that always accompanies such a situation. Bill even heard today that all officers were here until it's over. I discount that entirely but mention it to indicate how fast we are starting to move. Don't let it alarm you – No doubt it was only a cracked info rumor. No change in policy to return us home yet has been suggested as far as we know. I know that your headlines must be rather Far Eastern – but wanted you to know that I still go along about usual."

He went on to report that the general had allowed the Officers' Club to bring up Manila nightclub acts to put on a show. He said that two or three of the girls "were on the hot side" but were "well covered by clothes." Then, he reminisced about the time when "reserve officers" brought a nude whore into a party at Ft. Des Moines and how upset and embarrassed he was about the event. Fleeger continued about his morale. "Received your radiogram yesterday Lou – not to give up – and it was so good to get it from you – but it made me realize that I sort of hit the bottom there for a few weeks and must have written some dismal letters. I'm sorry Darling, I always try to do the right thing but I spent 3 very miserable weeks with a very bad cold – not in bed but felt like the Devil – bad cough – sore throat etc. – and it ruined me – never had suffered mentally so in all my life. – And there are many others – Bill [Chandler] is a wreck – and Jim [most likely Blanning] no better – helping himself with lots of rum – but I'm not that way Louise – my love is too great for me to ever act or be other than you'd want – and I am famous for my good humor and nature – every dam smile and word of which is as false as can be. But your despair has always been one of my

"BUT YOUR DESPAIR HAS ALWAYS BEEN ONE OF MY WORST WORRIES."

worst worries...When I thought that I couldn't live another day without your love, you sent the radio helping me. It was wonderful Louise – I've never been so helped in all my life – I was so discouraged and blue I almost hoped I'd be deathly sick – and then to hear from you – Be a good soldier.... Still I want you to know how one word of help from you has almost made me bungle along and do what I should."[43]

On the 15th, he wrote extensively about mail. "Clipper came in yesterday so today I have two more letters from you Dear. They're so sweet I can't stop reading them...Your letters have been so very wonderful I'm almost worried for fear that now you're being nice to me and not telling me everything...But Lou I can't say too often – or ask you too often – to write to me like that – always – send an air mail at <u>least</u> every three days Lou. That's the most you can do for me until I come home, I count on them very much Lou – so don't forget. This – over here – is so bad now that missing 1 Clipper is ghastly – I've never suffered so – and it make me realize that we are not quite so stable here as we might be. I'm trying to tell you how wonderful your letters are my Darling – how I live for them – and will – as long as I'm here – and to beg you to give me part of each day so I'll hear often – and over and over how you love me...after all its all I have to live for here – and its importance is so tremendous it leaves me weak."[44] He also wrote briefly about his reassignment: "...let me say again that so far as we know of no reason to prevent our return reasonably soon – and the policy to return us had been officially announced."[45]

ΩΩΩ

Out of the blue, Fleeger broached a new, disturbing subject: the morale of other officers. "I had a beer with Bill and Jim at the club this noon on the way home (usually do Sat and Sun noons honey – we live like machines) and they are both almost despondent. Very bad. Cistil [Blanning] facing 2 boy operations – tonsils etc – with no one to take care of the 3rd while she goes to the hospital and Betty [Chandler] almost crazy with ear punctures on Port [Clark Porter Chandler, II, age 4½ years] and no help for Stuart [William Stuart Chandler, age 2½ years] – both families hearing from the bank – no funds – dead broke. And literally going thru Hell. Rent, light, coal, bills, etc - Seeing Bill & Jim so extremely low made me do some heavy thinking Lou and I wanted to mention it to you. By

"...DON'T TRUST ANYONE WITH WHAT I WRITE LOU."

the way the way things are written home seem to fly back here is miraculous – Don't trust anyone with what I write Lou."[46] He added a little later: "You can't even know Lou ... what horror ... that Bill etc go thru. Bill is a wreck – mentally – not physically – and by looking at him I begin to see what your security has meant to me – it helps keep me well for one thing and that's important. And I need not add that the strain is starting to do strange things with health.[47]

The impact of separations on military families has varied greatly over the years. Not much has changed since 1941.[48] Families with "money problems" have often been unable to buy adequate food or pay bills, as illustrated in Fleeger's letters. Those with "separation problems" faced other crises: sometimes the military member broke down and turned to heavy drinking or running around, or became despondent and in some cases committed suicide; sometimes the wives felt abandoned or were not strong enough to cope with managing their families alone; and sometimes marriages collapsed under the new strains. But there was a difference in the post-war era and there is a difference today: soldiers know that they are going on "hardship" or separated peacetime tours. In Fleeger's era, most probably the only serving Army officers who had ever deployed overseas without their families did so during World War I.

Later in his long letter, Fleeger continued to talk about himself. "I'm <u>homesick</u> Lou – and only 3 pictures ... in months." Then, he talked again about returning. "As for the trip home Lou – guess we won't really know what we will want to do – or have to do to satisfy this long wait – until I'm enroute in Honolulu. So just make all plans Dearest – and we will decide at the time." Continuing: "As to when that will be there is not dope Lou. – A boat sailing there – are many – takes a few this week, but only one I've heard of going is Ed Grenade [medical officer assigned to Stotsenburg].[49] July boat still held temporarily.

We think it's for a boat last week of Nov but war news causes some to question that. General opinion seems to be that July and Oct. boats would straggle out anyway tho – even if war was declared. Probably only somewhat delaying departure. I still hold all that very remote – and will tell you at <u>once</u> when we know. Even if it should be duration Lou don't give up. That's just another way of saying emergent and it isn't even logical that it would be in our case. However, things over here are so big now that I can't even hint at it so you could understand and thank heavens. If worst came to worst it will save us. Your rumor about [Ft.] Ord is probably correct. We have heard also – en-route – but don't know if it is your barrio boys."

He included disturbing comments about a fellow officer. "John [Wheeler] has slept all P. M. – he's a pretty sober fellow but said (in the field last night) Jim [probably Blanning] drank all nite so he had to keep him company. Rather bad on Jim – may have to have Clinty move in on him for his own good. He used to bother me in bed at 4 A. M. but I threw him out a few months ago and he hasn't bothered me since."

ΩΩΩ

On 16 November, in a separate seven page letter[50] written on regular stationery in ink, Captain Fleeger wrote: "Up at 7 and played 18 holes of golf – picking up two Air Corps boys half way round. Nice day – fairly hot as usual – but pleasant on the golf course – and the sunshine has been good for my cold. So sort of tooled along thinking about you Lou – and wishing for your company. Met Col. Ramsey [probably Lt. Colonel Mott Ramsey, VC)* on the golf course – Vet – now USAFFE Vet and has been ill since he transferred to Manila. Said he hated the city – and he looked it. Visiting Col. Fields] I guess. My game was fair – broke 100 anyway and hope to play enough to have a fair game by the time I start to play with Jim and Larry. In at 10:30 – half hour in the office – an hour with Clinty at 5 O and loafing this afternoon."

> *"WE LEAVE ON MANEUVERS WITH SKINNY [WAINWRIGHT] DEC 1. DOPE IS THAT WE PROBABLY WILL NEVER RETURN..."*

Next he wrote about field maneuvers: "We leave on maneuvers with Skinny [Wainwright] Dec 1. Dope is that we probably will never return – in the field from now on – no doubt to make room here for your Parker boys if they are the ones – and to stand by in the field while they train. The prospect is not so bad. We should be in one place most of the time

---

* The *1943 Army Directory* listed only one Ramsey – Mott Ramsey - as being a regular officer in the Veterinary Corps. At that time, Ramsey was at Ft. Sam Houston, TX where he might have been hospitalized. No Colonel Ramsey shows up as a POW or as a war casualty on available lists.

– semi-permanent and should be gone by the rainy season – the hard part of the year in the field. Still focused on leaving, he continued: "So later this P. M. I have to sort of re-pack – putting my civilian clothes – and best things in your steel trunk. So if we don't come back I can come in a day – or write Honorio – to get the valuables – (I have very few fortunately) in storage etc. If it develops that we remain out John and I will try to have Honorio join us to take care of our tents – clothes – mail – etc and act as valet, house-boy – lavendera [laundress], and tent orderly. Haven't asked him yet but can get another if

"SOME POSSIBILITY THAT THE WAR SCARE MAY DELAY OUR RETURN SOMEWHAT – WE DON'T KNOW..."

he won't go. He is very good – and honest and reliable – so is worth the 10 pesos each we pay him – almost worth that for the care he gives our air mail – around which our entire lives revolve." Turning to the war situation, he added, "Some possibility that the war scare may delay our return somewhat – we don't know – but if it does – don't let it turn you over Dear. We old timers will get the breaks within a reasonable time, in spite of even a war – we believe. Our numbers now – compared to the total here is a drop in the bucket. Heavens I hardly know anyone on the post anymore." On a personal note, Fleeger added some steamy comments for his wife and ended the letter with; "start a bonfire with this, Just wave it at the pit and it will burn."

Fleeger must have been appointed the Regimental Adjutant (S-1) at this time because he spent time with his regimental commander, Colonel Pierce.[51] That would have been normal for the chief personnel and administrative officer of the regiment while the regiment remained in garrison.

ΩΩΩ

Four days later, a new American colonel – soon to be a brigadier general - arrived for duty in the Philippines. Crusty Bradford Chynoweth, an infantryman, did not like the outlook of officers in Manila. [52] He recalled that the officers attending the Reception Party in Manila "seemed wholly unaware that War was about to erupt." He disgustingly reported that "The Air Force officers flaunted grotesque beards and moustaches... They were overdue to return to the U. S. and they grew these hirsute appendages in *passive protest*. What a commentary on their discipline and morale! It all seemed unreal. Chynoweth concluded: "This sense of *unreality* remained with me throughout my stay in Manila. This *false calm*, like the eye of a hurricane!" Told that he would command the 61st Division (Philippine Army) on Panay, Chynoweth asked MacArthur's G-1, Colonel Paul Stivers, when he could leave, and he noted that Stivers said: "Oh, don't be in such a hurry! Stick around and enjoy the night life in Manila!" Next, the colonel reported that his West Point classmate, Charlie Drake, the USAFFE Quartermaster, took him to dinner at the Jai Lai Club where they sat in front of a "Japanese and his wife, looking haughty and not friendly." Later, he said that Drake "dragged me off to meet a special friend of his. It was Bud Coyle of the Artillery." He added, "Charlie Drake then steered me to the next night spot," and concluded "I was not a do-gooder, but felt then, and still do, that USAFFE Headquarters was gravely wrong to put night life ahead of war."[53]

Chynoweth would have been fascinated by Fleeger's comments to his wife on 17 and 18 November. Fleeger continued his story. I "sent an Air Mail today. But forgot something – while we are on maneuvers and after that Dec -1-15 – if we stay in the field I may not be able to send messages amateur radio. So don't worry! The Sig. Co. [Signal Company], McKinley, that sends them will be on maneuvers too and the station at McK may close for a while... Two years of tiredness – blue – and somewhat discouraged – and the house a dam dormitory....Guess we have both discovered that living without each other is just a series of days – sort of empty of living – except that you have our boys... Still no news about sailings Louise. And very little of anything else that I can tell you. We expect all of this area to look like Chicago in about a week – but you'll have to see it in your papers when it comes out. As a matter of fact we don't know how many or when – a great deal depends on the conference in Washington. - Very large and vicious war Louise – as you have said and I often think – What small pawns we are. - However I have constant faith in early return to you no matter what – also wanted to sort of warn you about mail Lou. If anything pops I suppose clipper service will be sporadic – if so my letters will be en-route 2 or 3 each week as usual and will get to you even tho they may be late, and as always I will live for yours. I knew Nov. would be an endless month and it is. I count days much as I did at West Point fourth year waiting to go home to marry you – I recall how endless those months were too." [54]

Fascinatingly, Fleeger did not seem to consider that any Japanese strike would terminate "civilian" air and boat traffic to the Philippines, much less military air and boat traffic. He had to have known about a critical American strategic dilemma in the Pacific, namely, that the Japanese occupied the mandated Caroline, Marshall, and Mariana Islands which dominated the small American possessions of Wake and Guam that served as stepping stones in the line of communications (and the Clipper route) that stretched from the United States to the Philippines. In case of war, Japan could easily block air and sea routes from Hawaii to the Philippines.

Marking Time

Just as fascinating, Fleeger appeared to be dealing with his remaining days in the Philippines as he most probably did as a cadet – marking time - and counting the days until good things would happen, much as American leaders seemed to be marking time until something dramatic happened in the Pacific. Cadets always focused on the time remaining to important events, especially happy ones, and as a consequence, upperclassmen required their Plebes, Fourth Class Cadets (freshmen), to recite "The Days" on demand and include official and unofficial information in their oral reports. On Fleeger's demand, a plebe might have responded:

"Sir the days!
There are four days until Army plays Harvard at New Haven.
There are sixty days until Army sinks Navy.
There are seventy-five days until Christmas Leave begins.
There are 247 days until your graduation.
And there are 280 days until Mr. Fleeger marries
Miss Susan Louise Morgan."

At Ft. Stotsenburg, Fleeger might have replicated his past with:

"Sir the days!
There are two days until Thanksgiving.
There are four days until the 26th Cavalry defeats the
Spanish Polo Team at the Manila Polo Club.
There are seven days until the next Clipper arrives.
There are thirty days until our boat sails.
There are thirty-eight days until Christmas.
There are sixty days until I see Louise again in San Francisco."

As the days dragged on for him, Fleeger started off his addition on the 18th with, "Not a dam thing good about today, honey. As I used to tell Gordon – except that it's another day gone that will not have to live without you. Same thing Lou – worked 6:30 to 8 – rode until 9 – weather fair and quite dry already – unusually hot – and with all the tanks – new roads everywhere etc – it is very dusty and dirty. Rode Flash Gordon as usual – and worked hard until 3 – just came home – earliest I've been here in months but I decided to quit anyway. No polo – General wants to use all the parades for athletics – so it is being batted around up at Post Hdqs now. I don't care – only ran it to keep myself busy – and the players out of trouble. Discovered today that Thanksgiving has to be on Thurs. here – so will have an easy day the 20th – it will be a rather dull Thanksgiving for me I'm afraid – I'll play golf – write to you – and think of you all day - No news yet Lou – all of the Cavalry officers still held - Something is bound to pop soon. – Chief [of Cavalry] hasn't ordered anyone over for 2 months so I know he's fed up – and Gen Grunert said he would try to crack it as soon as he lands. He's due in late Nov. and goes direct to Wash. – So we sort of suspect it will crack open early December for all concerned. – We have more in the Cav than we're entitled to and I know the Chief will raise heck about it eventually. I rather expect a letter from Harry Stadler soon so have held up on my letters for a couple of more weeks." He ended with "Hope I can send some better news soon - Just another day I've lived for you and loving you Dear. There has never been a love so steadfast and complete Louise."

ΩΩΩ

On Wednesday, 19 November he started a new letter.[55] He said: "Thought I'd write a while Lou – not a bit of news – but I know that I'll never be able to stand this month after month without many letters from you Lou – So I try to write a lot just so you'll have to. Some days I work at it for hours – much of the time just looking at your picture in misery honey – we heard yesterday that tomorrow is Thanksgiving – that's the way things happen over here. What turkey is ordered – has not arrived – so Dominick says we'll have chicken dinner again and that's that. Sounds very fine

"I'LL PLAY GOLF – AND HOPE THAT CLIPPER MAIL ARRIVES..."

doesn't it – but without you and the boys it's just another day Dear. I'll play golf – and hope that Clipper mail arrives – after lunch today I was so blue I got some of your letters and read them again...Finally out to play golf to keep busy – played with Bill. He's hard to handle. Very discouraged – as we all are – but shows it I guess. Money worries as much as anything." He continued; "Much activity, many things about to happen – but no rumors or dope as to anyone leaving. It's the Devil Lou – a dark outlook – and very hard to take. I feel the strain now definitely and admit – force myself at everything – and although my cold is gone, I feel washed up all the time, and dead. However, I can't help but feel that we over tour will leave soon – we're only a particle in the officer personnel now. So many have arrived. So it's a question of hanging on until it breaks for us. – If we all keep well Lou that's about all we can ask." And then for the first time, Fleeger talked about food: "I sort of got to going over what we had to eat – and what you'll have at home tomorrow. And wanted to tell you just to sort of remind you that the mental Hell – and physical – isn't glorified by food. We have no more fresh fruit – poor grapefruit or apples about once a week – since last May – lettuce only once that I recall since May – no celery in 7 months – no fresh fish – only usual tough tasteless beef – canned ham, salmon – etc. Use a lot of corned beef hash – rice (white) bread, etc. Still have butter but rancid and of poor quality, and that's what it's been. It sort of stupefies me to put it down in writing. Dominick does very well – mixing it around etc – but there isn't anything. It sort of makes me wonder about the content – over such a long period of time – no doubt I should take Vit[amin] capsules but don't remember what you said why don't you get them and send them to me Air Express (Clipper)." He went on to question whether the diet could have caused his "loss of condition" and then stated: "Dam [sic] as a matter of fact if Charley* moves in it will be rice, fish and carabao [native water buffalo] if we can get it."

ΩΩΩ

ON 20 NOVEMBER IN WASHINGTON, THE JAPANESE DIPLOMATS PRESENTED THEIR LAST PROPOSALS TO THE AMERICAN GOVERNMENT TO SETTLE THE SITUATION IN ASIA AND THE PACIFIC.

On 20 November in Washington, the Japanese diplomats presented their last proposals to the American Government to settle the situation in Asia and the Pacific. To the American Secretary of State "it seemed that the Japanese wanted American aid in establishing their hegemony of the western Pacific and eastern Asia."[56]

On that Thanksgiving Day in the Philippines, the 20th, Fleeger added to his letter: "Just came back from dinner honey. Dominick did the best he could – tomato juice – chicken – potatoes – pumpkin pie – Sauterne (reminding me of you) and coffee. The regimental chaplain said Grace – all of us probably

---

*Ironically, Fleeger used "Charley" as the nickname for the Japanese, and years later, Americans gave that nickname to the Viet Cong (Victor Charlie) during the Vietnam War.

secretly homesick – as I was – and then the usual wisecracks to cover it up, etc. Now I'm home resting. John is sleeping. He still has growing pains – and Pete [Bernd, Ordnance '33][57] up at Baguio – so I'm going to write to you until I run out of chatter and then dress for the evening."

There should not have been a shortage of good food at Ft. Stotsenburg at the time. The Filipino cooks employed by the officers could have easily found abundant fresh Philippine fruits – papayas, bananas, calamancies, avocados, chicos, guavas – as well as large quantities of native brown eggs, sweet potatoes, and rice in local markets. Local companies produced non-refrigerated margarine in quantity and American civilians used it used extensively. While Americans and Europeans generally avoided native pork because of possible trichinosis, they could purchase live chickens in the Filipino markets or buy butchered ones in the American Cold Stores in Manila. Normally, enterprising grocers had to import the items Fleeger listed – apples, lettuce, celery, and such. It sounds as if the Army Quartermaster had fallen down on the job.

Later on Thanksgiving Day, he began Letter No. 2.[58] He talked about receiving a letter from his mother and two from his wife at noon. He said he understood how difficult it was for Lou to write with the two boys but asked her to keep writing and then added, "And honey if you get an air mail off every 3 days I get them swell. So is that too hard? Those today were so

"FOR NOW THOUSANDS ARE ARRIVING — HAVING LEFT FAMILIES — AND I AT LEAST AM AT THE TOP AND WILL RETURN SOON IF ANYONE DOES."

fine. I'm quite overcome – having been half sick for 6 weeks – and extremely discouraged and blue more so than I have admitted." Fleeger immediately turned to his expected return. "For now thousands are arriving – having left families – and I at least am at the top and will return soon if anyone does. So we must be patient and not let the horrible misery of a Sunday afternoon or a lonely evening overcome us...I won't say yet that I won't be home Xmas – it could happen – but my best opinion is that I will not go until after the July Group and they go probably – we hope – about Dec 1. Don't take it too hard Dear – for the homecoming will be quite an event – even compared to Xmas – and that's what we really count on – and be very brave about it. Make yourself be patient and realize that all that really matters is my safe return no matter when – and peace again...This is Hell Lou – but I can do it for your loving me." The majority of the letter was quite passionate, and Fleeger realized it and wrote: "Gee lover – hope a censor never gets our letters. It would give him a total collapse no doubt." On Friday afternoon, the 21st, Fleeger added two and a half pages to his Letter No. 2. [59] "I'm home from work and have to close this out –

blackout tonite all over the islands 6 p.m. to 6 a.m. tomorrow morning. – So we have supper at 5 and I'll go over to inspect Hdqs – and to bed early no doubt. We've had 4 or 5 black out trials – longer each time – tonite won't be a light in the Phil except a few authorized by MacArthur in Port Area [Manila] where they are unloading a flock of ships with war supplies - By the way Ed Grenade leaves tomorrow.[60] They still go out a few at a time, and very suddenly. Long day Dear – thinking of you and working – conference with one of the new tank battalions this P M – their new barracks are between hospital and show ring – all the way to the dry river bed! More came yesterday – etc – quite a show – Tomorrow we inspect all of the cavalry troops – ready for the field – leaving Dec 1 unless confusion of your barrio boys arrival calls it off. Still don't know if we will ever return here – no one knows anything and I suspect the staff downtown of being in a Hell of a sweat." He continued about John Wheeler and unidentified people in the United States. "Last nite John and I had drinks until 7 – as usual and talked. He's a very fine and remarkable boy – unusually so, and it developed that his uncle is a doctor in Yankton – Dr. Auld. John is from Min[nesota]. John wants you to tell Fran and Hope to look up Doctor Auld and tell him of John. – John also knows Douglas Lodge very well...So we had dinner last nite and went to the movie. I came home at 11 but John went down to Pinios (new officers' bar) to drink a few with the mestizo whores – and look around. He was home by midnite." Then, it was back to golf and the naming of new people. "I was up at 7 and started golf. Col. Ives [probably Colonel Albert Ives, CO, 24th Field Artillery[61]] nearly always joins me at 7 – he can't stand the racket either I guess so we play together and talk about you all. ...signed papers at Hdqs. Home for a beer with Bob Lindsey [most likely James Robert Lindsay, 24th Field tillery[62]], it being a holiday. He stayed until about 1 P.M. – said he, Dougherty [probably Colonel Louis R. Dougherty, a field artilleryman[63]], Carl Baehr [24th Field Artillery Regiment[64]] and Lockwood [probably Major or Lieutenant Colonel Hansford N. Lock-

"I AM WRITING MY SECOND LETTER TO HARRY STADLER AND THE CHIEF TOMORROW TO POUR IT ON THEM AND REMIND THEM AGAIN OF MY ORDERS."

wood, Jr., 24th Field Artillery Regiment[65]] – and the July Boat were now rumored to be leaving around December 1st. That is the most I've heard in November. It all adds up with other dope tho, and I really believe is correct, leaving me on top in December, as I've predicted all along. Hope that I can verify that shortly honey so you'll know that it won't be so very long. I am writing my second letter to Harry Stadler and the Chief tomorrow to pour it on them and remind them again of my orders. More of that later this month I hope." Continuing he wrote about new people. "Boat day today Lou – not one but many –

escorted. Don't know who we get, but hear a regular Capt and Col of Cav are on board. Army has taken over all of Port Area and piers [in Manila] including pier 7 – and the activity is rather stupendous. This group today is apparently officers and supplies for us – and not your barrio troops. No definite dope but we suspect 147 etc are due in a few days. – In other words we expect all 14 – to break lose any minute and life to be very hectic. Will try to let you know what it amounts to in next few weeks. The one Cav officer Capt [Leland] Cramer – regular - just arrived - very nice boy – was a Thomason[66] act under Bill at Ft. Sheridan and recommended as being very outstanding so I had him assigned to our house. He seems to be very fine – bachelor about my age. Keen – and very pleasant. That makes 4 of us here† – all get along fine, and life alone – or when it's too quiet is unbearable – So - I think we will be glad to have a 4th. He says several ships came in with his, and more behind – not of the now expected divisions but more or less normal replacements. Replacements came to release Mac [Lt. Colonel Carter McLennan], Joe C[leary], and all those back to us here at Stotsenburg. The big show yet to come – your dope at Parker tells you about when they pay first insurance premiums here."[67]

ΩΩΩ

On Saturday, the 22nd, Fleeger wrote a two-page letter. He discussed his family and then reported: "Bill also heard today – radio from Betty – rather the climax of events for them the last few weeks. She said she had given up and wanted to know if she should move east or what - Louise – I'm afraid to say these things for fear I'll pressure you into something not too pleasant – but you can't know what it means to me to think of you all safe and taken care of and with someone who cares." He then returned to his reassignment situation. "Also heard from Paul Kendall today – nice letter.[68] Said he had written to Chief of Remount recommending me and reply was that I was listed on high priority – but that I probably would not be detailed until I wrote to push it – he advised me – as well as G'.I to try to get out first to the 2nd Div at Riley and then decide

"THINGS HAPPEN FAST NOW. YESTERDAY ONE OF MY INSTRUCTORS AT BENNING ARRIVED WITH A NEW UNIT OF NEW TANKS..."

what could best be done.* So my status is still temporary requested for the 2nd Cav Div. I will write to Harry S[tadler] soon to try and pressure my orders. Bill – etc haven't gone

---

† Fleeger, Cramer, Wheeler, and Peter Bernd.
* G'I. not identified, but he could have been Colonel George E. Isaacs, General Staff Corps (Major, Adjutant General's Department) who was serving in the Adjutant General's Office in Washington, DC in 1943.

yet but orders will help them when anyone goes and we still expect them to leave any day." And he talked about the war. [69] "Did I tell you that Terry [de la Mesa Allen] is going to major general and to Armored Division at Benning.[70] Things happen fast now. Yesterday one of my instructors at Benning arrived with a new unit of new tanks – you may remember him Col [James R. N.] Weaver.[71]

Then, he added inexplicable comments: "Every time I see them, thousands now – I think – well at least I've been here – and should go home – but they will no doubt be here for the war. News starting to leak out about more on the way – don't know yet how many." From probable war, he flipped to personal issues: "End of the day again Louise – the strain seems to get worse now day by day. And I'm numb with it. Worked hard all morning – inspected the regiment with the staff. Took me 5 hours out in the sun to inspect the shoeing - all the troops came in tired and hot as Heck...Blackout last nite – Carl Baehr came down and we talked till 9:30 – discovered Cramer and I knew each other. He was at Camp Custer when I was – that was a swell summer wasn't it." He finished with, "...All for today – have to change – and try to pass hours 5 to 7 with a couple of drinks – very lonesome without my swell family." At the end of his letter, Fleeger mentioned the officers living with him. "John is in Manila at a Harvard Yale drink fest. Pete [Bernd] moved out to Clark (Ordnance) leaving Lee and I here." At this time, John Wheeler probably commanded Troop E, Fleeger's prior command, and Leland Cramer probably commanded Troop A. After remarking that he would play golf the next day, he added a strange line: "Love me and don't give up Lou. I have night mares about the day we might – but know we won't."

"LOU, WILL NOT GO ON MANEUVERS DEC 1 – POSSIBLY NOT UNTIL JANUARY -"

The next day in a new letter, he wrote: "...usual Sunday – they are always the same – and long and dreary. I played golf 7 to 10:30, worked an hour and had lunch. Lee and I are writing letters, reading, etc. and that's about all. Sounds very dull doesn't it? And it's much worse than that...And still not a dam word what may happen – not even a rumor. Lou, will not go on maneuvers Dec 1 – possibly not until January – arrival of what's coming will keep the whole Dept turning over – don't know how much will come here, but guess most of it will." But, he added a warning: "I want to caution you about seeing orders on me or hearing of my return. Don't believe or even be hopeful over a damed rumor. Orders might come out on me today as they have on Bill – and still no return until Dept. says so. So don't pay any mind – it's too hard on us both – as it has been on Betty.

When it appears that I will really come back I'll send the radio we agreed on – at once – and until then we will save ourselves a lot by just not believing anything." [72]

Apparently, by this time, MacArthur had gained the final say about sending officers home. But Fleeger still focused on going home and went on to discuss the shipment of goods associated with his expected return to the United States.

ΩΩΩ

On Monday evening, the 24th, Fleeger reported that he had umpired polo after a hard workday, and he repeated that he felt quite low. [73] Then, he turned to the situation in the Philippines. "Things here are tremendous Lou – as you can imagine even at home. My personal opinion is that this becomes the jump off for the U. S. entry in to the war this spring. We are not like we were when you left. Even now quite secure here on Luzon – with more arriving by the hour until I can't see it as anything but the base for entry soon. Which will no doubt amaze many Americans. In fact, I can probably guess accurately where the expeditionary force will go – but can't even put it in a letter. Here it will amount to defense, evacuation, supply, and a few bombings, etc. all of that late spring – my guess – but I still hope to be home by then."

> *"WE ARE NOT LIKE WE WERE WHEN YOU LEFT. EVEN NOW QUITE SECURE ON LUZON."*

His comment about the Philippines becoming a staging base casts doubts on Fleeger's analysis of the military situation. The build-up must have impressed him, but more had to be done to form an expeditionary force. The tiny Asiatic Fleet had no amphibious ships to transport troops, no small ship-to-shore craft to land troops on hostile shores, and no aircraft carriers to protect an invasion fleet, and USAAFE had too few fighters to protect an invasion fleet and too few fighters to cover Luzon and protect the thirty-five B-17 bombers on any long range strike. Perhaps Fleeger assumed that the Pacific Fleet with its battleships and carriers would sortie from Pearl Harbor into the Western Pacific to cover the expeditionary force. But would the fleet bring troops? MacArthur had no American infantry divisions to send anywhere and the Army had none available to deploy to the Philippines for such an expeditionary force. Under the best of circumstances, MacArthur would not have been able to deploy the mobilizing Philippine divisions to other countries even if the Philippine Government approved such a deployment. More importantly, where would such an expeditionary force strike – heavily armed Formosa, or Okinawa, or Japan itself? Count this comment as bar talk – unfortunately, wishful thinking.

Fleeger continued on 24 November: "Wrote my follow up letter to Harry S[tadler] today but will not send it until the Clipper comes in – typhoon at Wake [Island] again so this will be delayed…life very unbearable Lou – but I live for return to you soon and that's all I can say."

On the 25th, Fleeger's morale dropped into the tank.[74] "Your radio came today – saying my letters hadn't sounded very good. Guess they don't honey but I'm sure you understand. I felt rotten for weeks – half sick in addition to worry – and guess I sort of gave up a bit. I usually can take quite a bit but recently I seem to be rather thin skinned Lou. And it gets to me sooner. Hope you forgive me dear – and only thought is not to alarm you or cause you undue concern about me. Now I feel better – physically although I still have a residual cough from the cold and can't shake it off. Very much like Gordon's old cough…So I'm sorry about some of my letters – and there may be more again so brace your feet Lou. I seem to go under about every ten days now and each time it's harder to recover and be human again." On a brighter note he added: "The poinsettias are blooming – several large bushes outside my screen by the road, and I see them as I dress each morning and evening." Changing subjects, Fleeger got back to army information. "Skinny [Wainwright] is due tomorrow to take over the forces here (post headquarters is lost in the storm it's so minor) – so we expect things to crack a bit. Will be glad to have him. Bob Lindsey was in Manila yesterday – snooping and although he hasn't called me he told Bill in passing that they still expect the July boat to go very soon, probably early Dec. Only darn rumor even that we've heard for weeks. All for now honey – time to change – I've just come in from umpiring and running polo. Keeps me going 15 hours a day but that is the only way I can live."

ΩΩΩ

ON THE 26TH IN WASHINGTON, THE U. S. GOVERNMENT ISSUED A WAR WARNING …

Wednesday 26 November became a critical day for everyone in the Philippines and the world. The Japanese Government had decided on war if negotiations failed, and early that morning, Admiral Isoroku Yamamoto's *Pearl Harbor Striking Force* sailed from the Kurile Islands to be ready to strike if needed. On the 26th in Washington, the U. S. Government issued a war warning to its commanders in the Pacific.[75] Having read the Japanese coded messages from prior days, American leaders in Washington rejected the Japanese conditions and assumed that war was imminent. Meanwhile at Ft. Stotsenburg, Fleeger reported: "Going out soon to umpire polo – That will use up most of the afternoon thank Heavens. Usual day – busy all morning – went over at 6:30 and sent a short note to you regular mail – and so on. Not a thing new Lou. But still we have not heard that officers will <u>not</u> go home – we still expect something to pop any day on Chandler etc – until then we try to stand it honey – on the way home with Bill this noon I told him I'd blow my brain out but I'm afraid it's so dam small it's behind a tooth and I'd miss it. Tomorrow – we have a turkey dinner – at nite – some turkey having arrived along with bombers and a few other gadgets. – By the way Lou this thing over here is starting to build up to quite definite proportions – and even tho I surmise in my dope to you – it might be quite accurate. In other words I wanted to remind you again to destroy everything I write and never talk about it - I know that you do – but it is more serious than it used to be. – All for now Lou - out to polo – I love you Dearest Lou – and each minute just rolls along with my dreaming of your love." [76]

When he returned from polo, Fleeger talked about "putting something on the tree for his boys and for his mother and father," and said that he felt badly about asking Lou to do that because he had "hoped to be home." After grouching about looking for presents locally, he talked again about returning: "As usual all can say now is that I still feel sure that it will be soon. Until they say not – we all believe that to be the dope."

ΩΩΩ

On Thursday night, 27 November Fleeger began his last pre-war letter. "This is sort of our second Thanksgiving – Turkey arrived so tonite we had turkey dinner – worked this morning as usual honey... At 1:30 Clinty – Bill and I played 18 holes of golf. Fair golf (I shot 92 to beat them both) and in at 4:30 for a drink at 5 O. Had to dress to be at the club at 6 for a drink and last toast to Gen. [Edward] King. He is leaving for Manila tomorrow – Chief of Field Art[illery]. – Phil. Theater – big crowd at the Club.

WAR WARNING FROM CHIEF OF NAVAL OPERATIONS
27 NOV 1941

"THIS DISPATCH IS TO BE CONSIDERED A WAR WARNING.

NEGOTIATIONS WITH JAPAN LOOKING TOWARD STABILIZATION OF CONDITIONS IN THE PACIFIC HAVE CEASED AND AN AGGRESSIVE MOVE BY JAPAN IS EXPECTED WITHIN THE NEXT FEW DAYS.

THE NUMBER AND EQUIPMENT OF JAPANESE TROOPS AND THE ORGANIZATION OF NAVAL TASK FORCES INDICATES AN AMPHIBIOUS EXPEDITION AGAINST EITHER THE PHILIPPINES, THAI OR KRA PENINSULA, OR POSSIBLY BORNEO.

EXECUTE AN APPROPRIATE DEFENSE DEPLOYMENT PREPARATORY TO CARRYING OUT THE TASKS ASSIGNED IN [WAR PLAN] 46 [RAINBOW 5.]..."

TOP SECRET MESSAGE FROM CNO TO CINCAF, CINCPAC

Ceiling hung with guidons [small flags for company-sized units] of new units – and all floor space filled with those officers who chose to come." [77]

On Saturday, eight days before the Japanese struck Pearl Harbor, he continued his letter and wrote three and a half more pages. "Had another reception at the club last night for Skinny. Went in groups by units – lasted from 8 to11 – in one door and out the other. Never have seen so many officers. Couldn't stay because of the congestion so came home to be at 10. Review today and busy all morning – things beginning to pop. This P. M. I'm loafing and writing letters and will play golf in the morning as usual. Besides I have a stomach ache! – so thought I'd take it easy. Had field onions last night and they're about to kill me. Rec'd your air mail this noon Lou –so good to hear again – and to know that you love me. I'll answer part of it now and read it again this evening – very swell let-ter Lou (a bit bitter in spots, but I feel that way too – except that it can't be helped and I try not to dwell on it – or let it leave me despondent and discouraged). [78]

Fleeger also wrote about two infirm officers. "Lou I don't know much about Ed Cahill. He was evacuated to Sternberg [Hospital in Manila] very ill some time ago, supposedly recovered and went back to China.[79] We were never able to discover what the trouble was. Gordon talked to him and said he looked terrible, but I didn't see him…By the way, Col. Andreas[*] was evacuated to Mayos [Mayo Clinic]. Very serious – prostate and cancer I hear."

"WE ARE AT A RATHER CRITICAL PHASE OF OUR FAR EASTERN POLICY LOU."

He then talked about officers shopping and reported that the new officers were paying much higher prices for the same goods, and added that "even the whores raised prices! (for the same old stuff)."

Unaware that the Japanese Fleet was enroute to Hawaii, Fleeger turned to the pros-pect of war. "We are at a rather a critical phase of our far eastern policy Lou. Thought I'd sort of run over it – without saying things that shouldn't be published in order to be per-fectly fair with you … trying neither to alarm you – or leave you in the dark. I rather guess (my personal opinion) that the heat from Wash[ington] is on Charley for the real McCoy – and it is possible that a fast war may develop. – It may take a few months – and I think it will – but unless Charley folds, it is a certainty. And apparently he won't back down. That would mean this department as home base for the ball game and your pa-pers will be full of it. However the picture has changed since you were here. And we should be reasonably secure. If it should come off – soon – mails will be considerably off schedule no doubt, and I didn't want it to frighten you." Then he returned to discussing

_____

[*] Not identified.

possible field duty. "And it is possible that we might take the field soon – to remain there. So my letters may be shorter – or not as regular as they have been. We are more or less clearing the decks – packing excess clothing etc and if possible I will ship out the gray chest next week – Keeping only my field and saddle equipment and bed-roll. Part of the regiment left this noon and will not return ... Rather hard to tell you what it looks like – because of secrecy – but from the above you can gather than it may break wide open - as usual be discreet with my remarks – read to Dad."

Then it was back to returning home. He said: "...not a rumor as to the return of the July boat – Col. Douguerty due to go with them – was in Manila this week – and says they will get out in about ten days. Of course now Charley may interfere – but probably not. Lee's [most probably Lt. Colonel Lee Vance, Regimental Executive Officer] orders leave Mac [Lt. Colonel McLennan] and I next and he may not want to go – (has a regiment of Phil. Army and may get a Division) so I am sending on this Clipper my second letter to Harry asking him to turn on the heat. Not much I can do except that – he and the Chief are the only ones who can pressure the Adj[utant] General and that's what it will take. – And I asked Harry to do it – he is on the job – for 3 more are on the way – over the Chief's objection possibly because we are already over – so barring interference from the Japs I should have orders during December Lou – and if war breaks anytime after that I feel sure it would not hold up the return of the over-tour officers. If the July group leaves I'll send amateur radio so you will know at least I'm the next to come home Lou. I live for the day – and for heaven's sake never worry about what I do honey – I work – eat – sleep – and live every minute for you...but don't ever make me feel that it was a misfortune to love me – the misfortune is that I am a soldier – that I can not help. – no matter how you put it – and I live for my return and the day when I can make up for some of the things you've gone thru. – I'll resign in a second if you ask Dear – and do anything – but I cannot escape my work here – until I'm ordered home." He ended this last letter with: "I adore you constantly."

> *"I SHOULD HAVE ORDERS DURING DECEMBER LOU – AND IF WAR BREAKS ANYTIME AFTER THAT I FEEL SURE IT WOULD NOT HOLD UP THE RETURN OF THE OVER-TOUR OFFICERS."*

The pre-war letters show clearly that Fleeger's separation from his wife deeply affected him, so much so that he seemed despondent at times and to such a degree that he focused intensely on his return to the United States at a time when war with Japan was most probable if not imminent. But war – possible or actual -- did not dampen his optimism that he would rotate home. Obviously, his personal unhappiness dominated his life.

War Clouds 1941

"War clouds reflecting from Europe and England cast shadows over the Philippines in the early part of the year, 1941.

The word 'emergency' crept into almost every conversation, then 'war' was added.

We knew Japan had been preparing for war for many years. I was there for a few months in 1934 and witnessed their practice blackouts."

Amelia Bradley, 1945

In one letter he wrote: "I've told you what the [letters] mean to me, Lou - please remember to flood me with your news – and your love letters – and assure me again and again of your love and passion for me. Lou it is all I have – and I mean all...."[80] His comments were precursors to those he would make as a prisoner of war.

Fog of Peace

It seems inexplicable with the deteriorating situation in the Far East that Fleeger still thought that he would rotate home because war would not start for several months. Why would the Army rotate experienced officers back to the United States at a time when it was hurriedly deploying inexperienced officers and units to the Philippines and at a time when they needed more American officers to advise and help train the newly recruited Philippine divisions? Many military people in late 1941, however, including General MacArthur, "still thought it would be several months before the Japanese struck. The month of April 1942 was commonly accepted as the critical date and most plans were based on that date."[81] Still having officers with two years experience on the ground on Luzon would trump bringing in replacements. It also seems inexplicable that commanders on Luzon did not have their units working twenty-four hours a day, seven days a week to prepare for war. The arrival of new officers, new units, and new tanks and aircraft, the construction of new roads and facilities all pointed toward a coming war threat. While he mentioned training and maneuvers, Fleeger wrote about them as if they were "asides" and not as if they were central to life in the 26th Cavalry. And his reports of playing polo and golf, attending receptions for general officers, and having dreaded late afternoon dead time certainly did not reflect any intense war preparation.

In contrast to these comments, William Chandler of the 26th wrote after the war the "Men and officers were convinced that combat was not far off."[82] Harry Fleeger's letters from November 1941 do not support Chandler's post-war report about high morale and excellent training. From Fleeger's reports, Chandler himself might have had a different outlook in 1941. He had been "almost despondent" about his wife and - like Fleeger - expected orders to return to the mainland. Only "Mac" seemed to be leaning forward in his saddle – looking forward to a more senior and demanding position with the Philippine Army.

While Harry Packard, much like Harry Fleeger, did not anticipate war, newly arrived Colonel Chynoweth did, and other officers in the Philippines must have. Many old Manila and Philippine hands, much like the soldiers, held diverse opinions about possible war. Some thought that Japan would not be stupid enough to attack the islands, and if she did, they believed that the United States and Great Britain would defeat Japan in a short war. Others expected war, but they continued their normal lives. Few Allied civilians left, even after the military evacuated dependents and even after relatives in the United States and in other places pleaded for them to do so.

ΩΩΩ

Roy Doolan, an old China and Philippine hand, had returned to the Philippines in December 1940, and his wife and son had followed in February 1941. He provided an exceptional perspective of life in the Far East before war began. Doolan wrote in *The Healdsburg Tribune* (CA) on 23 July 1953:

> The U. S. State department had cancelled the passages of all tourists and women and children bound for the Far East shortly before sailing date [December 1940]. Our consulates in Japan, China, [French] Indo-China, Thailand, Malaya and the Dutch East Indies had simultaneously advised American firms in these areas to send their dependents and non-essential personnel back to the United States because of the explosive polit-

REALITY 1941

"VERY FEW OF US WERE SERIOUSLY CONCERNED WHEN THE FAMILIES OF ARMY AND NAVY PERSONNEL WERE SHIPPED HOME AND MANILA STREETS WERE CROWDED WITH THOUSANDS OF NEWLY ARRIVED AMERICAN SOLDIERS. TO OFFSET THIS WARLIKE CONDITION VACATIONING FAMILIES OF MANILA BUSINESSMEN WERE RETURNING TO THEIR MANILA HOMES.

NEITHER MY HUSBAND NOR I WERE VERY WORRIED, AND WHEN A CABLE CAME FROM MY BROTHER JACK IN MELBOURNE BEGGING US TO LEAVE, WE MERELY LAUGHED AND THOUGHT THAT THE AUSTRALIAN NEWSPAPERS WERE JUST TRYING TO ALARM THEIR READERS."

AMELIA BRADLEY, 1945

ical situation in the Far East. Neither order affected the Philippines...

Then he commented on life in Manila: "Manila was a gay spot in 1941 with wartime prosperity at a peak. There were four air-cooled theaters featuring first-run movies, two horse racing tracks, one of which was equipped for night racing, a beautiful new Jai-Alai building with players imported from Spain, two fine 18 hole golf courses, polo matches, sailing races and places like the Elks Club, Army Navy Club, with exquisite cuisines." Next he spoke about evacuations: "In April 1941, all the women and children of the Armed Forces in the Philippines were ordered home. Families that had evacuated to Manila from other parts of the Far East on advice from the consulates were told to continue to the United States. At this time the Manila consulate assured American residents that they would receive notice in plenty of time to evacuate their families."

In addition, Roy Doolan reported that American officials had negotiated secretly with the University of Santo Tomas to use the university as an internment camp and that Manila had held its first blackout practice in September 1941. The blackouts led to "black out" parties. Earlier he had written about his experience with a man in Los Angeles with whom he had talked about the Philippines. When Doolan said that the United States should strengthen the defenses of the islands, the man replied bitterly: "Taxes are too high already. If the situation in the Far East was so critical, the Americans out there had better pack and come home."

MANILA HAD HELD ITS FIRST BLACKOUT PRACTICE IN SEPTEMBER 1941.

Doolan then summarized what he had heard at the 1941 Armistice Day Dinner of the American Legion in Manila. "The speakers were Colonel Willowby [Charles Willoughby, MacArthur's G-2] for High Commissioner [Francis] Sayre, General "Skinny" Wainwright for General MacArthur, and Admiral [Thomas] Hart for himself as Commanding Officer of the Asiatic Fleet." Fleeger and other soldiers would have been stunned at his next comment: "They all seemed to be recovering from emotional shock. I attributed this at the time to adverse reports from Washington as there was nothing particular in the newspapers. They all spoke with deep feeling on the imminence of an attack by Japan. None offered any words of hope that we might be able to repel an invasion."

If these senior people thought this way, why were the soldiers on the ground and the civilians in Manila apparently complacent? Why didn't the U. S. Consulate order Americans to evacuate? Did everyone believe that the Japanese armed forces could not successfully invade the Philippines? Did their thinking reflect their beliefs of Anglo-Saxon superiority and Japanese inferiority? Would a handful of Americans with their Filipino allies stop the more experienced, well-trained, and determined Japanese armed forces? Few Americans had seen the Japanese in action. MacArthur had when he visited the Mukden front with his father in 1905. He wrote:

> *I met all the great Japanese commanders: Oyama, Kuroki, Nogi, and the brilliant Admiral Heihachiro Togo – those grim, taciturn, aloof men of iron character and unshakeable purpose. It was here that I first encountered the boldness and courage of the Nipponese soldier. His almost fanatical belief in and reverence for his Emperor impressed me indelibly.* [83]

A young Robert Eichelberger who would lead troops in the war under MacArthur had also seen and commented on the skill of Japanese infantry in the same war.

> *In contrast to the Thirty-First Infantry in marching, discipline, their flankers, etc., I found the Japanese much better soldiers. I still feel that the Japanese soldiers were a commander's dream, e.g., they never exposed themselves unnecessarily, they never fired until they had a good target, and they obeyed the orders of their officers while taking perfect cover.* [84]

Both American generals knew that the Japanese Army could be very good. Similarly, American admirals should have expected the Imperial Japanese Navy to be equally good because it had destroyed the Russian Fleet at the start of the Russo-Japanese War and had modernized in the 1930s. But time had passed, and memories had dimmed.

ΩΩΩ

Looking back, there was "a disconnection" with reality in Fleeger's world and in the world of those officers expecting to rotate home in late 1941. There also was a disconnection in USAFFE Headquarters in Manila when Colonel Chynoweth arrived and there was a disconnection in the civilian world in Manila and in the rest of the Philippines. And there was a disconnection with reality in the United States. *Life* Magazine dated 8 December 1941 – and on the streets before that date - with a photo of General MacArthur on its cover, contained the following commentary.

> *For a nation poised on the precipice of a two ocean war, the U. S. was extraordinarily complacent last week. Washington cocked tense ears for the first sounds of shooting on the wide Pacific. Congressional leaders – even isolationists – predicted that a declaration of war on Japan could be shoved through both houses with as little difficulty as a minor appropriation.*

Life's editorial continued. "There was no question that the country was thoroughly aware of the situation. Newspaper headlines loomed heavy with portents. Yet, no one worried. From coast to coast Americans talked more, thought more about tactics in Libya, and two or three lively murder cases than they did about war in the Orient. Rear Admiral Adolphus Andrews, commander of the North Atlantic coastal frontier, orating at the launching of a destroyer, discoursed at the length on Nazi U-boats, said nothing about the great rival fleet on the far shores of the Pacific. New Yorkers watched with fascination the swift marrying-off of an octet of beauties in a Broadway musical show. Bewildered backers of Texas U. football team cheered up when Texas came out of its slump to beat the hitherto unbeaten Texas Aggies, 23-0." The editorial added, "All this indicated just one thing: that Americans were not frightened about the Japanese. Even scary Senators Wheeler, Clark & Nye faced war with Japan without blanching. Among the nation's big newspapers, only the capricious New York *Daily News* (which in the last decade has shrilled long and loud its anti-Japanese slogan: "Two ships for one") recommended appeasing Japan." And then the article prophetically analyzed the coming war:

> *What few pondered, in the enthusiastic nationwide endorsement of the administration's tough Pacific policy, were the immense strategical problems involved in fighting a war west of the Philippines. For the time being the classic American naval principle of an undivided fleet, acting as a unit, has been scrapped in the interest of aid to Britain. For the time being the classic naval theory that a Pacific conflict must involve three years of slow westward progress from fortified base to fortified base has been conveniently forgotten.*

Life's editors probably reflected the opinion of most of the Americans in the United States, British in the United Kingdom, and Dutch in Holland as well as the civilians, soldiers, sailors, airmen, and marines in the Philippines, Hong Kong, Singapore, and the Netherlands East Indies with the comment that, "The American people felt secure in the belief that America's superb Navy could cope with all the difficulties. Americans felt confident, rightly or wrongly, that the Japs were pushovers."[85]

The fog of peace still enveloped too many people.

Eve of War

By early December, the Philippine Army had expanded to over 100,000 soldiers, including dozens of American officers, so MacArthur had just over 132,000 air and ground personnel deployed around the Philippines. But the new Filipino divisions were neither

"THERE WAS NO QUESTION THAT THE COUNTRY WAS THOROUGHLY AWARE OF THE SITUATION. NEWSPAPER HEADLINES LOOMED HEAVY WITH PORTENTS."

well-trained, nor well-equipped for war. They would become cannon fodder or just disappear.[86] So the ground fight would rest on the men of the Philippine Division, the Scout artillery units, the new tank battalions, and the 26th Cavalry. Were they ready to fight? Bill Chandler said the 26th Cavalry was in good shape and implied it was ready to go. He wrote, "Although our material strength was low, as compared with similar units in the U. S., our state of training and morale was extremely high...There was never a period of more than a week when part of the regiment was not in the field. In addition to the constant field exercises ordered by the Regimental Commander, there were other serious tasks directed by higher headquarters...Troop and squadron marches and problems were held twice weekly by troops remaining in garrison and regimental problems were held at least once a month. The state of individual and organization training was of a high standard and the condition of the men and animals excellent...it is not believed than any unit in the U. S. Army was in better state of training or more ready for active service than the 26th Cavalry in the late fall of 1941."[87]

But was it? Fleeger's letters did not verify intensive training. Talk about such training might have surprised many of the Americans who called Manila home, because many of them saw only the easy-going, languid, garrison side of Army life in Manila. And on Sunday, 7 December Manila time, in line with that easy going life, Lt. Ramsey and another 26th Cavalry officer along with a couple of officers from the new tank battalions played a polo match against the superb Manila Polo Club Team. General Wainwright refereed the match.[88]

Why were American officers playing polo sixty miles from their home station after Washington had sent strong war warnings to the commanders in the Pacific on the 27th and 28th?

PUSHOVERS

"THE AMERICAN PEOPLE FELT SECURE IN THE BELIEF THAT AMERICA'S SUPERB NAVY COULD COPE WITH ALL THE DIFFICULTIES.

AMERICANS FELT CONFIDENT, RIGHTLY OR WRONGLY THAT THE JAPS WERE PUSHOVERS."

LIFE MAGAZINE
8 DECEMBER 1941

ΩΩΩ

MESSAGE FOR JAPANESE SOLDIERS

"THE NEW RESTORATION OF THE THIRTIES HAS COME ABOUT IN RESPONSE TO THE IMPERIAL DESIRE FOR PEACE IN THE FAR EAST.

ITS TASK IS THE RESCUE OF ASIA FROM WHITE AGGRESSION, THE RESTORATION OF ASIA TO ASIANS, AND — WHEN PEACE IN ASIA HAS BEEN WON — THE FIRM ESTABLISHMENT OF PEACE THROUGHOUT THE WHOLE WORLD."

JAPANESE PAMPHLET

Why was the senior American field commander refereeing a polo match after USAFFE had notified senior commanders on 28 November to "Be prepared for any eventuality" and his peer, Major General George Moore, Commander of the Harbor Defense Forces, had told his subordinates that the message meant "only one thing to me – War – be prepared for an attack" and then moved all his units into their war positions that night?[89]

Something was amiss.

ΩΩΩ

By 8 December, neither Fleeger nor Chandler nor any other cavalry officer had received a ticket home.[90] No July boat had left. No October boat had left. Like it or not, Fleeger and his American and Filipino comrades faced a devastating war.

Key questions loomed in the background:

1. *Were they personally prepared to fight?*
2. *Were they strong enough to defeat a Japanese ground force with so many new people and so much new equipment?*
3. *Did they have any idea what would happen to them in their far off outpost?*

In retrospect, one must conclude the answer to each of these questions was "no," because, while there had been a dramatic increase in air power, the only material increases in ground power were the 104 light tanks of General Weaver's Provisional Tank Group on Luzon and the small marine battalion on Corregidor. Therefore, a courageous, but ugly story was about to unfold.

Notes

1 "Ft. Stotsenburg" in *THE LOG LINE*, undated information sheet, c. April 1939. (James Fleeger's papers).

2 *Ibid.* See "Ft. William McKinley."

3 *Letter Harry Fleeger to Keith*, o/a 9 January 1940, 2 pages. The first page is missing. Postscript dated 9 January. Year of letter determined to be 1940 because Fleeger arrived in September 1940. Jim Fleeger provided information about Keith Selby, 12 June 2009.

4 *Ibid.*

5 *Ibid.*

6 Personal knowledge. I remember watching Clippers land as a child.

7 *Letter, Fleeger to Keith.*

8 Cy [Cyrus] Young, an insurance adjuster, lived in Scottsbluff, NE. He married Mildred (Mird) Morgan, Louise Fleeger's sister. During the war, Louise and her sons and Keith and Berta [Morgan]

Selby and their children lived with the Youngs. According to Jim Fleeger, Cy Young became the father figure for all the children there. Telephone conversation with Jim Fleeger, 12 June 2009.

9 *Letter, Fleeger to Keith,* for quotes.

10 *Ibid.*

11 "These Atrocities Explain Jap Defeat," *Life* Magazine, May 16, 1938, 14, carried a page of photographs about the Rape of Nanking. One caption read, "Typical fate by thousands in Nanking: execution with hands tied in back, bodies left to rot in roadside ponds."

12 Iris Chang, *The Rape of Nanking* (NY: Basic Books, 1997), 4 and 6. Most people in the Far East knew about the atrocities (See *Life* Magazine, May 16, 1938) but probably not the immensity of them. Personal knowledge.

13 *Letter, Fleeger to Keith.*

14 For details about the organization and strength of American units in the Philippines and about the mobilization of American and Filipino units, see Louis Morton, *The Fall of the Philippines* (Washington, DC: Government Printing Office, 1953), 14-50.

15 John E. Olson assisted by Frank O. Andrews, *Anywhere-Anytime, The History of the Fifty-Seventh Infantry (PS)* (Self-published, 1991), 218-220. (hereafter, Olson, *Anywhere-Anytime*).

16 Comment to author. See also Brigadier General Bradford G. Chynoweth, *Bellamy Park* (Hicksville, NY: Exposition Press, 1975), 195.

17 General Dwight E. Beach, "Handwritten Notes," n.d. and an undated, untitled newspaper clipping in possession of author about Lieutenant Kenneth Beach. Also, conversation with Dwight E. Beach, Jr., The Woodlands, TX, May 2008. Kenneth Beach died on the *Brazil Maru* in 1945.

18 Dr. Oliver W. Orson, DVM, "Service in the Far East, September 1, 1940 to August, 1945," 1. Paper in possession of author.

19 "Obituary for John Taylor Ward," *Assembly Magazine,* Winter 1970, 122-3.

20 For the chaplains, see Richard S. Roper, *Brothers of Paul, Activities of Prisoner of War Chaplains In the Philippines During WW II* (Odenton, MD: Revere Printing, n. d.), 34-35, 75, 77, 138, and 283.

21 Chynoweth, *Bellamy Park,* 188.

22 Ken Zitzman, "Obituary for Samuel Edward Jones," *Assembly Magazine,* January 1990. Full name, rank, and service found in *Army Directory-April 20, 1943* (Washington: War Department, 1943) (hereafter, *1943 Army Directory*), 407. In 1943, Zitzman was serving with the Air Force.

23 Lt. Gen. James M. Gavin, *War and Peace in the Space Age* (NY: Harper & Brothers, Publishers, 1958), 37.

24 *Ibid.*

25 Untitled newspaper clipping about Lt. Kenneth Beach, possession of author.

26 Letter, Brigadier General Paul D. Phillips to John B. Lewis, 10 July 2001, possession of author.

27 Letter, Brigadier General Paul D. Phillips to John B. Lewis, 27 June 2001, possession of author.

28 Students at Proviso East High School prepared the *Bataan Commemorative Research Project,* www.privoso.k12.il.us/Bataan. The source lists the names and National Guard units for the 192d Tank Battalion. The California State Military Museum, www.militarymuesum.org/Bataan, contains information about Company C and the other companies of the 194th Tank Battalion. For the 200th Coast Artillery Regiment, see *Bataan Memorial Museum Website.*

29 Max Hastings, *Bomber Command, The Myths and Reality of the Strategic Bombing Offensive 1939-1945* (NY: The Dial Press, 1979), 99. Hastings, 106, noted the impact of early bomber raids: "Most significant, however, were the results of the first careful analysis of target photographs. Gelsenkirchen oil refineries, the object of repeated attacks, appeared virtually undamaged. Mannheim,...was scarcely damaged." Peter Darman (Ed.), *World War II, A Day- by-Day History* (NY: Crestline, 2005), 240.

30 Chynoweth, *Bellamy Park,* 195.

31 *Letter, Harry Fleeger to his wife,* 20 August 1941.

32 *Letter, Harry Fleeger to his wife,* 26, 27, 28, 29 September and 1 October 1941, 2.

33 *1943 Army Directory,* 368 listed "Stadler, John H., Jr., O15731, col. (maj.), Cav., Ft. Bliss, Tex." No other male officers named Stadler were listed.

[34] Captain George M. Kaufman served in Headquarters, Ft. Stotsenburg. He survived the *Oryoku Maru* and was killed on the *Enoura Maru* in Formosa on 9 January 1945. His last address was Machenzie Farms, Hampton, NJ. Kaufman was awarded a posthumous Purple Heart. See also *ABMC Website* and www.oryokomaruonline.org. Kaufman is memorialized on the tablets in the Manila Cemetery.

[35] Louise Fleeger's sister and wife of Cy Young.

[36] *Letter, Harry Fleeger to his wife*, 1 October 1941, 4.

[37] "Fleeger Obituary," *Assembly Magazine*, July 1989, 175.

[38] Captain Harry Brown Packard, "Dear Gang" Letter, Ft. Stotsenburg, P. I., March 12, 1941 in *Cullum File #8856*, Association of Graduates, United States Military Academy, West Point, NY (hereafter, *Cullum File*). Packard was a member of the Class of 1930.

[39] Roper, *Brothers of Paul*, 74-75.

[40] Edwin Price Ramsey and Stephen J. Rivele, *Lieutenant Ramsey's War, From Horse Soldier to Guerrilla Commander* (hereafter, *Ramsey's War*) (Washington: Brassey's, 1996), 39.

[41] Captain, later Major, Joseph Aloysius Cleary, Class of 1934, *1989 USMA Register*, #10103, 391.

[42] *Letter, Harry Fleeger to his wife*, 14, 15, and 16 November 1941, 1.

[43] *Ibid*, 3.

[44] *Ibid*, 4.

[45] *Ibid*, 6.

[46] *Ibid*. Blanning had three sons, James, Jr., William Franklin, and Richard Bradford. His wife's name was Virginia. See: "Obituary for James Chester Blanning," *Assembly Magazine*, January 1995, 149. Chandler's children's names were found in "Vital Statistics Questionnaire, William E. Chandler," *Cullum File #9124*.

[47] *Ibid*, 7.

[48] Personal knowledge and observation. Fleeger's comments are most interesting. I had problems with several officers and NCOs in Korea who could not handle separation from their families. Consequently, I had to board, court-martial, punish, or serve court-martial charges on several because of their heavy drinking or inappropriate behavior. Some wives moved to divorce their deployed husbands. Some experienced soldiers committed suicide because of their despondency. Separation problems periodically make the news as military families deal with deployments to Iraq and Afghanistan today. Soldier suicides have become a serious problem in 2010.

[49] *Letter, Harry Fleeger to his wife*, 14, 15, and 16 November 1941, 10. Fleeger wrote "Grenade" rather than Granade. Irvin Alexander and Dominic J. Caraccilo (Ed.), *Surviving Bataan and Beyond, Colonel Irvin Alexander's Odyssey as a Japanese Prisoner of War* (Mechanicsville, PA: Stackpole Books, 1999), 262 (footnote 26) identified Granade.

[50] *Letter, Harry Fleeger to his wife*, 16 November 1941.

[51] "Fleeger Obituary," *Assembly Magazine*, July 1989, 175.

[52] Chynoweth, *Bellamy Park*, 192-93. General Chynoweth deployed to the Visayas where he commanded Visayan Force in 1941-42. He surrendered there and survived over three years as a POW. He was not on the Death March. Chynoweth received a Distinguished Service Medal for his service but was not promoted during or after the war. He retired as a BG in 1947. I met the general in the 1970s and corresponded with him for a time. He sent me a copy of the draft for this book, entitled *Visayan Castaways*. It has some different material in it. The general was a tough and intelligent man with strong convictions and he never pulled his punches. He died in 1985.

[53] *Ibid*, 192-93.

[54] *Letter, Harry Fleeger to his wife*, 17-18 November 1941.

[55] *Letter, Harry Fleeger to his wife*, 19-20 November 1941.

[56] Herbert Feis, *The Road to Pearl Harbor, The Coming of the War between the United States and Japan* (Princeton, NJ, 1950), 310. Feis quoted from *The Memoirs of Cordell Hull* (2 vols: New York: 1948), II, 1069-1070.

[57] Fleeger identified the individual as "Pete, Ordnance '34." There was no "Pete" in that class and none of the Ordnance officers in the class served in the Philippines at this time. Peter P. Bernd in

the Class of 1933 fits Fleeger's description. He was an infantry officer who transferred to or was detailed to the Ordnance Corps. The *1934 Army Directory, 169,* listed Bernd as a captain (1st Lt, Inf) of Ordnance and a POW. The *1989 USMA Register, #9747, 387* showed him as serving with the 745th Ordnance Company (Aviation) and the PI Ordnance Depot. Bernd perished with Fleeger on the *Arisan Maru.* He earned a Bronze Star and a posthumous Purple Heart. Bernd's son, David Paul Bernd, followed him to West Point, graduated in 1957, and became an Air Force officer. *1989 USMA Register,* #21342, 599.

[58] *Letter No. 2, Harry Fleeger to his wife,* 20-21 November 1941.

[59] *Letter No. 2, Harry Fleeger to his wife,* 21 November 1941.

[60] Ed Granade left. He is not listed on any POW lists available. However, there is a Lt. Colonel John E. Granade, MC listed in the *1943 Army Directory,* 240 as serving at Camp Carson Colorado. No other officer by that name is listed, so John E. should be "Ed" Granade.

[61] *1943 Army Directory,* 268 listed "Ives, Albert R, O4863, col. (lt. col.) FA, prisoner of war." No other Ives was listed as a field artilleryman or POW. See also *National Archives Website* (hereafter, *NARA Website*). Colonel Ives was listed as a POW of the Japanese. No other Ives was so listed. Additionally, Colonel A. R. Ives was listed as a POW in Formosa on the website, "Never Forgotten, The Story of Taiwan POW Camps and the men who were interned in them" @powtaiwan.org. (hereafter, *"Never Forgotten" Website*).

[62] *1943 Army Directory,* 268 listed "Lindsay, James R., Jr., O15374, lt. col. (maj.) FA, prisoner of war." The only other Lindsay listed is a Richard C. Lindsay in the Air Corps. All Lindsey's were in the US or Europe. The *NARA Website* lists James R. Lindsay as a POW. Only one Lindsey or Lindsay is listed with a "R" or "Robert" in his name. The *1989 USMA Register* listed James Robert Lindsay, Jr., #7218, as a member of the Class of 1923. No "Robert" was listed for a Lindsay or Lindsey who could have served in the Philippines at this time.

[63] *1943 Army Directory,* 215 listed "Dougherty, Louis R., O2494, col, FA, prisoner of war." No other officer named Dougherty was listed as serving in the Philippines. *NARA Website* lists two officers with the name of Dougherty. One was a 1st Lieutenant of Quartermaster; the second was an artillery officer with the rank of colonel. Additionally Colonel L. R. Dougherty is listed as a POW in Formosa in the *"Never Forgotten" Website.* A Louis R. Dougherty also was listed as a former member of the Class of 1907 at the U. S. Military Academy. As such he would have been one of the older officers in USAFFE. No additional information was found in the *1989 USMA Register.* Dougherty later served as the artillery officer with II Philippine Corps.

[64] Captain, later Major, Carl Baehr, Jr., Class of 1936. *1989 USMA Register,* #10628, 401. Baehr became the Commanding Officer of the 88th Field Artillery Battalion (PS), survived the Death March, and died on 15 December 1944 on the *Oryoku Maru.* He received a posthumous Purple Heart. Baehr's father, Class of 1909 and a classmate of George Patton, served as a brigadier general (colonel, FA) during the war. Later he commanded an artillery brigade and VI Corps Artillery in the Mediterranean Theater. See *1943 Army Directory,* 161 and *2002 USMA Register,* #4793, *Biographies,* 4-99.

[65] *1943 Army Directory,* 291 listed "Lockwood, Hanford N., Jr., O8248, lt. col. FA, prisoner of war." No other Lockwood was listed as serving in the Philippines. Also, on the *ABMC Website,* Colonel Hanford N. Lockwood, Jr., 24th Field Artillery Regiment (PS) is listed as killed in action on 9 January 1945 (the day the *Enoura Maru* was bombed in Takao Harbor, Formosa) and as memorialized on the Tablets of the Missing in Manila Cemetery. His awards were the Legion of Merit and a posthumous Purple Heart. His son, Hanford Nichols Lockwood, III, graduated from West Point in the Class of 1943. See *1989 USMA Register,* #13649, 459.

[66] www.trumanlibrary.org/oralhist/montague.htm. Consulted 20 Jan 2009. Samuel A. Montague explained the Thomason Act in an interview with Neil M. Johnson at the Truman Library on 30 October 1992: "It was an Act of Congress introduced by Congressman [R. Ewing] Thomason, and it authorized the government to select a thousand of the best ROTC graduates [annually] who wished to apply, to serve for a year in the Regular Army. At the end of the year it would offer regular commissions to the best 10 percent."

[67] *Letter No. 2, Harry Fleeger to his wife*, 21 November 1941.

[68] *1943 Army Directory*, 276 listed "Kendall, Paul G., O15419, col (maj. Cav.) QMC, Fort Jackson, S.C." He was probably Fleeger's stateside contact. The only other Paul Kendall listed was an infantry brigadier general.

[69] *Letter, Harry Fleeger to his wife*, 22 November 1941.

[70] Major General Terry de la Allen – a bit of a renegade - gained fame as the Commanding General of the 1st Infantry Division in North Africa and Sicily during World War II.

[71] Soon appointed a brigadier general, Weaver commanded the Tank Group during the Luzon and Bataan campaigns.

[72] *Letter, Harry Fleeger to his wife*, 23 November 1941.

[73] *Letter, Harry Fleeger to his wife*, 24 November 1941.

[74] *Letter, Harry Fleeger to his wife*, 25 November 1941.

[75] Joint Committee, *Pearl Harbor Attack Hearings*, Part 14, 1405. See Top Secret Message, CNO to CINCAF, CINCPAC, November 27, 1941.

[76] *Letter, Harry Fleeger to his wife*, 26 November 1941.

[77] *Letter, Harry Fleeger to his wife*, 27 November 1941.

[78] *Ibid.*

[79] May have been Colonel Edwin Martin Cahill, a cavalry officer from the Class of 1933, who was a language student in China from 1939 to 1943 and then served on the War Department General Staff (G-2) from 1944 to 1945. The *1943 Army Directory*, 185 showed Cahill assigned to the U. S. Air Force overseas. Retired in 1963, he died in1984. See *1989 USMA Register*, #9770, 384.

[80] *Letter, Harry Fleeger to his wife*, 16 November 1941.

[81] Morton, *Fall of the Philippines*, 50.

[82] Lt. Colonel William E. Chandler, "26th Cavalry (PS) Battles to Glory," *Armored Cavalry Journal*, Volume LVI, Number 2, Part One, March-April 1947, 11. (hereafter, "26th Cavalry," *ACJ, Mar-Apr*).

[83] MacArthur, *Reminiscences*, 30.

[84] General Robert L. Eichelberger, "Dictations," (25 July 1952), III-53.

[85] *Life Magazine*, December 8, 1941, 38.

[86] Morton, *Fall of the Philippines*, 22, 24, 42 (aircraft), 49, and 50 (troop strengths).

[87] Chandler, "26th Cavalry," *ACJ*, Mar-Apr, 11.

[88] Ramsey and Rivele, *Ramsey's War*, 40-43.

[89] Colonel Emil Ulandwicz. Extract from *Diary* under "War Time Events, Nov. 28, 1941," in possession of author.

[90] Biographical information came from James Fleeger and *Assembly Magazine,* 175.

Sidebar Notes

Four U. S. Negotiating Principles
Feis, *The Road to Pearl Harbor,* 178.

Warning Order from Chief of Naval Operations
See footnote 73.

Message in Pamphlet for Japanese Soldiers
Read This Alone - And the War Can Be Won, in Colonel Masanobu Tsuji, *Singapore, The Japanese Version* (Washington: 1962) translated by G. W. Sargent, Appendix 1, 304.

Three

"Regiment delayed astride the main road"

Captain John Wheeler leading a 26th Cavalry patrol.

L ate in his diary Fleeger wrote that he would prepare a "Brief summary of my war experiences – copies for Jim and Larry and file."[1] He probably planned to expand on his many comments because he wrote in the word "Reutel" with many entries. As mentioned, "Reutel" meant "Remind me to tell you."

He did, however, write a brief narrative about the 26th Cavalry, its people, and its operations on Luzon and Bataan. His historical summary told about the regiment from its bivouac on 8 December 1941 to its destruction in April 1942. He probably expected to use his notes to write a detailed history about his regiment after the war as Chandler did.

26th Cavalry (PS)

As the former Adjutant, Fleeger reported in his diary that the regiment was 789 strong just before war began, but Louis Morton, the Army's official historian, said that there were fifty-five officers and 787 enlisted soldiers, a total of 842 in the regiment on 30 November 1941.[2] The cavalry regiment approximated the size of a standard World War II infantry battalion. Besides its regimental headquarters and its Headquarters Troop, the 26th Cavalry had two squadrons made up of three horse-mounted troops each and a separate mechanized machine gun troop. The small troops or companies – one reported an average of eighty-nine men present for duty on its morning reports at Ft. Stotsenburg – could maneuver well on Luzon's Central Plain but would not move as easily in the mountainous jungles on Bataan.[3] The regiment had several motorized scout platoons, but Fleeger did not clarify whether the platoons belonged to the regimental headquarters troop, the squadrons, or to the individual troops. The regiment also had a transportation platoon. (See Appendix C) Based with the regiment at Ft. Stotsenburg were the:

- 3rd Pursuit Squadron, U. S. Army Air Corps,
- 12th Ordnance Regiment,
- 24th Field Artillery (PS),
- 35th Pack Train (PS), and
- 48th Motor Repair Section (PS).

Detachments from the 12th Medical Regiment and from signal, quartermaster, finance, and military police units also served at the large post.[4]

ΩΩΩ

Just before war broke out, Colonel Clinton Pierce commanded the regiment. Lt. Colonel Lee Vance served as the Executive officer. Vance had replaced Lt. Colonel Walter Buchly who had returned to the mainland with his family on the March boat.[5] Pierce's staff included Fleeger, the Adjutant (S-1), Captain Paul Jones, the Intelligence Officer (S-2), Captain William Chandler, the Operations Officer (S-3), and Captain Walter Buboltz, the Supply Officer (S-4). Jones also served as the regimental communications officer. Major Hubert Ketchum commanded the 1st Squadron, and Major Thomas J. H. Trapnell commanded the 2nd Squadron. Chandler and Fleeger were West Point classmates and regular officers; Trapnell, Ketchum, and Jones were also West Pointers and regular officers.

First lieutenants or captains commanded the troops. Forrest Richards led Headquarters Troop and Jack Ford led the Machine Gun Troop. Newly arrived Leland Cramer commanded A Troop, Captain Houston Farris commanded B Troop until transferred to the Philippine Army, and Ralph Praeger commanded C Troop. Fleeger's housemate, John Wheeler, led E Troop. Paul Wrinkle and Joseph Barker led F and G Troops, respectively. Barker and Praeger were West Point classmates and regular officers.

Young, reasonably experienced first lieutenants led the scout car sections and the platoons in the Troops. Most were reserve officers.

As war began, several senior cavalry officers belonging to the 26th Cavalry, all regulars, served with other units. USAFFE did send Lt. Colonel Carter McLennan to the Southern Islands where he worked for General Chynoweth and eventually assigned three officers to the newly organized I Philippine Corps on Luzon: Colonel Gyles Merrill became the G-4, Colonel Frank Nelson became the G-3, and Lt. Colonel Claude Thorp became the Provost Marshal.

USAFFE had also attached several 26th Cavalry majors, captains, and first lieutenants to Philippine Army units on Luzon and on the Southern Islands, where like many of their peers, they found themselves working as instructors to train the mobilizing Filipino units, or in

26TH CAVALRY REGIMENT (PS)

1 DECEMBER 1941

COMMAND

CO	COL C. PIERCE
XO	LTC L. VANCE

STAFF

S-1	CPT H. FLEEGER
S-2	CPT P. JONES
S-3	CPT W. CHANDLER
S-4	CPT W. BUBOLTZ

LINE

SQUADRON COMMANDERS

1ST	MAJ H. KETCHUM
2ND	MAJ T. TRAPNELL

TROOP COMMANDERS

HQ	CPT F. RICHARDS
MG	CPT J. FORD
A	1LT L. CRAMER
B	CPT H. FARRIS
C	CPT R. PRAEGER
E	1LT J. WHEELER
F	CPT P. WRINKLE
G	CPT J. BARKER

some cases where they gained command of Philippine Army companies or battalions. And, in some cases, the detached officers formally joined other regiments. (See: Appendix D).

On 3 December, MacArthur's Headquarters detached the 26th Cavalry from the Philippine Division and assigned it to General Wainwright's North Luzon Force (NLF) which had been directed "... to protect airfields and prevent hostile landings in his area, particularly at points opening into the central plains and the road net leading to Manila. In case of a successful landing the enemy was to be destroyed." MacArthur ordered Wainwright to hold the beaches at all costs. Wainwright had the most critical mission in the Philippines because MacArthur had shelved the old defensive plan that predicated a withdrawal into the Bataan Peninsula in order to defend at the waterline.

Besides the 26th Cavalry, Wainwright now commanded four Philippine Army divisions – the 11th, 21st, 31st, and the 71st. MacArthur, however, kept a string on the 71st Division. Wainwright also commanded several small Philippine Scout units: a battalion of the 45th Infantry Regiment; Battery A, 23rd Field Artillery (Pack); Batteries B and C, 86th Field Artillery; and the 66th Quartermaster Troop (Pack). He did not have a formidable force. The newly mobilized 31st Division's first regiment had mobilized in September, the second arrived in camp on 25 November, and the third regiment joined on 6 December. The new rifle companies had no machine guns - a glaring deficiency - and the small Filipino riflemen had to manhandle bolt-action, single shot, World War I Enfield rifles built for larger Americans and Europeans. Moreover, USAFFE issued World War I vintage 75 mm guns to the Filipino artillery units. To make matters worse, seventy percent of the artillery shells would turn out to be duds. Other new Philippine Army divisions experienced similar growing pains and similar problems.

> **MACARTHUR ORDERED WAINWRIGHT TO HOLD THE BEACHES AT ALL COSTS.**

Realistically, the 26th Cavalry, the battalion of the 45th Infantry (PS), and the supporting Scout artillery batteries formed the tough core of Wainwright's combat force. He had no all-American combat units so the Filipinos would have to shoulder incredible loads. Fortunately, they were Scouts and MacArthur considered that they "were fit, trained in combat principles, and ready to take the field in any emergency." The Scouts would give good accounts of themselves.

To General Wainwright's south, Major General George M. Parker, Jr. commanded South Luzon Force. He had two Philippine Army Divisions – the 41st and the 51st – and supporting troops.

MacArthur kept Wainwright's former command, the Philippine Division, with its American regiment less one battalion, in the Reserve Force along with the 91st Division (PA) and the 86th Field Artillery (PS).[6]

War: A Shocking Beginning

War began in the Philippines on 8 December 1941. At that time, Fleeger reported the 26th Cavalry was scattered around Luzon. He wrote: "The "26th Cavalry (Less Troops F & G) was in garrison; Troop F on D. S. [detached service] Nichols Field, Rizal, P. I.; and Troops B & C on reconnaissance mission to Baler and Dingalen Bays." [See Map 1 for Luzon Operations.] Nichols Field stood south of Manila. MacArthur's air commander had stationed most of the new P-40s there. Nichols abutted Ft. McKinley, the home base for most of the Philippine Division. Dingalen Bay pushes into the east coast of Luzon about 60 miles from Ft. McKinley and nearly due east of Ft. Stotsenburg. Farther north, Baler Bay cuts into the eastern coast, about eighty miles from Ft. Stotsenburg. Americans considered the two bays possible landing sites for Japanese troops, and both were closer to Manila than Lingayen Gulf.

Fleeger added more about the 8th: "... at 6:00 A.M. radio reported Pearl Harbor bombed, 9:00 A.M. Regiment (less Troops F and G) and rear echelon Regimental Headquarters moved to previously selected concealed bivouac about 2 kilometers north of Stotsenburg along the Bamban River. Troop F was directed by radio to march at once [from Nichols Field] to Stotsenburg." Troop G rejoined later on the withdrawal into Bataan.[7]

The information that the regiment had a previously selected "concealed bivouac" indicated that the USAFFE had developed some contingency plans about an expected Japanese invasion of the islands.

FLEEGER DID NOT MENTION THE DEVASTATING ATTACK ON ADJACENT CLARK FIELD...

Strangely, Fleeger did not mention the devastating attack on adjacent Clark Field on the 8th which destroyed about half of the modern P-40s and B-17s in the Philippines and put the ground forces in a terrible position for the expected battle for Luzon.

The same day, he reported that Troop F had rejoined the regiment, and "Regiment attached to North Luzon Force and held in reserve."[8] The next day, Fleeger noted that: "2d Squadron (less Troop C) with one section of tanks, one battery SPM [Self-Propelled Mortars], one section of scout cars – all commanded by Major Trapnell[9] – moved to Cabiao, east of Mount Arayat [about ten miles east of Ft. Stotsenburg]. Mission – to find and destroy large enemy parachute force reported by civilians to have landed near Cabiao. No enemy encountered." He added, "First Squadron established counter reconnaissance screen from Mabalcal to Angeles inclusive [Map 1]. No enemy encountered." And then, "Both squadrons ordered to return to Stotsenburg and to concealed bivouac in Baluca village area.[10]

After the Japanese struck Clark Field and after they bombed other places on Luzon, rumors and bad information swept through the countryside. Some Manilians said that the American pilots were sitting around fat, dumb, and happy at Clark when the Japanese struck. They were not! The fighter pilots had been up all morning, had returned to refuel, had done so, and began taking off when the enemy aircraft arrived. The heavy bombers - which MacArthur had directed be flown to Mindanao before war began and which had taken off about 0800 hours to patrol and not be caught on the ground - also had returned to base to refuel and then to arm for a strike on Formosa.[11] Bringing all the aircraft back at one time without maintaining any type of air cover over the field, set up the disaster. But, the incorrect story developed a life of its own as many civilians tried to understand the debacle. Even today, war histories perpetuate the wrong story.

...RUMORS AND BAD INFORMATION SWEPT THROUGH THE COUNTRYSIDE.

Another story developed about the first American hero of the war: Captain Colin Kelly. He did not bomb and sink a Japanese battleship and win a Medal of Honor as many said he did. Kelly did not sink any ship, but he did stay with his stricken B-17 bomber while his crew bailed out. For his sacrifice, MacArthur awarded him a Distinguished Service Cross.

More misinformation worried people. Many Filipinos alleged that the Japanese paratroopers had landed at many places on Luzon, but as Trapnell and his troopers had discovered, no parachute drops took place. The Japanese bombings, however, created confusion everywhere – sometimes bordering on panic.

ΩΩΩ

On the 11th, the Japanese Air Force brought the war to the cavalry. Fleeger reported: "Regimental area on post heavily bombed. Casualties – 2 enlisted men killed and about 40 animals dead or wounded at shoeing shops." The same day, he wrote that "Two sections scout cars, commanded by Lieutenant [Ethan] Cunningham, with extra ammunition dispatched to Cagayan Valley [the long north–south valley in north east Luzon], to be attached to infantry force operating there. Departure effected during bombing at regimental area." Then, "About December 12, regiment less detachments move to Pampanga to avoid daily heavy bombings of Stotsenburg."[12]

Fleeger did not name any enlisted men killed in his narrative, an interesting omission. They most likely were Filipino. His listing of animal casualties reflected the concern of the cavalrymen with their stock and highlighted the vulnerability of the horse-mounted unit to air attacks.

On the 13th, the regiment marched to Bamban (Map 1), just a few miles north of Ft. Stotsenburg and joined Wainwright's North Luzon Force (NLF). The next day, the cavalrymen shod their horses and prepared to march north again. They moved about twenty-five miles north to Gerona on the 14th and marched another twenty miles to Rosales on the 16th. For three days they bivouacked in Rosales. At this time, the commanders knew little about Japanese actions although the Japanese reportedly had landed at Vigan on the northwest coast of Luzon and at Aparri, on the northern tip of Luzon.[13]

Fleeger noted that Troop C, commanded by Captain Ralph Praeger, had been dismounted and on 20 December drove by bus to Bontoc "to prevent enemy from occupying the Bontoc area." Bontoc was in the Mountain Province, many miles

ON THE 13TH, THE REGIMENT MARCHED TO BAMBAN...

north of Baguio. There was only one road from Baguio to Bontoc. There were dangerous hairpin turns, some steep grades, sheer drops along the road, and in some places the engineers had literally cut the road out of the side of the mountains. In places, the road was one-way and cars, buses, and trucks alternated traversing the restricted, narrow road.[14] It was a strange place for cavalrymen, even dismounted ones. The troop never rejoined the regiment, and Fleeger noted, "its operations will have to be reported separately by Captain Praeger, troop commander." After the war, Thomas Jones, one of Praeger's lieutenants, did just that. That same day, Captain Thomas Dooley, General Wainwright's aide-de-camp, went to Manila where he went dancing with Matilda Zobel, a local belle. He stayed overnight at the Army-Navy Club and noted, "no evidence of war" in Manila.[15]

The regiment marched another fifteen miles to Pozorrubio (Map 1), near Lingayen Gulf, to be "in a position of readiness." There, Wainwright attached the regiment to the 1th Philippine Army Division commanded by Brigadier General William Brougher.

On 22 December, shortly after Japanese forces landed at Lingayen Gulf the 26th Cavalry entered the fighting. About 2 A.M., Fleeger brought news and orders to Colonel Pierce from Brougher's headquarters: the general ordered the regiment to march from Pozorrubio north to Rosario and await further orders. The regiment marched at 3:00 A.M. Then, Wainwright through Brougher ordered it to march west of the town of Damortis on the coast of Lingayen Gulf "in order to prevent the enemy advance south of the line Damortis – Camp One." That morning, "information indicated enemy landings in strength in Agoo area north of Damortis." Also that morning, Wainwright detached the regiment from Brougher's division and attached it to the 71ˢᵗ Philippine Army Division led by Brigadier General Clyde Selleck. The regiment retained the mission Brougher gave it, but gained a new one: "... cover the right flank of North Luzon Forces." Fleeger had brought these new orders back to the regiment from General Selleck's headquarters.[16]

Subsequently, Fleeger reported that contact was established between a "scout car section with enemy tanks, infantry and bicyclists [which had] entered Damortis from Agoo." He added, "About 75 Japanese transports were unloading troops. The resulting battle of Damortis was the first major engagement of the battle of Lingayen Bay." He continued, "[The] Regiment delayed astride the main road and during the afternoon was forced back to a position about 3 kilometers west of Rosario." (Map 2) Then, "At 5:30 P.M.," he added, "regiment was ordered to withdraw to the Bued River line, and occupy a position near Agat."

ALL EARNED D.S.C.

Trouble began when an enemy "attack was launched as the regiment started its withdrawal – and right flank was enveloped by about two companies of enemy infantry." Subsequently, Fleeger reported that "A sharp attack also developed along the main road at about 8:00 P.M. Troop F had been holding enemy advance along the trails from the north with difficulty and now had to act as rear guard." Consequently he noted, "The regiment, Troop F, and elements of the enemy attack all arrived at Rosario at about the same time. Considerable confusion resulted. Troop F in position in the barrio holding enemy attackers from the north just clear of the regimental column as it withdrew while every effort was made to expedite the withdrawal. Major Trapnell, Lieutenant Wheeler,[17] and Lieutenant [Clayton] Michelson[1] [Squadron Veterinarian], held, and destroyed by burning the bridge one kilometer west of Rosario. All earned D.S.C. [Distinguished Service Cross]."[18]

Wheeler wrote a more complete report of the action, and it appeared in _Life_ Magazine on 2 March 1942. He recalled: "After the battle of Damortis our cavalry was assigned to cover the withdrawal of the infantry to the south. Our tanks had just withdrawn through us, leaving us as the rear guard. Suddenly two more tanks came right down the middle of the road and stopped. I rode over and shouted, "What the hell's the idea?" A guy sticks his head out of the turret but didn't say anything. I cussed him out. He banged the lid

---

[1] Two spellings found: Michelson and Mickelsen. Have used Mickelsen found in NARA records.

down and all hell broke loose. They were Jap tanks." Wheeler continued: "There was barbed wire on both sides of the road so we couldn't deploy. If a man was knocked off his horse he was trampled. The rest of the regiment went galloping down the road with bullets going by on both sides. I heard Major T. J. H. Trapnell calling my outfit and found him by a bridge. He wanted to defend the bridge but we seemed to be the only ones left. At that moment Lieutenant Clayton Michelson of the Veterinary Corps came up with the Vets' truck. Why it wasn't blasted off the road I will never know. I helped them push it down

A GUY STICKS HIS HEAD OUT OF THE TURRET BUT DIDN'T SAY ANYTHING. I CUSSED HIM OUT. HE BANGED THE LID DOWN AND ALL HELL BROKE LOOSE. THEY WERE JAP TANKS."

and pour gas on it and the bridge and light it. The fire just barely stopped the tanks from crossing the bridge and getting at our infantry."[19]

Wheeler wrote the only known contemporaneous account by a participant in the action. Historian Louis Morton included an abbreviated account of this important action in the official U. S. Army history for the campaign, writing, "As the last tanks passed through the American lines, the rear guard of the 26th Cavalry was penetrated by Japanese tanks. In the confused action that followed, the Japanese tanks, merged in the darkness with the struggling men and terrified riderless horses, cut up the defenders and exacted a heavy toll. Only bold action by Maj. Thomas J. H. Trapnell in blocking the bridge over a small river a few miles west of Rosario with a burning tank halted the Japanese and prevented a complete rout."[20] General Wainwright highlighted the action in his memoirs, a summary of the action appears in the citation for the DSC awarded to Trapnell, and *Life* Magazine printed a photo of Trapnell with a short blurb about his heroics along with photos and comments about other soldiers and sailors who had performed courageously in the Philippines.

Fleeger then noted, "The rear guard was under fire of enemy enveloping forces and tanks throughout, but the withdrawal, more or less piecemeal to the Bued River line [Map 2, below Rosario], was completed by midnight. (175 men reached Bued)."[21]

During this short time, the cavalrymen gained their first experience against modern Japanese forces.[22] The horse soldiers maneuvered and fought Japanese infantry and tanks much as Polish cavalrymen had fought against the German panzer units that invaded Poland in September 1939. Moreover, they suffered tough blows from the Japanese dive bombers just as the Poles had suffered similar blows from the German Stuka dive bombers. No American aircraft supported the regiment. Although the American and Filipino troopers gave good accounts of themselves in these actions, they took a beating.

The cavalrymen then occupied a hasty position at Agat on the 23rd, held the river crossing there, and kept the road open so that troops from Baguio could withdraw north to the mountain city. On the night of 22-23 December, some troops from the 71st Division had reached Agat, but the Philippine Army units did not occupy the position and left on the morning of the 23rd. Ordered to cover the withdrawal of the rest of the 71st Division, the cavalrymen did so until 9:00 A.M., and then they withdrew through the division at Sibson and marched south to Pozorrubio where they planned to reorganize.

Fleeger continued. "Baguio troops did not withdraw via Route #3. At this time two sections of scout cars, First Lt Charles R. Bowers commanding ... covered the roads and trails north and east of Pozorrubio. At dark, December 23, the regiment was again ordered to withdraw to Binalonan [Map 2] at about 1:00 A.M. without food or rest since before Damortis action. Bivouac in southern area of barrio. Division headquarters 71st Division at town plaza."[23]

General Wainwright visited the 26th Cavalry at Binalonan, but Fleeger did not mention his presence. Obviously proud of his former regiment, the general noted that the cavalrymen had been in "furious combat," that the regiment "was reduced to not more than 450 men" and had held its position at Binalonan "against overwhelming odds," and "Here was a true cavalry delaying action, fit to make a man's heart sing." Wainwright reported that "little" Colonel Pierce's performance as regimental commander resulted in his promotion to brigadier general.[24]

CHRISTMAS EVE

"AT 5:00 A. M. REGIMENTAL OUTPOST WAS DRIVEN IN BY JAPANESE TANKS ADVANCING DOWN ROUTE #3."

On Christmas Eve, Fleeger recorded that "At 5:00 A.M. regimental outpost was driven in by Japanese tanks advancing down route #3. Hasty defenses were organized at regimental bivouac and attack of enemy infantry and tanks though Binalonan was held." Two hours later, he said that the regiment had "learned that all the troops and 71st Division [Command Post] had withdrawn during the night," and added that the "Regiment was unable to break off [its] engagement until early afternoon, during which time enemy was denied the barrio and routes east thereof toward Tayug." Enemy tanks eventually bypassed Binalonan and moved south to Urdaneta. Finally, the 26th withdrew in the afternoon under the cover of Troop F and a scout car section and became part of 71st Division's reserve at Tayug, five miles to the east (Map 2). At Tayug, Colonel Pierce combined the machine gun troop with Troop B because it had only three heavy machine guns remaining.[25]

Sometime, during all this action, Fleeger sent his wife a telegram wishing her a Merry Christmas. He added: "No news." (See Appendix V.)

As remnants of the 71st Division withdrew again to Umingan (Map 2) about five miles southeast, the regiment held the river crossing at Tayug "under heavy shellfire and enemy infantry attack, until 2:30 A.M. December 26, when the regiment was ordered to withdraw to Umingan." Fleeger noted that the 26th Cavalry

> **FLEEGER SENT HIS WIFE A TELEGRAM WISHING HER A MERRY CHRISTMAS. HE ADDED: "NO NEWS."**

"executed a model withdrawal, destroying 7 bridges enroute and suffering two casualties in breaking contact." Back again in 71st Division reserve, the exhausted and hungry troopers spent Boxing Day in place. Fleeger reported at this time that the regiment was "considerably depleted," that "all records were lost," and that "battle casualties from Damortis to include Tayug were estimated at roughly one third of effective regimental strength in officers, enlisted men, animals, and equipment, killed, wounded or missing in action."[26] The intense fighting over three days and about twenty miles had badly hurt the small regiment, but the Filipino troopers had fought their hearts out against the advancing Japanese and would continue to do so.

From its position in front of the main line, Pierce moved the regiment about twenty-five miles further south on the night of the 26th to Munos (Munoz, Map 2) and bivouacked. The next day, he marched the regiment to San Isidro [just west of Gapan] another twenty-five miles away. About 9:30 or 10:00 A.M. at Bamban on the 27th, Captain Thomas Dooley, General Wainwright's aide, recorded in his journal that "Dominick Truglia whom I lived with at Stots – came walking up. He was reported killed in the Damortis fight. He had escaped across country and came in with 10 E. M."[27] During this time, the 71st had left the regiment behind when it pulled out by bus on the 27th. On the 28th, Pierce moved his command to Mexico (Map 2). Finally behind friendly lines, he prepared to reorganize and planned to rest his troopers. A relatively fresh Troop G rejoined after being "relieved of its mission of maintaining observation at Baler and Dingalen Bay." But on the 29th, the cavalrymen moved north to Porac (Map 2) and became the reserve for Wainwright's NLF. There, Fleeger wrote: "At Porac, Troop B was organized into a motorized force with buses, trucks, sedans, and bren gun carriers [British-made open tracked vehicles mounting a machine gun] drawn from the Manila pool and combined with the remnants of the Machine Gun Troop. Captain Barker commanded the unit. The shattered Troops E and F were combined into Troop E-F. Troops A, E-F, and G formed the 2nd

...THE CAVALRYMEN ON LUZON DID NOT KNOW THAT THEY WERE CONDUCTING SOME OF THE LAST HORSE-MOUNTED OPERATIONS OF THE U. S. ARMY...

Squadron commanded by Major Trapnell." For all intents and purposes, the 1st Squadron had ceased to exist.[28]

On the 30th, Fleeger noted that the 26th Cavalry "Marched to San Jose [Map 2] and attached to the 21st Division, [Brigadier General Mateo Capinpin] commanding. Remained at San Jose covering left flank of 21st Division until January 3 – only patrol activity." On 4 January, he added, "[The 21st Division] withdrew to river line through Dampe covered by 26th Cavalry."[29]

Sometime during this fight, or perhaps on Bataan, the regiment recruited about 200 soldiers to replace its losses.[30] In retrospect, the recruitment was amazing because Filipinos had to have been the replacements, an impressive testimony to loyalty to the United States and their opposition to the Japanese.

During the fight and delaying action from Lingayen Gulf to Bataan, the cavalrymen on Luzon did not know that they were conducting some of the last horse-mounted operations of the U. S. Army, and they did not know that cavalrymen such as Colonel George Patton[31] would soon lead tank forces in Europe, and that other cavalrymen such as Colonel I. P. Swift[32] would lead infantry forces in the Pacific. Fleeger had been introduced to mechanized cavalry during his time at Ft. Knox, but he did not write anything in his diary about the future of horse-mounted troops in war. But his experience on Luzon should have convinced him that horse cavalry had seen its day and that cavalry units could only be effective when equipped with tanks and other armored vehicles.

On 4 January 1942, Fleeger wrote the first of two snippets about his own actions: "it was on the march to Porac 30 miles – cold rain – that I made the trip in reconnaissance car to Stotsenburg to destroy all secret maps."[33] He did not say why the maps were left behind or how he got there. That would be a story in itself. Considering the danger at the time on the 29th – the Japanese were attacking the town of Tarlac just north of the fort - and Wainwright's North Luzon Force was desperately holding the door open to Bataan for the South Luzon Force – Fleeger's action probably deserved a decoration. As with so much of the information about the early fighting, his story is lost.

War: A Tragic End

The Japanese forces that landed at Lingayen Gulf shattered MacArthur's plans to defend at the beaches. As Wainwright struggled to hold back the Japanese advancing from Lingayen Gulf and withdraw south under heavy pressure without stopping the Japanese at the planned defensive lines, Major General Parker with his South Luzon Force held back the Japanese who had landed at Limon Bay. It soon became clear, however, that the Japanese in the north could reach Manila and cut off Parker from Wainwright. Therefore, MacArthur ordered a general withdrawal into Bataan on the 26th, the same day that he declared Manila to be an "Open City" so that the Japanese would cease bombing it and his American and Filipino troops would not defend it. The general told Wainwright to hold the Japanese far enough north of Manila so that Parker could move his South Luzon Force north, pass around Manila, move north behind North Luzon Force, and then turn west and south into Bataan [Map 3]. Wainwright and Parker conducted flawless operations and guaranteed that

"26TH CAVALRY COVERED AND WAS LAST ELEMENT TO CROSS BEFORE BRIDGE WAS BLOWN. OUR TROOPS OCCUPIED THE FIRST DELAYING POSITION THROUGH KULIS."

the final defense of Luzon would take place on Bataan, just as planned under the abandoned War Plan Orange. But in 1942, no U. S. Pacific Fleet would dare to bring reinforcements to the Philippines and most likely could not have done so because the Navy did not have a sufficient number of fleet-oilers to support a drive to the Philippines.[34] Unfortunately, American leaders in Washington diverted the reinforcements, materiel, and supplies earmarked to go to the Philippines to Australia. They would remain there. The U. S. Asiatic Fleet would not help; Admiral Thomas Hart had abandoned the Philippines in December and joined other allied naval units in the Netherlands East Indies. MacArthur, Wainwright, Parker, and their troops would have to survive on their own. Soon they would become "The Battling Bastards of Bataan."

Fleeger highlighted the 26th Cavalry's role in the withdrawal into Bataan. On 5 January 1942, he said that the "11th and 21st Divisions [PA], already proceeded by other Luzon forces, withdrew into Bataan, a well-timed force withdrawal through the Layac Junction bridge [Maps 3 and 4]. 26th Cavalry covered and was last element to cross before bridge was blown. Our troops occupied the first delaying position through Kulis [Culis, Map 4]. 26th Cavalry arrived at Kulis at about 1:00 A.M., January 6, and moved at once to concealed bivouac on left flank of 31st Infantry, U. S. Army, [the] left unit of holding troops on the Kulis position."[35]

After moving into the Bataan Peninsula, Fleeger reported that the "Regiment suffered heavily all day under air directed artillery bombardment, about 25 animal casualties," and that "Reconnaissance by patrols and staff continued during day to left flank and front, and late P.M. regiment moved to bivouac area about two miles further west. During night contact with the left flank of 31st Infantry was lost because 71st Infantry fired on our patrols and prevented contact."[36] Major Fleeger continued: "At 2:30 A.M. [January 7] encoded message was received from commanding officer 31st Infantry which could not be decoded because code key had been changed January 6, and 26th Cavalry was not notified of change. Patrol reports indicated imminent withdrawal of 31st Infantry. The scout car section was sent out by only available motor route, that through the position of the 31st Infantry. At 4:30 A.M. section was ambushed with loss of three of four cars, and all regimental records, diary, etc. Also standards and colors." He went on: "Regiment was out of contact with any friendly forces and behind enemy lines with no apparent exit. Regiment marched more or less continuously over rugged mountain terrain, scorching all trails – without food or forage, to arrive on the left flank of the Abucay position [Map 4] noon of January 10. Regimental S-4 arrived in the afternoon with food and forage. Regiment was badly exhausted. All animals very weary and in need of shoeing."[37]

AFTER MOVING INTO THE BATAAN PENINSULA, FLEEGER REPORTED THAT THE "REGIMENT SUFFERED HEAVILY ALL DAY UNDER AIR DIRECTED ARTILLERY BOMBARDMENT, ABOUT 25 ANIMAL CASUALTIES,"

One thing was notable about all the withdrawals and movements: most were made at night to avoid Japanese air action.

On 11-12 January, Fleeger reported that the regiment "marched to bivouac in the 1st Philippine Corps reserve. The regiment remained at Bagac [Map 4] about two weeks." Continuing, he wrote, "From this bivouac, normal reserve functions were performed. These included a counterattack at Muron [Moron, Map 4] by Troop E, and one at [Kilometer] Post 168 by Troop G, both against enemy troops which had infiltrated through the lines of the Philippine Division (eventually surrounded and forced to withdraw). Casualties were suffered in both engagements...."[38]

Newly promoted Captain Wheeler reported Troop E's actions at Moron.[39]

About Jan. 16 we learned that the Japanese were moving south toward Moron with artillery, along beaches and over trails. The Philippine Army outfit was ordered to attack, with my mounted troops as advance guard. Under the very reassuring sound of our artillery, we moved forward across a stretch of rice paddies into the woods which surrounded the town. Lieutenant Ramsey there delighted and relieved me by volunteering to take my advance guard through Moron, knowing well that a battalion of roughly 300 Jap infantry was there. As we neared the town our artillery barrage lifted, leaving an unearthly quiet."

Riding in between the houses with pistols raised we did not know what was going to hit us but we knew something would. Halfway to the town square I heard a Jap machine-gun fire – a characteristic snapping sound caused by a higher velocity and smaller projectiles than ours, and unmistakable. I rode at the head of the advance party as we moved up, were fired upon, then turned around, rode back and went into dismounted action. We tied our horses between nipa huts, then moved forward down the road with men in each gutter along the sides of the houses."

Next, he wrote about one of the lieutenants: "A messenger came galloping back from Lieutenant Ramsey saying he had been ambushed by an enemy force with machine guns and he wanted support quickly. From there on it was simply a matter of cautiously moving up under heavy rifle fire to Lieutenant Ramsey and his men. They had taken cover as best they could behind coconut trees and in a ditch. One was dead, three wounded in a small area. It looked like more."

Wheeler then described the actions of one of his Scouts: "Pedro Euperio, Pvt. 1st Cl., a 19-year old raw recruit by Scout standards, saw three soldiers ahead wearing Philippine Army uniforms. He moved forward until they fired, then shot quickly – they were Japanese disguised as Philippine officers. Despite his wounds Euperio crept up until ordered to lie down. About the first thing I saw was Euperio drenched in blood, propped up against the house – pistol in his one good hand, directing us how to move up, indicating points under enemy fire."

"WE ATTACKED STRAIGHT THROUGH THE BEACH. WE FIRED WHERE WE HEARD FIRE..."

Then, the captain described the attack. "We attacked straight through the beach. We fired where we heard fire and were happy to see when we went through the bushes that there were dead Japanese. We got straight through to the water, reorganized and attacked around Ramsey, using him as a pivot, sweeping south and killing them under houses, in trees and under bushes. About 20 broke, throwing down all equipment, even guns, in the high grass. I was surprised to see two of my men with bullet holes straight through their helmets, yet unscratched. I had Private Gonzalez behind me and as I went along I grabbed the Japanese compasses and so forth, hanging them on Gonzalez.**"**

When he met Lieutenant Ramsey, he added: "...with all the shooting and hollering going on I was sure he said to me, "Come on, you yellow--- ---, let's get after them." Outraged, I "started doing silly things – going into bushes where no one else would go until I realized how foolish I was. He had meant that remark for the all the Japanese at the time." Following a lull, the captain reported, "Ramsey and I saw three inert Japanese. Two were dead – the third had been hit in the thigh and shoulder. He would make a begging sign, pull open his shirt and pull a bayonet toward him. He may have been told we killed all Japanese by torture, but I think he was just in terrible pain. We tried to give him water – I left him my canteen."

Wheeler continued his story.

Suddenly we heard a machine gun from the river and all hell broke loose again. We realized what we had been fighting was an advance group and a battalion was forming up across the river. We fought in small groups, every man for himself. Sergeant Tolentino ran forward under heavy fire and threw a hand grenade in a house that had been giving lots of trouble. Later, he grabbed a light machine gun and began chasing a squad of Japanese down the road – moving in on them absolutely alone and without fear. I grabbed a rifle and followed him because a machine gun does need a little security. We had no cover but it seems to me if you run around and fight hard you don't get hurt – you keep moving aggressively and it's the best defense. I hit one Jap who was trying to shoot Tolentino. He twisted, squirmed and finally ended hanging over a fence. Sergeant Tolentino closed in on one flank while I went around the other shooting another Japanese. Just then his companion leaned around behind a tree and shot me in the leg. I ran back under cover and saw that Sergeant Tolentino had been shot too. We got him out on a shutter later. About that leg wound of mine – have you ever been kicked in the leg by a horse? It felt just like that. Knowing how it feels is a great satisfaction – doesn't leave anything unknown to fear.

The captain summarized the action. "Moron was a hail of bullets and that never stopped. There were so many in the air that if you put out a sheet of cloth in five minutes it would have been riddled. At first, knowing Jap tactics, I had a nauseated sensation of being trapped – thinking that they had let us have our fun and sweeping around behind us on both flanks. We were outshooting them and could – any day. We fought all day. I can remember running through fire behind some little houses trying to get a drink but all the pumps were dry – our lips were so swollen we could hardly talk. But the Scouts were loyal to the nth degree – all they said were things like: "don't go there, sir, I will go." – "They are shooting from that, sir." "Be careful Cap-

"Be careful Captain."

tain." Late that afternoon my mission had been accomplished – the town was seized and held adequately and I was to fall back again in reserve."

So went one of Fleeger's "bivouac reserve actions."

On the 16th, the cavalrymen lost their mounts, and the regiment deployed as infantry. Fleeger noted that the change became necessary because of "the mountainous terrain of Bataan and by enemy control of the air." When the food situation became critical, the quartermaster slaughtered all the animals for food. About the same time, the regiment assigned Bren Gun carriers to each troop and to squadron headquarters. Apparently, the machine gun troop ceased to exist. With their horses gone, the regiment used buses for transportation.[40]

Several days later, on 25-26 January, Fleeger reported: "Regiment covered the withdrawal of the 1st Philippine Division (two battalions Philippine Constabulary were attached to regiment for the mission). 1st Philippine Division withdrew, after suffering heavy losses, to the reserve battle position on Bataan along the Orion-Bagac line [Map 4]." About this time, USAFFE promoted Colonel Pierce to brigadier general and assigned him to command a Philippine Army division, and Lt. Colonel Vance took command of the regiment. Major Trapnell took over as Executive Officer and became a lieutenant colonel about a month later. Major James Blanning, Fleeger's classmate, returned from duty with I Philippine Corps and took over the remnants of Trapnell's 2nd Squadron, and Fleeger took command of the decimated 1st Squadron.[41]

"REGIMENT COVERED THE WITHDRAWAL OF THE 1ST PHILIPPINE DIVISION..."

After covering the withdrawal, Fleeger reported that "...the regiment was again placed in I Corps Reserve in bivouac along Trail 9 where it remained until moved to Bobo Point in support of Corps and Army troops against enemy landings, at and near Aglóloman and Quinauan Points [23 January-8 February]."[42] At first, "The regiment was employed only for patrol activities." But he added, "A few days later the regiment was moved to bivouac on Trail 17 and prepared for counterattacks against the enemy penetration in the Tuol pocket but was not committed in this action." Next, he recalled that "During the reconnaissance and training period Troop F was ordered to and destroyed an enemy force which had escaped from the Agloloma battle and was making its way north through the mountains in an attempt to join enemy forces north of the M.L.R. [Main Line of Resistance]."

The new battle position, which stretched from just below Bagac across the rugged mountains to just below Orion, became critical for the defense of Bataan. General MacAr-

ON 8 FEBRUARY 1942, LT. GENERAL MASAHARU HOMMA, THE JAPANESE COMMANDER, CONCLUDED THAT HE WAS "TOO WEAK TO CRACK THE USAFFE LINE," thur planned "to fight it out to complete destruction" of his forces on the strong mountainous position. Commanders reorganized their forces because of the loss of officers, men, and equipment. A "conglomeration of units" soon held various defensive sectors. While American and Filipino commanders organized their defenses, the Japanese struck the M.L.R. and launched coastal attacks, but they could not break through. On 8 February 1942, Lt. General Masaharu Homma, the Japanese commander, concluded that he was "too weak to crack the USAFFE line," withdrew to more defensive positions, and "asked Tokyo for reinforcements." While many USAFFE units had suffered greatly in the campaign they had punished the invaders: some Japanese units had ceased to exist. In fact, Homma estimated that "he had only three effective infantry battalions." At the time, the morale of the Americans and Filipinos was high, but the "effects of short rations and general shortage of supplies were being felt."[43]

ΩΩΩ

Bataan provided excellent terrain for the Filipino-American units to defend. The new M.L.R. crossed the peninsula on high ground between 4,222 foot Mt. Natib and the Mariveles Mountains to the south. But the tropical insects, leeches, scorpions, and snakes that inhabited Bataan made it an inhospitable area for the weary troops who were running short of quinine and medicines needed to sustain their health. Only twenty-five miles across and twenty miles long, the small peninsula with its jungles, mountains, and its many lateral streams provided the weakened defenders several advantages that they did not have in the open central plains of Luzon. They had less ground to defend and had shorter supply lines. They also had relatively safe flanks: on the west, the rugged mountains dropped down close to the sea; on the east, there were swamps and high ground. Only one well-surfaced road penetrated the new position, and it ran along the east coast. And, the Japanese could not see many of the Filipino-American defensive positions from the ground or from the air. But much of the pre-war stockpiles of food, and medicine, and ammunition had been moved out to support the defense of the beaches, so the returning troops did not have those valuable assets. To complicate the defense, thousands of Filipino civilian refugees had moved into the defended areas to escape the Japanese. And, unfortunately, they needed food as well.

Fleeger wrote little about life on Bataan in February or March. February became a critical month. The Japanese on Bataan began to refit and reinforce for a new offensive. On the 11th, Douglas MacArthur with a small party left Corregidor for Australia.[44] Fleeger did not comment about his departure, but wrote: "Upon change of command in I Philippine Corps (General Wainwright assumed command of all Philippine Forces), the regiment was ordered to Bobo Point and attached to Luzon Force Reserve, remaining at Bobo Point until April 4. Training and reconnaissance for counterattacks along the beaches or on the front of I Corps were constant during this period but there was no action."[45]

On 15 February, the British surrendered 100,000 British, Indian, Ghurka, and Australian troops at Singapore. On the 19th, the Japanese bombed Darwin in Australia, a few days later they destroyed allied naval forces in the Java Sea and in the Sunda Straits, and then they invaded Java. March brought more Japanese successes. The Dutch surrendered Java on 8 March, and the Japanese seized Rangoon in Burma the same day. At the end of March, the Japanese occupied Sumatra and began landing in the Solomon Islands. By that time, Fleeger reported that the 26th Cavalry Regiment consisted of a "Regimental Headquarters, a Headquarters Troop, with about 6 scout cars remaining of 13, 1st Squadron with Troops and B present. Troop C on detached mission at Bontoc – 2nd Squadron made up of Troop E-F and Troop G, and Machine Gun Troop with Bren carriers."[46]

The situation on Bataan was not good. Fleeger, however, in his letter of the 27th of February tried to convince his wife that all was well when it was not. "I am well Lou – about as usual – and assure you that nothing unusual has happened to me in the way of injury. I was ill a few days but nothing serious in case you were notified. Clinty, now a B.G., Lee [Vance], Trap [Trapnell], Paul [Jones], Bill

BREAKING OUT

"THE TINY CONVOY RENDEZVOUSED AT TURNING BUOY JUST OUTSIDE THE MINEFIELD AT 8 P.M. THEN WE ROARED THROUGH IN SINGLE FILE, [LT. JOHN] BULKELEY LEADING AND ADMIRAL ROCKWELL IN PT34 CLOSING THE FORMATION.

ON THE RUN TO CABRA ISLAND, MANY WHITE LIGHTS WERE SIGHTED — THE ENEMY'S SIGNAL THAT A BREAK WAS BEING ATTEMPTED THROUGH THE BLOCKADE. THE NOISE OF OUR ENGINES HAD BEEN HEARD, BUT THE SOUND OF A PT ENGINE IS HARD TO DIFFERENTIATE FROM THAT OF A BOMBER, AND THEY EVIDENTLY MISTOOK IT. SEVERAL BOATS PASSED.

THE SEA ROSE AND IT BEGAN TO GET ROUGH. SPITEFUL WAVES SLAPPED AND SNAPPED AT THE THIN SKIN OF THE LITTLE BOATS; VISIBILITY WAS BECOMING POORER."

DOUGLAS MACARTHUR

[Chandler], Jim [Blanning] – are also fine. That is about the most I can tell you." He did say that he had been promoted to major on 19 December along with Bill Chandler, and he wrote about his boys. "Have been so homesick for Jim and Larry – How they must be growing. Take good care of them Lou – as I know you are – Remind them that I expect them to be very good American boys – and very wonderful to the mother. Also assure Larry that I thought of him on his birthday." (See: Appendix W)

With the quiet on Bataan and the Japanese victorious everywhere else, Fleeger and his troops began to starve and starvation soon took its toll. As Fleeger explained late in his diary, there was little food on Bataan after 5 January: "1/2 rations. Rice and salmon – not enough – a few canned goods salvaged enroute – limited sugar, flour, coffee, milk, salt, cigarettes. Also eaten during this period: - rice harvested under fire – milled by hand in bivouac – native method – leaves of several native trees cooked as vegetable – roots of trees also – green guava tree leaves – coconut palm hearts – native pig – wild pig (few) – carabao from QM – also shot in camp – horse meat – mule meat – monkey meat – iguana meat – wild birds."[47] Moreover, as the troops began to starve, medicines ran low. Quinine – needed to combat malaria - began to run out, and by the end of March the American and Filipino defenders were weak and sick and hardly fit for more savage combat in the heavy jungles and mountains of hot, humid, and insect- ridden Bataan. But they held on!

ΩΩΩ

April brought an end to the 26th Cavalry. Fleeger wrote: "Night of 4-5 April the regiment moved to junction of Trails 7 and 9 and prepared to counterattack possible penetrations on the right flank of I Philippine Corps sector, from left of II Philippine Corps Sector which had already been penetrated by the enemy in force. Troop B with two sections scout cars attached, all commanded by Major Fleeger, squadron commander, moved to the corps boundary but no action developed."[48] The following night, he reported that "... the regiment moved by bus to Mariveles [Map 4] to a position on Trail 10 in the II Corps area just in the rear of the Corps M.L.R.

"ON ARRIVAL AT ABOUT 4:00 A.M. THE ENTIRE II CORPS WAS IN RETREAT."

On arrival at about 4:00 A.M. the entire II Corps was in retreat. Regiment was attached to the 31st Division which consisted of the commanding general [Brigadier General Bluemel] and his staff, all troops being dispersed." He continued. "April 7, the regiment fought delaying actions along Trails 2, 12, and 18, in conjunction with remnants of the 31st Infantry, U.S.A., 57th Infantry (P.S.) [Colonel Edmund Lilly,

Jr., Commanding] and the 14th Engineers (P.S.) [Lt. Colonel Frederick Saint, Command-ing] to arrive at a final position on Trail 20 just south of the Alangan River and west of Lamao at daylight of April 8. The actions of the day were more or less continuous, cha-racterized by pressure from the enemy ground troops in force – constantly supported by light and medium (105) artillery, and dive bomber attacks."[49]

Fleeger set the stage for the end: "Marched all night [8-9 April] to the Alangan River ridge position to arrive at dawn – exhausted – decimated – to fight gallantly the last battle before surrender."[50] That day, he said that "… a thin line was established behind the Alangan River, with the remnants of the following units in order from left to right – 14th Engineers (P.S.), 26th Cavalry (P.S.), 31st Infantry U.S.A., 57th Infantry (P.S.), 803rd Engi-neers, and Provisional Air Corps Regiment. The terrain was rugged, the time limited, and large gaps existed all along the front. General Bluemel had been given command of the entire force and employed the regimental staff, 26th Cavalry, as his command group. Communications had entirely broken down." General Bluemel summarized the situation. "I am lying here in the pitch black dark, with no map and only a vague idea where I am. I have been fighting and falling back on foot for the last 72 hours. I have no staff, no transportation, no communications except the phone I hold in my hand. My force con-sists of the remnants of the only units that have fought the enemy, not run from them. The men are barely able to stagger from fatigue and lack of food, which we have not had for over 24 hours… Where is the food we need to revive our starving bodies? Where is the ammunition we need to fire at the enemy? Where are the vehicles and medics to treat and evacuate our wounded and disabled? I'll form a line, but don't expect it to hold much past daylight."[51]

> *"DURING THE NIGHT OF 8-9 APRIL SURRENDER WAS ORDERED BY LUZON FORCE, AND DURING THE MORNING OF APRIL 9 ALL ECHELONS SURRENDERED TO THE NEAREST ENEMY ELEMENTS."*

Fleeger continued his story. "Early on the morning of April 8, the enemy supported by artillery, tanks, and dive bombers, attacked the left sectors. (Major Chandler was shot in this action.) The line crumbled and the right flank of the 26th Cavalry was enveloped. Withdrawal down Trail 20 was directed and the regiment moved south, delaying enroute, until after dark."[52]

Finally, the desperate fighting ended. Fleeger noted: "During the night of 8-9 April surrender was ordered by Luzon Force, and during the morning of April 9 all echelons surrendered to the nearest enemy elements. At this time Regimental Headquarters and Headquarters Troop included only one section of scout cars and a few Troopers, 1st Squadron included only remnants of Troop E-F, Troops B, C, and M.G. having disintegrated, become lost, or casualties."[53] Apparently, there was one last flicker of a fight. Colonel Vance reported that the action did not last over thirty minutes.

The troops of the 26th Cav., (PS) were deployed and an engagement commenced. At this time the attention of the C. G., 31st Div., was called to the fact that Headquarters Luzon Force surrendered at daylight and directed firing to cease at that time, that it was now almost noon and a fight was commencing; if the command fought its way out of this situation, it would be to surrender at Mariveles or some other places as there was no place to go or other troops to be reached and that many casualties would be incurred for no useful purpose. It was decided to stop the fight and surrender.[54]

Fleeger did not say how he came to surrender or how he dealt with the surrender.

FLEEGER DID NOT SAY HOW HE CAME TO SURRENDER OR HOW HE DEALT WITH THE SURRENDER.

His fellow squadron commander, Jim Blanning, however, called his officers and men together and asked them what they wanted to do. Several in the group who had been cut off from the main force, chose not to surrender. Blanning then divided the remaining rations among the escapees, and they moved out from Bataan to other locations on Luzon. Captain Joseph Barker and Lieutenant Ramsey chose to escape. Blanning did not surrender. He moved into the nearby hills to take care of malaria-ravaged Major Paul Jones who was "too sick to move without assistance." The Japanese eventually captured both officers, but fortunately for both of them – especially Jones – they both missed the Death March.[55]

ΩΩΩ

As recorded, Fleeger mentioned himself only twice in this operational history, neither of which involved combat operations. As the regimental adjutant and a squadron commander, he had to be privy to many key operational matters and he had to have been involved in several combat operations. He must have had more to report, but for unknown reasons chose to write a bare-boned summary of his regiment, nothing about the squadron he commanded, and nothing of substance about himself.

But his friend, Bill Chandler, did write about him. His first entry said: "At about 2 P. M., December 22, Major H. J. Fleeger, Regimental S-1, arrived from General Brougher's headquarters with orders and grave news. The regiment was to move on Rosario at once where we would receive further orders." Later, he wrote: "This dispatch from Lieutenant George had no sooner arrived than Major Fleeger returned from General Brougher's Headquarters with more definitive orders...Major Fleeger had received orders for the regiment from General Wainwright through General Brougher. ... The mission of the 26th Cavalry was a hard one: to hold the enemy north of the Damortis-Rosario road and, if forced to withdraw, to execute maximum delay along the axis Damortis-Rosario thereby protecting the north flank of North Luzon Force."[56]

Chandler added the following information after the regiment lost contact with the 31st Infantry on Bataan. First, the officers realized that the "regiment was cut off behind enemy lines" and, second, "Colonel Pierce elected to try the mountain trails." Third, Chandler said that "No one in the regiment was familiar with trails, although the S-1, Major Harry J. Fleeger, and one noncommissioned officer had made a trip from Abucay Hacienda to Dinalupihan [Map 4] some two years before. Jungle trails change considerably in two years and neither was confident of the route, but the regime started off generally southwest at 7:00 A.M. ...At daylight, January 9, Major Fleeger went ahead with an orderly to find a crossing of the ravine and with considerable difficulty managed to reach the other side, where by a fortunate coincidence, he ran into First Lieutenant Robert Cunningham, Platoon Leader of the Scout Car Platoon.[57] Lieutenant Cunningham reported that Captain Barker, with his motorized unit of the regiment, was bivouacked about three kilometers west of Pilar on the Pilar-Bagac road [Map 4] and that he had sent several patrols to likely spots where he thought that the regiment might possibly debouch from the mountains. Lieutenant Cunningham had arrived in time to see Major Fleeger's head appear over the edge of the ravine. Major Fleeger immediately sent Cunningham back to Barker with orders to get food and forage to this point as soon as possible while he returned to guide the regiment over the ravine."[58]

"MAJOR FLEEGER WENT AHEAD WITH AN ORDERLY TO FIND A CROSSING OF THE RAVINE AND WITH CONSIDERABLE DIFFICULTY MANAGED TO REACH THE OTHER SIDE..."

In early April, Chandler wrote more about Fleeger. "A reconnaissance and contact detachment, under Major H. J. Fleeger, consisting of Troop B and one section of scout cars, was dispatched to contact the 45th Infantry and to keep the 26th Cavalry advised of the progress of their attack. Major Fleeger located the rear echelon of the 45th Infantry Command Post, but the jungle was so thick and the terrain so rough that even these officers did not know what progress their regiment was making."[59]

Fleeger also did not write about rampant disease on Bataan, and he did not explain his sickness. He did not report his personal thoughts or concerns; he said nothing about his own morale; he did not write about the deaths of his troopers or of the wounded and the impact the casualties had on him; and he did not speak about any church services or of the actions of chaplains as he did later when in prison camp. He mentioned a few people, made some perfunctory comments about American generals, but did not mention MacArthur. His silence about so many actions and people left big gaps in his story.

"Missing at Surrender"

Weeks after the surrender on Bataan, the major listed fifteen cavalry officers as "missing at surrender": two colonels, one lieutenant colonel, two majors, three captains, and seven first lieutenants.

The two missing colonels had not fought with the 26th Cavalry on Bataan. Colonel Merrill had served as Wainwright's G-4 at I Philippine Corps. He had surrendered, but

...THE MAJOR LISTED FIFTEEN CAVALRY OFFICERS AS "MISSING AT SURRENDER"...

unknown to Fleeger he had escaped and remained at large. Fleeger knew that Colonel McLennan had been with the Philippine Army in the "Southern Islands," but he did not know he had surrendered because the Japanese kept colonels such as McLennan separated from the lower-ranking officers. Brigadier General Chynoweth, commanding Visayan Force and the 61st Division (Philippine Army) provided the best information about McLennan. The general had placed McLennan in command of Filipino forces on the island of Negros. Chynoweth described McLennan as "a dour Scot who never said more than one sentence at a time – but it was always to the point." When he sent the colonel to Negros to replace the American colonel who had suffered a nervous breakdown there, he commented: "Nothing ever broke Mac's nerves."60   After the surrender of Corregidor, and during the time that officers in the Visayas were debating whether to comply with surrender orders that General Wainwright had issued under the threat that the Japanese would kill the captured soldiers on Corregidor, Chynoweth reported McLennan to be the deputy commander on Negros. The cavalry officer eventually went to Iloilo on 20 May 1942 to arrange for the surrender of Filipino and American troops on the island.61

Lieutenant Colonel Claude Thorp, Provost Marshal of I Philippine Corps, also had not officially fought with the regiment and he had evaded capture and had gone into the field to lead guerrillas.

Fleeger did not know the status of Troop C, so he reported Major Praeger, the Troop Commander, and Captain Jones of Troop C (he was a lieutenant when he left in December) as missing. However, for some unknown

FLEEGER DID NOT KNOW THE STATUS OF TROOP C...

reason he did not report the troop's third officer, Captain Warren Minton as missing at surrender. Fleeger listed three other captains as missing: Barker, Spies, and Van Nostrand. The aristocratic Barker, who had come to the Philippines on his first assignment as a cavalry officer, had risen quickly to command Troop G, and had fought extremely well as the commander of Troop B and the Machine Gun Troop. Barker had evaded capture and had quickly joined up with Colonel Thorp. Jack Spies also had evaded capture and joined up with Thorp on Luzon. The third missing officer, William Van Nostrand, had deployed to the southern islands. Unknown to Fleeger, Van Nostrand, who Chynoweth considered a fine and enthusiastic officer, had risen to become the executive officer of the 61st Infantry Regiment (Philippine Army) and had deployed from Negros to Mindanao on 1 January 1942. Like McLennan, the captain surrendered rather than continue to fight as a guerrilla because of the threats against the Corregidor garrison. The Japanese imprisoned young Van Nostrand in the POW Camp at Davao.[62]

Fleeger did not know what had happened to seven missing first lieutenants. He reported Lieutenant Ramsey as missing. He apparently did not know that Ramsey had joined Thorp. He noted that that James Bickerton, Robert Burlando, David Coale, and Frederick Thomas were serving with the Philippine Army. At the surrender on Bataan, Thomas was dead, Bickerton continued to fight on Iloilo, and Coale and Burlando continued active

> *FLEEGER DID NOT KNOW WHAT HAD HAPPENED TO SEVEN MISSING FIRST LIEUTENANTS.*

operations on Mindanao. At the surrender, Fleeger also could not account for Arthur Whitehead of Troop E and he reported First Lieutenant Carol Cahoon as "missing in action." Cahoon like Thomas was dead.

Fleeger also reported that First Lieutenants William Cummings and James Seay were on detached service. Seay had been serving with the 71st Infantry (PA). He had been the senior instructor with the 1st Battalion on the island of Negros before war started. In October, the 71st redeployed to Camp O'Donnell on Luzon, and when war began it moved north to Manoag and became part of USAFFE Reserve as part of the 71st Division (PA). The 1st Battalion eventually moved into defensive positions along the beach at Lingayen Gulf, may have moved north to Baguio, but eventually returned to the south and withdrew into Bataan. What Seay did during these actions, has not been determined.[63] But he did survive the fighting and became a POW.

At the time of the report, Fleeger probably assumed that all the officers he listed as missing in action had probably been killed, but by the time he made his list in the notebook, he must have known that most of the officers had surrendered. Most likely he had

KILLED IN ACTION

LUZON

LTC HUBERT KETCHUM

1LT PAUL ALLEN
1LT CHARLES BOWERS
1LT JOHN GEORGE
1LT ARCHIE HENDRICKS
1LT HENRY MARK

BATAAN

MAJ JOSEPH CLEARY

CPT PAUL WRINKLE

1LT CAROL CAHOON
1LT ETHAN CUNNINGHAM
1LT CLIFFORD HARDWICKE
1LT STEVEN GRAVES
1LT FREDERICK THOMAS
1LT DOMINICK TRUGLIA

met the cavalry survivors who wound up in Cabanatuan POW Camp, but he never mentioned meeting any of the previously missing officers in camp.

Cost

The fight on Luzon and on Bataan cost the regiment fourteen, or twenty-five percent (25%), of its fifty-five line officers killed in action. Two of the fourteen, Fleeger had listed as missing. The five medical and veterinary officers survived combat. Fleeger identified the six deaths on Luzon, one lieutenant colonel and six first lieutenants. Two of the dead lieutenants led Scout Car Platoons.[64]

Three lieutenants died on the first day in action, 22 December 1941. First Lieutenant John George, a Scout Car Platoon Leader who had led his platoon about 1,000 yards north of Damortis, but found that he could go no farther, became the first casualty when a bomb killed him near the town. Before his death, George had reported that he had sighted "at least 12 transports and six naval craft off Agoo and the enemy was thick just north of there," and he found "only scattered groups of Philippine Army troops in the area with no unified command."[65] His news did not help the regiment. Two other young officers also fell near Damortis. Japanese tanks had overrun First Lieutenant Paul Allen and most of his platoon from the Machine Gun Troop,[66] and according to Fleeger, Troop E lost First Lieutenant Archie Hendricks, Jr.[67] The Army awarded the three officers posthumous Purple Heart Medals.

Two days later, on Christmas Eve, three more officers fell. George's replacement, First Lieutenant Charles Bowers, died in action on "North Manila Road." The Scout Car officer had led a 26th Cavalry reconnaissance patrol that "covered the roads and trails north and east of Pozorrubio." Bowers apparently had ridden his motorcycle ahead of his scout section and had hit a Japanese tank column around daybreak. One report said that "Bowers was last seen struggling with a group of Japs and firing his pistol." No one ever saw him again. Fleeger reported him first as missing in action and then as killed in action on the 22nd, not on the 24th. The West Pointer from Los Angeles was twenty-six. "Russ" had been appointed to the Military Academy from Ft. Winfield Scott in California where he soldiered as a private in the 6th Coast Artillery. As a cadet, Bowers gained a reputation as "a complex and thoroughly likeable character." He was awarded a posthumous Purple Heart.[68]

ΩΩΩ

A senior officer, the commander of the 1st Squadron, Major Hubert Ketchum, Jr., died in action at Binalonan on the 24th.[69] At the time, Ketchum faced the brunt of the Japanese attacks. Early on, he had spotted several enemy tanks that he assumed were preparing for another attack. To counter them, he gained permission to go forward with two self-propelled 75mm guns from the 24th Field Artillery (PS) that had just arrived. He moved out quickly with an artillery lieutenant and the guns and disappeared. One cavalry officer reported that Ketchum had "leaped on one of the self-propelled 75's that had come up and took off chasing the tanks." Another reported that the 75s fired twice and that no one ever saw the two officers, the gun crews, and the guns again.[70] General Wainwright, who had been up at Binalonan with Colonel Clinton Pierce, provided an epitaph for the hard-charging cavalry commander: "the gallant Sandy Ketchum, of my old 26th Cavalry."[71]

...MAJOR HUBERT KETCHUM, JR., DIED IN ACTION AT BINALONAN... ON THE 24TH.

Born at Columbia Barracks, Cuba on 14 August 1901, Ketchum was the son of Hubert and Alice Ketchum. According to Ketchum, his "Father served 30 years as an enlisted man in 7th Cavalry," and he retired in October 1914 as the Regimental Commissary Sergeant. He noted that his father had been appointed a captain in the Quartermaster Reserve Corps in 1917 and had been discharged as a major in the corps in July 1919. The senior Ketchum served as an Assistant G-4 in the "3rd Army Corps throughout the World War and with [Army of Occupation] in Germany." As an Army Brat, Ketchum had attended grammar school at Ft. McKinley, just outside Manila, and had attended schools in Kansas and California before going to West Point. Originally appointed a second lieutenant in the Air Service, Ketchum transferred to the Cavalry the year after he graduated from the Academy. In 1930, he attended the Troop Officers Class at the Cavalry School at Ft. Riley, was still a second lieutenant, and still was single. After five and a half years of service, Ketchum pinned on the silver bars of a first lieutenant and four years later received his promotion to captain. He attended the Company Officers' Course at the Signal School in 1936. Appointed a major in January 1941, he began the war in that grade. On the day he died, the Army promoted Ketchum to lieutenant colonel, but he probably never knew about his promotion. He received a posthumous Silver Star and a posthumous Legion of Merit for his service. He was forty-two.[72] The regiment suffered a great loss. Ketchum's death highlighted the intensity and closeness of the fighting as the 26th Cavalry covered the withdrawal of the Philippine Army divisions.

First Lieutenant Henry Mark of Troop B died on the same day as his squadron commander. The Japanese killed Mark, who was from Los Angeles, when he made a "singlehanded attack on a hostile tank that was cutting his platoon to pieces." Mark had "led one attack forcing the Japs to draw back a little," but then "Mark himself went across an open rice field with the Japs pouring fire on him. Mark carried some grenades and was going to try to throw them into the tanks but a Jap machine gunner in a tree got him before he was 20 yd. away." The Army awarded the lieutenant a posthumous DSC and a posthumous Silver Star for his combat service.[73]

THE JAPANESE KILLED MARK … WHEN HE MADE A "SINGLEHANDED ATTACK ON A HOSTILE TANK THAT WAS CUTTING HIS PLATOON TO PIECES."

ΩΩΩ

Following the six initial deaths, Fleeger reported that eight cavalry officers died on Bataan, one major, one captain, and five first lieutenants. The three remaining Scout Car lieutenants fell in action. First Lieutenant Carol Cahoon became the first fatality. He had died on 5 January 1942 as MacArthur's forces closed into the jungle-clad peninsula. Young Cahoon, who entered service from California, led another Scout Car section or platoon. He must have just disappeared during combat for Fleeger to first have listed him as "missing since the surrender." The Army awarded him a posthumous Purple Heart.[74]

First Lieutenant Ethan Cunningham, another Scout Car leader, and First Lieutenant Clifford Hardwicke, Jr. of Troop G, died in action near Moron, on the west coast of Bataan on 11-12 January 1942, just a few days before Wheeler's action there. Edwin Ramsey of G Troop, who was with Hardwicke the night before, reported that a sniper had killed his friend when he went forward to recover the troop's horses. The loss shook Ramsey badly. Chandler similarly reported that Hardwicke had been sent to Moron to regain horses, and that he believed he could retrieve the animals by stealth and with little fighting. Joined by Major Thorp, the Provost Marshal of I Corps, Hardwicke moved out with a small detachment and ran into an ambush, apparently set up by a Japanese soldier wearing a Philippine Army uniform. The Japanese killed Hardwicke and wounded Thorp. Thorp took immediate control and withdrew the detachment. Cunningham and Hardwicke each earned a Silver Star and a posthumous Purple Heart.[75]

Major Joseph Cleary, who fought with the Philippine Army, died in action on 16 January near Abucay on the east coast of Bataan. According to a later newspaper report he "had been last seen on Bataan attempting to establish some forward positions." Commended by a brother officer as a "fine and gallant officer," Cleary earned a Silver Star and a Bronze Star for his combat actions and a posthumous Purple Heart. In addition to being listed as a 26th Cavalry casualty, Cleary is listed as a battle death for the 2nd Cavalry Brigade's Headquarters & Headquarters Troop on the rolls of the 1st Cavalry Division. The New Jersey officer was thirty at his death.[76]

First Lieutenant Steven Graves, another Scout Car officer, and First Lieutenant Dominic Truglia from the Machine Gun Troop perished on Bataan in January. Graves died on the 16th. He won a Silver Star for gallantry in action, most likely posthumous, and a posthumous Purple Heart. Fleeger reported that a bomb killed Truglia near Mariveles on the southwest tip of the peninsula. He provided no other details.

Then, on 17 February, the Japanese killed Captain Paul Wrinkle, commanding Troop E-F. Fleeger reported that his comrade died on 25-26 January. Wrinkle - he had replaced Captain Wheeler in command after Wheeler had been wounded – had gone forward as part of a task force under Major Blanning to destroy a large group of Japanese which had gotten behind the 91st Philippine Army

FIRST LIEUTENANT ETHAN CUNNINGHAM ... AND FIRST LIEUTENANT CLIFFORD HARDWICKE, JR. OF TROOP G, DIED IN ACTION NEAR MORON...

MAJOR JOSEPH CLEARY... "HAD BEEN LAST SEEN ON BATAAN ATTEMPTING TO ESTABLISH SOME FORWARD POSITIONS."

FIRST LIEUTENANT STEVEN GRAVES ...DIED ON THE 16TH.

WRINKLE LED HIS TROOP INTO A RAVINE TO DESTROY OTHER JAPANESE TROOPS. HE WAS "KILLED AT THE HEAD OF HIS MEN."

THE LAST CAVALRY OFFICER TO FALL IN COMBAT ON BATAAN, FIRST LIEUTENANT FREDERICK THOMAS, DIED DURING THE FINAL JAPANESE OFFENSIVE ON 8 APRIL 1942...

Division. After the planned attack hit thin air that morning, Wrinkle led a patrol that found some of the fleeing Japanese and pinned them down. As reinforcements came up, a serious fight ensued. Finally, after most of the cavalrymen stormed up a ridge and wiped out the Japanese there, Wrinkle led his troop into a ravine to destroy other Japanese troops. He was "killed at the head of his men." An unnamed NCO died alongside Wrinkle. Chandler noted, "Our losses... were hard to bear because of the value of these two men to the regiment." Wrinkle earned a Silver Star, most likely a posthumous one for this action, and a posthumous Purple Heart.[77]

The last cavalry officer to fall in combat on Bataan, First Lieutenant Frederick Thomas, died during the final Japanese offensive on 8 April 1942, the day before the surrender on Bataan. Young Thomas, on detached duty with the Philippine Army, won a Silver Star. Fleeger had reported him "missing since surrender" in his diary.[78]

Only Truglia's death remains a puzzle. No source besides Fleeger mentioned it. Truglia is not listed as a casualty in any written source. His remains are not buried in the Manila Cemetery; moreover, his name is not recorded on the list of the missing there. Truglia's name is not on any POW list. A search of similar names produced no results. There are three possible explanations to this puzzle. First, the Army recovered no remains because of the bomb blast. Second, the Army recovered Truglia's remains but could not identify them and then buried them as an "Unknown" in the Manila Cemetery. Third, the Army recovered Truglia's remains, buried them temporarily, and then after the war repatriated them to the United States where the family buried them in a private cemetery.[79] The third possibility might be the correct one because if Truglia was listed as missing in action and no remains were found, he should have been memorialized in the Manila Cemetery.

ONLY TRUGLIA'S DEATH REMAINS A PUZZLE.

The Army recovered the bodies of Allen, Hendricks, and Mark and buried them under sparkling white marble crosses in the magnificent Manila Cemetery. The American Battle Monuments Commission memorialized the other officers, excepting Truglia, on the giant, white *Tablets of the Missing* devoted to Army and Army Air Force casualties in the cemetery.

Fleeger noted in his diaries that he planned to write to Betty Cleary about her husband's death, Gladys Ketchum about her brother's death, and to write Tom about Joe Cleary's death at Abucay.[80] Most likely, Gladys Ketchum found out about her brother's death before the Japanese interned her in Santo Tomas Internment Camp in January 1942 or at least after American and Filipino forces liberated her from Los Baños Internment Camp in February 1945. If she had not gained the information at those times, she certainly would have found out about her brother from General Wainwright in late August 1945, when as a member of President Sergio Osmeña's party, she greeted the general at Nichols Field when he returned to the Philippines after the surrender of Japan.[81]

No one knows exactly how many of the loyal, determined Philippine Scouts perished during the campaign.

Glory

Bill Chandler entitled his short history of the regiment's action on Luzon and Bataan as "The 26th Cavalry (PS) Battles to Glory." There is little that is glorious in defeat, but the 26th Cavalry fought its guts out before the Japanese overwhelmed and destroyed the regiment. Pierce, Vance, Ketchum, Trapnell, Blanning, Fleeger, Barker, Wheeler, Wrinkle, Mark, all the scout platoon leaders, the other officers, and the Filipino Scouts of the regiment did battle to glory, but they paid a high price for doing their duty to the United States. Many of the officers earned personal glory. Four earned DSCs "for heroism so notable."

Fleeger, as mentioned, reported the award of three DSCs to Trapnell, Wheeler, and Clayton Mickelsen for their actions near Rosario in December 1941 during the first fight with the Japanese. But he did not report that Trapnell also earned a Silver Star, and a Purple Heart for his combat actions. Fleeger also did not mention Wheeler's action near Moron, Bataan on 16 March 1942 after fresh enemy troops had struck the 1st Philippine Division, but General Wainwright did. Wainwright wrote:

> *I went up to Maubon Ridge that morning, called on a troop of the 26th Cavalry to help a battalion of the 1st Philippine Division, and we managed to drive the Japs back across the Moron River. But the infantry battalion's commander suffered a severe head wound during the fighting. The next senior officer, Captain John Wheeler, took command and though painfully wounded in the leg he stuck with his men until they scored this delaying victory.*[82]

The general's report differed a bit from Wheeler's previous account. Wheeler most likely earned his Silver Star for this action and his Bronze Star for a lesser action. He wrote, apparently a short time later, "I haven't seen the Silver Star or the D.S.C. they say I am getting but am curious to see how they look because somehow they mean a lot. I guess all I ask for after we win is that some day I may be able to take them home with me."[83]

Fleeger did not make much out of Mickelsen's award, but it was truly special. A veterinary officer, not a line cavalry officer and supposedly a non-combatant, Mickelsen

A VETERINARY OFFICER, NOT A LINE CAVALRY OFFICER AND SUPPOSEDLY A NON-COMBATANT, MICKELSEN PROBABLY WAS THE ONLY VETERINARIAN TO RECEIVE A DSC IN THE ENTIRE WAR, OR PERHAPS AT ANY TIME. *

... DENTAL OFFICER, CAPTAIN EDWIN LARAGAY, ANOTHER NON-COMBATANT, EARNED A SILVER STAR. *

SGT GUADENCIO M. GARIFE

CPL LEO TALLUNGAN*

CPL FIDEL TOLENTINO*

*AWARDED PURPLE HEARTS

probably was the only veterinarian to receive a DSC in the entire war, or perhaps at any time.

Fleeger must have known about other awards because as the Adjutant for much of the time, he probably prepared the recommendations for the awards either during the war or in POW Camp. Unfortunately, he did not speak about young Henry Mark's DSC or his Silver Star Medal, but fortunately, Chandler did.[84] Also, he did not report that other officers earned at least thirteen Silver Stars or that the Regimental Dental Officer, Captain Edwin Laragay, another non-combatant, earned a Silver Star. And, regrettably, neither he nor any other officer reported awards earned by the Filipino Scouts or any of the American NCOs in the regiment.

ΩΩΩ

Fortunately, available death records provide some insight into the bravery of the enlisted Scouts. Three Philippine Scouts stand out: Corporal Leo Tallungan earned two Silver Stars, a Bronze Star, and two Purple Hearts, Corporal Fidel Tolentino earned two Silver Stars and a Purple Heart, and Sergeant Guadencio M. Garife earned two Silver Stars. Tolentino and Garife appeared to have died in Camp O'Donnell.

Corporal Fidel Tolentino might have been the "Sergeant Tollentino" whom Captain Wheeler cited in the action against Moron. Wheeler's Tolentino certainly warranted a decoration for gallantry.

Fourteen other Philippine Scouts earned Silver Stars for gallantry in action. Among them, Staff Sergeants Matias Gacgacao and Severo Masangcay and Privates First Class Leonilo Miole and Epemaco Villanueva probably died in action on Bataan.

Thirteen known Scouts earned Bronze Stars. Two earned two Bronze Stars and a Purple Heart each: American Staff Sergeant Louis G. Heuser and Filipino Corporal

Atanacio Games. Two Filipino First Sergeants earned Bronze Stars that further highlighted the combat bravery of the Scout NCOs.

The Army awarded a Purple Heart to 120 Philippine Scouts and a second medal to five of them.[85]

After many tough fights and many personal acts of bravery, Fleeger and the veterans of the 26th Cavalry could reasonably claim that pound-for-pound their small regiment was the best Filipino-American combat unit in the Philippines as it fought its way to glory.

Corregidor

When the fighting ended on Bataan, the Japanese began an intense shelling of Corregidor from the peninsula and simultaneously began overwhelming air bombardment of the island fortress that drove nearly all the troops into Malinta Tunnel. Counter-battery fire from Corregidor struck the advanced Japanese gun positions near Cabacan, Bataan and caused casualties among the American POWs collected there. One POW remarked, "They're using us as a shield to fire on Corregidor."[86] Because of the situation, General Wainwright suspended fire for three days to permit the Japanese to move the POWs north. That did not stop the Japanese from firing on Corregidor.[87] In early May after bettering the fortress for nearly a month, the Japanese successfully invaded Corregidor and forced General Wainwright to surrender Corregidor and then all U. S. and Filipino troops in the Philippines.

During these dismal days, two bright spots emerged. On 18 April, Lt. Colonel Jimmy Doolittle led Air Force B-25 bombers, launched from the aircraft carrier, USS *Hornet,* on a raid on Tokyo. On 8 May, the Navy gained a tactical tie and a strategic victory at the Battle of the Coral Sea and stopped the planned Japanese invasion of Port Moresby in New Guinea.

PVT ANTONIO AGAMON

SGT JULIAN ALMONTE

PVT EUSTAQUIO ANASTACIO

PVT FREDERICO BULATAO*

T5 MARTIN DOMALANTA

PVT SAMSON ESPIRITU

SSG MATIAS GACGACAO*

SSG SEVERO MASANGCAY*

PFC LEONILO MIOLE*

SGT FRANCISCO PACULANAN

PFC SELVINO SELIDE

PVT ANGEL SIBAL

PFC EPEMACO VILLANUEVA*

PVT NARCISO C. VIRAY*

*AWARDED PURPLE HEARTS

The New York Times

NEW YORK FRIDAY APRIL 10, 1942

JAPANESE CAPTURE BATAAN AND 36,000 TROOPS;
SINK TWO BRITISH CRUISERS; ITALIANS LOSE ONE;
INDIA REPORTED AGREEING ON NATIVE COUNCIL

DEFENSE CRUSHED

Stimson Reveals Defeat

Followed Failure to

Get in More Food

CORREGIDOR IS HELD

Wainwright on the Isle

Free to Set Course

Roosevelt Tells Him

By CHARLES HURD

Special to THE NEW YORK TIMES

WASHINGTON, April 9 – An overwhelming Japanese Army aided by the allies of hunger, fatigue and disease, today crushed the small mixed force that held the Bataan Peninsula since December.

Japanese forces, heretofore estimated at 200,000 men, including fresh assault troops, and supported by tanks, artillery, bombers and attack planes in profusion, enveloped an exhausted defending army of 36,853 men, as counted officially yesterday afternoon...

As far as was known today the rocky fortress of Corregidor Island still held its own astride the entrance to Manila Bay and other troops held adjacent fortified islands. The decision as to whether they should continue fighting was laid squarely on Lieut, Gen. Jonathan M. Wainwright, to whom President Roosevelt dispatched a message giving him absolute authority to continue the fight or make terms, as he might see fit...

Notes

1 *Diary,* 15.

2 *Ibid,* 51, listed strength of regiment. Morton, *Fall of the Philippines,* 49 gave the 30 Nov 1941 strength figures.

3 Bernard Norling, *The Intrepid Guerrillas of North Luzon* (Lexington, KY: The University Press of Kentucky, 2005) (hereafter, *Intrepid Guerrillas*), 48.

4 *Fact Sheet,* Ft. Stotsenburg, c. April 1939.

5 Conversations with William Buchly, o/a 26 May 2008 at West Point, NY.

6 Morton, *Fall of the Philippines,* 28-29 (Status), 69 (mission), and 70 (NLF).

7 *Diary,* 40.

8 *Ibid.*

9 Lt. Colonel Thomas John Hall Trapnell, Class of 1927, *1989 USMA Register,* #8071, 354. Also, personal knowledge.

10 *Diary,* 40-41.

11 Morton, *Fall of the Philippines,* 81 (patrol), 82 (strike on Formosa), and 88 (move).

12 *Diary,* 41.

13 *Ibid.*

14 Personal knowledge.

15 Thomas Dooley, *Journal,* 20. The Journal is located at the Cushing Memorial Library and Archives at Texas A&M University, College Station, Texas. Dooley graduated from Texas A&M in 1935. He had previously served with Troop G of the 26th Cavalry Regiment (PS). Dooley remained with General Wainwright during imprisonment on Formosa and in Mukden. He survived the war.

16 Chandler, "26th Cavalry," *ACJ,* Mar-Apr 1947, 14. Chandler reported Fleeger's activities. The times are a bit confused. Chandler reported that Fleeger arrived at 2 p.m. on the 22nd and that the regiment marched at 5 am on the 22nd, but Fleeger reported that the regiment marched at 3 a.m. *Diary,* 42.

17 Later captain and commander of Troop E.

18 *Diary,* 42-43.

19 Captain John Wheeler, "REAR GUARD IN LUZON, Winner of the D.S.C. tells how U. S. Cavalry covered withdrawal of MacArthur into Bataan," *Life* Magazine, 2 March 1942, 51.

20 Morton, *Fall of the Philippines,* 135.

21 *Diary,* 43.

22 *Ibid.*

23 *Ibid,* 43-44.

24 General Jonathan M. Wainwright, *General Wainwright's Story* (Garden City, NY: Doubleday & Company, Inc., 1946), 38-39.

25 *Diary,* 51.

26 *Ibid,* 44-45.

27 Dooley, *Journal,* 30. This is the only reference to Truglia's actions in combat found in any source besides one in Fleeger's Diary.

28 *Ibid,* 45-46 and 51. See also William E. Chandler, "26th Cavalry (PS) Battles to Glory," *Armored Cavalry Journal,* Volume LVI, Number 3, Part Two, May-June 1947, 12-13. (Hereafter, *ACJ,* May-Jun).

29 *Diary,* 45-46.

30 *Ibid,* 51.

31 In the small pre-war army, many of the cavalry officers had served together in other units. When Wainwright commanded the 3rd U. S. Cavalry at Ft. Myer, VA, George Patton commanded one of his squadrons and 1st Lieutenant Thomas Trapnell served as a troop officer. Comments by Lt. Gen. Trapnell to author, August 2001.

32 Swift commanded the 1st Cavalry Division which had been dismounted and fought as infantry during World War II. Upon returning to Luzon in 1945, Swift commanded I Corps.

[33] *Diary*, 46.

[34] Conversations with the late Captain Robert Morrison, USN-Retired, Houston, TX, 9 May 2008. Morrison emphasized that the fleet did not have a sufficient number of fleet oilers to support a move across the Pacific after the loss of the US base at Guam.

[35] *Diary, 46.*

[36] *Ibid*, 46-47.

[37] *Ibid*, 47.

[38] *Ibid*, 47-48.

[39] Wheeler, "REAR GUARD IN LUZON," 53-55.

[40] *Diary*, 51.

[41] "Fleeger Obituary," *Assembly Magazine*, July 1989, 175, and William E. Chandler, "26th Cavalry (PS) Battles to Glory," *Armored Cavalry Journal*, Volume LVI, Number 4, Conclusion, July-August 1947, 16-17. (Hereafter, *ACJ*, Jul-Aug). Chandler wrote the obituary so all the information about command changes are based on his writings. What is very interesting is that apparently no officer commanded the 1st Squadron after Lt. Colonel Ketchum died in December. The information presented about Major Trapnell by Chandler may not be correct. Trapnell wrote that he was the Executive Officer from 1 January 1942 until 9 April 1942. His official biography as Commanding General, Third U. S. Army (6 February 1962) reported that he became the Executive Officer in January 1942 and assumed command of the regiment on 7 April 1942. See *Cullum File* #8071.

[42] *Diary*, 47-48. See also Colonel Vincent J. Esposito, *The West Point Atlas of American Wars*, Volume II, 1900-1953 (NY: Praeger, 1959), Map 124.

[43] Esposito, *West Point Atlas*, Map 124.

[44] Douglas MacArthur, *Reminiscences* (NY: McGraw-Hill Book Company, 1964). See 143 for quote in sidebar.

[45] *Diary*, 48-49.

[46] *Ibid*, 51.

[47] *Ibid*, 118.

[48] *Ibid*, 49.

[49] *Ibid*.

[50] *Ibid*, 57.

[51] Olson, *Anywhere-Anytime*, 187.

[52] *Diary*, 49-50.

[53] *Ibid*, 50.

[54] Olson, *Anywhere-Anytime*, 190.

[55] Ramsey reported: "Blanning called us back together and asked for our decision. No one chose to surrender. Accordingly, he divided up our few remaining supplies equally among us, one can of fish and two handfuls of rice for each two men. We chose our companions and said good-bye." Ramsey and Rivele, *Ramsey's War*, 86. For Jones, see "Obituary for Paul Montgomery Jones," *Assembly Magazine*, April 1946, 20.

[56] Chandler, "26th Cavalry," *ACJ*, Mar-Apr 1947, 14.

[57] Ethan R. Cunningham.

[58] Chandler, "26th Cavalry," *ACJ*, May-Jun 1947, 14-15.

[59] Chandler, "26th Cavalry," *ACJ*, Jul-Aug 1947, 19-20.

[60] Chynoweth, *Bellamy Park,* 197 and 247.

[61] Morton, *Fall of the Philippines*, 581. Morton did not report that Chynoweth had relieved the commander on Negros. He still reported that officer to be in command with McLennan serving as his deputy.

[62] Colonel (posthumous) William Starr Van Nostrand, Class of 1934, 1989 Register, #10105, 391. See his obituary in *Assembly Magazine*, September 1978, 135, and Chynoweth, *Bellamy Park*, 199.

[63] Wm. J. Priestley, "History of the 71st Infantry," *Notebook 1, Priestley Diary*, 9-12. Extracts in possession of author.

[64] *Diary*, 53-56.

65 1st Lieutenant John A. George. See Chandler, "26th Cavalry," *ACJ*, Mar-Apr 1947, 14-15. George was a reserve officer.

66 *Ibid*, 16. 1st Lieutenant Paul K. Allen. Allen was a reserve officer.

67 *Diary*, 55. Fleeger listed Hendricks' death as occurring at Damortis on 22 December 1941. *ABMC Website* lists his death as 6 May 1942. The National Archives does not list Hendricks as a POW and does not list a date of death. Chandler in his articles about the regiment did not list Hendricks as a casualty anywhere. I have chosen to use Fleeger's information.

68 1st Lieutenant Charles Russell Bowers, Class of 1939, *1989 USMA Register*, #11443, 418. Fleeger listed him as "R. M." Bowers, *Diary*, 56 and as Charles R. Bowers, *Diary*, 44. Also see *ABMC Website,* the *Howitzer,* 1939, 110, and "Graduating Class Questionnaire" in *Cullum File #11443.* For his death, see Chandler, "26th Cavalry," *ACJ*, May-Jun 1947, 10. I have used the later date for his death.

69 Lt. Colonel Hubert Whitney Ketchum, Class of 1925, *1989 USMA Register,* #7788, 349. Awarded Legion of Merit and Purple Heart. Also see the *ABMC Website.* The latter shows an award of a Silver Star; the former does not.

70 Chandler, "26th Cavalry," *ACJ*, May-Jun 1947, 11 reported Ketchum's death. Wheeler, "REAR GUARD IN LUZON," 51 reported that Ketchum leaped on the guns.

71 Wainwright, *General Wainwright's Story*, 276.

72 *Cullum File #7788.* See "Vital Statistics Questionnaire," completed 14 February 1930 and "Military History of Hubert Whitney Ketchum (O-16197)."

73 1st Lieutenant Henry D. Mark. See the *ABMC Website* for his decorations. For his death, see Chandler, "26th Cavalry," *ACJ*, May-Jun 1947, 11 and Wheeler, "REAR GUARD IN LUZON, 51.

74 *Diary*, 55 and *ABMC Website.*

75 1st Lieutenant Clifford Hardwicke, Jr. See the *ABMC Website.* For his death, see reports of 1st Lieutenant Edwin P. Ramsey of G Troop, Ramsey and Rivele, *Ramsey's War,* 70 and Chandler, "26th Cavalry," *ACJ*, Jul-Aug 1947, 15.

76 Major Joseph Aloysius Cleary, Class of 1934, *USMA 1989 Register*, #10103, 391. See also the *ABMC Website.* Cleary is listed in "Battle Deaths of the 1st Cavalry Division, By Organization, as of 30 June 1947," a copy of which was found in the Archives of the 1st Cavalry Division Museum, Ft. Hood, TX on 19 June 2006. Also see "Major's Death Brings Award," in *Union City, N.J. Hudson Dispatch,* 12 March 1943, found in *Cullum File #10103.*

77 Captain Paul Wrinkle. *Diary*, 48, Fleeger reported that Wrinkle died on 25-26 January with one soldier, but on page 54, he reported Wrinkle killed in March. The date shown is from the *ABMC Website.* For combat summary, see Chandler, "26th Cavalry," *ACJ*, Jul-Aug, 1947, 19.

78 *Diary*, 54 and *ABMC Website.*

79 A search of the casualties in the American Battle Monument Commission's website found no one named Truglia. Other searches produced no results. Truglia's body may have been recovered, buried in one of the temporary Army cemeteries in Manila after the war, and then repatriated to the US. Families of the deceased interred in the temporary cemeteries were given the option of repatriating their dead or having them buried in the American Cemetery in Manila. Truglia was one of many who just disappeared from all records.

80 *Diary*, 60-61.

81 Wainwright, *General Wainwright's Story*, 276.

82 *Ibid*, 51 and 34-35.

83 Wheeler, "REAR GUARD IN LUZON," 55.

84 Chandler, "26th Cavalry," *ACJ*, May-Jun, 11.

85 *ABMC Website.* Other Bronze Star recipients included Corporal Marcelino Aquino, Private Mauricio Baldivicio (and Purple Heart), Sergeant Eligio Elias (and Purple Heart), First Sergeant Ididro Jamoral (and Purple Heart), Private Rosendo Labog (and Purple Heart), First Sergeant Urbano Marquez (and Purple Heart), Corporal Illuminado Monsanto (and Purple Heart), Private Alejando Novarro (and Purple Heart), Private Desiderio C. Orfiano (and Purple Heart), and Private Castor Ybay (and Purple Heart).

[86] Donald Knox, *Death March, The Survivors of Bataan* (San Diego: HarcourtBraceJovanovich, 1981), 123.
[87] *Ibid*. See footnote.

Sidebar Note

Breaking Out
MacArthur, *Reminiscences*, 134.

Four

"Prevent the enemy from occupying the Bontoc area"

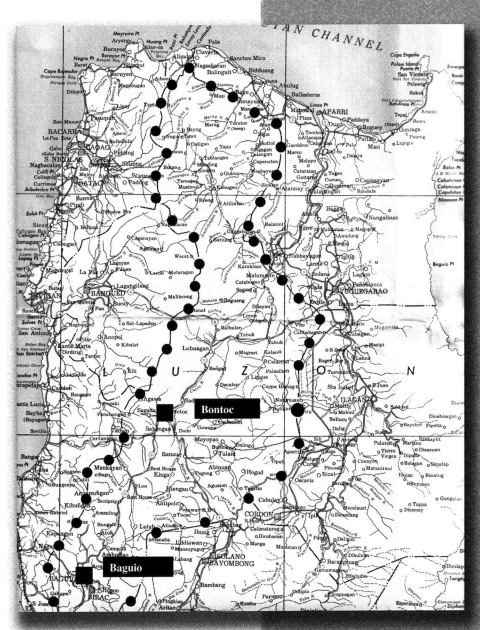

Plate 1 - Baguio, Bontoc, and the Mountain Province

Troop C had fought well in the north while the rest of the 26th Cavalry fought in the south, but it earned a special niche in the regiment's history by continuing active operations before and after Bataan fell. Fleeger reported that the troop had deployed to Bontoc, a small town deep in the Mountain Province north of Baguio, "to prevent the enemy from occupying the Bontoc area."[1] Similarly, another source reported that General Wainwright "wanted them to keep him informed of developments there and, if possible, to prevent the Japanese from significantly penetrating the Cordillera Central."[2]

Victory at Tuguegarao

As the regiment fought around Agat, Lieutenant (soon Captain) Thomas Jones had led the first element of the troop into Baguio on 23 December. Praeger arrived later in the day by bus with the remainder of his sixty-eight Philippine Scouts. In late December, unable to defend Baguio and unable to re-join his regiment as it withdrew toward Bataan, Praeger moved his dismounted Scouts across the mountains toward the Cagayan Valley in the east. After reaching Aritao, he found that he had fifty-nine of his original troops, but also he found that thirty to forty other Philippine Army soldiers who had become separated from their units had joined his troop. So had four or five Filipino officers, two American civilians, and Technical Sergeant William Bowen of the 228th Signal Service Company, which had been stationed at Camp John Hay.[3]

Bowen – described as movie actor handsome and charming - turned out to be a tremendous asset to Praeger and selfless like Praeger. A "natural professional," cool, and courageous, he did many tasks well. His enlisted American subordinates were "devoted to him." Deemed decisive for his first actions with the troop, Bowen "always seemed to face the most severe tests with an airy grace, [and] to get things done without apparent effort." Praeger soon gave Bowen a jungle promotion to second lieutenant, and consequently he is listed on some records as an officer of the 26th Cavalry. Praeger also gave a jungle promotion to one of the civilians, Francis A. Camp, but Camp is not listed anywhere as a member of the 26th Cavalry. Camp, the former China marine, proved fearless and had a "cold, settled hatred for the Japanese." Because of his aggressiveness, Praeger eventually limited Camp to attack missions only. A few days later, more stragglers and additional Filipino officers had joined Praeger's unit.[4]

From his new position in Bambang, Praeger and his officers decided to strike the Japanese airfield near Tuguegarao - farther north in the Cagayan Valley (see Map 5) - to destroy the remaining aircraft there. Early in January, Praeger began the 125 march to his objective. On the 5th, Troop C entered Santiago. From there, Praeger sent Lieutenant Warren Minton, Bowen, and four Scouts forward to reconnoiter eighty miles to the north. On the 8th, Captain Praeger reorganized: he left fifteen older Philippine Scouts in Santiago and incorporated thirty more Philippine Army "stragglers" into Troop C. By the 10th, the troop reached Mallig #2 west of Ilagan.[5] The same day, Lieutenant Minton returned from his reconnaissance and reported to Praeger. Minton then left for Tuao. Praeger marched to Mallig No. 1 on the 9th. Three days later, Praeger and his men bivouacked near Enrile, just west of Tuguegarao. Minton rejoined and "submitted plans for the attack." He also brought a map sketched by one of the Scouts after he had breakfasted with the Japanese flyers at the airfield. That evening, the raiders moved into Solana. There they found Lieutenant Bowen who wanted to attack the estimated 2,000 Japanese with the 150-man troop. Eager to attack immediately, Praeger led his men the final two miles to the objective. He found that "Despite all the people who knew of the impending assault, the over-confident Japanese were asleep, apparently certain that no American troops were within a hundred miles. A guard had been posted but few sentinels were out, so the attackers were able to crawl onto the airfield without detection." Some Scouts began searching for airplanes, but they did not locate them for several hours in the dark night. About the time they did, the Japanese detected the raiders and began firing machine guns in the direction of the main body. After the Japanese reacted, different groups took different actions. One tried to destroy the airplanes, Lieutenant Bowen's group tried to destroy the fuel dump, and Lieutenant Camp and his men shot up an enemy barracks. Bowen destroyed a Japanese ma-

TROOP C

COMMANDER

CPT (MAJ) RALPH PRAEGER

OFFICERS

1 LT (CPT) THOMAS JONES
1 LT (CPT) WARREN MINTON

ADDED

SGT (1 LT) ARTHUR FURAGGANAN
TSG (2 LT) WILLIAM BOWEN
CIV (2 LT) FRANCIS CAMP

chine gun crew with homemade grenades. Camp estimated that his group killed fifty or more Japanese in their barracks. In another action, Corporal Andres Montiadora and his patrol "denied a critical road junction to the enemy for thirty minutes, then proceeded to the rallying point, only to learn that the rest of Troop C was still on the airfield." The young corporal reacted quickly: he "hurried his men two and a half miles back to their original position and held it until dawn."[6]

All in all, the Troop C raiders killed between 100 and 200 Japanese (probably an overestimate) before they withdrew to Solana by dawn on the 13th. In addition, they destroyed Japanese weapons and radios, burned or wrecked "the houses of Japanese officials in the city, and disrupted the enemy's communication system in the Cagayan Valley." But to Praeger's disappointment they did not destroy any of the nese aircraft.[7]

THE JAPANESE RETALIATED AGAINST THE FILIPINOS. THEY QUICKLY DESTROYED A NEARBY BARRIO, BURNED HOUSES IN ANOTHER, AND MASSACRED SEVERAL CIVILIANS IN TUGUEGARAO.

Two raiders turned up missing after the raid. One, a young private had gotten lost, and returned to the troop quickly. The second, Lieutenant Bowen, found himself surrounded by the Japanese on the airfield. Fortunately, he managed to hide himself off the runway that night. The Japanese returned to the area on the 13th and repeatedly fired at where he was hiding. They missed Bowen, however, and after they stopped looking for him, Bowen escaped during the night and returned to the troop on the 14th.

The Japanese retaliated against the Filipinos. They quickly destroyed a nearby barrio, burned houses in another, and massacred several civilians in Tuguegarao. They took these actions because of the legitimate actions of a U. S. Cavalry troop and attached Philippine Army troops against a Japanese base before the surrender of U. S. Forces in the Philippines.[8]

Shortly after the raid, Minton reported the operation to another guerrilla leader who sent a report of the action to Corregidor where the Americans flashed the good news to the world. The small victory came at a time when the 26th Cavalry had just begun its fight on Bataan. USAFFE awarded Minton a DSC for his action and promoted him. After the war, the Army awarded posthumous DSCs to Praeger and Bowen for their roles at Tuguegarao.[9]

Following the action, Praeger and Jones contin-ued to fight with Troop C, but Minton left and joined another guerrilla command, the 14th Infantry, Philip-pine Army.[10] So eventually, did Francis Camp.[11]

ΩΩΩ

The big and slightly balding Praeger had quickly gained the respect of his soldiers and the Filipino civi-lians he dealt with. Down to earth, non-emotional, he took his responsibilities seriously and had worked hard to make Troop C an effective unit before war started. Following the Tuguegarao Raid, Troop C be-came part of the Cagayan-Apayao provincial forces (CAF) which Praeger led. "Only three years out of West Point," Praeger worked effectively with the Filipino governor of the province to improve intelligence ga-thering, deal with legal problems, and aid in the ad-ministration of the province. Norling summarized the major's accomplishments:

> *... uninstructed in guerrilla warfare, and with only three months experience of war of any kind, Praeger soon had Troop C admirably organized... He separated civilian from military authority – with the latter subordinated to Governor Adduru – set up what was probably the most fair and efficient legal system in any of the guerrilla groups in the islands, established price controls, issued paper money, and stabilized the economy within his do-main. He split his command into small groups to make it more difficult for the Japanese to strike a mortal blow at his organization.*

Praeger also "lightened the burden on Filipino farmers of feeding and protecting guerrillas in any one locality. In March and April of 1942 he ambushed supply trains, captured Japanese couriers, and fended off enemy patrols. As time passed, however, he steadily reduced military activities and concentrated on ga-thering intelligence and transmitting it to Australia.

PRAEGER TO MACARTHUR

JANUARY 1942

"AM CONDUCTING GOVERNMENT WITH UTMOST CARE LEGALLY AND MORALLY DEVOID OF POLITICAL AND PERSONAL CONSIDERATIONS.

MILITARY AND CIVIL AUTHORITIES IN PERFECT ACCORD HELPING ONE ANOTHER.

I HAVE PROVIDED ALL NEEDS OF THE ARMY COMPOSED OF SCOUTS, CONSTABULARY, AND PHILIPPINE ARMY IN THE CAGAYAN AND APARRI."

PRAEGER ADDED: "IF I MAY BE PERMITTED I CAN ORGANIZE FIVE THOUSAND ADDITIONAL MEN."

Most remarkably, he did all this so skillfully that he was supported by virtually the whole population of Apayao Subprovince."[12]

As time went by, other people joined Praeger. One well-cut Filipino civilian, Arthur Furagganan, joined the troop to work as a communications specialist. Praeger brought him in as a sergeant and eventually appointed him a first lieutenant in the 26th Cavalry. The Americanized Filipino officer loved the United States and his native land, and he proved invaluable to Praeger because after collecting radio parts from all over Luzon he built a workable radio transmitter that could communicate with stations in Australia and the United States. Captain James Needham from the 121st Infantry also joined Praeger, followed by his wife who had refused to meekly become a prisoner of the Japanese in Baguio. Needham helped the troop by manufacturing new grenades.[13]

After the fall of the Philippines, Troop C and CAF under Praeger continued to operate effectively as a guerrilla force for over a year. Unfortunately, in August or September of 1943, after some Filipinos betrayed them, the Japanese captured Praeger and Jones, Furagganan, and four sergeants, two from the 26th Cavalry.[14] Retribution followed quickly. One of Praeger's loyal lieutenants discovered who had been responsible for Praeger's capture and then "rounded up all the pro-Japanese local officials and killed almost everyone involved."[15]

Executions

Praeger and his subordinates faced immediate execution because the Japanese had threatened grim action against anyone resisting them after the formal surrender of the Philippines. Unexpectedly at first, the Japanese treated their new captives well, but they soon placed them in grim prisons – first Bilibid, then Ft. Santiago, and then Bilibid again, interrogated them, and lodged charges against them. Finally, they court-martialed Praeger and the others for:

1. *operating a radio transmitter,*
2. *espionage,*
3. *maintaining an enemy government,*
4. *printing enemy currency, resisting the Japanese army, and*
5. *disseminating Allied war propaganda.*[16]

There is no record of any sentence they handed out to Praeger.

The Japanese held Major Praeger in prison for many months – perhaps because he had treated captured Japanese soldiers so humanely, but they eventually executed – most likely they shot - him. One historian said the Japanese killed Praeger in August 1944. His former regimental commander, Clinton Pierce, however, reported his death as 3 December 1944. Other sources reported his death on 31 December 1944, nine days before American forces landed at Lingayen Gulf to begin the tion of Luzon.

For his wartime service, the thirty-year old Praeger earned two DSCs and a Legion of Merit.[17] General Pierce wrote that, "In his devotion to duty he set a shining example for soldiers everywhere. To him more than any other man, is due the credit for initiating the great resistance movement in the Philippines."[18] And General MacArthur wrote to his father and said: "In your son's death I have lost a gallant comrade and mourn with you."[19] The United States morialized Praeger on the *Tablets of the Missing and Buried at Sea* in the Manila Cemetery.

...PRAEGER COULD BE JUDGED TO HAVE BEEN THE MOST REMARKABLE AND PRODUCTIVE COMBAT OFFICER IN THE 26TH CAVALRY ON LUZON.

In retrospect, Praeger could be judged to have been the most remarkable and productive combat officer in the 26th Cavalry on Luzon.

Miraculously, the Japanese did not court-martial Captain Jones because he had been so ill in 1943 and 1944, and they "thought he would die in a few days anyway." Praeger had continually given them that impression as he nursed Jones during their eleven months together. In July 1944, the Japanese moved Jones to the military hospital at Bilibid where American POW doctors cared for him. Jones arrived at the hospital weighing seventy pounds. Fortunately, the doctors got him additional food and gave him some life-saving vitamins. Jones' delirium soon subsided, his eyesight improved so he could read again, and he gained about fifteen pounds. However, he never regained his health during the war. He survived, in part, because the Japanese forgot about him, and, in part, because troops from the 37th Infantry Division liberated Bilibid Prison in early February 1945. His illness saved his life. Better medicine and good food supported his recovery, and they came in the nick of time. Even with the help of the doctors, Jones would not have been able to survive many more days under the Japanese. After the war, Jones, who by that time was the only American survivor of CAF, wrote a valuable history of Troop C and CAF from which Norling wrote a larger history.[20]

BRIEF LIVES

"MOST OF THE CAF LEADERS WERE KILLED IN WORLD WAR II. MOST OF THE RANK AND FILE ALSO DIED, OR MERELY WENT HOME, ALTHOUGH SOME WERE ABSORBED INTO [COLONEL RUSSELL] VOLCKMANN'S GUERRILLA ORGANIZATION, USAFIPNL [U. S. ARMY FORCES IN THE PHILIPPINES, NORTH LUZON]...

THOSE WHO LEAVE BEHIND THEM EXAMPLES OF RESPONSIBILITIES ACCEPTED, PERFORMANCE OF DUTY EMBRACED, AND BLOOD SHED FOR WORTHY CAUSES MAY LIVE ONLY BRIEF LIVES, BUT THEY ENRICH THE NATIONAL LEGACY FOR GENERATIONS TO COME. "

BERNARD NORLING

The Japanese initially sentenced Arthur Furagganan to fifteen years imprisonment, but they changed their minds and executed Praeger's Filipino lieutenant on 4 February 1945, a day after the 1st Cavalry Division had liberated the internees in Santo Tomas and the day the 37th Infantry Division freed Captain Jones at Bilibid Prison. An American, Stewart Barnett, told Jones that "I saw that guy go out to die, and I never saw a man so brave in all my life – and I saw thirty-seven others die the same day. They ought to put up a monument to Arthur Furagganan in his hometown and write on it, 'Here is a Hero.'"[21] Furagganan earned a Bronze Star Medal and a Purple Heart. The Americans recovered his body and buried it in the Manila Cemetery.

The Japanese killed the Staff Sergeant Earl Brazelton and Staff Sergeant Louis Heuser (26th Cavalry) whom they had captured with Praeger. They also executed Captain James Needham, the homemade-grenade maker, who had helped Praeger and his group in the mountains. Edda Needham, whom the Japanese captured with her husband, survived the war, but she never recovered from the loss of her husband.[22] Brazelton from California and Heuser from Virginia each earned two Bronze Stars and a posthumous Purple Heart; New Yorker Needham earned a Bronze Star and a posthumous Purple Heart. The three are memorialized on the *Tablets of the Missing* with Praeger.[23]

The Japanese, however, did not execute Captain Warren Minton from Troop C or the newly-recruited Lieutenant William Bowen. Both officers had surrendered - Minton in 1942 and Bowen in 1943 – and both wound up in Cabanatuan. Minton had apparently surrendered on the call of the Japanese; Bowen had surrendered to protect his family.

The Japanese eventually moved Minton to Japan and Bowen to Bilibid hospital. In Bilibid, Bowen met and talked with Thomas Jones, and the irrepressible lieutenant scrounged food to help his sick comrade.

Pride

Fleeger reported no details about Troop C's remarkable operations in his diaries and he did not mention Praeger, Jones, and Minton after they went north. That is somewhat surprising because Major Chandler wrote after the war that "It was during this period [January 1942] that the regiment learned with pride of Troop C's successful raid on the enemy airfield at Tuguegarao."[24]

Some news about Praeger and Jones should have seeped into Cabanatuan after their capture, but it apparently never reached Fleeger. Moreover, Fleeger only mentioned Minton once in his diary, but did not indicate that he talked with him about any of the northern operations or that he even met him occasionally. While Fleeger must have known about the Tuguegarao Raid, he most likely never learned that Praeger had inducted Bowen or Furagganan into the 26th Cavalry. Perhaps this was an unlisted Reutel story.

Notes

[1] *Dairy*, 42.

[2] Norling, *Intrepid Guerrillas*, 27.

[3] *Ibid*. Norling reported different number of troops: 89 Scouts at Ft. Stotsenburg (48); 68 Scouts on 19 December (27); and 59 Scouts at Aritao on 31 December (48). At one place, he reported that 45 other Filipinos had joined Fleeger (27) and at another, he reported that 40 soldiers plus 4 or 5 Filipino officers joined Fleeger (48).

[4] *Ibid*, 48-50 (troop strength), Bowen (50-52), and Camp (49, 52-3).

[5] *Ibid*, 55. Mallig #2 was a "Philippine government farm project for landless peasants."

[6] *Ibid*, 58-9 for raid actions.

[7] *Ibid*, 59-60 covers the results.

[8] *Ibid*, 64.

[9] *Ibid*, 60.

[10] *Ibid*, 53-60 (raid) and 63-64 (Minton). In another account of the raid, Dr. Eugene C. Jacobs in his book, *Blood Brothers, A Medic's Sketch Book* (NY: Carlton Press, Inc., 1985), 29, 31 (raid), and 32, attributed the raid to Major Everett Warner and Minton. He wrote: *"Captain Minton selected some of his outstanding Scouts for his patrol. Under cover of darkness, Minton and his men surrounded the Japanese barracks at the Tuguegarao Air Field, killed some one-hundred Japanese soldiers as they emerged, and destroyed two planes on the ground. MacArthur was delighted! He promptly decorated the patrol and promoted Majors Warner and Nakar to lt. cols. and Minton to major."* Jacobs reported that he had served as the Regimental Surgeon to the so-called 1st Guerrilla Regiment.

Something is amiss because Jacobs did not mention Praeger and Troop C, 26th Cavalry (PS). According to Bernard Norling, "Lieutenant Minton carried news of their success to Maj. Everett Warner in Nueva Vizcaya, who radioed it to Corregidor, from whence it was sent off to the rest of the world." (Norling, *Intrepid Guerrillas*, 59) He added, "In an action that became typical for him, Warner sent his own version of the raid to HQ USAFFE. He placed himself in command and portrayed Minton as the leading hero in the action. Ignorant of the true course of events, HQ USAFFE responded with promotions for both men plus a DSC for Minton." (*Intrepid Guerrillas*, 94). In addition, Minton did not join Warner's command until 19 January, several days after the raid. I have to conclude that Jacobs reported in his book what Warner and Minton had told him about the raid, essentially what Warner reported to USAFFE, giving himself and Minton complete credit for the operation and leaving Praeger out of the story.

[11] According to the *ABMC Website*, Captain Francis A. Camp served with the 14th Infantry, a Filipino guerrilla regiment, once commanded by Lt. Colonel Guillermo Nakar. Camp earned a Silver Star, two Bronze Star Medals, and a Purple Heart for his service. He is shown as joining the regiment in the Philippines and dying on 31 January 1944. Camp is listed as Missing in Action or Buried at Sea in Manila Cemetery. The master list for POWs in the Pacific War does not list Camp. Norling provided no information about his final actions, but two endings seem possible: the Japanese killed Camp during one of his aggressive operations against them or they captured and then executed him. His website listing is similar to that for Nakar whom the Japanese executed in November 1943.

[12] Norling, *Intrepid Guerrillas*, 77.

[13] *Ibid*, 120-21 and 123-24 (grenades).

[14] *Ibid*, 230.

[15] Robert Lapham and Bernard Norling, *Lapham's Raiders, Guerrillas in the Philippines*, 1942-1945 (Lexington, KY: The University Press of Kentucky, 1996), 107.

[16] Norling, *Intrepid Guerrillas*, 232.

[17] Major Ralph Burton Praeger, Class of 1938, *1989 USMA Register*, #11167, 412. The *Register* and the *ABMC Website* list Praeger's death as 31 December 1944. According to Norling, *Intrepid Guerrillas*, 232, the Japanese executed Praeger in August 1944 at Ft. McKinley. Praeger was promoted to major while commanding the guerrilla forces in the mountains.

[18] Brigadier General C. A. Pierce, "Obituary for Ralph Burton Praeger," *Assembly Magazine*, April 1947.

[19] Quoted in Norling, *Intrepid Guerrillas*, 233.

[20] *Ibid*, 232 (Praeger), 233 (Furagganan), and 234-35 (Jones). Minton left Troop C before CAF was formed so he was never part of the new organization.

[21] *Ibid*, quoted at 80.

[22] *Ibid*, 232 (Praeger and Brazelton) and 233 (Needham, Edda Needham, and Furagganan).

[23] *Ibid*, 232. Norling assumed Brazelton died on or about 26 August 1944, but he did not give a date of death for Heuser. *ABMC Website*, however, lists the 26th of August as the date of death for both sergeants. *ABMC* lists 18 July 1944 as the date of Needham's death. The website shows Brazelton to have been assigned to the 228th Signal Operations Company and Heuser to have been a member of the 26th Cavalry (PS). It shows no organization for Needham.

[24] Chandler, "26th Cavalry," *ACJ*, Jul-Aug 1947, 17.

Sidebar Notes

Brief Lives
Norling, *Intrepid Guerrillas*, 239 and 241.

Praeger to MacArthur
MacArthur, *Reminiscences*, 204.

Five

"Establish a resistance movement"

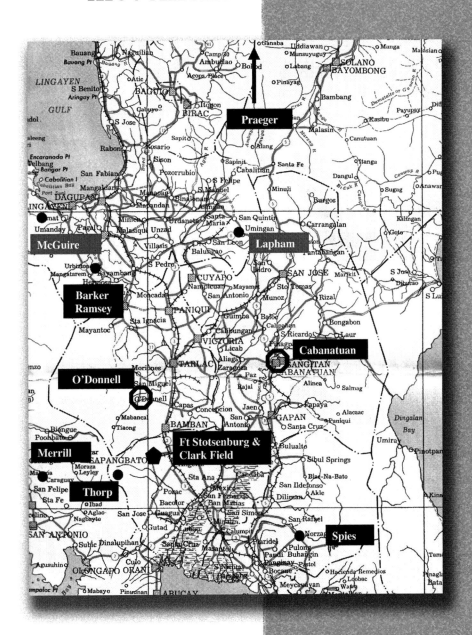

Plate 2 - American Guerrilla Leaders, Central Luzon, 1942

While Captain Ralph Praeger operated in the far north, four 26th Cavalry officers – Lt. Colonel Claude Thorp, Captains Joe Barker and Jack Spies, and Lieutenant Edwin Ramsey – escaped into the nearby countryside and became guerrilla leaders on Luzon. Fleeger did not know much about these guerrillas, but Ramsey did. He wrote about Barker, Spies, and Thorp – especially about Barker[1] after the war and added details about them that Fleeger did not know.

Guerrillas

Colonel Thorp became a senior guerrilla commander. Ramsey said that MacArthur sent him out "to establish a resistance movement."[2] Another source reported that Thorp told Colonel Merrill, his comrade from the 26th, that "General MacArthur had personally appointed [him] to raise guerrilla forces on Luzon."[3] Neither MacArthur nor his intelligence chief confirmed this directive in their own books. However, Lieutenant Robert Lapham, who worked under Thorp as a military police officer and then as a guerrilla, said that Thorp had met with General MacArthur on Corregidor and the general approved Thorp's plan to start up a guerrilla operation on Luzon. According to Lapham, Thorp was to sabotage Clark Field and gather intelligence about the Japanese.[4] Lapham also recalled that "The headquarters that now-Colonel Thorp established at Camp Sanchez clearly reflected considerable planning. Years before the cavalry [most likely the 26th] had erected several buildings on the site for use on maneuvers..." [5]

After Thorp organized his force, called *Luzon Guerrilla Force* (LGF), he broke it into four sections. In July 1942, he appointed three cavalry captains, Praeger, Spies, and Barker, to command different areas of Luzon. He assigned Praeger to control northern Luzon, Spies to oversee southern Luzon, and Barker to command Bataan and all the Central Plain from Lingayen Gulf to Manila, respectively.[6] Thorp then appointed Captain Ralph McGuire to head up west central Luzon, the area between Barker and the coast. By establishing this organization, Thorp tried to unify all the guerrillas on Luzon under his control. He failed, and others who also tried to unify the guerrillas failed because most guerrilla leaders were suspicious of their peers and of any centralized control. Moreover, with poor communications systems, a reliance on runners, and little physical contact with subordinates, no commander could exer-

IN JULY 1942, HE APPOINTED THREE CAVALRY CAPTAINS, PRAEGER, SPIES, AND BARKER, TO COMMAND DIFFERENT AREAS OF LUZON.

cise any centralized control effectively. Any attempt to do so would prove impossible. Realistically, Thorp could not control Praeger in the far north, and realizing this, Praeger just ignored him.

According to some, Thorp was probably the wrong man to try to control the various groups because many of the American leaders did not respect him, and, like many, he was over-confident of his probable success. In the summer of 1942, he reported to General MacArthur that "he could reconquer Luzon from within if given effective air support."[7] One wonders what MacArthur might have thought about his comment given the fact that the Japanese had decimated his forces with their air power and he certainly did not have air forces on hand in Australia and New Guinea that could have supported any force in the Philippines. But Lapham wrote that Thorp, a veteran of Pershing's Punitive Expedition to Mexico and World War I and a private soldier who had gained a commission, "was not an imaginative man, but he was tough, fearless, and well liked by his fellow officers and by enlisted men." Another guerrilla officer commented that Thorp "was a real leader: a serious officer devoid of any vanity or pretense."[8] Not everyone, however, thought highly of him. A senior Filipino guerrilla leader who worked for an American officer on Luzon thought Thorp to be an incompetent; another Filipino officer in the same unit thought that Thorp was just one of five tired old American colonels who were trying to sit out the war in the mountains.[9]

Shortly after Thorp announced his organizational plans, the Japanese captured him. Barker, Praeger's classmate who was leading East Central Luzon Guerrilla Force, took over from Thorp. The energetic youngster, who reportedly spoke Tagalog, made an excellent start, but less than three months later,[10] Barker, apparently desiring to get more accurate information about the Japanese and "probably from a sheer desire to defy the Japanese as well, had disguised himself as a priest and gone down to Manila." There, the Japanese captured him in January 1943.[11]

SHORTLY AFTER THORP ANNOUNCED HIS ORGANIZATIONAL PLANS, THE JAPANESE CAPTURED HIM.

Young Ramsey, Barker's deputy, took command of the Eastern Central Luzon Guerrilla Force. He inherited legitimacy that some other guerrilla leaders did not have because "By virtue of being under Colonel Thorp's authority, [Ramsey's] men were "official" USAFFE guerrillas, not bandits like other guerrillas roaming Luzon."[12]

During the war, Ramsey also tried to unify guerrillas all over central Luzon. He failed, but he did continue to operate his force for the duration of the war.[13]

ΩΩΩ

Colonel Gyles Merrill also became a guerrilla leader. On detached service as General Wainwright's supply officer at I Philippine Corps, he had surrendered on Bataan, but then he escaped from the Death March. Merrill, a full colonel when war broke out, became the senior American officer among the guerrillas.[14] Described as a tough, hard-drinking, weather-hardened cavalryman, and a tough disciplinarian, the fifty-year-old Merrill had been in the Regular Army all his adult life and was a stickler for regulations but generally liked by his peers and his men. Some Filipinos thought highly of him including Captain Ramon Magsaysay, one of his subordinates, who became the Secretary of Defense of the Republic of the Philippines and then President several years after the end of the war. Other Filipinos, however, thought he was one of the tired old American colonels mentioned earlier.[15]

Merrill's military experience might not have given him an advantage as a guerrilla, but he certainly was conditioned to survive on Luzon because "Long service in the tropics had made his skin so tough that he simply ignored the trillions of mosquitoes that swarmed over every square foot of Luzon and bit everyone in relays."[16] As the senior officer on the ground, Merrill also attempted to take control of all the guerrillas, but he became frustrated and angry when all of the American commanders of guerrilla units in central Luzon refused to attend a meeting that he called. Most of them told him that they reported directly to General MacArthur and not to anyone else.[17] So Merrill also failed to unify the guerrilla effort.

AS THE SENIOR OFFICER ON THE GROUND, MERRILL ALSO ATTEMPTED TO TAKE CONTROL OF ALL THE GUERRILLAS...

ΩΩΩ

Fleeger did not mention Ramsey or Merrill in his diaries. Neither did he speculate about whether the guerrillas in the nearby areas would try to liberate Cabanatuan. In fact, in the middle of 1944, as the Americans neared the Philippines and then after the Leyte landings, Lapham (headquartered nearby at Umingan) and another American guerrilla leader considered raiding the camp and freeing the prisoners. They went so far as to urge MacArthur's headquarters to authorize such an action because they feared that the Japanese would kill the prisoners once an invasion of Luzon became imminent. Both were confident that they could free the POWs, but neither could determine what they could do with the inmates after they rescued them. So they did not take action until after the Americans returned on January 1945. Then, Lapham's Filipino guerrillas helped rescue the remaining POWs.[18] Only one cavalry officer remained.

More Executions

Three of the cavalry officers Fleeger reported missing and who had become guerrillas did not survive. Fleeger only kept track of two of them: Captains "Little Joe" Barker and Jack Spies.

On 4 February 1943, Fleeger reported that "have just heard that Little Joe is in Ft. Santiago," and that a "later rumor is that Little Joe tried to escape and has lost his mind." Ft. Santiago was an infamous place. Few imprisoned there ever left alive.[19] Frederick Stevens, who survived Ft. Santiago, reported that "Capt. Barker... was kept in solitary confinement and not allowed out. As far as is known no extra food or cigarettes were given him [like Thorp]." He also said that a Filipino there told him that "Capt. Barker refused to talk or give them any information so he is being treated harshly."[20] Months later on 1 September 1943, Fleeger wrote that Little Joe was in Bilibid and "Should be O. K. from now on."[21] He was wrong. The Japanese executed Barker on 1 November 1943. He was twenty-eight. But Fleeger did not know of his death because five months later on 15 March 1944 he wrote: "Little Joe to McKinley? Rumor."[22]

After the war, Amasha B. Windham, a newspaper writer, reported that Barker had prepared a newsletter and distributed it in Manila in December 1942. "It taunted the Nipponese," she wrote, and "inspired the Filipinos to resistance and flung barbs into the very teeth of the aggressor." She added that Barker "was a dangerous prisoner and his captors knew it." A fellow officer reported that when

BARKER "WAS A DANGEROUS PRISONER AND HIS CAPTORS KNEW IT."

the Japanese interrogated Barker in Bilibid Prison, Barker told the Japanese that they could kill him for not giving them information and said "I would rather die than go home ashamed." The same officer said that the Japanese executed Barker in the Chinese Cemetery in northern Manila and buried him with five others in an unmarked, undiscovered grave. An unnamed American Chaplain told the reporter that Barker had "resisted every threat or bribe" of the Japanese, had "attempted to escape

JOE BARKER

GENERAL WAINWRIGHT PRESENTED A DSC TO BARKER'S FAMILY "IN RECOGNITION OF THE WORK DONE IN THE GUERRILLA CAMPAIGN."

ATTENDING WERE:

• BRIG. GENERAL

• CLINTON A. PIERCE

• BRIG. GENERAL

• WILLIAM E. BROUGHER

several occasions," and that if "he'd had half a chance, he'd have torn all the lousy Nip guards to pieces." He added: "The enemy admired him and his spirit. They also feared him. They knew his spirit could not be broken." Another story came from friends of Mr. George Litton who had supplied Barker and his guerrillas when they were in the hills. The Japanese captured Litton, and when they asked Barker if he knew Litton, Barker said he had never seen him. The Japanese eventually freed Litton; he credited Barker with saving his life.[23] Fleeger's comment that Little Joe had gone mad most likely reflected Barker's "fire" during his captivity. Barker's tragic end overshadowed the fact that - given his proven combat skills - if he had been less impulsive, he could have had a greater impact on the guerrilla movement on Luzon.

Major Chandler highlighted Barker's actions during combat. After the initial fights on Luzon, Barker assumed command of the dismounted remnants of the 26th Cavalry – Troop B and Machine Gun Troop - that were not under Major Trapnell's command. He fought the makeshift unit, which, mounted on buses and remaining trucks, served as a motorized force until the regiment reorganized on Bataan in late February.[24] Two comments stood out: "Captain Barker attacked late in the afternoon of January 22, driving the enemy northward along the road four and one-half kilometers, but was there stopped by a deep ravine and almost impenetrable jungle;" and, "Late in the afternoon of January 25, Captain Barker's force, having executed repeated brilliant delaying actions along the heavily wooded and winding Moron Road, passed through Troop A and ... marched past Bagac to an assigned bivouac area...."[25]

The Army awarded the dynamic Alabaman a "Silver Star for gallantry in action at Binalonan" on 24 December 1941, a "Legion of Merit for skilled handling of his troops throughout the Battle," and a "Purple Heart for wounds in action, resulting in his death." And then at a formal memorial ceremony after the war, General Wainwright presented a DSC to Barker's family "in recognition of the work done in the guerrilla campaign." Brigadier General Clinton Pierce, 26th Cavalry, attended, as did retired Chaplain John Duffy, 26th Cavalry.[26]

ΩΩΩ

On 10 May 1943, Fleeger wrote, "Jack Spies – who commanded Troop B – was my good friend – did not surrender but went into the mountains. Today I received rumor that he had died on October 25 – malaria – dysentery – starvation – pneumonia – even as so many have died here in prison. About 1/3rd of our 26th Cavalry officers remain alive."[27] Fleeger seemed to have gotten this information right, unlike his reports about Barker.

Father Forbes J. Monaghan, a Jesuit, reported that "Captain John Spiess [sic] was a young American officer who escaped to the camp maintained by the Ateneo in Zambales. Dissatisfied with the conditions there, he moved over to Bulacan and established himself with two other American officers in the hills near Norzagaray. From time to time he sent for Father Hurley for help. A red-haired *mestiza* girl with whom he was in love also helped him. Captain Spiess was Catholic, and every Saturday night he slipped into Norzagaray for confession to the parish priest, Father Alvarez. After staying at the rectory for the night, he would receive Holy Communion early, and be off again to the hills before daybreak."[28] Monaghan added that Spies had had been trapped inside the rectory one night by a Japanese raiding party. He laid his two pistols on a table and told Father Alvarez, "Go down and see them Father...You know nothing of my presence. If they come in here, I will fight it out with them." Later on he made a second escape, but as before Spies received Holy Communion before he left for the hills. Spies apparently had other priest friends. Father Carberry at Ft. McKinley, wrote home before the war and reported "I had Jack Spies out for cocktails one evening."[29]

> *AFTER STAYING AT THE RECTORY FOR THE NIGHT, HE WOULD RECEIVE HOLY COMMUNION EARLY, AND BE OFF AGAIN TO THE HILLS BEFORE DAYBREAK.*

Sometime later, Monaghan reported that Father Alvarez, who had gone to Spies' hideout in the hills, "found Spiess sick with pneumonia [and concluded] without medicine or a physician, recovery was hopeless." "The priest," he added, "gave him the last sacraments and a few days later, he died."[30] Guerrilla officers offered different stories. Lieutenant Ramsey said that the Japanese killed Spies "on his way to take up his command in Southern Luzon,"[31] and Captain Lapham reported, "Jack

No National Fame

THE FOUR CAVALRY OFFICERS THE JAPANESE EXECUTED FOR FIGHTING AS GUERRILLAS GAINED NO NATIONAL FAME AND GLORY – ALTHOUGH GENERAL MACARTHUR AWARDED THREE OF THEM POSTHUMOUS DSCS.

THORP RECEIVED A POSTHUMOUS DSC AND TWO PURPLE HEARTS.

Spies did not get along with Filipinos and was killed before he ever assumed his command." Lapham later commented, "Spies had been killed by somebody."[32]

Fleeger wrote one brief note about the missing Lt. Colonel Thorp. Fleeger said Thorp was in Bilibid and as with Barker "Should be OK from now on." He was wrong again: the Japanese executed Thorp with Barker on 1 November 1943. However, while he was in Ft. Santiago, the Japanese treated Thorp very leniently. Stevens reported that "[Thorp] had books, cigarettes, and special food. He was also was permitted to leave his cell every day to smoke and exercise."[33] Thorp received a posthumous DSC and two Purple Hearts.

The Army also memorialized Barker, Spies, and Thorp on the *Tablets of the Missing* in Manila Cemetery.

Courage Not Glory

Cavalry officers won eleven DSCs and twenty-one Silver Stars during the war. In comparison, only seven American officers earned DSCs and ten earned Silver Stars in the 57th Infantry Regiment (PS), a much larger unit.[34] The bravery and sacrifice of the officers of the 26th Cavalry Regiment reflected great credit on each of them and brought great glory to the entire regiment.

But, the four cavalry officers the Japanese executed for fighting as guerrillas gained no national fame and glory – although General MacArthur awarded three of them posthumous DSCs. However, Barker, Furagganan, Praeger, and Thorp displayed an extraordinary level of courage that differed from their comrades who fought the Japanese on the battlefields of Luzon. Knowing their fate, and knowing that the Japanese would kill and probably humiliate them by publicly beheading them, they apparently conducted themselves with tremendous dignity and sangfroid under terrible conditions and in some cases under severe torture. At their deaths, they fully merited the requirements for their DSCs, namely: "The act or acts of heroism must be so notable and involve risk of life so extraordinary as to set the individual apart from his comrades." In fact, each may have deserved a Medal of Honor for his courage during captivity and his actions at his execution that were in every sense "above and beyond the call of duty."

Fleeger did not know about these tragedies.

Notes

1 Captain Joseph Rhett Barker, II, Class of 1938, *1989 USMA Register*, Class of 1938, #11137, 412. Also see *ABMC Website*. Executed 1 Nov 43 at age 28. Lt. Ramsey wrote: "I had never been close to Joseph Rhett Barker, II; indeed, I had never particularly cared for his aristocratic Alabama manner and his West Point hauteur. But there was little of that left now. Barker too was emaciated; it was a brother hood we all shared, an inescapable fraternity of malnutrition, exhaustion, and doom." Ramsey escaped with Barker and reported their activities with the guerrillas in his book. Ramsey and Rivele, *Ramsey's War*, 75.
2 Ramsey and Rivele, *Ramsey's War*, 94.
3 Chris Schaefer, *Bataan Diary, An American Family in World War II, 1941-1945* (Houston: Riverview Publishing, 2004), 113. Schaefer covered the actions of Lt. Colonel Frank Loyd who was a successful evader.
4 Lapham and Norling, *Lapham's Raiders*, 13-14.
5 Lapham and Norling, *Lapham's Raiders*, 19.
6 Ramsey and Rivele, *Ramsey's War*, 110-11.
7 Norling, *Intrepid Guerrillas*, 149.
8 Lapham and Norling, *Lapham's Raiders*, 19-20.
9 Norling, *Intrepid Guerrillas*, 76 and 95.
10 *Ibid*, 148-9.
11 Lapham and Norling, *Lapham's Raiders*, 56.
12 Schaefer, *Bataan Diary*, 141.
13 Norling, *Intrepid Guerrillas*, 74.
14 *1943 Army Directory*, 309 listed Merrill as a full colonel. It listed two other guerrilla "colonels" – Martin Moses, 317, Arthur Noble, 322, as lieutenant colonels at the time. The third "colonel," Thorp, actually was a major on the Army list, 379.
15 Schaefer, *Bataan Diary*, 80-81 (Merrill), 322 (Filipino support) and Norling, *Intrepid Guerrillas*, 96 and 253 (fn 42) (tired old men).
16 Lapham and Norling, *Lapham's Raiders*, 37 and 248 (fn 8).
17 Schaefer, *Bataan Diary*, 250-52.
18 Lapham and Norling, *Lapham's Raiders*, 177.
19 *Diary*, 87.
20 Frederick A. Stevens, *Santo Tomas Internment Camp, 1942-1945* (Stratford House, Inc., 1946), limited private edition, 337.
21 *Diary*, 115.
22 *Ibid*, 145.

23 *Cullum File #11137.* See Amasa B. Windham, "Tale of Hero Who Fought, Died follows an Illustrious Pattern," unidentified Chicago newspaper, c. Nov 1945; Aaron D. Miller, "Letter to Commandant, U. S. Military Academy, 1 June 1951"; and undated copy of "Memorial Service, Captain Joseph Rhett Barker, II, 26th Cavalry, Philippine Scouts, U.S.A."
24 Chandler, "26th Cavalry," *ACJ,* May-Jun 1947, 13.
25 Chandler, "26th Cavalry," *ACJ,* Jul-Aug 1947, 16-17.
26 *Cullum File #11137.* See "Memorial Service, Captain Joseph Rhett Barker, II, 26th Cavalry."
27 *Diary,* 94.
28 Forbes J. Monaghan, *Under the Red Sun, A Letter from Manila* (NY: The Declan X. McMullen Company, 1946), 149.
29 Roper, *Brothers of Paul,* 77.
30 Monaghan, *Red Sun,* 149-50.
31 Ramsey and Rivele, *Ramsey's War,* 136.
32 Lapham and Norling, *Lapham's Raiders,* 36 and 54.
33 Stevens, *Santo Tomas,* 337.
34 Olson, *Anywhere-Anytime,* 218.

Sidebar Note

Joe Barker

Memorial Service Brochure, possession of author. *Brochure* stated that a previous Silver Star had been awarded "for gallantry in action at Binalonan, Luzon on December 24, 1941," and Legion of Merit had been awarded for "skillful handling of his troops throughout the Battle," and a Purple Heart awarded "for wounds in action, resulting in his death." The Purple Heart most likely was awarded because of Barker's death by execution.

Appointment to West Point
Signed by the Secretary of War

Barracks at West Point

Cavalry Drill in the Riding Hall at West Point

Second Lieutenant, U. S. Cavalry

Capt. Glenn S. Finley, Second Lieut. Harry Fleeger, and First Lieut. W. Nutter
14th Cavalry

Louise Fleeger
(center) on "Friday"

Louise Fleeger
*(right) winning
Department
Horseshow,
Ladies Hack, 1940*

Harry Fleeger, Jim Fleeger, Louise Fleeger, Larry Fleeger
In the Philippines, c. 1940

Six

"Tired – hungry – hell of a life"

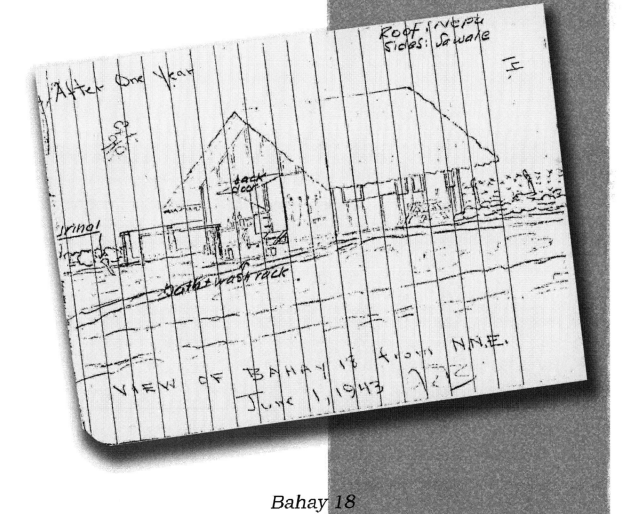

Bahay 18

Early on, Fleeger decided "My notes will not contain reference of prison camp experience. They will not bear repeating – and although I will never forget I pray that the memory dims – a stout heart, a clear conscience – and never despair – the last is the hardest – you will never know."[1]

In that regard, he did not write about his experiences on the Bataan Death March [Map 6] during which about 650 Americans and somewhere between 5,000 and 10,000 Filipinos died.

"Death was Easier than Life"[2]

Fleeger's experience on the Death March probably fell between those of two 26th Cavalrymen: David Miller and Thomas Trapnell.

Second Lieutenant Kermit Lay of I Philippine Corps reported Miller's story. "In our group there was a cavalry captain from Kansas City named Miller who I had known before the war in Manila and who I used to hang around with. When he was captured he still was wearing Cavalry boots. During the March the boots got so heavy that they began to rub huge blisters on his feet. He also had dysentery and was real sick. A former MP company commander and I tried to hold him up. We were on either side of him, but it was hard going on us and we began to fall further and further back. Finally, one of the men at the rear of our column, who kept watching for guards, yelled at us that a Jap was coming. By now we were dragging Miller. When the guard got to us he rammed his bayonet right through Miller. Naturally we dropped him and ran up and got into the middle of the column."[3]

"WHEN THE GUARD GOT TO US HE RAMMED HIS BAYONET RIGHT THROUGH MILLER."

Stanley Falk recorded a quite different story about Trapnell. "About 400 Americans who had been with General Bluemel on the last II Corps line had been promised food several times on their march up the East Road. Yet each time they had been disappointed. Finally at Balanga [vicinity Abucay, Map 6], Major Thomas J. H. Trapnell, the senior officer in the group, decided to do something about the situation. He caught the attention of some of the Japanese, told them forcefully that his men were exhausted and starving, and demanded food for them. Surprisingly enough, his bold stance paid off. The Japanese gave each man a large serving of rice and a big piece of rock salt…" Falk added, "The 400 Americans in Major Trapnell's group boarded Japanese trucks at Balanga and rode all the way to Camp O'Donnell without stopping.[4]

Miller was doomed as so many men like him were. Trapnell and his men were fortunate as were some other small groups that the Japanese trucked north.[5] Trapnell in his later years said that his group had it pretty easy on the Death March and that the groups ahead and behind his suffered greatly.[6] But he never spoke about his own actions at Balanga.

Fleeger did not report the worst story about the Death March: the Japanese reprisal against the Filipino soldiers of the 91st Division who allegedly had surprised and overrun the Japanese 65th Brigade on 6 April and who had not surrendered early. The story was grim: "Then, at a given signal, the execution began. Japanese officers moved down the line from one end, mercilessly beheading the luckless Filipinos with their gleaming sabers. From the other end, the Japanese enlisted men worked toward them, methodically plunging their bayonets into the backs of the prisoners...For two hours the grisly slaughter continued, the Japanese sweating at their work in the hot sun, pausing to wipe away the perspiration, and then returning to their grim task."[7] A handful of Filipinos survived. Between 350 and 400 died for an action they did not take. The Philippine 41st Division, not the 91st, had conducted the attack on the 6th. Perhaps, this was to be one of Fleeger's Reutel stories."[8]

Fleeger also did not comment about his weeks at Camp O'Donnell. After arriving there, Fleeger and the other Americans learned how terrible POW life would be for them. The Japanese commander told Americans that they would be treated as captives not as POWS. 1st Sergeant Houston Turner, 31st Infantry, reported his speech: "A Japanese officer gave us a little talk about what we could expect. He told us that Americans were dogs, that they'd always been dogs, and that they were going to be treated like dogs."

DEATH MARCH

"EVERY FEW YARDS JAP NONCOMS MATERIALIZED LIKE GARGOYLES FROM THE GRAYISH WHITE PALL AND SNATCHED AMERICANS OUT OF THE LINE TO BE SEARCHED AND BEATEN. BEFORE WE HAD GONE TWO MILES WE HAD BEEN STRIPPED OF PRACTICALLY ALL OF OUR POSSESSIONS.

THE JAPS MADE NO MOVE TO FEED US. FEW OF US HAD HAD ANYTHING TO EAT SINCE THE MORNING OF APRIL 9. MANY HAD TASTED NO FOOD IN FOUR DAYS. WE HAD A LITTLE TEPID WATER IN OUR CANTEENS, BUT NOTHING ELSE."

CAPTAIN ED DYESS

Camp O'Donnell

"In O'Donnell our boys were dying forty, fifty, sixty a day. We couldn't bury them fast enough."

One survivor correctly labeled the camp, "Camp O'Death and the "Andersonville of the Pacific."

Soon death overwhelmed the POWs in the camp. PFC Andrew Aquila, 192nd Tank Battalion, said: "In O'Donnell our boys were dying forty, fifty, sixty a day. We couldn't bury them fast enough." First Lieutenant Mark Herbst, M.D., added: "They would bury forty a day on our side and 100 a day on the Filipino side." Some POWs just gave up and died. PFC John Falconer of the 194th Tank Battalion reported: "Death was easier than life. All I had to do was just lay back and die. I didn't have to worry about that. It was as easy as letting go of a rope. A lot of people quit hanging on."[9] But, Sergeant Turner and others hung on. He explained: "I damned near died in O'Donnell from malaria. I got an attack there. Somehow I must have lost consciousness and I woke up in the morgue, what they called zero ward. I was laying on a woven sawali grass mat, like a shutter that came off a window. There were stiffs all around me. I crawled over to a medic who was sitting around and asked him what I was doing there. He told me because I was supposed to be dead, that I had already been counted as dead and was on a list. I got up and he asked whether I could make it back to my company areas. I sure tried."[10]

Eventually about 1,500 of an estimated 9,300 Americans died from dysentery (866), malaria (433), lack of medical treatment, malnutrition, and brutality at Camp O'Donnell. Young soldiers and young officers perished in the greatest numbers. Fortunately, no 26th Cavalry officer died in O'Donnell. Tragically, about 25,000 Filipinos died in their segregated area of the camp. One survivor correctly labeled the camp, "Camp O'Death" and the "Andersonville of the Pacific."[11]

Fleeger was in the middle of all this. He suffered from malnutrition. He had been sick himself. He must have dealt with the dying, and he must have seen men give up. Luckily, he did not see his Filipino Scouts suffering. Perhaps, Fleeger drew a lucky straw as Trapnell had on the Death March, but more than likely he did not. He certainly experienced the worst at Camp O'Donnell where the worst was the daily norm. Again, this probably was a Reutel story.

Cabanatuan

Fleeger did not describe much about his new home at the Cabanatuan POW Camp, located near Cabanatuan City, which was about 100 miles north of Manila [Map 6]. When the Philippine Army mobilized in 1941, engineers built three camps – 1, 2, and 3 - near the town to house three regiments. Each camp occupied about fifty acres and the engineers subdivided each camp into three battalion areas. Each area had a large administrative building with small offices, a wooden dispensary building, a long shelter that functioned as a garage, a guardhouse with a jail in it, and a number of nipa-roofed, sawali-sided barracks. The Philippine Army planned to billet forty Filipino soldiers in the sixty-foot long barracks.

The Japanese took over the camps to house the American prisoners they held in Camp O'Donnell and the others they imprisoned in Bilibid in Manila. They erected eight-foot barbed-wire fences around each camp and built several four-story guard towers at the camps. Across the road from the camps, the Japanese used many small buildings to house their guards.

Beginning in late May 1942, the Japanese moved the sick and wounded from the field hospitals on Bataan into camp No. 3. They also moved in the much healthier POWs from Corregidor whom they had held in Bilibid. Shortly after that, the population in Camp No. 3 reached 6,066. To fit the large number of POWs into the camp, the Japanese stuffed 120 rather than forty men into each of the existing barracks. Colonel Napoleon Boudreau, a Coast Artillery Commander, became the POW's first commander and remained so until October 1942 when the Japanese transferred all the POWs in Camp No. 3 to Camp No. 1. Before that, around 31 May, with Camp No. 3 filled, the Japanese moved the remaining Corregidor POWs from Bilibid to Camp No. 2. But Camp No. 2 had no water, so they soon moved these POWs into Camp No. 1.

"THERE WAS ABSOLUTELY NO HOPE IN THEIR EYES."

The Japanese began moving POWs from Camp O'Donnell to Camp No. 1 on 2 June. About 5,850 – the sickest, weakest, and most disabled POWs – eventually arrived in late June, about the time the Battle of Midway took place in the middle Pacific. Navy Ensign William Berry described the incoming O'Donnell POWs: "Back on Corregidor we had heard rumors of how badly they were being treated, but we were unprepared for the shock of what we saw. Those guys all had malaria and dysentery and were so skinny that they looked like walking skeletons with skin hanging from their bones. There was absolutely no hope in their eyes. These were relatively young men in their late teens and early twenties – people who only a few months before had been in prime physical condition. But they looked so old. So downtrodden."[12] And, Fleeger and his friends were part of the incoming groups.

After the Japanese moved the 3,000 POWs from Camp 3 into Camp 1 in late October, the camp's population rose to about 8,700. Now the only camp, Camp No. 1 became "Cabanatuan POW Camp." An American agricultural experiment station before the war, it took its name from the town of Cabanatuan four miles to its east. The camp sat on flat, arid ground and measured about 600 by 800 yards in size. While Cabanatuan became the primary POW camp for military personnel on Luzon, not all the American POWs wound up in Cabanatuan. The Japanese kept about 2,000 on work details around Luzon, held many others in Bilibid, kept many at Ft. McKinley, and, as mentioned, they eventually sent several hundred to the Davao Penal Colony. And many of the very sick POWs captured on Bataan and Corregidor never made it to the camp. They just disappeared, never to be seen again.

Not the Ritz

Cabanatuan was not a pleasant place. Fleeger and the other POWs lived in rather primitive conditions in 20 foot by 20 foot nipa huts (*bahays*) with no running water, no rudimentary bathrooms, and no screens. They did, however, have one improvement from their previous buildings – they had raised floors. Disease was everywhere. So were nasty bugs and insects. Lacking long-sleeved shirts, long trousers,

FROM THE START, THE JAPANESE PROVIDED INADEQUATE QUANTITIES OF FOOD...

insect repellent, DDT, and mosquito nets, the POWs provided fleshy targets for mosquitoes producing dengue fever and malaria. Lacking shoes, the Americans were subject to all sorts of earth-borne infections such as hookworm and ringworm and fungus infections such as Hong Kong foot (i.e., severe athlete's foot). Moreover, cut feet invited general infections.

From the start, the Japanese provided inadequate quantities of food and seldom provided adequate protein for meals. Consequently, *beri-beri* became rampant. Additionally, the Japanese did not provide sufficient medicine to treat the sick for malaria, pellagra, or dysentery. And then a diphtheria epidemic broke out and killed 130 in June. That same month, 610 other POWs died from malnutrition and various diseases. In September 1942, Major (Dr.) Eugene Jacobs reported the pathetic situation of the sick POWs: "I was the Chief of Medical Service in the camp hospital and had some 2000 patients in 20 wards. I visited each patient daily. There was actually very little that I could offer them except some hope for a better tomorrow. The patients all suffered from multiple diseases. Many had lost from one-third to one-half their body weight. Most of them had one or more vitamin deficiencies. Nearly everyone had beriberi."[13] With so many sick, Zero Ward – the death ward – remained a tragic reality in the Cabanatuan just as it had been in Camp O'Donnell. Jacobs described it. "The ward usually contained 30-40 extremely debilitated patients lying naked on the floor, frequently in their own vomitus or dysenteric stool. Flies walked casually over the leathery skin of the dying men. Rarely did one arouse himself sufficiently to threaten a fly. In fact, most did not desire to be disturbed and typically responded: "I have suffered enough. Just go away. Let me alone."[14]

By the end of 1942, nearly 2,000 more prisoners died in the main camp. Another sixty-one had died in Camp No. 3 before the Japanese closed it.[15]

ΩΩΩ

Fleeger's new address for the duration was *Bahay* #39. It was not the Ritz, but with nipa and sawali, it could keep the rain out most of the time (though not the heat and the bugs). In his first entry about his *bahay*, Fleeger listed his *bahay* mates, and identified six of them as his "blood brothers" – members of his "shooting squad." They were mostly infantry officers.

He listed seven other officers – mostly field artillerymen - as living in his *bahay*. Fleeger did not explain their bunking arrangements. Perhaps they had double-decked bunks in the early days.

Nine of the officers - Bauer, Bidgood, Browne, Dunmyer, Blanning, Chandler, Fitch, Howard, and Johnson – graduated from West Point. Three of them -

BAHAY MATES & "BLOOD BROTHERS"

KAROL A. BAUER, INF
45TH INFANTRY (PS)

CLARENCE BIDGOOD, CE
71ST ENGINEER BATTALION (PS)

CHARLES A. BROWNE, INF
91ST DIVISION (PA)

WILLIAM J. DUNMYER, INF
HQ, II PHILIPPINE CORPS

EVERT S. "POP" THOMAS, CAC
ADJUTANT GENERAL
PHILIPPINE DIVISION

ALBERT B. ZWASKA, INF
45TH INFANTRY (PS)

OTHER *BAHAY* MATES

JAMES BLANNING, CAV
26TH CAVALRY (PS)

ALBERT W. BRAUN, CH
(CATHOLIC)
200TH COAST ARTILLERY
REGIMENT

WILLIAM E. CHANDLER, CAV
26TH CAVALRY (PS)

ALVA R. FITCH, FA
24TH FA REGIMENT (PS)

CHARLES E. N. HOWARD, FA
88TH FA REGIMENT (PS)

CHESTER L. JOHNSON, FA
24TH FA REGIMENT (PS)

HARRY PACKARD, FA
24TH FA REGIMENT (PS)

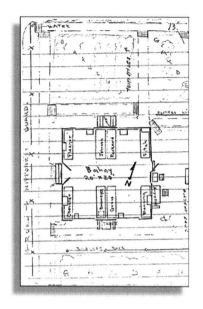

FLEEGER DRAWING

BAHAY MATES
JUNE 1943

JAMES BLANNING, CAV

BILL CHANDLER, CAV

BILL DUNMYER, INF

ALVA FITCH, FA

HARRY FLEEGER, CAV

GARDNER GROSS, INF

CHESTER JOHNSON, FA

HARRY PACKARD, FA

Blanning, Chandler, and Howard were Fleeger's West Point classmates. Two of them – Blanning and Chandler – were cavalry comrades.

Except for the grim situation, the lousy quarters, and the poor food, the group of POWs should have been very compatible and should have enjoyed each other's company. And having a Catholic chaplain in the mix who was a World War I veteran and who had been wounded in the war and recommended for a Distinguished Service Cross for his actions in that war must have added a special flavor to the group.[16] Fleeger and his mates probably missed Father Braun when the Japanese transferred him to Davao. Howard could have added interesting stories to any "bull" session because his father had been a regular Army officer and had served in the Philippine Insurrection, along the Mexican Border, and in World War I.[17]

Fleeger sketched views of *bahay* in his diary in June 1943. By then, the Japanese had moved several hundred POWs to Davao and reduced the congestion in the camp, and Fleeger noted that there were only eight in his *bahay* - mostly field artillery majors. Bauer, Braun, Browne, Howard, and Zwaska had gone. Major Gardner B. "Spade" Gross, an infantryman from Nebraska,[18] had joined Blanning, Chandler, Dunmyer, Fitch, Fleeger, Johnson, and Packard in the hut.[19]

The major never described a typical day in the camp, but his boss at the camp library, Lt. Colonel David Babcock, penned the following: on 30 September 1942:

6:20 a.m. – 1ˢᵗ call- 6:30 reveille – calisthenics – Bahay coffee – b'fast of Lugao, yeast and salt to which I add sugar – half awake, arguments usually start at this time. Usually stiff and sore from sleeping on hard boards, tho still able to sleep soundly. After b'fast, do some writing either morale or personal or both.

Babcock continued:

- *About 10 start out on rounds of Group I, camp hdqrs, or elsewhere on morale business.*
- *Return for chow at noon – steamed rice, gravy or soup, cucumbers, or commotes or possibly fried eggplant.*
- *In p.m. either read, write or have welfare or morale meetings or arrange for shows.*
- *5 p.m. evening chow-steamed rice, gravy or soup, commotes or cucumbers – occasionally a roll or bread. Every second or third day we open a can (when in the money) and have patties or a loaf or straight. Once had corn beef and shirred eggs.*
- *After chow – roll call and evening morale program – show, quiz program or lectures. All during the day conferences with Burrell, Gamble or others on morale, welfare, rumours, etc.*
- *After the show mosquitoes so bad nothing to do but go to bed (usually around 8). Sleep well tho up about twice a night to go to the Johnny because of the diet. And so to bed.*
- *Varied by inspections, trips to hospital, guard duty, etc.[20]*

From his report, Fleeger seemed to be getting plenty to eat at this time, but in November he reported that his feet were bad and his eyes were so bad that he had to hire soldiers to read and write for him. Moreover, he had contracted *beri-beri*. By the following May, he weighed only138.5 pounds.

A year after he arrived, Fleeger reflected on the continued dismal conditions when he began one diary entry with: "We have rats in the rafters of the *bahay*, Bill almost killed one with a wooden scivvie.[21] (Later killed it)."

Surviving

The first issue of importance in the POW camp was survival. Fleeger had mentioned that months before in a letter to his wife. As noted earlier, Fleeger said that he had been sick for two months – April and May - and had nearly died before he entered Cabanatuan. Moreover, he had developed *beri-beri* in May.[22]

Fleeger initially dealt with survival by developing rules to live by. In July 1942, he wrote "My Prisoners Creed."[23]

1. *To be willing and anxious to sacrifice anything for a friend, the reward to be complete in the sacrifice.*
2. *To be ever willing and anxious to give, cheerfully, the reward to be complete in the giving.*
3. *To devote my post war life – first to Louise – second to my sons Jimmy and Larry – third to the service – the devotion to be sincere, conscientious and humble.*
4. *To review past events periodically attempting to make each day hereafter justify both itself and one day I have lived as a prisoner.*
5. *To strive daily to live a more Christian life.*
6. *To enjoy each hour.*

The impact of the war and the deprivations of imprisonment clearly underpinned Fleeger's comments about sacrifice. He certainly knew first-hand about sacrifice as he had witnessed his comrades help others at the risk of their lives during combat, on the Death March, and during imprisonment. And he knew about giving because he and his friends often shared their meager rations to survive. His priority of wife, sons, and service most likely reversed an earlier priority of service, wife, and sons. And Fleeger's emphasis on daily living probably reflected his uncertainty of surviving as a prisoner and at the same time provided him a means to survive hour-to-hour, meal-to-meal, and day-to-day in the POW Camp.

On 16 August 1942, Fleeger expanded his philosophical base and wrote down twenty of his favorite quotations.[24] Eight came from the Bible or from Christian prayers. Two reinforced his earlier rule to live a more Christian life:

AND FLEEGER'S EMPHASIS ON DAILY LIVING PROBABLY REFLECTED HIS UNCERTAINTY OF SURVIVING AS A PRISONER...

"But be ye doers of the word and not hearers only, deceiving yourselves (James 1:26)" and "for as the body without the Spirit is dead, so faith without works is dead also (James 2:26)." And death would have been on his mind when he was considering his future in Cabanatuan and when he wrote, "Intreat me not to leave thee, or to return from following after thee, for whither thou goest I will go; and where thou lodgest I will lodge, thy people shall be my people, and they God my God, where thou diest I will die and there will I be buried, the Lord do so to me and more also it ought but death part thee and me (Ruth 1:16,17)."

Fleeger then quoted a French Army captain, who was killed riding in a steeplechase, and who provided a fitting assertion for the captured cavalryman: "We must be ready to ride, yes to fall, for only those who dare to ride can fall, and we will not meet our end until the time comes." Fleeger had ridden well, fallen, and could not predict his end, but, after witnessing rampant death all around him, he must have realized that his odds for survival were not great. Then, as if to give himself hope, he wrote: "While there is life there is hope," and added with POW humor, "While there is rice there is hope." Next, as if to strengthen his will and encourage himself, he wrote down Winston Churchill's admonition to "Live dangerously – Fear naught – and all will end well." In 1942, the hope that "all will end well" was as critical to survival in the Philippines as it was in England. Soon General MacArthur codified that hope in his famous comment: *"I Shall Return"* that became the beacon of hope for the Filipinos and the military and civilian POWs who dreamed of the day they would be free again and that, in turn, infuriated their Japanese conquerors.

"WHILE THERE IS RICE THERE IS HOPE."

Fleeger also reflected on his West Point heritage.[25] On 18 October 1942, he added: "During War and Prison Camp days, conversation has turned to West Point (after food) most frequently. This acid test has made us realize that *Honor, Duty, Country* – and memories of Alma Mater have unconsciously become probably the strongest influence of our precarious existence. Reminiscing has aroused a new longing to visit the Academy again, there to renew our ties – with old barracks, the Chapel, The Corps, and scenes of peace and beauty along the Hudson. I hope to spend a short time myself on such a trip, leisurely planned with a view to learning a new acquaintance with something too old and deep for any of us to overcome – *Where they of the Corps have trod.*"[26]

On the other hand, in contrast to Fleeger's desire to revisit places at West Point, an older POW told me years later when he visited West Point for a reunion, that each time he returned, he could not wait to leave the place.[27]

Fleeger's listing of the motto of his *alma mater* as "Honor, Duty, Country" provides an intriguing sidebar to his story because the modern motto lists a different order, namely "Duty, Honor, Country." What triggered the variation? Did Fleeger just give the motto his personal twist, did he misstate it, or had "Honor" become more important in prison camp than "Duty?" Had Fleeger made Honor his top concern because he had witnessed problems in camp? All this is interesting because he had been an honor representative while a cadet at West Point.

And then Fleeger listed the quotation which he had developed with Bill Dunmyer[28] on Bataan: "I pray that I may never be tired, hungry, or lonely again." He never said how these quotations helped him during captivity.

As a follow-on to his musings, Fleeger listed what he thought about most as he went about the task of surviving. First he focused on his family:

1. *Louise*
2. *Does Larry still get soap in his eyes?*
3. *Has Jimmy worried for me?*
4. *Is the Judge [his father] still sweating out my return?*

Then he turned to food.

5. *Hot Fudge Parfait*
6. *T Bone Steaks*
7. *Cold chocolate milk*
8. *Mother's kitchen table*

    9. All food

Miscellaneous thoughts followed.

    10. Things to buy and places to go on return leave
    11. Many pitchers of ice water
    12. Cliffie's ice box
    13. Lou-Larry-Jim
    14. Roses for Lou
    15. Good humor bars
    16. Lou and Mother at church
    17. The Buick

He finished with Lou.

    18. Each day another rough day gone – away from Lou – how many more?
    19. The old days at [Ft.] Stotsenburg and living with Lou
    20. Riding Sunday A.M. through Forage Farm with Lou
    21. The War
    22. Lou – Lou – Ever

ΩΩΩ

Religion did not make his list. That seemed strange because so many of his favorite quotations came from the Bible. But, obviously religion became important to his survival. In August 1942, Fleeger reported attending the "first communion service since evacuation," apparently given by Chaplain Frederick "Ted" Howden of the 200th Coast Artillery Regiment. Then, on Thanksgiving Day, 26 November 1942, he mentioned "have just returned from communion service – quite unlike yours I'm afraid amid surroundings and in an atmosphere that leave me a bit done up – I know that I could feel your prayers for me my lover - they constantly keep me from total despair."[29]

"CHURCH – WE MUST BE FAITHFUL – IS THIS OUR TEST?"

As the diaries progressed, Fleeger dealt more with religion. On Mother's Day in May 1943, he wrote "Church – dreams of home – prayers for you two Mothers." And in his next entry on Palm Sunday, 18 May 1943, he wrote: "Church – 'We must be faithful' – Is this our test?" Then he added, "Warren Minton was baptized."[30] Fleeger never said when Minton had rejoined his comrades after being with the Troop C, 26th Cavalry and with Major Warner's guerrilla unit in the northern mountains or why Minton chose to be baptized. On 27 June, he continued: "This is Sunday – but a work day. Our rest day – if we get it – is on Friday – known as Frunday. I go to church – knowing that you would want me to and it has prompted me to develop some very firm resolutions. Some day I may record them but this is a reminder to you to ask me about them – and to remind me to some day have them on my pad." About two weeks later, he reported that there was no church, just Bible Study, and a couple of days later he noted it was "Time for church."[31] Another "Frunday" fell on 13 August, and Fleeger noted "Communion at 10." The next Frunday, he wrote "Communion Service at 10 – St. Luke – the Prodigal Son – I have a debt to pay when this is over – Sam – Reutel." Two weeks later he reported that he had missed church. On 15 October, he reported taking communion again.[32]

> *I HAVE A DEBT TO PAY WHEN THIS IS OVER – SAM REUTEL."*

An interesting sidelight to Fleeger's comments about church services are those found in a book about Chaplain Robert Preston Taylor of the 31st Infantry, a Baptist, and Chaplain Zerfas of the 26th Cavalry, a Catholic. The biographer wrote: "Now the chaplains needed a new approach to ministering to the prisoners, an approach that would keep morale high and help the men occupy their minds... Zerphas (sic) suggested they renew their request to conduct open religious services on the parade ground. Taylor thought organized activities would be helpful, since the prisoners' health had improved to the point where many of them could participate." He reported further that the senior chaplain spoke to the Japanese official and said, "For more than a year we have wanted to conduct religious services for our men, but permission has been refused. We would like to ask once more for permission to conduct such a service" This time, the Japanese approved the church services and said that "All the guards will also attend." [33]

There is a disconnect between the two stories: Fleeger reported that he had gone to church in August 1942, but Chaplain Taylor's biographer placed the beginning of church services "over a year" after Cabanatuan opened. Perhaps the explanation is that Fleeger attended small, private services, and did so before chaplains held the first large public service on the parade ground. There is also an interesting omission: Fleeger never mentioned Taylor or Zerfas in his diaries.

Fleeger should have known Zerfas well. He most likely reported to Fleeger, the Regimental Adjutant. Moreover, according to one source, his commander cited Zerfas "for bravery for having stayed exposed in the open in order to comfort a badly wounded soldier while other able-bodied men sought [cover], and reported that "Fr. Zerfas accompanied units of the cavalry on seventy missions behind enemy lines."[34] Fleeger would have known that. The Catholic priest, apparently a big man and an active one, said Mass very early every morning, delivered milk to 600 men twice daily,

"FR. ZERFAS ACCOMPANIED UNITS OF THE CAVALRY ON SEVENTY MISSIONS BEHIND ENEMY LINES."

volunteered to replace other POWs on labor details, and met each evening with other priests to pray the Rosary and other prayers in public. Fleeger may not have known that.

A brother chaplain wrote about the evening prayers: "It was an experience to hear several hundred men speak out to God night after night" while "All the rest of the camp listened respectfully." Fleeger never mentioned those occurrences. One explanation of Fleeger's omission might be that Zerfas went to the Davao Camp in October 1942 and he forgot the chaplain until he returned to Cabanatuan in June of 1944. [35]

It seems, however, as if these POWs lived in separate worlds in Cabanatuan. Moreover, later statements add to the puzzle. For example, one report said that "The chaplains discussed the change that was taking place among the prisoners. They realized the potential danger inherent in such a religious awakening, for they knew that over the centuries man had used religion as a cloak to cover his fears, but when the danger passed he threw the cover away...Many of these men, too, would do the same, Taylor knew, and yet he was convinced that the risen Christ was walking up and down the corridors of Cabanatuan...Most of the events that led to the transformation of Cabanatuan from a morgue to a mountaintop were spontaneous and caught even the chaplains by surprise."[36]

Fleeger, who seemed religiously conscious, never mentioned religious changes in many other POWs, never wrote that the POW camp had become a "mountaintop," and never reported in his diaries that "a new light shines in Cabanatuan."[37] But the religious activity had some impact. It changed one officer, Lt. Colonel Ovid O. "Zero" Wilson. A friend wrote, "Never a religious man before, as a prisoner Zero found and embraced the Catholic Church." And, "He became strong in his faith and remained so throughout his life."[38] Another POW, Harold K. Johnson, wrote about religion and was impressed by the devotion of one Catholic chaplain and influenced by other chaplains. He said that "during the years of my time in Japanese prison camps I turned to the Bible and derived a great deal of comfort from it." After the war, Johnson became the President of a new movement, Protestant Men of the Chapel, and "influenced the expansion of the movement into the Air Force and Navy" and to "principal U.S. bases in Turkey and North Africa."[39] He became one of the most outwardly religious senior officers in the Army.

On 5 December 1943, Fleeger received Communion. He next noted, "Boxing Day – Another Xmas gone – My third away from Louise – I pray the last alone" and "Midnite Mass Xmas eve was a beautiful service" – "God grant peace with honor."[40]

After 1943, Fleeger's comments about church decreased.

In January 1944, he noted "barefeet in church" but nothing more.[41] On the 7th of April, he mentioned Good Friday and reported that "Tomorrow is Easter." And then on the 9th, Fleeger reported: "Sunrise service – in camp – camp church now has 982 members – 47 states – 52 denominations – 8 foreign countries. I think of you 3 at sunrise service also."[42] Perhaps the 982 members indicated that there indeed had been a religious revival of some sort in the camp.

"MIDNITE MASS XMAS EVE WAS A BEAUTIFUL SERVICE" — "GOD GRANT PEACE WITH HONOR."

On 11 June, Fleeger said: "I want to go to church at Congregational Church at Soo Falls some day where we were married."[43] On 14th, the Birthday of the U. S. Army and Flag Day, the major wrote an interesting entry: "Reading 'Anno Domini' by Latourette – 'The Return to Religion' by Link (Psychologist) and 'The Man Nobody Knows' by Bruce Barton. Want to buy and re-read Link's book at home – excellent in nearly all respects – also want Kempis' "Following of Christ" – (Prayer Book.)."[44] Eleven days later Fleeger noted: "Church today – so many Sundays and Sunday afternoons without you."[45]

Shortly thereafter, Fleeger wrote about what he was going to do when he was back with his family. He wrote nothing further about religion or attending church or about how he was going to "live a more Christian life" in his diaries. Perhaps he had just worn down and had become too weak or too numb to write or do much. He wrote only one long entry and eight short ones after that.

Tough as life was in Cabanatuan, Fleeger never reached the religious conclusion that Abraham Lincoln did in the middle days of the American Civil War:

I am almost ready to say this is probably true – that God wills this contest, and wills that it shall not end yet. By his mere quiet power, on the minds of the now contestants, He could have saved or destroyed the Union without a human contest. Yet the contest began. And having begun He could give the final victory to either side any day. Yet the contest proceeds.[46]

But he could have.

Rice Lugao & Carabao Blood

EARLY MENU

BREAKFAST

LUGAO AND RICE

DINNER

STEAMED RICE AND

CORN GRAVY

SUPPER

STEAMED RICE —

COMOTIES (SWEET

POTATOES)

OTHER ITEMS

CARABAO

DRIED FISH

EGG PLANT

PURICO-PIG

While Fleeger may have thought more about his wife in camp as he looked to the future, thoughts about food dominated his present in Cabanatuan. For most POWs, food became the common obsession. Fleeger began his entries about food by briefly listing prison camp foods:

Rice lugao and steamed carabao – native pig – camoties – egg plant – kong kong – coconuts – green papayas – squash – cucumbers - ginger – limes – rice coffee – salt – sugar – purico – string beans – mongo beans – carabao brains – carabao tripe – carabao blood, tail etc., dog – civet cat – cats -.

Sufficient quantities of the foods would have kept the POWs healthy, but the Japanese never provided sufficient quantities day-in and day-out. The listing of dogs, cats, and carabao blood illustrated the lack of adequate food.[47] Fleeger listed an early menu.[48] Months later, he would have been delighted to have so much.

Lugao or "mush" was soft rice – Fleeger said it was "cooked in 50 gallon *kawa* (pot)" - that was meant to be thick as oatmeal, but as the months wore on it became more and more watery. POW cooks prepared lugao from their meager stocks of grain as did the internee cooks in Santo Tomas in Manila. Never very tasty or nutritious, lugao became a cruel joke as cooks added more and more water to provide some kind of meal to the prisoners. As time went along the diet of polished rice – which has little nutritional value – and the ever watery lugao and virtually no protein could not sustain the health of the POWs.[49]

The importance of food grew with the length of imprisonment. In December 1942, Fleeger wrote about eggs. "The war and prison months have been punctuated by terrific mental upheaval, turmoil or agony, on countless occasions: for instance, under heavy artillery barrage, advance under fire, ever constant daily bombings, loss of friends, physical exhaustion, decay of health, all out loneliness, homesickness, and thoughts of Lou. However, of all these, the most poignant, and the most morale destroying memory has been a simple thought. It has haunted me daily since the surrender, has returned to mind each waking forlorn hour at nite, and caused fretful dreams. No other mental hazard has been so difficult. The memory, strange to record, has been this: Of that heavenly, delicious sound of the crackle and sputter of frying bacon and eggs of a morning back in mother's kitchen...."[50]

This haunting note which placed his wife below food in importance showed the impact of starvation or near starvation on prisoners. Hungry as they were, these Americans, however, never turned to cannibalism, although later on some thought about it.

On Christmas Day 1942, Fleeger wrote that "we received our first good food in quantity." He explained: "Authority permitted entry of British Prisoner of War Bundles – packed in South Africa – and routed via Geneva Red Cross – each man got a 10 pound box – tea, pudding, mutton, chocolate, jam, and cans of food that we have dreamed of for 9 long months. So our day is plentiful for the first time - also bundles from the people of Manila."[51] Ten pounds of food would not last long, but that day, Fleeger reported that "we had 14 here for Xmas dinner – chicken – corned beef stew – rice flour cake – and coffee – a feast. – But our stomachs have shrunk – now we are resting and trying to overcome the meal. I gave Bill Dunmyer and Spade Gross 2 small bananas each."[52] The impact of rich food could have been disastrous, but the POWs survived. With so many months behind them and so uncertain a future, the POWs should have been more conservative with their food supply. But, given the conditions and the fact that Fleeger hoped that he would be with his family the following Christmas, he could not have been expected to "hoard" his precious provisions.

EGGS

"...THE MOST POIGNANT, AND THE MOST MORALE DESTROYING MEMORY HAS BEEN A SIMPLE THOUGHT. IT HAS HAUNTED ME DAILY SINCE THE SURRENDER, HAS RETURNED TO MIND EACH WAKING FORLORN HOUR AT NITE, AND CAUSED FRETFUL DREAMS. NO OTHER MENTAL HAZARD HAS BEEN SO DIFFICULT. THE MEMORY, STRANGE TO RECORD, HAS BEEN THIS: OF THAT HEAVENLY, DELICIOUS SOUND OF THE CRACKLE AND SPUTTER OF FRYING BACON AND EGGS..."

IN MARCH, HE MENTIONED THAT THE JAPANESE WOULD GIVE THE POWs EXTRA FOOD AS A REWARD FOR THE PRISONERS CATCHING 6,000 CANS OF FLIES (ESTIMATED 12,236,000 FLIES) AND 317 RATS.

FLEEGER SAID THAT THE BOUILLON CUBES HAD THE "MOST DELICIOUS TASTE UNDER HEAVEN ... AND THEN SAID THAT THE SHAVING CREAM WAS "GOOD ENUF TO EAT."

Then on 1 January 1943, the Japanese delivered Red Cross boxes from the United States to the POWs. Fleeger noted "so we have plenty of food."[53] That would not last long. In February, the Japanese paid the POWs for the last three months. Fleeger had eggs and fruit again. He noted that with the food, all were recovering from their various ailments: sore feet, nasty hemorrhoids, and poor eyes. But the food did not cure malaria.[54] In March, he mentioned that the Japanese would give the POWs extra food as a reward for the prisoners catching 6,000 cans of flies (estimated 12,236,000 flies) and 317 rats.[55]

On 3 June, the major wrote "We are using syrup made from cakes of native sugar (very vile and amoebic) boiled down – ants added of course. Corporal Bramley [most likely Clarence Bramley, Air Corps][56] makes pretty good cup cakes with rice flour and peanuts." He went on to say that they held a birthday party for "Johnnie" Johnson, his *bahay* mate and served carabao meat, rice, rice cake, and fruit that night. His note ended with "Not bad."[57] Later in June, Fleeger complained: "We are still on rice and a little carabao meat – maintenance – and I haven't had a good meal for almost two years now." [58] This contradicted his comments about the recent "good food." The next month, he wrote that the "Prisoners ate cats, dogs, snakes, and angleworms" and added "Had a protein bath last week. Pappy [Archer] bought us a hind quarter of a small carabao – 3 meals of Lucy – She had big brown eyes."[59] In August, he reported that while working in the heat, he had "...thought of Mrs. Johnson's maple ice cream all day – torture."[60]

On Thanksgiving Day 1943, Fleeger expected the arrival of additional Red Cross boxes of food. "Last was a year ago – December '42 – 2 1/2 boxes per man. This year expect more. Means life itself – food, medicine."[61] After the boxes were distributed on 1 December 1943, he noted: "Wonderful Day. Faces like boys at Xmas tree – examining labels, quality, quantity – date manufactured, taste, etc. But we know hunger – no one excuses his excitement. I like to think Lou prepared mine – cans of grape jelly, ham and eggs, pork loaf, butter, dried milk, Spam, corned beef, pate, bouillon cubes – sugar, chocolate, kup café, soup, prunes, Kraft cheese, crackers, cocoa, orange concentrate, Vitamin C pills, a few cigarettes – also toilet articles in kumfort kits, shave cream, blades, razors, toothpaste, etc."

Fleeger said that the bouillon cubes had the "most delicious taste under Heaven – after so long on rice," that the few cigarettes were the "first in year and a half," and then said that the shaving cream was "good enuf to eat." Fleeger, however, nearly became a casualty from the issue: "Dam near cut my thumb off on a Ham and Egg can from my Red Cross Box – Now recovering."[62]

There would be no more Red Cross kits for the POWs. Whether the Japanese received anymore is not known.

A few days later, Fleeger wrote an entry for his Dad. He explained that rice cost 180 pesos a sack, a meal for a family in the market cost 60 pesos [U. S. $30 in prewar money], and rice 40 pesos per kilo.[63] On 26 December, he added: "Our Red Cross Boxes gave us enough to eat – and make. Bill, Jim and I exchanged bits of sugar – or a few cigarettes for presents.[64] The Red Cross boxes had arrived in Manila on November 1943 aboard the Japanese ship, *Teia Maru*. The ship had carried allied diplomatic personnel, press people, and varied allied interned personnel from Shanghai, Hong Kong, Manila, Saigon, and Singapore to Portuguese Goa where they boarded the Swedish luxury liner, *Gripsholm*, which then took them to the United States. At Goa, Red Cross supplies were transferred from the *Gripsholm* to the *Teia Maru* for transportation to the war zone. The repatriated people from Manila brought out information about the POWs and many smuggled out letters from internees.

MS *GRIPSHOLM*

"HOPE THE GRIPSHOLM BROUGHT YOU SOME GOOD NEWS FROM HARRY...:

MRS. O. O. WILSON

"...PLEASE TELL THEM THAT HARRY, JIM, TRAP ARE VERY FIT."

GLADYS KETCHUM

Unbeknown to Fleeger, Mrs. Ovid O. Wilson, wife of the former G-1 Officer, I Philippine Corps, wrote Mrs. Fleeger about him on 16 December 1943. Mrs. Wilson wrote: "Hope the Gripsholm brought you some good news from Harry. I had three wonderful cards from Zero which assured me that all was well." Continuing, she added, "Yesterday I received a letter from a friend of mine [Phyllis Barth] who is interned in Santa [sic] Tomas... The letter stated that Gladys Ketchum [sister of deceased Lt. Colonel Hubert Ketchum] is interned in Santo Tomas also." Betty Wilson then reported that her friend said: "If you know where to find Lou F., Sisty B., and Alys Trap,[1] please tell them that Harry, Jim, Trap are very fit. Wish you would all write us letters thru Red Cross and by all means enclose pictures of all the families. The boys are learning all about planting, shodding (not horses) and latrine duties...." Still focusing on the other wives, she asked, "Lou, I can't think of Sisty B's last name to save my soul. Do you know it, and do you know where to reach her? If you do, will you please pass this news on to her. If not, let me know, and I'll start a search. Also Alys Trapnell." Later in the typed letter, Mrs. Wilson wrote that, "All the news I have

MRS. WILSON'S OPTIMISM ABOUT THE END OF THE WAR DID NOT MATCH THE REALITY IN CABANATUAN.

heard since the arrival of the Gripsholm has been most encouraging, and I really believe there is going to be an end to this nightmare after all. Someday we'll all have a reunion," and then added, "Anyway, let me have the dope about Sisty and Alys.[65]

Mrs. Barth's positive report that, "We have plenty of food [in Santo Tomas], all the native vegetables have been quite a surprise"[66] and Mrs. Wilson's optimism about the end of the war did not match the reality in Cabanatuan. Since there were no Cabanatuan POWs evacuated on the *Gripsholm,* the news about Cabanatuan had to be secondhand at best. One American POW, Air Corps Lieutenant Edgar Whitcomb, did escape on the *Gripsholm*, but he had never been in Cabanatuan. Whitcomb had not surrendered and had evaded the Japanese for some time after the fall of the Philippines, but the Japanese eventually captured him, imprisoned him in Ft. Santiago, and interrogated him there. Somehow, he convinced the Japanese that he was not a soldier and they released him from Santiago and sent him to Santo Tomas. Once there, Whitcomb feared that other internees would identify him as an Air Corps officer and that such a discovery would infuriate the Japanese and be fatal to him. Incredibly, he managed within a few days to get transferred with other internees to Shanghai. After his miraculous escape from

---

[1] Louise Fleeger, Sissy Blanning, and Alys Trapnell

the Philippines, and after some time in Shanghai, the unsuspecting Japanese repatriated Whitcomb with other Allied personnel in Shanghai to Goa where they boarded the *Gripsholm* and sailed to the United States. [67]

Just a few days after the last food packages arrived in Cabanatuan as well as in Santo Tomas, the Japanese Army took control of the civilian camp in January 1944, and life would get worse there as the Japanese reduced the food ration to about 1,000 calories a day by the end of the year. Soon the starving civilian internees – now for all intents and purposes civilian POWs – would resemble the starving POWs in Cabanatuan.

Even with the extra food, however, Fleeger reported that he lost three pounds in December and was "on the way down again" and "so low that vitamins absorb per day barely enuf."[68]

At about the same time that Mrs. Wilson wrote Louise Fleeger, Major Fleeger wrote a note about "Zero" Wilson: "Zero had a story I enjoyed – an Englishman was married and when asked by his friends how it was he replied: "Well – fornication is no novelty to me don't you know, but my wife enjoys it."[69]

ON 17 MARCH 1944, FLEEGER REPORTED THE ARRIVAL OF SPECIAL BOXES FROM FAMILIES...

"MOE [DALY] GOT A FOOTBALL – ONE MAN GOT RICE – 1 MAN A BUS TICKET FRISCO TO PEORIA!"

On 17 March 1944, Fleeger reported the arrival of special boxes from families. "Boxes coming – Dust of toothpowder all over camp and men at dobe [smoking] sit – looking – Many wet or broken – Intense interest in all – another mill-stone. - Betty sent all food – OK – clever. – Jim's mostly food – I wonder what mine will be and if ruined -- Should get it today – Need food and vitamins the most – But how would you know." One comment voiced a special concern – "Jim's [box came] from Virginia W. Blanning – not Mrs. James C. Blanning. With one foot in the grave we have thought of course but it's a shock to see it." Continuing, he added, "Jim sorting cocoa and sugar out of his box, etc. Phil Lauman[70] had a grand box from his mother – Pappy [Archer] from Alice – Mine maybe today – You're so smart honey." Next, he reported that "Moe [Daly] got a football – one man got rice – 1 man a bus ticket Frisco to Peoria!" He concluded his entry: "... for the first time in almost 3 years have had gum, life savers, bull durham – candy..."[71]

Two asides were noteworthy. Fleeger judged that the prices for the items were about the same as he had known, adding "our first news of the cost of living," and he reported that there was a newspaper from the East Coast "first paper we've seen since November '41" and a Readers Digest from the summer of 1943. [72]

Two days later, he opened his box which his wife had mailed eight months before and recorded that "...all O. K. but bouillon cubes. I was all thumbs until I had found the vitamin pills – they mean life to us. – And you sent plenty Lou – I <u>knew</u> you would. No damage – And I'm taking 3 or 4 a day – when Bob put the dose on the box – 1 tablet – he had no idea what we look like after 2 years in prison. So I am mighty happy – the vitamins mean the most. Box appeared to be sent in a hurry - but everything else most useful – slept in pajamas last night first time since 1941. And we are all enjoying the fruit – candy – etc.[73]

The POWs should have stretched out their vitamins to supplement their deteriorating diet. One a day for 100 days or so probably would have helped them more than loading up on 3 or 4 a day for a shorter period of time.

In 1944, Fleeger highlighted growing starvation. On Easter and the third anniversary of the surrender of Bataan, Fleeger wrote: "Wish I could have had eggs with you this morning – We are again losing weight rapidly – Year after year." He added, "Have lost 5 pounds." A few days later he added: "picture of you very good – odd to us to see anyone who looks so well (and you do) and so well fed! – for we are so thin and hungry." On 25 April, Fleeger wrote: "Here very rough – thin – hungry again – ever – and powder keg days of '44 ahead. The next day he wrote: "<u>Very </u>hungry." On 7 May, he continued: "Belt up a few more notches... Wish I had some of your cake Susan –

"*VERY HUNGRY.*"

or Blanche's donuts – or Cliffie's meat loaf – or just some bread sorghum and coffee like Dad used to eat when he was a kid on the farm in Missouri. Have lost about 7 or 8 pounds this time – Hope I don't go down to 95 again." On 11 June, Fleeger said it was "another hungry day," and wrote "Today my rice ration at noon wouldn't have filled one of Cliffie's tea cups. Beri-beri and pellagra returning – etc. – endless." Sixteen days later, he continued: "Very little to eat. Have lost about 15 pounds." On Independence Day, he wrote "Wish I could picnic with you all today...Scoshi [little] chow.[74]

His comments reflected his poor diet and showed that starvation had increased as it had for civilian POWs in Manila. The chances of survival diminished as POWs got weaker and weaker. Many became desperate. On his last Fourth of July, Fleeger highlighted their desperation: "Trap has kidney stones – very sick – Baked a cat for him yesterday – eating dogs also – when they can be caught." He added, "I wonder if I ever did eat sausage and buckwheats – we think, talk and dream of food." And, then reported that he "Ate canna lily roots last nite made me sort of sick." Later, he added "hungry."[75] Canna lily roots were probably semi-poisonous. Fleeger was lucky. The dried and ground roots of banana plants, however, produced thick, cassava-like flour that provided some bulk and nutrition to watery lugao. While baked cats and dogs sound terrible, many people eat them as part of their normal diet.[76]

In August, the major reported that he was "very thin" and weighed only 115 pounds. Fleeger reported that he had "no energy - no mental ability." "[Two and a half] years of this has reduced us (we that remain) to thin – rather scarred – skeletons – pushing ourselves to work on a handful of calories and living in hope. I feel fair – hunger headaches – beri beri etc." On 21 September 1944, the day U. S. Navy aircraft appeared over Luzon, he noted further: "...tired – hungry – hell of a life."[77] Not even the sight of American aircraft and the possibility of liberation made up for the lack of food.

ΩΩΩ

In the early days, the availability of "Quan" provided the only good news about food in Cabanatuan. Quan according to the major was the "Most common word of prison vocabulary – specifically meaning special articles of smuggled or unusual food, i.e. – sardines, tuna, tobacco, etc. etc. – also a gulash made from fish, rice, peppers, etc. etc."[78] Quan saved lives. Gavan Daws wrote about "quan" in his comprehensive history of POWs. He said: "Getting hold of extra food became an obsession. It took time and trouble, cost a lot, and meant a great deal. It turned into a ritual...Quan came to be the high point of life...For intensity the only thing in life to compare with it was sex. And because sex was long gone, quanning turned into the very sex of existence."[79]

> *"QUAN ...WAS THE "MOST COMMON WORD OF PRISON VOCABULARY..."*

Quan became available for a time because the Americans could buy food in the local markets and Filipinos and Americans in and around the camp smuggled food and medicines in to the POWs. The Japanese should have been pleased that outsiders tried to feed the POWs and keep them healthy at no cost to the Imperial Japanese Army, but they were not and went out of their way to prevent smuggling and to punish those who tried to help.

In August 1942, Fleeger mentioned that the Quan cook and orderly for Bill Dunmyer and himself was a PFC Reynaldo Trujillo from the 200th Coast Artillery Regiment (AA) from New Mexico. The major liked the young soldier and planned to dine with him in the Hotel Hilton in Albuquerque after the war and also have Trujillo carve some mahogany furniture for him. That would not happen; "Ray" died with Fleeger on the *Arisan Maru.*[80]

On 30 September, Fleeger said that he would have Quan for supper and that Pappy will cook. The menu would be "Beef –vegetable soup – other quan."[81] In October after reporting that he and Bill were in charge of Mess #1, Fleeger reported that "Cooks Ray [Trujillo] and [Aaron] Drake, and Mess Sgt [John] Reynolds, having put the bite on Tracer for Quan, served us a surprise birthday supper, rice pancakes, mongo beans, and banana pudding. Pappy [Captain Herman N.] Archer was guest...(can of fish quan saved by Pappy for the occasion had been stolen.)"[82]

On Thanksgiving 1942, Fleeger wrote: "Quan dinner at our *bahay*: duck donated by Harry Packard – Quan supper at my mess hall – can of peas donated by Pappy ...

ON THANKSGIVING 1942, FLEEGER WROTE: "QUAN DINNER AT OUR BAHAY: DUCK DONATED BY HARRY PACKARD..."

First fowl for me since December a year ago – Our diet still rice." Guests for the evening included Pappy Archer, Jack Batchelor, Jim Blanning, Bill Chandler, Bill Dunmyer, Alva Fitch, "Spade" Gross, and Johnnie (Chester) Johnson.[83]

In June 1943, he reported: "Tonite we will have a Quan – to put on our rice – in celebration. Bill is making it from a can of hoarded mackerel – our last – mongo beans, peppers, etc. Pappy Archer and Morris Cummings[84] will be over. And Jim of course. I've thought all day of angel food cake – fried chicken – and ice cream."[85]

Quan – little as it was -- and the food and vitamins from Red Cross and family kits saved many POWs from reaching terminal starvation. Without the additions, POWs probably would have started dying from malnutrition in early 1943. As it was, they began dying from malnutrition late in 1944. With hoarded food supplies available, the Japanese deliberately starved the POWs and caused countless unnecessary deaths.

ΩΩΩ

To cope with the lack of good food, Fleeger wrote eclectically about food topics. He listed cooks from New Mexico that he should contact after the war, recipes for egg nog and *Torte de Huevos*, and places to eat in the U. S. after the war. He placed the following restaurants at the top of his list: the Palace and Mark Hotel in San Francisco which he noted were expensive, Wolf's Inn on Fredericksburg Road in San Antonio, also expensive, and the San Jacinto Inn in Houston, sixteen miles south of the San Jacinto Battleground. He seemed most taken with Frenchy's Black Cat Café on Alamo Street in San Antonio, noting "low prices – original setting – good oysters – very excellent."[86]

He prepared a long lists of foods that he considered "the end of all good things." The resultant list grew "after months of hungry prison camp discussion."

Fleeger and his friends "spent hours and days and weeks making these lists and menus." He identified thirty-two meats, twenty-six vegetables, eighteen salads, thirty-four desserts; wrote down breakfast options that included sixteen fruits and juices, seven meats, sixteen possible main courses, eleven optional breads and rolls, ten possible cereals, chocolate pudding and coffee; and listed forty miscellaneous favorite foods starting with peanut butter sandwiches.

He went so far as to place asterisks by his most favorite foods, some of which were T-Bone steak (medium), roast rolled rib, fried chicken, broccoli, new beans, new peas, lettuce with Roquefort or Thousand Island dressing, banana and peanut butter, hot fudge pecan parfait, hot fudge Sunday with almonds, chocolate pie with whipped cream, pork sausage and bacon, and raisin toast, bear claws, and butter rolls.[87]

IF FLEEGER COULD HAVE GENERATED CALORIES BY DREAMING, HE WOULD HAVE GAINED WEIGHT.

If Fleeger could have generated calories by dreaming, he would have gained weight.

Soldiers were not the only Japanese captives who dreamed about food. In nearby Santo Tomas, one internee wrote:

> *Food, food, no one talked of anything else. Old cookbooks traveled backwards and forwards over the entire campus as starving internees copied recipes. I wasn't interested in such a crazy project, but [my husband] was. He spent a lot of time making a chart of what we should eat during the first three months after we were freed. He said that we must have carefully balanced diets, being graduates of a cooking school that used no oils, fats, eggs or milk. It would take a long time for digestive systems to manage real food if it ever came our way again.*[88]

Interestingly, Fleeger did not list cigarettes on his wish list of foods. In different parts of his diaries, he mentioned cigarettes, but he did not seem to be addicted to them, although, in August 1944, he reported: "Tobacco almost gone – Will be hell then."[89] Cigarettes, however, played an incredible part in the lives of all POWs.

In Santo Tomas, the civilian POWs hungered for tobacco. Their addiction was nearly incomprehensible. Children hunted the grounds for left over cigarette butts for their parents. At one time, adults searched for substitutes for tobacco. Some dried hibiscus leaves to smoke, only to find out that the leaves were poisonous.[90] In the military camps, the demand for tobacco often became fatal. Gavan Daws reported that many POWs traded their meager rations for "smokes" in Korea and Japan, and, consequently, many of them starved themselves to death.[91]

"No deaths yesterday"

The terrible conditions in Cabanatuan and the lack of food caused POWs severe health problems. Fleeger highlighted the gravity of their situation in two of his comments. The first concerned the camp. On 17 December 1942, he wrote: "No deaths yesterday – first zero day since surrender – total so far about five thousand." The second concerned his condition on his birthday, 27 June 1942: "...I was dying – almost – as it later developed. The men on either side of me did die – but those experiences have been common."[92] He did not explain what had caused his problem or why he recovered.

Because of the poor food, Fleeger came down with *beri-beri* - caused by a deficiency of vitamin A – in September 1942. *Beri-beri* stayed with him for the duration.

"MY HEALTH — GOOD BUT FOR DRY BERI BERI — FEET AND LEGS IN BAD SHAPE."

On 22 November, he reported that he had dry *beri-beri* "and had intense pain and ache in feet, legs, arms, hands – Pappy gave me 16 Betaxin today – May save me – Can't sleep." Continuing, he wrote: "My health – good but for dry beri beri – feet and legs in bad shape." A month later, when he wrote about eggs, he wrote: "Beri Beri has my feet and ankles badly crippled – No remedy but good food so I expect to have it for some time."[93] He was right: his *beri-beri* never went away.

In December, Fleeger said: "I need eggs, (Vitamin A for the eye ulcers), fruit for scurvy, a duck for Christmas and a pound of tobacco to roll skags."[94]

In January 1943, he said that hoped that his *beri-beri* would improve because as mentioned the Japanese had distributed Red Cross boxes to the POWs and Fleeger reported that he had plenty of food. That was a short-lived dream for the malnourished prisoners; the *beri-beri* did not abate. Just after getting the food packages, Fleeger noted: "Severe case of hemorrhoids – good food but much pain. Feet are better."[95] On 27 June, he wrote: Today I am thankful to be well – back to my old weight of 130 (from a low of 95) and with no ill effects but a certain amount of dry *beri-*

beri."[96] In July, he still had *beri-beri* and in October, still suffering, he reported *"20 more shots – B1 – hydrochloride — for my *beri beri*."*[97]

In August, he noted that cholera had broken out in Manila, and he had taken "Jap shots – cholera, dysentery, typhoid, bubonic."[98]

Sterility became a health concern. In November 1943, he noted that, "Most of us are possibly sterile from this racket and the subject of impotency is sometimes discussed. A camp cartoon shows a beautiful blonde – a negligee standing in her bedroom saying, "You needn't apologize Major – I enjoyed hearing all about Bataan."[99]

> *IN AUGUST, HE NOTED THAT CHOLERA HAD BROKEN OUT IN MANILA, AND HE HAD TAKEN "JAP SHOTS — CHOLERA, DYSENTERY, TYPHOID, BUBONIC."*

In January 1944, Fleeger noted that he had "Numbness from poor circulation."[100] The next month, he began a course of thiamin for his *beri-beri* and hoped that it would help. He wrote: "Don't mind the pain but don't want to come out of it with a weak heart."[101] By March, he reported that he had completed the thiamin treatment and his "beri beri feet are better – best since '42". But by May, *beri-beri* was back and he reported having pellagra blisters. On his 36th birthday, he reported that he had some pellagra again and scurvy for the third time and added: "Very little to eat. Have lost 15 pounds. Wish I could see this day 37th birthday – home I hope."

But that would not happen because the United States forces had just begun their twin drives across the Pacific and would not reach Luzon for another year. Admiral Chester Nimitz had invaded the Gilberts in November 1943 and started forward in the Central Pacific. General MacArthur had moved into the Admiralties in the Southwest Pacific in February 1944 before he began his advance along the coastline of New Guinea in April. As the American forces headed toward the Philippines and Japan, they triggered the fateful Japanese evacuations of all their military POWs.

In March, the major reported that he was pretty sick because he had a "Bad infection in my left hand and arm. Hot packs and sulfa thiazol." He then reported that the pajamas he received "were swell" and implied that they were valuable because they covered him and protected him from insects and added that "our resistance so low we are a perfect culture for every dam infection in existence."[102] More short comments followed: in August 1944, "Sore feet and mouth" and "no malaria or amoebic at present." In September, "very thin, *beri beri* again – also some edema – sore eyes" and "– pellagra worse – *beri beri* so so." [103]

In his final commentary about food, Fleeger said on 8 October 1944: "Very hungry – Weigh 119 – want to recall these days when I have food again – Want Klim – Peanut butter – Ovaltine on the table – gifts of food – etc. – and want to feed someone else who is hungry at home..."[104]

Malnutrition affected Fleeger's weight. At 119 pounds he had lost thirty to forty pounds from his prewar weight of 150-160 pounds. As a small man, he could ill afford such a drop in weight. Earlier, at 95 pounds he must have been a skeleton, but he remained considerably heavier than young Thomas Jones of Troop C who dropped to seventy pounds before his liberation.[105]

"VERY HUNGRY – WEIGH 119 – WANT TO RECALL THESE DAYS WHEN I HAVE FOOD AGAIN..."

Fleeger's comments about food showed how the unsatisfactory diet led to malnutrition and starvation and then the lack of food led to sickness – particularly *beri-beri,* and the combination threatened Fleeger's survival as well as the survival of other POWs. His small size probably saved him. Bigger, heavier men suffered more grievously from starvation and malnutrition than smaller men. Fleeger was lucky.

All of this misery was unnecessary. Allied governments had shipped tons of food and medicine to the Japanese for distribution to the POWs, but the Japanese often deliberately failed to distribute all of the supplies. Additionally, they failed to provide suitable food and adequate quantities of food to their POWs, in part, because they did not consider or ignored the fact that their larger Western POWs needed more food than their own soldiers did. Consequently, too many POWs died of malnutrition in POW camps and too many starving and sick POWs died en route to Japan because they did not have the energy, strength, or stamina to survive the terrible conditions they faced in the POW ships. And all were in such terrible physical condition when they landed in Japan in February 1945 that they shocked Japanese officials there and many – including three cavalry officers - died nearly immediately.

The Japanese had sufficient food stored at Cabanatuan. There was no reason for the POWs to be starving in January 1945. When the Japanese left the camp just after the Americans invaded Luzon, they left behind Pet condensed milk, canned goods, sugar, and rice in their warehouse, as well as well as "medicines, mosquito nets, shoes, cigarettes, underwear and blankets." The POWs could not believe what they found. Many consumed the food immediately and fell sick, but within a few days the good food began to help the starving men. Quickly, "Astonishing things began to happen to their bodies. For some the throbbing aches of beriberi diminished. Their night vision improved. With stronger immune systems, the men recovered from all sorts of miscellaneous low-grade infections that had persistently tormented them. Tropical ulcers shrank, rheumy eyes cleared up. "Many men put on a pound a day in weight. One soldier gained thirty pounds in two weeks."[106] While the nutritious food helped the remaining five hundred or so POWs in January 1945, even small amounts of the rich milk and canned goods would have helped many more men such as Harry Fleeger as similar food from the Red Cross packages had done months before. The Japanese starving of the prisoners of war was criminal.

Killing Time?

While thoughts of his wife and food filled his days, Fleeger recorded more prosaic matters in his diary. He wrote about the thousand books and magazines that were in the camp library. He said that the books were "worn and torn, or rebound by our clever binders using scraps of paper." He added: "I have read hundreds of books trying to cover all of those at all educational in which I could arouse an interest," and then he listed in alphabetic order by title the 223 books that he apparently read or consulted. He commented that "Since the Japanese authority would not allow entry of a library all books were singly smuggled in by men returning from outside detail. "Andrew Jackson" even appeared from my quarters in Stotsenburg." Most probably, some of the poems, commentary, and quotations in his diaries came from the books he read. Fleeger listed biographies of Abraham Lincoln, Benjamin Franklin, Andrew Jackson. Robert E. Lee, Chiang Kai-shek, and Napoleon, some plays by Shakespeare and by Eugene O'Neil, *The Iliad,* and an assortment of fiction. He identified a few history books – *Development of China, History of the Orient, Berlin Diary, Civil War* (S. V. Benet), *History of the World* (Wells), *Military*

RED CROSS SUPPLIES

"ACCORDING TO ARTICLE 29 OF THE GENEVA CONVENTIONS, EACH PRISONER WAS TO BE ALLOWED ONE RE D CROSS PACKAGE PER WEEK."

LINDA HOLMES

"...THE LACK OF MEDICINE, SUPPLIES, AND SURGICAL EQUIPMENT WAS HEART-BREAKING – ESPECIALLY BECAUSE RED CROSS BOXES CONTAINING SUCH SUPPLIES AND VITAL LIFESAVING EQUIPMENT REMAINED LOCKED UP IN WAREHOUSES AT JUST ABOUT EVERY PLACE WHERE POWs WERE CONFINED."

LINDA HOLMES

"...WE FOUND SEVERAL WAREHOUSES PACKED WITH RED CROSS FOOD AND MEDICAL SUPPLIES. THE DATES OF RECEIPT INDICATED THAT THESE ITEMS HAD REACHED JAPAN PRIOR TO AUGUST 1943."

DR. THOMAS HEWETT

WHY FLEEGER DEVOTED SO MUCH TIME TO LISTING BOOKS IS A PUZZLE.

History of the US, Secret History of the American Revolution, War, and *History of American Diplomacy* (Bemis) – some of which could not have been favorable to Japan. The availability of the history books was ironic because the Japanese prohibited the teaching of history in Santo Tomas.[107] Perhaps the strangest book that Fleeger listed was *Eugenics and Sex Harmony.*[108] I wonder how many women-starved POWs checked out that best-seller? Why Fleeger devoted so much time to listing books is a puzzle. The only probable answers were "to kill time" or "to exercise the brain."

Additionally, Fleeger listed books that he planned to have in his post-war library[109] and for his sons. At number one, he listed *Harvard Classics,* and he listed the *Bible in Prose* as number two. At number twenty-four, he listed *The Constitution of the Presbyterian Church in the U. S.* At number twenty-nine, he listed the *Following of Christ* which he noted was "My prison camp prayer book taken from a dead soldier." He designated "Long Fellow's works," "Shakespeare's works," "Kipling's works," and "O Henry's works" as numbers four, five, six, and twelve. He selected Freeman's *R. E. Lee,* as his top-ranking biography, at number eight, and then placed Carl Sandberg's *Lincoln* and Jomini's *Napoleon* at numbers thirteen and fourteen." At fifteen, anticipating the future, Fleeger listed *History of World War II.* Fleeger chose *Captain Horatio Hornblower* as his top novel. Most interestingly at twenty-eight, he listed another future book:

Mister Archer USA –
as told to Rutherford Platt
– Pappy Archer – Friend – Prison Camp
Age 64 – wars – about 6 – H. N. Archer,
Princeton, New Jersey – Service – 47 years

Probably one of the stories for that book was the one Fleeger reported in his diary. "During the war – Capt. (Pappy) Archer was in charge of the 12,000 Filipino refugees in Bataan and of their refugee camps. Just before the surrender, Pappy caught a bomb fragment in his back and was taken to No. 1 hospital seriously wounded. While he was there, refugee women walked the many kilometers daily to bring him extra food or to remake his hospital bed. On one occasion – a Sunday – they arrived complete with a priest for a special service at his bedside – On another occasion one of the Filipino women told Pappy – "There are only 2 good people left in this world – you and God." He added that, "The events reflect in general the attitude of the Filipino towards we Americans." [110]

ΩΩΩ

More seriously, Fleeger logged all his personal property losses in his diary with the apparent intent of submitting a claim for reimbursement to the Army after the war. He carefully listed each article of personal property that he had lost during the campaign or that the Japanese had taken from him.

Painstakingly, he entered the details in his log: quantity, quality, original price of each item, and estimated the cost of replacement, approximate date of purchase, the length of time in use, and the condition and estimated value of each item at the time of loss. In some cases he wrote remarks about items. He listed cavalry boots made in the United States and the Philippines, uniform shoes made by Florsheim, Nunn-Bush, and Stetson, a tuxedo made by Hart, Schafner, Marx, and Rayban sunglasses. He estimated his financial loss as $1,491.30.[111]

As with his library listings, Fleeger must have spent hours putting the claim together. While today it appears to be a minor problem, the financial losses to a poorly paid officer in the 1940s were a major concern. Fleeger recorded his highest pay during imprisonment as $223 a month so his losses exceeded six months pay. After preparing his log about his losses, the major prepared a list of clothing that he planned to purchase after he returned to the United States. That action seemed to be one step toward the future and a renewed life.[112]

The major also recorded his pay data.

1. *Last paid to include November 30, 1941, by Finance Officer, Ft. Stotsenburg, P. I. (Brinkemeyer) (In grade of Captain).*
2. *Partial payment of $25.00, against my pay in December 1941 or January 1942.*
3. *Due U. S. for war rations: - About December 15 to January 5, 1942 - 25¢ per day – January 6 to April 8 inclusive - ½ ration - 12½¢ per day.*
4. *Promoted to Major – 1942 – Dec 24, 1941 Hdqs. USAFFE – pay and allowances dues from Jan – 1942.*

5. *Allotment to 1ˢᵗ National Bank, Junction City, Kansas (for wife) increased effective January 1, 1942 – from $195 to $300.*
6. *10% of base pay for foreign service due from Dec 7, 1941.*
7. *Commutation of quarters due entire period.*
8. *Allotments-*
   - *1ˢᵗ Natl Bank – Junction City, - Kansas, $195 to January 1, 1942 – thereafter $300.*
   - *$10,000 Government Life Insurance - $13.90 per month.*
   - *$3,000 Army Mutual Aid Life Insurance – about $4.00 per month (exact amount no known).*
   - *Reliance Life Insurance Co. – Pittsburgh – about $18.00 per month for life insurance (exact amount not known.*
   - *If promoted to Lt. Col. During prison tour – pay due me would be increased by amount due as Lt. Col.*
9. *1 Check written in Bataan, P. I. against Junction City Bank - $25.00 to Farrell – who may have died – so check might be lost.*
10. *December 7, 1941 – balance in Philadelphia Trust Co., Manila, about 40 pesos – exact amount not known.*
11. *Pay due me in September 1, 1942 – roughly $1200.00 – and not paid at that time (more if I am Lt. Colonel).*

He then listed his current pay.

Base and Longevity	*$287.50*
Rental	*$100.00*
Subsistence	*$54.00*
Foreign Service	*$25.00*
TOTAL	*$466.50*

And he added: "Above pay in grade of Major – If promoted to Lt. Col. after surrender, increase of about 50 dollars per month is due from date of promotion."[113]

Fleeger apparently anticipated a promotion to lieutenant colonel. That should have happened because Fleeger had held a lieutenant colonel's billet as a squadron commander in 1942.

Most of the surviving Army POWs found that they had not been promoted while captured, but the Army promoted them one grade after they were liberated. The survivors, however, often found later that the Army had promoted their peers and many officers junior to them who had fought with other units in World War II or who had fought as guerrillas on Luzon to higher ranks. As an example, Lt. Ramsey, 26ᵗʰ Cavalryman turned guerrilla, ended the war as a lieutenant colonel while Trapnell, who was much older and experienced, remained a lieutenant colonel during imprisonment. The Army promoted Trapnell to colonel on the day he was liberated, but soon afterwards demoted him to his previous rank as the army downsized. Strangely, the Army did not posthumously promote Fleeger and other POWs who perished – except for Van Nostrand - to higher grades after the war even though by the time of their deaths in 1944 they would have earned higher ranks if they had not been POWs.

In June 1943, Fleeger noted: "Complete 12 years service June 11th – another fogey of about $13.00 [a month]. Pay due me now about $2500 – all for Louise and dam hard earned."[114]

In August 1943, Fleeger wrote that he had given Pappy Archer 15 pesos in May, 20 pesos in June, and 6.00 pesos in August and that while he was in Camp O'Donnell he "wrote one check to Farrell for $25.00 for cash." He also noted that he earned sixteen dollars a day for his wife and sons.[115] In August 1944, he commented that: "I take great pride in earning each day my 16 dollars for you three Lou - it adds up as the days go by and provides some small consolation – each month that passes at least I earn that much for you and it proves a symbol of my consuming devotion to you Dearest – I know that you will understand my thought."[116] In late 1943, he charted the pay he had received from the Japanese. The Prison Headquarters posited 110 Japanese pesos a month into a nese Postal Savings account from August 1942 to December 1943. Fleeger "received" between ty-five and forty Japanese pesos each month. In February 1943, he donated 100 pesos to camp welfare and he deposited fifty more in March and May 1943.[117] Fleeger did not mention why he did not draw out the ance of the pay due him. In 1943, before life got really terrible in camp, he might have been able to "buy" food with the additional money. He also did not list any pay deposited to his account in 1944. In April 1944, Fleeger continued about his pay: "very proud to have earned over 15,000 dollars since this mess started – at least I have done that much for you three. If you have only drawn 300 per month – I have 4,000 due me – all for you."[118]

IN AUGUST 1944, HE COMMENTED THAT: "I TAKE GREAT PRIDE IN EARNING EACH DAY MY 16 DOLLARS FOR YOU THREE LOU..."

All of these entries in the diaries – particularly the long lists - seemed to be exercises in killing time, although Fleeger obviously cared about his financial status and that of his family.

"No Work - No Food"

Fleeger worked at several jobs during his imprisonment: Mess Officer, Assistant Librarian, and laborer.

"CHANDLER'S KITCHEN – QUIT YOUR BITCHEN," Early in Cabanatuan and before the consolidations of all the messes on 1 December 1942, Fleeger and Bill Chandler ran a mess hall that fed 600 POWs a day. Dubbed "Chandler's Kitchen – Quit Your Bitchen," the kitchen "employed" a crew of thirty-two enlisted men. Sergeant J. E. Delanty of Bakersfield, CA, served as the Mess Sergeant, and Ray Trujillo and Philip Travera from New Mexico served as the cooks.[119]

Fleeger did not write about his stint as a Mess Officer. However, on 9 December 1942, Major Harry Packard, the Mess Officer in Group II, commended Fleeger for his work, and he provided a good insight into running a mess in Cabanatuan.

During this period [August-November 1942] the health and morale of five hundred men depended in no small measure on the ability of your kitchen to utilize the meager supplies received and produce palatable meals under abnormal working conditions. Rain and mud in the kitchens – meals prepared in darkness – wet and green wood that would not burn – kitchen equipment limited to a few cawas – five gallon cans and gasoline drums – rice and concong, and concong and rice. These were but part of the obstacles that had to be overcome.

Due to your superior work in the organization and supervision of your mess, your men were fed three meals a day without fail. Your services merit the thanks of the entire group...

The Commanding Officer of Group II, Lt. Colonel Trapnell, indorsed the report and added more detail.

I heartily concur in the above report. The trying conditions and difficult disciplinary problems involved in the administrative work in prisoners of war camp with the shortage of material, food, and medicine and the resultant poor physical condition of the men make the proper performance of duty exceptionally difficult. Major Fleeger has functioned under these conditions exceptionally well. I rate him superior throughout.

Typed on lined paper, the commendations seemed aimed at keeping some sort of administrative normalcy in operation of the camp.[120]

Fleeger worked at two other places. In December 1942, he wrote: "I still work all day at the library to pass the hours – yesterday was on farm detail at prison farm – terribly hot – cutting grass.[121] On Christmas Day 1942, Fleeger reported: "My health good but for dry beri beri in my feet. I'm marked quarters and still work in the camp library."[122]

He did not talk much about his work except for his entries about all the books in the library. Apparently, he worked there because of his poor health. In another letter commending his work, the Camp Librarian, Lt. Colonel David Babcock, said that Fleeger had "been relieved from such special duty in order that he may be replaced by a permanent quarters [invalided] officer." Babcock, in his commendation of 8 August 1943, wrote further.

> *I desire to commend Major Fleeger's services in the highest degree. He joined the library staff at a time when field officers[2] had no duties and solely in the interests of camp morale. He has worked steadily, capably, and loyally, and has contributed materially to the growth of the library from its early beginnings. As an Assistant Librarian his work has been efficient and capable in the highest degree. His relief has been merely a matter of administrative routine. Were I to rate this officer at this time on his duties under me, I would give him a rating of "superior.[123]*

Trying to maintain pre-war normalcy, Babcock added: "Request that this letter be filed at this Headquarters with a view to later filing with his efficiency record at the War Department."

One wonders how the post-war leaders in the Armor Branch in the War Department would have evaluated the professional skills of a cavalry major who had served as an Assistant Librarian under a field artillery lieutenant colonel and as a Mess Officer under another field artillery major. How would those "superior" ratings have stacked up against peers who had commanded cavalry or armor battalions in extended combat in North Africa or Europe?

ΩΩΩ

No Work — No food.

"Prisoners of War must be placed under strict discipline as far as it does not contravene the Law of Humanity. It is necessary to take care not to be obsessed with a mistaken idea of humanitarianism or swayed by personal feelings toward those prisoners which may grow in the long time of their imprisonment.

The present situation of affairs in this country does not permit anyone to lie idle doing nothing but eating freely.

With that in view, in dealing with the Prisoners of War, too, I hope you will see that they may be usefully employed."

Prime Minister Hideki Tojo
30 May 1942

---

[2] Field grade officers – i.e., field officers – were majors, lieutenant colonels, and colonels.

Upon leaving the library, Fleeger worked on the prison farm and on the airport. Early in the war, Japanese commanders decided to require POWs – including officers and as noted above eventually field grade officers – to work. The Japanese high command made "No work – no food" a national policy, one that devastated sick soldiers.[124] More importantly, the Japanese decreed that POWs would work on war-related projects and in their war industries in deliberate violation of the Geneva Conventions regarding the working of POWs. Because of a shortage of manpower in Japan, the senior commanders then decided to move POWs to Japan, Korea, and China to work in factories and mines there.

On 27 June 1943, Fleeger reported that "We are working a large prison farm – daily. I was out all morning. Very hot. And rough work with the guards on the drive – that like so many other unpleasant events – I will not describe it now – but want you to remind me to tell you of some of it – when I am home."[125] About a month later he continued: "working on the farm daily – Most rough – Reutel... One less on the farm – Is heaven merciful? ...[126] Met a man on the farm named Cater who knows Sam [Fleeger] well. Was like news from home. Reutel."[127]

"WORKING ON THE FARM DAILY – MOST ROUGH – REUTEL... ONE LESS ON THE FARM – "

Another POW described working on the farm in more detail. "We had to do everything by hand, for we did not have any machines to help in the digging or harvesting, and we put in long hours to accomplish the tasks required by the Japanese. We started at 6:00 in the morning and lasted till 11:00, when we were given a bowl of rice and a cup of colored water called soup for lunch. We could rest until 2:00 in the afternoon, and then we worked on the farm till dark. This routine went on day after day, without a break, and we were not allowed to talk while in the field planting, picking, or digging. We thought the food was for us, we were so foolish. The Japanese either ate the food or traded what we grew for favors in town from the local Filipinos. The farm produced large quantities of beans, squash, corn, sweet potatoes, okra, and eggplant. As a rule, we POWs got the tops, while the Japanese ate the vegetables. And of course if anyone were caught eating any of the vegetables while working on the farm, a beating was the price he paid."[128]

On 21 July, Fleeger wrote: "Today on the farm I developed my "P-J idea."[3] Reutel Louise. Also the altar." His notes provided no decoding for his comments. Eight

---

[3] Not explained.

days later he added: "Farm everyday – feet sore with *beri-beri.*" Later, he wrote, "Farm everyday – over two months now." In August, he still worked on the farm every day and said that it was hot. He added a twist - "someday I want to get that hot again – and have a cold beer when it's over – After all – I can stand a lot of these days knowing that each is 16 dollars for Lou, Jim and Larry –" The next month, still working on the farm every day, he reported "quanned off [punished] last week – Mental Hell." Fleeger did not say what the Japanese punished him for or how they punished him. He reported doing the same work in November while suffering from *beri-beri* etc."[129]

All reference to work disappeared after that entry until 2 March 1944, when Fleeger wrote, "Working at airport." The next month he noted that he worked at the airport daily and had lost five pounds. In May, Fleeger noted more punishment, -- "Sun treatment twice this week—I'm exhausted," [130] but did not say why.

*"**SUN TREATMENT TWICE THIS WEEK—I'M EXHAUSTED...**"*

August began with work at the airport. Fleeger commented: "Same old grind – work on airport – very thin – *beri beri* again – also edema – sore eyes. We hope – and try to be patient." Then, work changed again. "Work at airport stopped today [15 August] so I'll no doubt be back on the farm working barefoot – Rather rough in our condition." On the 20th, he added "feet cut and sore from grass detail – work everyday – heat – bare feet – cuts – sores – misery – and on a carbohydrate diet only maintenance." In September he continued: "Work every day – tired hungry – hell of a life" and "have lost five pounds working on the farm everyday." And in his last entry on 8 October, he reported "Farming every day."[131]

There were two terrible side effects from the various work details. First, the Japanese brutalized the POWs while they worked on the prison farm and on other projects. Second, the Japanese deprived the POWs of the food they grew while they watched the POWs starve.

"For dreams are the arms that prisoners bear"[132]

Fleeger's devoted many pages of his diary to returning to the United States – his future. First, he listed twenty seven "customs or projects" that he would continue without fail in the States after the war. At the top of his list were:

1. *Family games including ping pong, rummy, pinochle, cribbage, hearts, and bridge, chess.*
2. *Family movies – to make a record of the boys' events.*
3. *Breakfast in bed for Lou to be served by the men on Sundays -- ? or more?*
4. *Wine with dinners frequently.*
5. *Appropriate gifts for Lou on all important remembrance days, etc. from the 3 of us.*

As item 16, he listed: "Family attendance at church and participation in church activities. Next he listed Charity, and added a note, "this to include the boys sharing trips, their money – or possessions with other boys not so fortunate." As #22, he listed: "For my den – a 'quan' can – as a constant reminder of rugged days." His last item stated "Life long contacts with Bill and Betty [Chandler]." I wonder how his listing of "Coca-Cola, Fanny Farmer Candy, assorted salted nuts, always in ice box" would sort out with his plan to have "Morning calisthenics for all (me too)."[133]

"FOR MY DEN — A 'QUAN' CAN — AS A CONSTANT REMINDER OF RUGGED DAYS."

Shortly after arriving in Cabanatuan, Fleeger outlined future activities of his sons, Jim and Larry.[134]

1. *Continuous instruction and participation in numerous sports to include especially football, basketball, volleyball, swimming, shooting, boxing, wrestling, baseball, softball, gymnastics, hockey, golf, tennis.*
2. *Attendance at good opera or musical events.*
3. *Summer jobs during high school years.*
4. *Supervised high school program to include in order: English and English Lit, History, Mathematics, Bookkeeping, typing, and shorthand, Penmanship, Spelling, Economics, Spanish, Manual Training and manual course, Athletics – Music.*
5. *One year at home after high school and before college. (No compromise).*
6. *Travel to South America – one college summer.*
7. *Travel over all of 48 States – one college summer.*
8. *College education as selected by them.*
9. *States travel for pleasure to parks, etc. during high school summers.*
10. *One or two summer camps pre-high school.*
11. *High school age golf instruction.*
12. *Work with me in basement wood-work shop.*
13. *Boy Scout Activities.*
14. *Chess.*
15. *Dancing.*
16. *YMCA.*

In another list of things to do, Fleeger added more activities for his sons:[135]

1. *"Indoctrination of the boys by contract, agreement, reward, example - frequent discussion – not to mix drink and driving.*
2. *Trips for boys to dairy, large newspaper, factory (Bendix), hospital, packing plant, famous churches –*
3. *School in driving and state auto laws – for the boys – when they are about 14-17 years old.*
4. *Hunting trips for Jim and Larry.*
5. *Basement workshop for myself and boys.*
6. *Fishing trips for boys.*

As mentioned earlier, Fleeger had identified twenty-nine books that he would purchase for his library and for his sons. His ambitious programs and activities probably would have terrorized his sons because they would have had no time to be boys when dad returned home. Along with school demands, Fleeger might have made their lives pressure cookers.

In September 1943, Fleeger focused on what he would do when he got home.[136]

1. *Consider Lou first always -*
2. *Stay up! and go to evening events -*
3. *Work on our home or garden -*
4. *Confine my athletics to things I can enjoy with Lou and Jim and Larry –*
5. *Make new friends and remember old –*
6. *Read!*

Looking forward, Fleeger planned several trips. During his return leave he planned to drive to Ft. Riley, KS and budgeted $50 for it. He planned to take the boys and while there, he would order new uniforms, and would visit the school library, book store, and the Post Exchange. He was going to write his cavalry comrade, Captain John Wheeler, in St. Paul, MN and expected him to join his group. He next planned to visit Washington and New York and budgeted $400 for the trip. He would not take the boys on this trip. Fleeger planned to drive to see his Aunt Florence [Morgan Stout][137] in Ames, IA and then take the train from Des Moines to Chicago and stop over in South Bend. There, he would host a dinner party for Lou's friends. In Washington, he planned to see the Chief of Cavalry and visit Walter Reed Hospital and friends at Ft. Myer. Then, he would move on to New York where he would check on uniforms and see stage shows. Driving north to Lake Placid, he intended to spend two days

IN WASHINGTON, HE PLANNED TO SEE THE CHIEF OF CAVALRY AND VISIT WALTER REED HOSPITAL AND FRIENDS AT FT. MYER.

there if "in season," most likely meaning the ski season. Returning south, Fleeger hoped to make an overnight visit in New Jersey on Pappy Archer in Trenton.

Even more ambitious than his Washington-New York trip, Fleeger planned a "Motor trip for the family to Southwest." He also budgeted $400 for this trip. He proposed to plan the trip with his brother Sam who had gone to Houston to work in a naval shipyard there.[138] He expected to go to Kearney, NE to Uncle Trum's [Truman Falgatter],[139] to Scottsbluff, NE to see Cy and Mird [Young], then to Denver to the Russell's, and onto the Grand Canyon. In Silver City, NM, he planned to visit Major John Turner and Pryor [Prior] Thwaits from 200th Coast Artillery. In Ft. Bliss and El Paso, he planned to look up old Cavalry friends. In San Antonio, Fleeger hoped to visit Harry Fischer. [140] He expected to end his trip in Houston "for the hunting season," spend a week there with Sam Fleeger, and while there he would visit the Gulf and "hunt if possible." Next, he would go to New Orleans if that were possible; if not, he would drive north to Ft Leavenworth. He noted that he would seek good cabin camps or hotels, cook his own breakfast, "lunch part time," and eat "all dinners in good restaurants or hotels." He planned to give "gifts, flowers, candy, whiskey" for those he visited on the trip.[141]

FLEEGER NOTED SEPARATELY THAT WHEN HE REACHED NEW MEXICO HE SHOULD CONTACT ELEVEN SOLDIERS FROM THE 200TH COAST ARTILLERY INCLUDING THE ENLISTED COOKS ASSIGNED TO MESS #1 IN CABANATUAN.

Fleeger noted separately that when he reached New Mexico, he should contact eleven soldiers from the 200th Coast Artillery including the enlisted cooks assigned to Mess #1 in Cabanatuan. Among them were Carl Clemmons [actually Clemons] from Albuquerque, Aaron Drake from Carlsbad, Syd Hudgens from Hobbs, Kunnally [actually Billy Kanally] from Albuquerque, J. E. Reynolds from Clovis, Bert Sandoval from Chacon, and his wood cutter friend, Reynaldo Trujillo, in Albuquerque. In addition, he planned to see Sergeant [Robert] Davis from Gallup who had been a Mess Sergeant with Battery D, 515th Coast Artillery and who had run a restaurant in Gallup before war began.[142]

He also planned to see the officer cooks - Major Dores [probably Winnifred Dorris] and Lt. Clinton Seymour.[143] At this entry, Fleeger did not indicate that Seymour served as a 26th Cavalry officer as he had previously; he listed him as a member of the 200th Coast Artillery Regiment. But there was only one Clinton C. Seymour shown as a POW. Perhaps Seymour had served on detached service with the cavalry from the coast artillery regiment which had once been a cavalry outfit. Fleeger also included Lt. Colonel John Turner in this list.

He also listed a number of friends to whom he planned to send messages or gifts on their birthdays. At the top of his list were Bill and Betty Chandler and Captain "Pappy" Archer and his wife, Alice. He planned to send Pappy a half dozen tablespoons. Then, he listed his comrades: Paul Jones, Harry Fischer, Gardner Gross, Bill Dunmyer, John Wheeler, and Jim Blanning. He included two NCOs – Sergeant J. E. Reynolds and Corporal E. Rada of Lodi, Wisconsin, and three other officers, Air Force Captain Jack Batchelor from Arkansas, and Signal Corps Major Roy Herrick, and a Ray Doran [most likely Major Roy Doran] from San Antonio. Fleeger also listed his blood brothers – Chester Johnson

> *THEN, HE WOULD SEND A FOLLOW-UP LETTER TO THE PERSONNEL OFFICER IN THE OFFICE OF THE CHIEF OF CAVALRY "FOR DOPE AS TO THE BRANCH SET-UP," "ORDERS FOR ME," AND "MY PROBABLE ARRIVAL IN WASHINGTON ON TRAIN TRIP."*

and his wife, Kay, and Harry Packard, and his own family - his dad, his mom (Cliffie), his wife, his two sons, and a "Bubs" [Berta Morgan Selby].[144] Fleeger expected to send a wedding anniversary greeting to Ray Doran of San Antonio.[145]

Fleeger planned to dictate several letters when he returned to Parker. One was to go to his brother to "re-establish of letter writing," another to the Chief of Cavalry to announce his return and send best regards. Then, he would send a follow-up letter to the Personnel Officer in the Office of the Chief of Cavalry "for dope as to the branch set-up," "orders for me," and "my probable arrival in Washington on train trip." Next, he planned to write the Adjutant at Fort Riley "for roster officers – and dope about uniforms," and the Sergeant Major, 26th Cavalry "for regimental news" to be sent on to others of the 26th." He would have been surprised to learn in 1945 that the 26th no longer existed on Army rolls.

On a personal note, he expected to write the 1st National Bank in Kansas to set up a bank account and "secure loan pending payment by finance if necessary," write to General Brougher "requesting he buy Colt 22 pistol for me – thru NRA" and sending family news, write Bean & Company in Freeport, Maine "for a catalogue of sport and camping equipment for purchase of fishing equipment for Jim – Larry – myself [and] picnic equipment," and write Tiffany's in New York "for information regarding the purchase of a new West Point ring."

FOR HIS FAMILY, FLEEGER PLANNED TO WRITE A "CIRCULAR LETTER WITH ALL NEWS FOR ALL MEMBERS OF OUR FAMILY — 12 COPIES,"

AND A

"BRIEF SUMMARY OF MY WAR EXPERIENCE, COPIES FOR JIM AND LARRY AND FILE."

To catch up on what had happened while he was imprisoned, Fleeger planned to write to *Life* Magazine, *Time* Magazine, *The Cavalry Journal*, and *The Army-Navy Journal* to get the publishers to send him "all copies since October 1941." In addition, he would seek news from several friends: Gordon Bartlett,[146] Bugs Cairns,[147] his old polo teammates Bill Nutter and Glenn Finley, and Bill Chandler.

As with Trapnell, he would ask Chandler and Lee Vance for "recommendations." He did not say for whom he wanted them or if he wanted personal recommendations to send to Cavalry Branch.

For his family, Fleeger planned to write a "Circular letter with all news for all members of our family – 12 copies," and a "Brief summary of my war experience, copies for Jim and Larry and file."

He ended his list of letters stating that he would send one to "Clinty Pierce enclosing Regimental History." He did not clarify whether he meant the brief history he wrote in his diaries or an expanded one.[148]

From his comments, Fleeger's future seemed to be "a cloudless sky."

Apocalypse

By the time Fleeger left Cabanatuan he had met the apocalyptic horsemen. War had overrun him and forced him to surrender. Famine had trampled him, but weak and withered, he had survived. Meanwhile, Pestilence had kicked him sharply, but he still stood. Then, he had stepped aside to let Death gallop by. In the meantime, addictive tobacco arrived to replace Famine, but still withered, Fleeger withstood its addictive charge."[149] And loneliness had come and brought along Despair. But War would return, find him, and finally bring Death to bear.

Notes

---

[1] *Diary*, 15.

[2] Donald Knox, *Death March* (San Diego: Harcourt Brace Jovanovich, 1981), 203. Quote *"Death was easier than life"* from PFC John Falconer, 194th Tank Battalion.

[3] Knox, *Death March*, 139.

[4] Stanley Falk, *Bataan, The March of Death* (NY: W.W. Norton & Company, Inc., 1962), 150 and 155.

[5] *Ibid, 155.*

[6] Personal knowledge.

[7] Falk, *Bataan*, 108-09.

[8] Estimated deaths, see Falk, *Bataan*, 197 (Americans) and 198 (Filipinos).

[9] Knox, *Death March*, 203.

[10] *Ibid*, 157 (dogs), 165 (Aquila), 168 (Herbst), and 170 (Turner).

[11] John E. Olson, *O'Donnell, Andersonville of the Pacific, Extermination Camp of American Hostages in the Philippines* (c. 1985), 155-9. Olson provided detailed numbers. He reported that 9,180 reached the camp by July 1942, the Americans disinterred 1,547 bodies, and that total deaths may have been as high at 1,567. The cited death list showed 1,508 deaths by July 1942 (when most of the remaining POWs were moved to Cabanatuan) and 1,547 by the end of November 1942. Camp strength reports showed a smaller number, 1,449. See 162 for causes of death.

[12] William A. Berry, *Prisoner of the Rising Sun* (Norman: University of Oklahoma Press, 1993), 95-96.

[13] Eugene C. Jacobs, M.D., "From Guerrilla to P.O.W. in the Philippines," *C.M.D.* [Current Medical Diary], April 1971, 384. Major Jacobs had been the Surgeon at Camp John Hay, a medical officer in the 43rd Infantry Regiment, Philippine Army, and then the Medical Officer of the 1st Guerrilla Regiment (reorganized as the 14th Infantry Regiment, PA). The Japanese shipped Jacobs out on the *Oryoku Maru*. He made it to Japan and then Manchuria. He was evacuated on 24 August 1945 from Mukden POW Camp.

[14] *Ibid.*

[15] *Ibid.* Jacobs reported 2,400 deaths during the first eight months of the camp. The reported deaths come from Knox, *Death March*, 196-97.

[16] Roper, *Brothers of Paul*, 33-38.

[17] Charles Edward Nason Howard, Jr., "Vital Statistics Questionnaire," *Cullum File #9215.*

[18] Gross is listed as a Lt. Colonel in the *NARA Website*. No unit found for him. His last POW camp was in Keijo, Korea.

[19] Diagram, *Diary*, 165.

[20] *Diary of Lieut. Colonel D. S. Babcock, U. S. Army, American Prisoner of War Camp Cabanatuan, Phil. Islands,* (hereafter, *Babcock Diary*), 8. Typed copy in possession of author.

[21] A homemade wooden sandal.

[22] *Babcock Diary*, 112-13.

[23] *Diary*, 6.

[24] *Ibid*, 1-2 and 8-11.

[25] James Fleeger provided the information about his dad being an honor representative during a telephone conversation, 28 Jan 2006.

[26] *Diary*, 69. Italics added.

[27] Chynoweth, *Bellamy Park*, 303.

[28] Major William James Dunmyer, Class of 1937, *1989 USMA Register*, #10845, 406. See: *Diary*, 10, 12, 68, 74, 88, and 131. Also see the *ABMC Website*.

[29] *Diary*, 12 (15 August 1942) and 74 (26 November 1942/Thanksgiving). Fleeger listed him as Houden rather than Howden.

[30] *Ibid*, 94.

[31] *Ibid*, 108 and 110.

[32] *Ibid,* (church) 113-14, 115, and 125.

[33] Billy Keith, *Days of Anguish, Days of Hope* (NY: Doubleday, 1972), 146-47.

[34] Roper, *Brothers of Paul,* 283-84.

[35] *Ibid,* 284-85.

[36] Keith, *Days of Anguish,* 148-49.

[37] *Ibid,* 148.

[38] Joseph C. Wilson, "Obituary for Ovid O. Wilson," *Assembly Magazine,* June 1983, 133.

[39] Lewis Sorley, *Honorable Warrior, General Harold K. Johnson and the Ethics of Command* (Lawrence, KS: University of Kansas Press, 1998), 70 (quoted by Sorley) and 124.

[40] *Diary,* 129 and 135.

[41] *Ibid,* 139.

[42] *Ibid,* 150 (7 April and 9 April).

[43] *Ibid,* 154.

[44] *Ibid,* 155.

[45] *Ibid.*

[46] Ronald C. White, Jr., *The Eloquent President* (NY: Random House, 2006), 153.

[47] *Diary,* 118.

[48] *Ibid,* 76-77.

[49] *Ibid,* 65 and personal knowledge. Italics added.

[50] *Diary,* 80-81.

[51] *Ibid,* 82.

[52] *Ibid,* 82-83.

[53] *Ibid,* 86.

[54] *Ibid,* 88.

[55] *Ibid,* 90.

[56] A Sergeant Clarence H. Bramley, 21st Pursuit Squadron, 5564 Lewis Avenue, Long Beach, California, survived the war.

[57] *Diary,* 95-96.

[58] *Ibid,* 107.

[59] *Ibid,* 111-12.

[60] *Ibid,* 115.

[61] *Ibid,* 127.

[62] *Ibid,* 128-29.

[63] *Ibid,* 130.

[64] *Ibid,* 135.

[65] Letter from Mrs. O. O. Wilson, 233 Howard Street, San Antonio Texas to Mrs. H. J. Fleeger, 2409 4th Avenue, Scottsbluff, Nebraska, postmarked Dec 16, 1943. (James Fleeger's papers).

[66] Phyllis Ludwig Barth ended the war in Los Baños Internment Camp, step-child of Santo Tomas. So did Gladys Esperanza Ketchum. *Stevens, Santo Tomas,* 541 and 549.

[67] Edgar R. Whitcomb, *Escape from Corregidor (NY: Regnery, 1958),* 211-15.

[68] *Diary,* 138.

[69] *Ibid,* 129.

[70] Major Philip Gatch Lauman, Jr., Class of 1937, *USMA Register 1989,* #10844, 406. Also see the *ABMC Website.* Killed on the *Oryoku Maru, 15 Dec 44,* at age 29. The *Register* shows the award of a Silver Star and Purple Heart; *ABMC Website* shows a Legion of Merit and a Purple Heart.

[71] *Diary,* 145.

[72] *Ibid,* 145-46.

[73] *Ibid,* 146.

[74] *Ibid,* 150, 151, 153, 155, and 156.

[75] *Ibid,* 156 and 158.

[76] Personal experience.

[77] *Diary,* 159 (15 Aug) and 163 (10 Sep).

[78] *Ibid,* 64.

[79] Gavan Daws, *Prisoners of the Japanese,* (NY: William Morrow, 1994), 113-14.

[80] *Diary,* 11. *ABMC Website* listed Trujillo as a member of the 515th Coast Artillery Regiment (AA). He was awarded a Purple Heart posthumously.

[81] *Diary,* 63.

[82] *Ibid,* 70.

[83] *Ibid,* 68 and 74. Fleeger listed three nick names for Major Chester Johnson: "Johnnie," "Chump," and "Johnsonelli."

[84] Probably William M. Cummings, 26th Cavalry, who was on detached duty with the 53rd Infantry Regiment (PA) when the forces on Bataan surrendered. Cummings died on the *Brazil Maru.* He earned a Bronze Star and a posthumous Purple Heart. *ABMC Website.*

[85] *Diary,* 107.

[86] *Ibid,* 18 (cooks), 18-20 (restaurants) and 20-21 (egg nog).

[87] *Ibid,* 118-124.

[88] Amelia M. Bradley and John H. Bradley, *MacArthur Moon,* unpublished manuscript, 135.

[89] *Diary,* 162.

[90] Personal knowledge.

[91] Daws, *Prisoners,* 308-09.

[92] *Diary,* 79 (17 Dec 1942) and 107 (June 1942).

[93] *Ibid,* 73-74 and 79.

[94] *Ibid,* 79.

[95] *Ibid,* 86.

[96] *Ibid,* 107.

[97] *Ibid,* 125.

[98] *Ibid,* 115.

[99] *Ibid,* 126.

[100] *Ibid,* 139.

[101] *Ibid,* 143.

[102] *Ibid,* 147.

[103] *Ibid,* 158-9 and 163.

[104] *Ibid,* 164.

[105] James Fleeger reported that his dad was about five foot eight in height and weighed about this amount. *Conversation,* 25 January 2006. *Diary,* 94, Fleeger reported that he weighed 130 pounds on 18 May 1943 up from 95 pounds. Fleeger himself in his Questionnaire found in his Cullum File listed his height as five foot seven and his weight as 130 when he was in high school.

[106] Hampton Sides, *Ghost Soldiers, The Forgotten Epic Story of World War II's Most Dramatic Action* (NY: Doubleday, 2001), 239 (food found) and 243-244 (impact of food).

[107] The Japanese prohibited the teaching of history and geography in the internee run schools in Santo Tomas Internment Camp. Personal knowledge.

[108] *Diary,* 96-105.

[109] *Ibid,* 106.

[110] *Ibid,* 72-73.

[111] *Ibid,* 24-38.

[112] *Ibid,* 36-38.

[113] *Ibid,* 22-23.

[114] *Ibid,* 96.

[115] *Ibid,* 114-15.

[116] *Ibid,* 159 (15 August 1944).

[117] *Ibid,* 134.

[118] *Ibid,* 151.

[119] *Ibid,* 77-78.

[120] *Ibid,* 168.

[121] *Ibid*, 80.

[122] *Ibid*, 83.

[123] *Diary*, 167.

[124] E. Bartlett Kerr, *Surrender & Survival* (NY: William Morrow and Company, Inc, 1985), 83. Tojo's "...government would require that the Allied prisoners be governed by the dictate then being applied to the Japanese people which had come to be expressed in a national slogan, "No work – no food.""

[125] *Diary,*107.

[126] *Ibid*, 109-10.

[127] *Ibid*, 110. Cater was probably Private Jack A. Cater from Battery F, 515th Coast Artillery Regiment. Cater survived the war. See: the *Names Project- 200th/515th Coast Artillery - Roster of the 200th Coast Artillery and 515th Coast Artillery Regiments*, Bataan Corregidor Memorial Foundation of New Mexico, Inc. See http://www.angelfire.com/nm/bcmfofnnm/names/d.html (hereafter, *"Names Project-NM")* and *NARA Website.*

[128] Lester I. Tenney, *My Hitch in Hell, The Bataan Death March* (Dulles, VA: Brassey's, 2000), 110.

[129] *Diary*, 111, 112, 113, 114, 115, and 126 for farm information and 117 for "quanned off".

[130] *Ibid*, 144, 151, and 153 (sun treatment).

[131] *Ibid*, 158, 159, 162, 163, and 164.

[132] Charles Brown, *Bars from Bilibid Prison* (San Antonio: The Naylor Company, 1947), see 8, "Bataan Surrender" ("For dreams are the arms that prisoners bear to attack their bitter foe Despair.").

[133] *Ibid*, 16.

[134] *Ibid*, 13-14.

[135] *Ibid*, 15-16.

[136] *Ibid*, 117.

[137] *Telephone conversation with Jim Fleeger, 12 June 2009.* Louise Fleeger's sister Florence Morgan. She married a gentleman named Stout.

[138] *Ibid.*

[139] *Ibid,* Uncle Truman Falgatter, maternal uncle of Louise Fleeger.

[140] Fleeger listed Major John W. Turner, Jr. as a member of the 200th Coast Artillery, but the *ABMC Website* listed Turner as a member of the 515th Coast Artillery Regiment, NM. The *"Names Project-NM"* does not identify his regiment. He is listed only as "Officer." Prior Thwaits is listed on the NM Website. Harry O. Fischer, an engineer officer, is listed on the *NARA Website*. Thwaits and Fischer survived.

[141] *Diary*, 17-18 and 59.

[142] Yvonne Boisclaire, *In the Shadow of the Rising Sun, The True Story of Robert Davis, POW and Battery D 515th CAC, Orphan Unit of Bataan* (Bella Vista, CA: Clearwood Publishers, 1997), (hereafter, *Shadow*), 37 and 46.

[143] Names verified on *"Names Project-NM,"* "Dores" [Not Dures as in the typed diary] could only be "Dorris." The only name similar to Kunnally is Kanally. The only Seymour listed is Clinton Seymour. For list of names, see *Diary*, 18.

[144] Louise's sister Berta married Keith Selby. During the war, they lived in Scottsbluff, AR with Louise and the Cy Youngs. During the Vietnam War, Berta's son, David, served as an Army Surgeon commanding a medical battalion at Danang. As a result of his conversation with a brigade commander of the 3rd Brigade of the 82nd Airborne Division, apparently that officer decided to recruit a "bored" Jim Fleeger to replace his departing artillery battalion commander. *Telephone conversation with Jim Fleeger, 12 June 2009.*

[145] *Diary*, 131.

[146] Most likely William Gordon Bartlett, Class of 1933, *USMA Register 1989*, # 9676, 383. Bartlett served with the OSS in Europe in 1943 and 1944 and with the G-1 Section of the Army Ground Forces in 1945 and 1946. The New York-born cavalry officer retired in 1959 and died in 1971. No information was found about his service in 1941 and 1942. The *1943 Army Direc-*

---

tory, 164 listed him with the Army Ground Forces in 1943 and as a lieutenant colonel (permanent rank of 1ˢᵗ Lieutenant).

[147] Possibly Bogardus Snowden Cairns, West Point 1932, *1989 USMA Register*, #9463, 379. A cavalry officer, Cairns commanded an armor battalion in North Africa and Europe during World War II. He later became an army aviator and died in a plane crash in 1958 as a major general. The *1943 Army Directory*, 185, listed him as serving with the 13ᵗʰ Armored Regiment overseas as a lieutenant colonel (permanent rank of captain).

[148] *Ibid,* 59-60.

[149] Brown, *Bars from Bilibid Prison* see 38, "Bataan Surrender" ("For dreams are the arms that prisoners bear to attack their bitter foe Despair.") and 100, "The Fifth Horseman" ("This Fifth one, called Tobacco, rides to soothe the stricken man.").

Sidebar Notes

Death March
Lt. Col. Wm. E. Dyess, *The Dyess Story, The Eye-Witness Account of the DEATH MARCH FORM BATAAN AND THE Narrative of Experiences in Japanese Prison Camps and of Eventual Escape* (NY: G P Putnam's Sons, 1944), 73.

MS *Gripsholm*
U. S. Navy photograph on website for the *Gripsholm.*

Red Cross Supplies
Linda Goetz Holmes, *Unjust Punishment, How Japan's Companies Built Postwar Fortunes Using American POWs* (Mechanicsburg, PA: Stackpole Books, 1961), 51, 52, and 102.

No Work – No Food
Kerr, *Surrender & Survival*, 84-5.

Seven

"Then again it will be roses for Lou"

Louise with son, Jim

Susan Louise Fleeger dominated her husband's thoughts in prison camp just as she dominated his thoughts after she left Manila with their children in early 1941. She had been part of his life since childhood and seemed key to his psychological survival in Cabanatuan. Fleeger thought about the past with his wife, considered some of the present, and focused mostly on the future.

Louise

He began his saga on 30 September 1942, noting: "...Another day gone away from Lou – smoking – no clothes – lonely – hungry—but never despair – only life and friends – memories."[1] Reflections followed. They included a self critique.

1. *"Notes for Re-write – As Soon as Released – in form of letter to Lou – to review our pre war years – and detail my hopes for her and us.*
2. *Story of narrow escape at surrender – with Johnnie – and my thoughts of her that hour.*
3. *Our growing up together at Ft. Des Moines – and Jimmy joins us.*
4. *How I come to know how fine she is – how selfish I can be.*
5. *Life at Benning and Stotsenburg finally all perfect – but my never telling her so.*
6. *The war – my hopes to live for her – and boys – and my plans for all."[2]*

Then on his wife's birthday in 1942, Fleeger wrote about the past and the future and included his adaptation of "this too shall pass." "Your last birthday, 1941, I was alone as today Louise, but with the assurance that my Baguio gift and my message has reminded you of my ever constant love. Today I can only try to realize that your thoughts and prayers are for me too – and I feel the strength of your hopes across the months of war." Continuing, "This has been rough – but then I remember how you have suffered – almost a year now with no word from me. – Soon I pray, and on other birthdays I can wake and wish you that "Happy Birthday" of old days – and make up in part for all of this - then again it will be roses for Lou. This cannot make me suffer enough to ever dim that picture – it is but a passing hour – our love will bring us through with a real devotion and only fading scars."[3]

"YOUR LOVE KEEPS ME FROM DEATH TODAY."

In November 1942, Fleeger emphasized his spiritual connection with his wife: "you were all at church this morning as I read a Psalm - you wished for me at Mother's dinner – as I had my rice... I'll be remembering other Sunday afternoons with you – and waiting for their return – Your love keeps me from death today. How Long? –

For ever Lou."[4] He did not explain his comment about death. Was Fleeger critically ill? Was he seriously depressed? Was he suicidal? On Thanks-giving, after returning from a communion service he continued: "I know that I could feel your prayers ... they constantly keep me from total despair – I have so much to be thankful for – first my life – so far – and then for having had you and Jim and Larry for so many years. After all we have lived quite a life – and the later years will repay doubly – after this difficult lesson. I will think of you each minute today..."[5]

Fleeger's entries during the first six months in Cabanatuan sway back and forth from despair to hope. He, no doubt, realized the situation he was in. With despair always at hand, Fleeger clung desperately to the hope of a better life in the future with his wife, the center of his hope.

Obviously looking to improve his relationship with his wife, Fleeger turned to Dale Carnegie's book for advice and imbedded Carnegie's questions to husbands in his diary.

FLEEGER'S ENTRIES DURING THE FIRST SIX MONTHS IN CABANATUAN SWAY BACK AND FORTH FROM DESPAIR TO HOPE. HE, NO DOUBT, REALIZED THE SITUATION HE WAS IN. WITH DESPAIR ALWAYS AT HAND, FLEEGER CLUNG DESPERATELY TO THE HOPE OF A BETTER LIFE IN THE FUTURE WITH HIS WIFE, THE CENTER OF HIS HOPE.

1. *Do you still court your wife with an occasional gift of flowers, with remembrances on her birthday or wedding anniversary or with some unexpected attention, some unlooked for tenderness?*
2. *Are you careful never to criticize her before others?*
3. *Do you give her money to spend entirely as she chooses above the household expenses?*
4. *Do you make an effort to understand her varying feminine moods and help her thru periods of fatigue, nerves, and irritability?*
5. *Do you share at least half of your recreation hours with your wife?*
6. *Do you tactfully refrain from comparing your wife's housekeeping or cooking with that of your mother or of Bill Jones' wife except to her advantage?*
7. *Do you take a definite interest in her intellectual life, her clubs and societies, the books she reads, or her views on civic problems?*

8. *Can you let her dance with or receive friendly attentions from other men without making jealous remarks?*
9. *Do you keep alert for opportunities to praise her and express your admiration for her?*

And, "Do you thank her for the little jobs she does for you such as sewing on a button, darning your sox, and sending clothes to the cleaners?"

He ended the section with the following entry: Dale Carnegie's *"For Wives* is interesting but when scored by me – my score *For Husbands* was so low by comparison that I have omitted *For Wives.*"[6] Fleeger placed his wife on a pedestal in these months while he gave himself a lower and lower grade as a husband.

Then after reading quotations from Admiral Richard Byrd, the explorer of Antarctica, Fleeger wrote down one of Byrd's comments:

> *Thinking things out, alone on the barrier, I became better able to tell what in the world was wheat for me and what was chaff – I learned that a man can live profoundly without masses of things – I came to believe that a man's primary objective should be to seek a fair measure of harmony within himself and his family circle. - It wasn't the fear of death – <u>but a terrible anxiety over the consequences to those at home</u> – I realized how I had failed to see that the simple, homely, unpretentious things of life are the most important – <u>at the end only two things matter to a man – the affection and understanding of his family.</u>[7]*

Fleeger agreed with Byrd's many comments and then added this note for his wife: "One who had not been through the frequent threat of sudden death could never gain the import of the [Byrd] quotations. For me they express some of the thoughts that have been mine and they are apt with striking similarity and effect. I have lived each thought a thousand times."[8]

On Christmas Eve, 1942 the cavalryman complained about being homesick. On Christmas Day, he repeated many previous themes. "My every thought, as usual, has been for my Lou." Fleeger could hear his sons' prayers. He wrote: "I live for them –

"MY EVERY THOUGHT, AS USUAL, HAS BEEN FOR MY LOU."

and knowing the safe and secure American life they enjoy I consider no sacrifice of mine too great. May next Xmas have us all together with our own Xmas tree – God bless you three – and I'm living for the day with you in my thoughts my dearest lover." Then he turned to the subject of giving to others: "Louise - This Xmas has taught me true giving and I'll give my life and years to you when we are together again – in a more considerate, understanding and humble manner, I pray."[9]

On 15 January, 1943, Fleeger sent out his first post card to his wife. He reported "All Well" - a required lie – which did not in any way reflect his condition or the condition of any POW. But the post card at least confirmed that he was alive on that date.

On 8 February 1943, a day he called a "red letter day," Fleeger received a form Christmas letter/card from his wife: "Xmas greetings – proud of you – praying for welfare, reunion - Louise." It was the first contact he had had since receiving his wife's last letter before war began. Elated, he wrote: "Our thoughts are all a turmoil – word from home after so long – and the heartbreak of that wonderful "Louise" – I think of you three constantly Lou." Continuing, he noted, "after so long at least one of my prayers has been answered because we must assume now that you know we are alive and well." He added: "The message was a wonderful experience – it renews my hopes – and you three are in my prayers as always." And then, "Now I'm wondering why Lou chose a message which did not include "All Well" – I feel that they are alright but if anything has happened to Dad it will be my most bitter war experience."[10]

In April, he returned to his unworthiness as a husband: "I am 'earning' you Lou – the hard way – life will owe me to you forever after this – I dream of you every night – God how sweet you were – my ever constant love..."[11] The same month, he continued his reflections with a long entry. "During our

> *"I AM 'EARNING' YOU LOU – THE HARD WAY – LIFE WILL OWE ME TO YOU FOREVER AFTER THIS – I DREAM OF YOU EVERY NIGHT..."*

service, I recall quite distinctly that you were bitter on the few occasions when you believed us to have been [shoddily] treated by the Army. Now that you experience real injury I wonder how you have reacted. In fact I have spent hours of agony wondering and have wished of course that I had been able to bring myself to a resignation – for your sake – But would civilian life have been a solution? We must have an aim for living – in addition to love – and a loyalty. My loyalty has always been to you Dear but also to the service. We who are here now realize that some of our people must be lost – that you and those at home may live as you have and will live – That is brutal but part of the scheme of affairs. In my heart I know you have been brave and true – but still I have worried – I will want to be assured often – when I am with you again." He closed with, "Bad day I guess – They are rather frequent — This stinks."[12]

Nothing seems to have changed much over the years – which comes first for the professional soldier, the Army or family? How many officers have resigned because of family needs or demands and regretted it because they lost all sense of purpose? How many did not resign and regretted the consequences on their families? The war and extended separation had already taken their toll on Fleeger. Things would get worse.

May 1943 found Fleeger upbeat: "A beautiful sunrise this day. My thoughts of Jim and Larry and my eternal devotion and love for Louise." A few days later on Palm Sunday, he wrote: "sunsets still beautiful, friends sincere, and my thoughts always of Lou and my boys." But just before those words, he had written "Guards shot a boy this week, food is now maintenance."[13] The next month after talking about work on the prison farm, he reported: "I was out all morning. Very hot. And rough work with the guards on the drive – that like so many unpleasant events -- I will not describe it now – but want you to remind me to tell you of some of it – when I am home." Then, he turned to their projected reunion: "It [unpleasant events] should explain partially what a strange creature has returned to you. However I can do it if it means that it will never happen to my Jim and Larry – that's the constant thought that prevents despair."[14] Later in the entry, Fleeger continued talking about being home for his next birthday because "conservative estimates" said the Allies were moving. Those estimates were terribly wrong. MacArthur did not begin moving north fast until after February 1944, and it would take him until late October to return to the Philippines. Fleeger ended the day by writing "We have known nothing but misery and misfortune

"...YOU COULD NEVER UNDERSTAND THE ANIMAL RETURNED TO YOU WILL BE MENTALLY AT LEAST 60 PERCENT OSSIFIED..."

for eighteen months – but hope never dies and patience can be almost endless – for you Lou – I can feel your love across the suffering and hear Jim's and Larry's prayers. Until 1944."[15]

On Independence Day 1943, despair returned. "Patience Dearest, love me well for you could never understand the animal returned to you will be mentally at least 60 percent ossified from exposure to 5 years of tropical sun and several years of prison, physically intact perhaps, but with all reserves exhausted by starvation, quite unaccustomed to writing anything except to sign his name once or twice a year, bewildered by electric lights, traffic, trains, and autos, overcome by the vision of swaying hips and breasts...anxious to wolf all food everywhere – without manners or tools, terrified by conversation – especially feminine, vitamin insane, love intoxicated, work allergic, and to top it all – subject to horrifying nightmares."[16]

Fleeger got it right. The POWs returned different people. PFC Robert Brown, 17th Pursuit Squadron, a survivor, said that "Coming home was very confusing. I couldn't stand anyone to give me a hard time. I'd shake and go to pieces...I came home but I was still in jail. I bought a car. I also drank a fifth of booze a day, but couldn't even get drunk. I was so goddamn nervous. I couldn't sit still...I couldn't sleep... I couldn't converse with anybody."[17] Moreover, many POWs continued to have frightful nightmares. J. J. Carter reported "I still get captured about once every month. Actually, it's harder on my wife. I never wake up, but she does. She doesn't know how to cope with this nightmare. I'm always captured in different places and the circumstances are always different. But it's always by the Japanese. Sometimes in these nightmares I say, "You know this is strange, but I was captured once before."[18] And Fleeger's comrade, taciturn Tom Trapnell, had nightmares all his long life.[19]

In August, Fleeger asked: "Why didn't I ever kiss you when we were out riding? I always thought of it as I looked across at you." [20] Three weeks later, he recorded: "Lou – your love <u>never</u> leaves me. And I pray that what I have been thru will make you love me even more someday – So long without you – over two years now – I still dream of you almost every night – you are part of me – our memories dim but your sweet smile never fades lover. (The diet makes us forget almost our own names.)"[21]

In mid-September, the POWs learned that Italy had surrendered and their morale improved, "but we are numb with the long imprisonment."[22] Fleeger looked backward again. "Always thinking of Louise – finding her on the beach at Lakeside – meeting her at the hotel in Hot Springs – our evacuation goodbye – in the sally-port at West Point – we have lived and loved...Another day gone without you - you were so cute in riding habit Louise..."[23] Then, he said that when he got home he would "Consider Lou first always."[24]

On 20 October, his wife's birthday, Fleeger repeated again that his wife had never been out of his thoughts, and he added "Surely this sacrifice and misery will leave us real love forever - Happy Birthday

"SURELY THIS SACRIFICE AND MISERY WILL LEAVE US REAL LOVE FOREVER..."

my old Sweetheart Lou -- You <u>have been loved</u> – never forget that Louise – You are so fine – I often wonder why you took me."[25] On Thanksgiving, he reminisced again. "Another day – 900 days since we kissed goodbye Louise...These lonely hours worshipping you Lou reminded me of walking guard at West Point when I used to dream of you so much. You were adorable in New York – we were so naïve – and the night train to Chicago – God – how sweet. ...And no snapshots of the boys or you – so often begged for – then no mail since December 1941 (Now November '43). What a hell of a long weary road."[26] Apparently, the major forgot he had received at least one card in early 1943.

In December, as Christmas approached, Fleeger wrote several entries. He started with: "Lou when I'm home there will be nothing I want as badly – after I have you – as to be useful, livable, and loveable. I count on you to help me and I will need your help always."[27] Then, "Memories fade – it has been so long but I still dream of you almost every night Lou – Where are you today – and how are you all – my third year with no word of any kind,"[28] and "I hate to think of my third Xmas alone." And finally, "Very homesick thinking about you Lou – And Jim and Larry. I held you by the hand Louise that most difficult hour after you put the boys in bed on Xmas Eve and I kissed you goodnite and Merry Xmas."[29]

ΩΩΩ

On New Year's Eve 1943, the POWs produced a two-hour show and ended the evening singing "Auld Lang Syne." The next day, Fleeger said that the music made him homesick for his wife, and he remembered other New Years' Eves, dancing with his wife, and having fun with friends. He reported that the POWs in his *bahay* had coffee and sat around talking about their families. He and his friends were miserable, but they could not think about anything else. Then he said: "My prayer is that the New Year will give you back to me Susan. There are so many things of you – and for you I did poorly – and I've dreamed a million dreams of the better way to do them." [30]

"MY PRAYER IS THAT THE NEW YEAR WILL GIVE YOU BACK TO ME SUSAN."

On Sunday 14 January 1944, Fleeger reminisced some more. "I thought of you Lou when your house was quarantined and you lived with us. I remember Cliffie fixing your Curls – I don't know when I started loving you but it must have been then."[31] After noting on 1 February 1944, that 25,000 letters allegedly arrived for distribution of 50 to 100 a day, Fleeger complained "After 2 years and 2 months its Hell to know a letter is so close and not get it – I pray Lou you say where you are. And what of our love? If I hear only that I'll be happy..." [32]

The lack of communication had obviously worn him down. And his introspection seemed more destructive as he wrote: "...<u>I am coming to know myself for the first time</u> – You may not like me – and I love every hour with faith that goes back to starry evenings on your back porch – and you were <u>very</u> Susan – and utterly adorable. And the memories of the chicken pox at Benning leaves me weak with homesickness. 'I luf you very much you.'"[33]

On 7 February 1944 after he had read a letter from his wife that had been mailed on 16 January 1943, his spirit soared. "And so typical of you Louise and our love – perfect. - Told me all that I wanted to know – said so bravely – and so wisely – and after so many months of misery it was a greatest experience." Learning that his wife now had a home of her own, he wrote: "...now I have a home too – to dream of – with the three of you – and I can be at peace now – knowing you are safe and comfortable – and living for me." He went on to comment about the photos of his sons, and then wrote: "I was awake last nite for hours and will memorize your letter Louise reading it over and over. Most important was your saying you loved me – as always. I was weak until I had found it. So good to know I'm loved by so sweet and perfect a lover – God – how homesick today."[34]

The underlying fear that his wife no longer loved him bubbled just under the surface in many of his entries. After reading two more short letters, he added, "I could read between the lines and know how you've suffered Dear heart – and your picture (the square one) indicated it too – If my prayers could only help you –this silent love and devotion is all I can give you. If you could feel how great it is you'd not be so hurt – Someday I'll kiss those cares away – forever – I love you unceasingly my lover and darling wife – How long?" Continuing on, he analyzed the photos: "I've been looking at your picture Louise and I can see the hurt in your eyes – I'm so sorry – my Dear – and your small lips look so the same – I can almost feel them ... Dearest in being so devoted to Jim and Larry – and in loving me as you <u>always</u> have – you make all of this bearable. Those two things are <u>all I ever ask</u>."[35] About a week later, still focusing on letters, he added a new twist: "Louise -- So many letters have omitted many important things." Refocusing on the letters, Fleeger said: "Reading your letters every day Lou – and dreaming of you with all my strength – Had a terrifying nightmare last night of you and Paul back at State – awoke screaming – God how long – <u>I love you so</u> – I'm re-

> *THE UNDERLYING FEAR THAT HIS WIFE NO LONGER LOVED HIM BUBBLED JUST UNDER THE SURFACE IN MANY OF HIS ENTRIES.*

minded I started writing to you in school notes 18 years ago – and so to the end of time – I love you so darling lover Susan."[36]

After receiving a box from home, Fleeger wrote "...made me awful homesick to see the things you packed yourself and I could almost hear Jim and Larry talking

"THIS IS A LONESOME DAY."

about it – you three are so dear to me – and I love you so tremendously... This is a lonesome day – the things make me think of you so hard. God send peace and your arms around me again. I love you."[37] A few days later after receiving another letter, and some photos, he reported that he "Never had such a wave of complete homesickness. Made me want to hold you close with my arm around your small waist -- God Lou – this misery – we can only live for the day I can have you again. – I will make up to you for so much lover and never leave you ... I love you with love so deep Lou that it seems that 12 years ago we had never learned of love – Wish I could kiss you – My Dearest own Lou – forever – Your devoted H."[38]

ΩΩΩ

The letters from home seemed to have a dual effect: initially they raised Fleeger's morale and spirit; then they depressed him. But homesickness continued. On 2 April, Fleeger wrote: "Have read your August 8th letter many times Lou – It was brave. And very sweet. You have always been wonderful in every respect – Have been very homesick this week – Remember the nite Pudy drove us home from Manila – you were angry – but so dear – Your lips had a special sweetness that nite lover – I have never forgotten."[39] Two days later, he continued: "Your letter haunts me Lou. So sweet to read that you love me even more than August 8, 1931. Our love is founded on so many fine and permanent things Louise – it can never die – I keep telling myself – and nothing else in the world is of any importance to me now. In the picture I've just noticed your short skirts – gives me a funny feeling in my heart – You still have those beautiful legs Dearest – there are none so lovely – and your hair do looks different – yesterday – (Sunday PM) was long Lou – and lonely. I thought of you in the old way – and love you so desperately my Darling Lou ever – H"[40]

On Good Friday, 7 April, Fleeger reported that he had received a radio gram – one of thirty–eight received. The radio gram was three weeks old. Considering himself blessed, Fleeger wrote: "wonderful to have it. And your words "loving you" will be in my thoughts – every minute for all the time yet to live this out – Tomorrow is Easter – I'm looking at your picture taken last Easter – so sweet." On Easter he added: "I think of you 3 at sunrise service also – and love you all – So very much."[41] Later in the month, Fleeger talked about being homesick because his wife went to Ft. Knox without him and complained that on earlier trips they had not had the money to buy "little things that would have helped." But he added, "At least in all this misery its consoling that I still earn money for you Lou so you can travel – dress – eat (So important I now know)."[42]

On the 4th of July, Fleeger noted that he had received fifteen letters from his wife and said "If you could only know what they mean in these years of Hell and misery." Continuing, he wrote "After over 2 years in prison I'm prompted to list some of the things I want when I'm out of this – first of course – a true and wonderful love and companionship with Lou – all life will begin again for me with that."[43] On 15 August in a long entry, Fleeger reflected: "On looking over my notebooks I find very little Lou but my lonely thoughts of you on days I have written a note of love – but of course I have restricted this record because of Charles – he may see it some day and so our life - and events as a prisoner will have to be told later."[44] His reference to the Japanese may explain Fleeger's lack of detail about POW life.

Then, he returned to the subject of his previous Army life. "I know how over concentrated my efforts were for my work – and how selfish and unpleasant I

"AFTER THIS HORROR I HAVE A NEW SET OF VALUES..."

was because of that. After this horror I have a new set of values and a new philosophy that I pray will mean a great deal to you three some day soon – I think I've been through too much to ever omit any important act of my own that can possibly enrich your life or the life for Jim and Larry...thousands of plans to talk over with you – and some sincere apologies to make to you – more fully."[45]

POW life had changed Fleeger and had definitely changed his perspective as a professional soldier. Would he have been happy in the Cold War army? Would he have been able to compete successfully with the combat veterans who stayed in the Army? How would he have dealt with the "hardship" or "separated tours" of thirteen months or so after the war? He may not have been able to handle any long separations considering the pre-war reflections and his camp commentaries.

In August, after identifying gifts for his dad and for a friend, the major announced out of the blue, "Am sure that I want to adopt a little girl soon after return home – have thought it out and hope I can persuade Lou."[46] He never returned to the subject again or commented on his wife's possible reaction.

On 21 September, the day that U. S. Navy pilots from Vice Admiral William Halsey's Third Fleet raided Luzon, Fleeger noted that "Sky was black today – Great event!" He added that he received four more short letters, one from March 1944.[47]

The twenty-first and the next day were great days in the Philippines. For the first time since 1941, POWs in Cabanatuan and Bilibid and the internees in Santo Tomas saw American planes, and there were dozens of them. Colonel Irwin Alexander wrote that the "strikes were a tremendous boost to our morale because they spelled an end to Nip air supremacy." The air strikes boosted spirits in Santo Tomas and internees began hoping for an early rescue. [48] Great disappointment followed when the American aircraft did not show up again for many days. Fleeger noted that with a terse comment: "Still waiting for them to come back." [49] No one realized that these first aircraft came from Halsey's prowling Third Fleet and they were part of an unplanned reconnaissance of the islands. Because of them, Halsey reported that the central Philippines were lightly held, and he recommended canceling the invasion of Mindanao that was scheduled for November and recommended that MacArthur invade the Central Philippines immediately. Within days, the U. S. Joint Chiefs of Staff approved the invasion of Leyte for 20 October. MacArthur's return became imminent. Soon Halsey's pilots would be back. Fleeger must have dreamed that he would see his wife soon.

MACARTHUR'S RETURN BECAME IMMINENT.

Nine days later, he said just that, "...we hope to stay here now – will get me back to you about nine months earlier," and he estimated liberation around 20 December 1944.[50] Fleeger's hope was forlorn. He and his buddies apparently feared the dark side of the return of the Americans: the Japanese would move them to Japan as they had done with hundreds before them.

On 8 October 1944, as mentioned earlier, Fleeger reported that he had "Received 4 more short letters. And he mentioned his wife for the last time, ending with – "My love is more each day of Lou – will it ever end --"[51]

Had his dreams of Lou and the appearance of the American planes driven off Despair?

Sons

While Fleeger concentrated so much on his wife, he did write some interesting comments to his boys. On 30 November 1942, he wrote; "Hi Little Man Larry – 10 months is such a long time to go without talking to a little boy, Larry! Today I saw a little boy. He came into camp with his Father to deliver food. He was the first boy I had seen since 10 months ago when a little fellow was wounded and slept in the bed next to mine in a Bataan hospital. They made me very homesick for you and Jimmer." He added, "I hope that you had a fine Sunday dinner with Mother and that you all remember me. Be a good trooper Larry – and grow to do fine things – You will have all my help when I am home again. I think of you boys each hour – and I can hear

you calling toodle oo – You were such a scamp – Love boy – Your Dad."[52] On 29 December, he wrote Larry again, saying "Larry – I have missed you so today – Happy Birthday my boy – and many many more – when I am home again I will always try to be with you and Jimmy on your birthdays. Your Dad."[53]

On 21 August 1943, he wrote, "Happy Birthday Jimmy. Wish that I could see you today – be a good boy son – The year has been so long without you"[54] In April of the next year, Fleeger wondered if "Jim and Larry remember me." He added to a note to his wife, "Jim must be quite grown up – I miss them so."[55] Jim Fleeger was ten.

Missed You So

Years later, Larry and Jim Fleeger would discover what their dad had planned for them, and Louise Fleeger would discover what she had meant to her husband. But there would be no roses for Louise.

Notes

[1] *Diary*, 63.
[2] *Ibid.*
[3] *Ibid*, 69-70.
[4] *Ibid*, 73.
[5] *Ibid*, 74.
[6] *Ibid* 75-76. Italics added.
[7] *Ibid*, 81.
[8] *Ibid.*
[9] *Ibid*, 83.

[10] *Ibid*, 87-89.

[11] *Ibid*, 91.

[12] *Ibid*, 93.

[13] *Ibid*, 94.

[14] *Ibid*, 107.

[15] *Ibid*, 108.

[16] *Ibid,* 108-09.

[17] Knox, *Death March*, 462-63.

[18] *Ibid,* 475.

[19] Family members told me on 12 May 2002 that General Trapnell suffered nightmares all his life. One would never have guessed that such a taciturn and disciplined man such as Trapnell would still be dealing with nightmares from World War II late into his nineties.

[20] *Diary*, 113.

[21] *Ibid,* 116.

[22] *Ibid,* 117.

[23] *Ibid.*

[24] *Ibid.*

[25] *Ibid,* 125.

[26] *Ibid,* 127.

[27] *Ibid,* 129.

[28] *Ibid.*

[29] *Ibid,* 135.

[30] *Ibid,* 137. Susan Louise Fleeger was his wife's full name.

[31] *Ibid,* 139.

[32] *Ibid,* 140.

[33] *Ibid.*

[34] *Ibid,* 141.

[35] *Ibid,* 142.

[36] *Ibid,* 143.

[37] *Ibid,* 147.

[38] *Ibid,* 148.

[39] *Ibid.*

[40] *Ibid,* 149.

[41] *Ibid,* 150.

[42] *Ibid,* 151-52.

[43] *Ibid,* 156-57.

[44] *Ibid,* 160.

[45] *Ibid,* 160-61.

[46] *Ibid,* 162.

[47] *Ibid,* 163.

[48] Caraccilo, *Surviving Bataan and Beyond,* 181 (raid) and 182 (movement). Personal knowledge.

[49] Personal knowledge. *Diary,* 163.

[50] *Diary,* 163-64.

[51] *Ibid,* 164.

[52] *Ibid,* 74-75.

[53] *Ibid,* 84.

[54] *Ibid,* 114.

[55] *Ibid,* 151, 25 April.

Eight

"It was rough –
I was a survivor"

Row of Unknowns, Manila Cemetery

On Memorial Day 1943, about a year after he entered Cabanatuan, Fleeger wrote: "Service at the prison camp cemetery. 1500 prisoners allowed to attend. Japanese Major presented a wreath – the camp improvised a small wreath. Prayers in Hebrew, Latin, English, - choir – about 3000 dead. About 1600 died at O'Donnell prison camp – we were there April-May 1942. Of the total of 20,000 American prisoners between [one third and one half] are now dead. Of our group which surrendered Bataan almost 70% died – most as a result of prison march out of Bataan. It was rough – I was a survivor....[1]

Fleeger's overestimated the loss of the 26th Cavalry - "our group" - at seventy-percent at this time, but he would be correct after more cavalry officers perished on the POW ships in 1944 and 1945 and in Japan.

POW Casualties, 26th Cavalry

Fleeger reported the deaths of Captain David Miller and First Lieutenants Stephen Chamberlin and William Ward in 1942. As mentioned earlier, the Japanese bayoneted Miller to death on 16 April during the Death March. Miller had been on detached service as the Assistant Provost Marshal at I Philippine Corps. Chamberlin, the Assistant S-4 for the 26th Cavalry, and Ward, a platoon leader in Troop E, died in Cabanatuan on 14 June and 20 August 1942 respectively, most likely from malnutrition, disease, or abominable treatment in Camp O'Donnell. The Army awarded Chamberlain and Ward a Silver Star for gallantry in action. The deaths of the lieutenants highlighted the fact that many young officers, who should have been the strongest and healthiest of the officer POWs, died early during imprisonment. The Army did not award posthumous Purple Hearts to these officers.

POW Ship Casualties, 26th Cavalry

Many more cavalrymen perished at sea. With the imminent arrival of American forces in the Philippines, the Japanese decided in 1944 to evacuate most of the remaining POWs to Japan. They wanted the starved and diseased survivors who were still able to work to join the earlier POWs who worked as virtual slaves in mines and factories in Japan, Korea, and Manchuria. In addition, they wanted to remove the POW survivors from the grasp of the Americans when they returned to Luzon. Fourteen cavalry officers, including Fleeger, who had surrendered, survived the Death March, Camp O'Donnell, and imprisonment in Cabanatuan, died on three unmarked POW ships that sailed for Formosa and one that sailed to Japan.

Arisan Maru

In October, the Japanese began moving POWS – including Fleeger and some of his officer and enlisted friends - from Cabanatuan to Bilibid Prison in Manila. On the 11th of October, they crammed them and a total of 1,783 American POWs into the holds of the 6,886 ton cargo ship, the *Arisan Maru*. The POWs came from camps on Luzon and included civilians from several countries. Enlisted soldiers made up the bulk of the POWs. Many had served in the New Mexico coast artillery units. The Japanese planned to send about 600 of the POWs to the Kwantung Army in Manchuria.

The planned voyage began poorly. Large quantities of coal partially filled Hold #1 of the ship. Consequently, the POWs found little space to stand or sit in all the holds. Once the prisoners moved into the cargo holds, the heat became unbearable and the Japanese failed to provide drinking water to offset the heat. Several POWs died quickly from the heat. To make matters worse, in violation of international rules,[2] the Japanese did not mark the *Arisan Maru* as a POW ship.

Because of frequent American air raids on Manila, the Japanese loaded the ship quickly and sent it south toward the island of Palawan. It remained off the southern island while the Americans raided Manila from the 15th to the 18th, raids which preceded and supported the American invasion of Leyte on 20 October. On the day MacArthur returned to the Philippines, the *Arisan Maru* returned to Manila and became part of Japanese Convoy MATA-30, a convoy of eleven other cargo ships, a fleet supply ship, and three destroyers. MATA-30 sailed on the 21st, and the Japanese hoped that the ships would reach Takao on Formosa in three days. Unfortunately for the POWs, the convoy moved slowly because a torpedo had damaged one of the cargo ships and that ship and the *Arisan Maru* could make only seven knots.

Around dawn on 23 October, the escorting Japanese destroyers picked up radio signals from American submarines, and at about 0900 one of the destroyers picked up more signals. Unknowingly, MATA-30 had sailed into a concentration of nine American submarines that had deployed between Luzon and

UNKNOWINGLY, MATA-30 HAD SAILED INTO A CONCENTRATION OF NINE AMERICAN SUBMARINES...

Formosa because the submarine captains expected to find many Japanese targets in the area. Reacting to the radio signals, the Japanese immediately broke up their convoy and let the fastest ships sail for Takao without escort. The two destroyers stayed with the slower ships, but they would be unable to stop the resultant carnage. At 1730 on 23 October, the nine lurking American submarine skippers began their attacks on the slow cargo ships. The USS *Sawfish* made the first kill when the boat torpedoed the previously damaged *Kimikawa Maru.* The Japanese ship sank in less than three minutes. Another submarine fired a dud torpedo into the *No. 1 Shinsei Maru* about midnight and slowed her down. Covered by darkness, the USS *Snook* torpedoed the *Kokuryu Maru* around 0100 on the 24th, at 0315, the *Snook* sank the *Kikusui Maru,* and then at 0605 she sank the *Tenshin Maru,* bringing the total sinkings to four. As morning dawned, after over twelve hours of attacks, the USS *Drum* added a fifth sinking, torpedoing the *Shikisan Maru* at 0758. Then at 1100, the USS *Seadragon* blew up the *Taitan Maru,* and at 1225 *Seadragon* finished off the *No. 1 Shinsei Maru.* With seven ships destroyed, the Americans continued their attacks. At 1405, *Seadragon* sank the *Eiko Maru* which just had completed rescuing some of the crew and passengers from the *No. 1 Shinsei Maru.* With eight ships sunk and one damaged, the remaining ships scattered. The *Arisan Maru* with the two escorts became a prime target.

...ONE TORPEDO HIT THE STERN OF THE *ARISAN MARU,* FATALLY DAMAGING THE SHIP.

At 1750 on the 24th, about twenty-four hours after the first attack by *Sawfish,* Commander E. A. Blakely in USS *Shark II,* spotted the POW freighter and her escorts and fired his torpedoes. Two hit the empty number three hold on the starboard side and one torpedo hit the stern of the *Arisan Maru,* fatally damaging the ship. As the cargo ship started to sink, the two Japanese destroyers closed in on *Shark II's* position and one dropped seventeen depth charges and then returned and dropped more. *Shark II* disappeared with all hands.[3]

Aboard the *Arisan Maru,* according to survivors, hundreds died from the initial explosions, but the surviving POWs did not panic, and the ship sank slowly. Sergeant Calvin Graef, 200th Coast Artillery, had gone topside on cooking duty when the torpedoes hit. Guards forced him below and shut the hatch behind him. He reported that "There wasn't any hysteria, in fact, if anything it was more or less that if the ship were sunk, it could be that some people would get out and that would be better than what we had been going through." Corporal Donald L. Meyer who was in the forward hold with about 600 men crawled out after the guards had left. After POWs lowered a rope to those remaining below and others got out, "Meyer found a canteen of water, threw some planks overboard, and slid down a cable into the ocean." As the POWs came topside, they found that most of the Japanese had left. Some POWs "took out their frustrations on any Japanese they could find." Graef killed one. He said that no Japanese guard got off the ship alive.

The POWs also saw that the Japanese on one of the destroyers had beaten off about thirty-five survivors who had swum toward the destroyer seeking to be rescued. Likewise, Japanese on a nearby lifeboat clubbed Robert S. Overbeck, a civilian, back into the water. Overbeck had gone into the ocean from a hole in the ship's side and had swum to the lifeboat. Seeing such incidents, many POWs chose to stay aboard even though by this time the ship had broken in two. Strangely, both halves floated.

On the ship, many POWs headed for the galley before looking for life preservers and chowed down on sugar and ketchup. Some smoked two cigarettes at a time. Private Anton (Tony) Cichy of the 194th Tank Battalion scoffed up food and water before looking for a life preserver. Many of the POWs could not swim and there were insufficient life preservers for them. Many others just gave up as their last trauma unfolded.

AS WATER COVERED THE DECK OF THE ARISAN MARU, THOSE WHO STAYED ABOARD WENT DOWN WITH THE SHIP.

As water covered the deck of the *Arisan Maru*, those who stayed aboard went down with the ship. Those who stepped into the icy sea faced fifteen foot waves, remnants of recent storms. Many hundreds in the sea died the first night. The frail and weak drowned. Soon few swimmers or floaters remained. Some of the survivors drank sea water and went crazy. Others died of thirst. After a few days, only nine survived.

ΩΩΩ

By a stroke of good luck, Overbeck found an abandoned lifeboat with some fresh water in it. Eventually, four other POWs wound up on his boat – Cichy, Graef, Meyer, and Private Avery E. Wilbur. After raising a mast, they traveled about 300 miles west toward the China coast. Some Chinese sailing a junk found them up and steered them to a safe area on the China coast. From there the five Americans made their way through Japanese lines and reached an American outpost. Their incredible story ended when they flew to Washington, DC and freedom.[4]

A Japanese destroyer picked up two other Americans, Sergeant Philip Brodsky and Corporal Glenn Oliver, four days after the *Arisan Maru* sank. According to one source,[5] the two had initially found hatch covers to hold on to, but eventually found empty rafts and climbed aboard them. Without food or water during the time, both men thought about possibly eating a corpse if they found one. They agreed, finally, that they "wouldn't shove the other over and eat him." Aboard the destroyer, the Japanese interrogated the two men repeatedly believing them to be survivors from a sunken submarine. After many trying hours, the Americans found themselves on Formosa where the Japanese imprisoned them once again" and questioned them some more.[6] On Formosa, Brodsky and Oliver met two other survivors: Navy Boatswain Martin Binder from the sunken sub-tender, *Canopus*, and Private Charles Hughes. Hughes died on Formosa, leaving only eight POW survivors of the *Arisan Maru*.[7]

ΩΩΩ

No one knows how Major Fleeger and the three other cavalry officers – Major Paul Jones, Captain James Seay, and Lieutenant William Leisenring – died.

Fleeger's good friend Jones, another redhead, had been the Regimental S-2 when Fleeger was the Regimental Adjutant, and he took Fleeger's job when Fleeger took command of the 1st Squadron. Jones had earned a Silver Star, Bronze Star, and Purple Heart in combat.[8] Jones was born in Tennessee and had been educated there and in Alabama before he entered the Military Academy. And while still in secondary school, at age fifteen, he had joined the Tennessee National Guard and performed strike duty service as a private and a non-com.

CAVALRY OFFICER CASUALTIES

MAJ HARRY FLEEGER

MAJ PAUL JONES

CPT JAMES SEAY

LT WILLIAM LEISENRING

"Red" became a conscientious cadet and chose to be commissioned in the cavalry when he graduated. Assigned first to 6th Cavalry at Ft. Oglethorpe, he soon became the Regimental Signal Officer and later assumed command of Troop F. After attending the Cavalry School, Jones joined the 5th Cavalry at Ft. Clark, TX and "participated in the Louisiana Maneuvers in the summer of 1940." During this period, Jones served as the aide-de-camp to Brigadier General Jonathan Wainwright, the commander of the 1st Brigade of the 1st Cavalry Division, and in September sailed with the General to the Philippines. On arrival, Jones joined the 26th Cavalry. According to one source, Jones "worked so hard during the long Department maneuvers in Bataan in January that his commanding officer on more than one occasion had to give him a direct order to rest, and in one instance was so exhausted that he slept 19 hours straight." Reportedly, "the hardest working member of a regiment which abounded in hard-working officers," Jones "was given C Troop to organize and train up to the high Scout standards of the remainder of the regiment." When war began, the Colonel Pierce detached him to be the Headquarters Commandant of North Luzon Force and "instructed him to organize the enlisted component of General Wainwright's headquarters from the trained communications and other personnel of Headquarters and Headquarters and Service Troop, 26th Cavalry." Jones accomplished his mission. "After selecting key men from all sections of Regimental Headquarters and the Communications Platoon, he merged them. And with those few special-ists already assigned to the North Luzon Force Headquarters and such men as the Chief of Staff was able to obtain from other units the nucleus was formed of what was to be-come not only North Luzon Force Headquarters but eventually Headquarters I Philippine Corps." When Jones returned to the 26th Cavalry, he joined the staff once again as the Regimental Intelligence Officer and served as the Commander of Headquarters Troop. As mentioned, Jones did not surrender. After capturing him, the Japanese sent him to Ca-banatuan, and shortly thereafter, they shipped the still-sick Jones to the POW Camp on Davao. They returned Paul Jones to Cabanatuan in 1944. He had regained most of his health by the time the Japanese shipped him out with Fleeger on the *Arisan Maru*.[9]

Seay had been on detached service with the Philippine Army.[10]

Leisenring must have suffered a special hell if he survived the torpedo explosions. He had been a platoon leader in Fleeger's Troop A, had been sent to the Davao Penal Colony on Mindanao, and had survived the sinking of the POW ship *Shinyo Maru* off Mindanao in September. The *Shinyo Maru* carried POWs from the closed penal colony. Following their rescue, the Japanese returned the ship's POW survivors to Cabanatuan.[11] One can only imagine what went through Leisenring's mind during his second sinking. The lieute-nant earned a Silver Star for his combat service.

Lieutenant William Bowen of Troop C, whom Fleeger never listed as an officer in his regiment, perished with Fleeger and the other cavalry officers on the *Arisan Maru*. The *NARA Website* listed him as a regimental casualty. As mentioned earlier, Bowen had been awarded a DSC. He also had earned a Bronze Star.

> **WITH 1,674 DEATHS, THE SINKING OF THE *ARISAN MARU* BECAME THE GREATEST SEA DISASTER IN AMERICAN HISTORY.**

With 1,674 deaths, the sinking of the *Ari-san Maru* became the greatest sea disaster in American history. More POWs died in the East China Sea than passengers died on the *Titanic*. More POWs died than sailors died on the cruiser *Juneau* during the fight off Guadalcanal, and more POWs died than sailors died after a Japanese submarine torpe-doed the heavy cruiser USS *Indianapolis* at war's end.[12] The POW deaths were unneces-sary. The Japanese could have marked the *Arisan Maru* as a POW ship and could have asked the International Red Cross to notify the U. S. Government of her sailing and re-quested safe passage. While such action might not have guaranteed a safe passage, it could have. But the Japanese took no such action. Moreover, the Japanese made no at-tempt to rescue the POWs, and consequently hundreds of POWs perished in the cold, stormy, and dangerous East China Sea at the hands of their own countrymen. The United States awarded posthumous Purple Hearts to virtually all of the victims and memorialized them on the *Tablets of the Missing* in the Manila Cemetery.

Fleeger had been right to "fear a trip north."[13]

Oryoku Maru

Others in Cabanatuan should have feared such a trip also because many of them would not survive their trip north. Following the sinking of the *Arisan Maru*, the Japanese decided to ship most of the remaining "able-bodied" POWs in Cabanatuan and Bilibid to Japan. Many were Fleeger's friends. The Japanese left behind the sickest prisoners or those being punished for disciplinary infractions. They became the fortunate ones.

Unlike the POWs who shipped out on the *Arisan Maru*, officers – about 1,000 in all - made up the bulk of the group sent out on the *Oryoku Maru*. On 13 December, the Japanese loaded 1,589 Americans and thirty non-Americans onto the 7,362 ton ship. They also loaded 1,500 Japanese troops, 547 Japanese women and children, and 1,127 crewmen and passengers from other destroyed Japanese vessels on the small cargo ship. The Japanese also loaded aboard General MacArthur's Packard automobile and the ashes of 728 Japanese war dead.[14]

The Japanese placed 600 POWs in the first hold, 200 in the second, and 800 in the third, aft hold. The conditions became ghastly as they had on the *Arisan Maru*. After the

THAT NIGHT MEN REACHED THE LIMITS OF THEIR ENDURANCE. SOME WENT MAD. ... SOME OF THEM DRANK HUMAN BLOOD TO QUENCH THEIR THIRST.

ship left Pier 7, it anchored in the harbor. Soon temperatures in the holds of the stationary ship reached 120 degrees. Overheated men cried out for water. The Japanese provided none, and when the yelling did not cease they closed the hatches. As conditions below worsened, the Japanese interpreter threatened to shoot the POWs because they were disturbing the women and children. Finally, the Japanese permitted groups of four men at a time to move on to the deck, and in the early evening they sent a meal of "rice and seaweed" to the POWs.[15]

That night men reached the limits of their endurance. Some went mad. Some suffocated to death. Some trampled fellow POWs to death. A few killed others, and some of them drank human blood to quench their thirst. By dawn about fifty POWs had perished.

Filipinos knew about the POW ship and sent out reports to MacArthur's headquarters and to U. S. Navy carrier forces near the Philippines. POWs hoped that the information would prevent American attacks on the ship. However, once again, the Japanese did not mark the ship as a POW ship, and they even exchanged the number on the ship's funnel with another Japanese ship's number in order to confuse the Americans.

A few hours after the ship sailed from Manila Bay, American carrier planes from the new USS *Hornet* and the USS *Hancock* bombed and strafed the *Oryoku Maru* west of Bataan, killing and wounding over 300 Japanese sailors and merchant seamen as well as Japanese women and children. During the attack, flying metal fragments wounded about twenty POWs. After the attacks American POW doctors helped treat all the wounded. One report says that for their services, the Japanese beat doctors "as punishment for the air attack."[16] Another report said that the Japanese gave them each a glass of water.[17]

The Navy planes attacked the ship and others with it twice more that day and killed POWs as well as more Japanese. During these attacks, Lt. Colonel Trapnell, the assistant to the officer-in-charge in the aft hold, and another officer "stationed themselves on the exposed ladder leading to the deck in order to relay information of the action to the men below. Despite bullets, flying bomb fragments, and steel slivers striking all around the ladder they remained exposed during the attacks and by their calm words of encouragement and humorous comments, were successful in preventing panic from breaking out among the unnerved and exhausted prisoners of war."[18] Badly battered, the damaged *Oryoku Maru* limped slowly into Subic Bay. There, the crew offloaded the Japanese women and children but kept the POWs aboard.

The second night brought more horror to the men in the holds after discipline broke down completely. Yelling turned to screaming. POWs killed other POWs to keep them from killing their comrades. Some drank their own urine; others drank sewage. The POWs justly feared that

OTHER CAVALRY OFFICER CASUALTIES

ORYOKU MARU

MAJ JAMES BICKERTON
CPT WALTER BUBOLTZ

ENOURA MARU

CPT ROBERT BURLANDO
CPT DAVID COALE III
CPT JACK FORD
LTC WILLIAM VAN NOSTRAND
CPT (CHAP) MATHIAS ZERFAS

BRAZIL MARU

MAJ JAMES BLANNING
CPT WILLIAM CUMMINGS
CPT EDWIN LARAGAY, DC
CPT JOHN WHEELER

AFTER LANDING IN JAPAN

CPT ROBERT CARUSSO
CPT LELAND CRAMER
CPT CLAYTON MICKELSEN, VC
CPT FORREST RICHARDS

the Japanese had left them behind to be killed when the carrier planes returned.

On the 15th, planes from the *Hornet* hit the aft hold with at least one 500 pound bomb and six rockets. The Japanese interpreter finally told the POWs that they could leave the hold, but they would have to swim to the shore 300 yards away. When they reached the main deck, more Navy planes arrived, but after the American pilots realized that the white-skinned men who were desperately waving to them were not Japanese, they did not attack.

Most of the survivors swam to shore. Two were Fleeger's comrades from the 26th Cavalry. "Captain William E. Chandler...was in the rear hold. He was roused out of a stupor by the explosion of a bomb which seemed to have dropped right through the hatch opening. Dazed and shocked by the concussion, Chandler and other survivors crawled and dragged themselves to the deck. There Maj. Thomas J. H. Trapnell... gave Chandler sugar, helped him over the side, and swam with him for awhile. Chandler, semiconscious and swimming instinctively, later found himself on the sand – naked and exhausted."[19] Some POWs tarried and hunted for food. A Japanese officer killed at least one. Japanese crewmen shot others who they thought were trying to escape. Then on shore, Japanese machine gunners shot the POWs who strayed away from the main group of swimmers.

Once ashore, the Japanese placed the 1,333 survivors into an enclosed tennis court and kept them there without food or water until the 20th and 21st. More POWs died from the extreme heat and from cold at night. The Japanese then trucked the survivors to a jail and movie house in San Fernando, the railroad terminus of the Death March. While there the Japanese removed and bayoneted and beheaded fifteen of the sickest POWs. Finally, the Japanese moved remaining POWs to Lingayen Gulf. After spending two days on the beach, 1,070 POWs embarked on the *Enoura Maru* and 236 embarked on the *Brazil Maru* and sailed for Formosa. Twenty-one died en route.

Two of Fleeger's comrades from the 26th Cavalry, Major James Bickerton and Captain Walter Buboltz, died on the *Oryoku Maru* on 15 December. Bickerton had been on detached service at the time of surrender and Fleeger had reported him missing. He actually was fighting on the island of Iloilo around 16 April. A short report said: "Jap scouting parties coming ashore under the cover of darkness surprised and captured the outpost, cut telephone wires and generally paved the way for the

...MAJOR JAMES BICKERTON AND CAPTAIN WALTER BUBOLTZ, DIED ON THE ORYOKU MARU ON 15 DECEMBER.

pre-dawn landing of assault troops. Strong flanking parties reaching north and east seriously threatened the line of retreat of one Philippine Army battalion under Major Bickerton, defending Iloilo [City]. After dark that night however, having held their delaying positions according to plan sufficiently long for all demolitions to be executed, most of the battalion withdrew toward the mountains, and reached the regimental security area...in safety."[20] After his surrender, the Japanese imprisoned Bickerton on Mindanao. In September 1944 with Lieutenant Leisenring, he had survived the sinking of the *Shinyo Maru.* No one knows how Bickerton, who entered the Army from Illinois, and Buboltz, who had entered from Wisconsin, died. They may have been killed during the bombing of the rear hold, died of wounds from the bombing, or have been killed by the Japanese guards.[21] Buboltz, the Regimental S-4, had won two Silver Stars during combat.[22]

Enoura Maru

The two POW ships arrived safely in Takao Harbor, Formosa. Once there, the Japanese kept the prisoners locked in their holds. Men continued to die on both ships. On 6 January 1945, while the huge American invasion fleet headed for Lingayen Gulf on Luzon, the Japanese moved the POWs from the *Brazil Maru* to the *Enoura Maru.* The next day, they removed thirty-seven British and Dutch POWs who had survived another POW ship sinking and took them ashore. Their fate is not known. On the 8th, the Japanese loaded sugar aboard *Enoura Maru.* Hungry POWs immediately stole some of the precious food.

U. S. Navy pilots struck ships in Takao Harbor on 9 January. One of their bombs detonated near the forward hold of the *Enoura Maru* and killed at least three hun-

U. S. NAVY PILOTS STRUCK SHIPS IN TAKAO HARBOR ON 9 JANUARY.

dred POWs. The explosion also dropped a hatch cover into hold number two and killed several more men. The Japanese offered no medical aid for the wounded and prevented the removal of the dead from the holds for three days. Finally on 12 January, they removed about four hundred bodies and according to first reports burned them.[23] Apparently, however, the Japanese buried them because U. S. authorities exhumed the bodies many years later and buried them in several mass graves at the Punchbowl Cemetery in Honolulu.[24]

ΩΩΩ

Five 26th Cavalry officers - Burlando, Coale, Ford, Van Nostrand, and Zerfas - died as a result of the attack on the second POW ship. Captain David Coale, III had survived the earlier sinking of the *Shinyo Maru* off of Mindanao. Originally from Headquarters Troop, he perished on 9 January. He had been detached for duty with the Philippine Army dur-

WILLIAM VAN NOSTRAND ..."WAS HIT BY A BOMB FRAGMENT AND APPARENTLY DIED OF INTERNAL BLEEDING."

"FATHER ZERFAS KNEW THAT HE WAS GOING TO DIE. HE WAS READY TO GO. HE TOLD ME HE WAS READY AND WANTED TO DIE — THAT HE HAD SEEN ALL OF THIS WORLD AND ITS DEGRADATION...THAT HE WANTED..."

ing the war and had been sent to the Davao Penal Colony. Coale previously had been decorated with a Bronze Star.[25] Captain Jack Ford, the Commander of the Machine Gun Troop, died on the same day. So did William Van Nostrand who "was hit by a bomb fragment and apparently died of internal bleeding." A lieutenant colonel at the time of his death, he had been decorated with a Silver Star and a Bronze Star Medal with an Oak Leaf Cluster for combat service. As a cadet at West Point, Van Nostrand had been exceptional athlete in hockey and soccer, winning seven letters in the two sports.[26] His athleticism certainly helped him when he became an infantry officer and when he joined the mobilizing 61st Regiment of the 61st Division of the Philippine Army in September 1941 on the rugged islands of Panay and Leyte. Initially assigned as an instructor, he was given a command in the Philippine Army and promoted to major as war approached. As the Regimental Executive Officer of the 61st, he served on Negros and then on Mindanao.[27] On Mindanao, Van Nostrand transferred to and assumed command of the 81st Infantry Regiment on 4 April and he fought that unit well. An American commander there wrote that "Van Nostrand's 81st Infantry in the vicinity of Hijo, meanwhile having received a small increase in ammunition for the caliber .50 machine guns and 3-inch mortars, launched an attack against the Nip positions at Kilometer 62 north of Davao on 14 April. Fire was returned by both mortars and artillery pieces throughout the night, but without casualties to our forces." He was still fighting on 10 May after the order to surrender had been published. Van Nostrand survived a punishing attack, successfully withdrew, and reportedly surrendered on 20 May.[28] The Japanese imprisoned him in the Davao Penal Colony until June 1944 when he was transferred to Cabanatuan. Van Nostrand received a posthumous promotion to full colonel, but there is no explanation for the promotion. While the Army promoted some surviving officers one grade after their liberation, it generally did not promote other officers who died as POWs the one grade. The West Pointer was thirty-four at his death. [29]

Captain Mathias Zerfas, whom Fleeger listed as the Chaplain of the 26th Cavalry, nearly missed the trip north. The Japanese kept Zerfas in Cabanatuan when they moved the 1,000 POW officers to Bilibid before embarking them on the *Oryoku Maru*. Apparently, they moved him to the POW ship at the last minute. Officially, Zerfas died on 9 January, but Chaplain John Duffy reported a later date. Duffy wrote: "Father Matt had his left leg practically blown off at the knee. He was in great agony and shock. After administering the sacraments to him, with the help of a couple of others I moved him to a clearing where I covered him with the rags we salvaged from the dead to try and warm him as he was chilled and shaking badly. Father Zerfas knew that he was going to die. He was ready to go. He told me he was ready and wanted to die – that he had seen all of this world and its degradation that he wanted and he asked me someday to look up his father if I should ever get back to the States and tell him he had died like a man. Father Zerfas died about dusk on the evening of January 11, 1945, and we had to put him over with the other cadavers. On the 13th, the dead were taken from this hold and buried in a common grave on the beaches of Takao Bay, Formosa."[30] Zerfas, who was born in Wisconsin, had become a priest in 1934, served in the Civilian Conservation Corps during the Depression, and had deployed to the Philippines in April 1941, was thirty-six when he died. Ten other chaplains died en route to Japan.[31]

Days later, Captain Oliver Orson wrote that Robert Burlando, who Fleeger had reported to have been on detached service with the Philippine Army, was "sick and fading" and then "They kept dying: Major Burlando [and others] – diarrhea, malaria, despair, pneumonia, and infection were taking them. Some just gave up."[32] His death on the 9th probably was unnecessary. Rudimentary medical help might have saved Burlando's life and the lives of other wounded survivors. Burlando was from Dorchester, MA. The young cavalryman had fought well as an infantry officer on Mindanao, to wit: "In the early afternoon of the 7th, Captain R. C. Burlando with one rifle company and a section of caliber .30 machine guns was ordered ... to Sankanan to establish an outpost. Just at daylight the following day Burlando's outpost began taking heavy machine gun fire from the west. When ten truck loads of Japanese started de-trucking

RUDIMENTARY MEDICAL HELP MIGHT HAVE SAVED BURLANDO'S LIFE AND THE LIVES OF OTHER WOUNDED SURVIVORS.

about 500 yards to northwest of Sankanan on the Tankulan-Sankanan road, Burlando decided to withdraw across the gorge to the southeast of the barrio and join forces with

Lieutenant Weiland's command, which already occupied a position on the east rim of the canyon. During the withdrawal Burlando lost two of his platoons via the "buckwheat" route, one machine gun destroyed by a direct hit from a Nip mortar and another captured. Burlando and Weiland, reinforced by a section of mortars, stubbornly contested the Jap thrust."[33] On the 9th, Japanese snipers who had infiltrated between the Philippine Army units fired from the rear of Burlando's battalion. The captain immediately "sent out patrols and was successful in silencing the snipers." But the action proved futile because the next afternoon his regiment surrendered.[34] Burlando's cavalry training obviously had paid off because he performed similarly to the 26th Cavalry during its fighting withdrawal from Lingayen Gulf in 1941.

Brazil Maru

On 13 January 1945, the Japanese transferred 900 or so survivors of the *Enoura Maru,* including several cavalry officers, to the *Brazil Maru.* Fifteen more POWs died that night from unknown causes. The next day, the ship sailed with the *Melbourne Maru* - with 500 other prisoners embarked - and other ships and headed slowly north along the China Coast to the Yellow Sea and then to Korea. As the ships sailed north, the scantily clad POWs faced a new danger: biting, cold weather. On the 22nd it snowed all night. Two days later it snowed again and remained bitterly cold. On the 26th, one POW reported that it was "Coooold! Many have died! There were only three chaplains alive of twenty-three starting the trip. The medical service had completely evaporated." Only one medic remained on his feet.[35] Forty men died on the 27th and by the time that the *Brazil Maru* docked at Moji, Japan on 29 January, only 450 men – about half of the 900 who had boarded sixteen days earlier - still lived. The *Brazil Maru* turned out to be the deadliest of the last three POW ships: more POWs had died from malnutrition, disease, and cold on it than from the American attacks on either the *Oryoku Maru* or *Enoura Maru.* In comparison, only one man died on the *Melbourne Maru.* As on the

...ON 29 JANUARY, ONLY 450 MEN – ABOUT HALF OF THE 900 WHO HAD BOARDED SIXTEEN DAYS EARLIER – STILL LIVED.

Death March, position often meant everything.

Four more cavalry officers perished on the trip to Japan. Captain William Cummings who had been on detached duty with the Philippine Army (he is shown as a member of the 53rd Infantry Regiment of the 51st Philippine Infantry Division on the *Tablets of the Missing)* died on 21 January. Cummings earned a Bronze Star. Another William Cummings, "Father" Cummings, died on the ship. The priest had inspired so many, especially on the *Brazil Maru,* when many had given up hope, some had turned to stealing, and survival of the fittest began to reign. Cummings prayed and performed last rites. Reports said that the priest died while being held aloft and saying the Lord's Prayer.[36] Captain Edwin Laragay, the Regimental Dental Officer, died on the 23rd. The doctor, who had entered the army from New Jersey, won a Silver Star, a remarkable achievement for a dental officer. Major James Blanning, Fleeger's classmate, brother squadron commander, and *bahay* mate, perished two days later of "malnutrition and exposure." Whether he died of cold in one of holds or whether the Japanese placed him on deck to die is not known. Blanning's loss was tragic because he had been instrumental in saving a sick POW on the *Oryoku Maru.* He encouraged the weak comrade to go over the side and told him "You swim as long as you can and when you can't swim any longer, stretch out in the water and stiffen your body...I'll come up behind you and shove you by your feet. When you are rested enough, continue under your own power. We'll repeat this routine until we both get ashore."[37] Both made it while the Japanese fired randomly at the POWs swimming slowly to shore. The former Details Officer of Group 1 and Group 2 was thirty-six.[38] Heroic Captain Wheeler – he had earned a DSC, Silver Star, Bronze Star, and Purple Heart for his combat actions against the Japanese – died on the next day. As reported earlier, he had lived with Fleeger at Ft. Stotsenburg before war started, and he commanded Troop E before the Japanese decimated it.

The Japanese threw all the dead into the sea.

Japan

Deaths did not stop when the *Brazil Maru* reached Japan. Cavalry Captain Forrest Richards, who had been captured while serving with the Philippine Army, died on 30 January at the Moji Hospital, and Captain Leland Cramer, formerly the Commander of Troop A, died in the Kokura POW Camp just five days later.[39] There were no cavalry officers with Richards, but cavalrymen Chandler, Fowler, and Trapnell were in the camp with Cramer, and hopefully were with him when he died. The same day, the heroic veterinarian, Captain Mickelsen, died in the Fukuoka #1 Camp.[40] Captain Orson, a fellow veterinarian, reported that after getting into camp the Japanese sent the filthy prisoners to the bathhouse "where there were huge vats of hot water, sufficient for ten men at a time." He wrote: "Lt

"LT FRANK AND I CARRIED CAPTAIN MICKELSON DOWN FOR HIS BATH AND BACK. I THINK IT WAS TOO MUCH. WITHIN A WEEK HE WAS DEAD FROM PNEUMONIA."

Frank and I carried Captain Mickelson down for his bath and back. I think it was too much. Within a week he was dead from pneumonia."[41] The loss had to have been tough on Orson because he deployed to Manila with Mickelsen in May 1941 along with eleven other veterinary officers. To make it even tougher, he witnessed the death of four brother veterinary officers during the trip to Japan or as a result of it. The next day, First Lieutenant Robert Carusso, who had been on detached service to the Provost Marshal's section of I Philippine Corps and apparently had been reassigned to the 808th Military Police Company, died in Moji Hospital. No cavalry comrades were with Mickelsen or Carusso.[42]

The Army awarded posthumous Purple Hearts to all the officers of the 26th Cavalry who perished at sea.

ΩΩΩ

The Army recovered and identified the remains of the some of the Filipino POWs who died on Luzon and buried them in the American Cemetery in Manila. The Army, unfortunately, only recovered, identified, and buried the remains of three cavalry officer POWs in the cemetery: Captain Robert Carusso and Lieutenants William Ward and Arthur Furagganan. Carusso's burial is surprising because he died in Japan. Most likely his ashes rather than his body were buried in Manila. Ward, as mentioned, perished in Cabanatuan, and the Japanese executed Furagganan. There is no information about where the remains, if any, of Captain David Miller and Lieutenant Stephen Chamberlin were buried. They may be among the many unknowns buried in the cemetery. The Japanese buried the cremated remains of one officer POW - Captain Forrest Richards - in charnel (combined with others) at Moji. There is also no information about the remains of Captain Leland Cramer who died in Korea.

The United States memorialized Fleeger and the cavalry officers who died on the POW ships or in Japan and Korea – except Mickelsen and Cramer - on the giant *Tablets of the Missing and Buried at Sea* at the cemetery (Appendices I and K).

Disappeared into the Sea

For the cavalry survivors, the loss of so many of their comrades in the POW ships must have shocked and numbed them. While they could have anticipated heavy casualties in combat against a larger, more modern force, they could not have suspected that they would lose so many friends as a result of the American attacks on unmarked Japanese POW ships and from terrible treatment by the Japanese in the POW camps. With all the casualties, the Japanese decimated the officer leaders of the last U. S. cavalry regiment to fight on horseback. Whatever glory the cavalrymen had earned on land in 1941 and 1942 disappeared into the sea in 1944 and 1945.

Notes

1 *Diary*, 95.

2 Gladwin, "American POWs on Japanese Ships Take a Voyage into Hell."

3 Most of the information about the *Arisan Maru* came from Michno, *Hellships*, 249-52.

4 *Ibid*, See 257 (Binder); 253, 255-56 (Cichy); 252-53, 255 (Graef); 257, 252, 255 (Meyer); 254, 256-57 (Oliver); 253-56 (Overbeck); and 254-56 (Wilbur).

5 Michno, *Hellships*, 252-54 and 256-58 (Brodsky and Oliver).

6 Brodsky told a slightly different story in another source, Robert S. LaForte, Ronald E. Marcello, and Richard Himmel (Eds.), *With Only the Will to Live, Accounts of Americans in Japanese Prison Camps 1941-1945* (Wilmington, DE: SR Books, 1994), 103-105. He said that "...when the water came up to me us, I just floated off the ship and swam away." He did not mention covers or rafts. He did not mention his companion, Oliver, although he reported "We were afloat four days and four nights" and "we did see ships coming." He did not mention eating any dead or making any pact. He did not mention interrogation on the rescue ship, but he recalled interrogation by the Japanese *Kempei-tai* on Formosa: "I told the guy in charge that we were American prisoners of the Japanese on a ship that was sunk by Americans, and I was picked up by the ship that delivered us here. They didn't want to believe that. They thought we were sailors off of a submarine that they had sunk and then were picked up" (71). Brodsky was from New Jersey. He had served as a medic on Nichols Field and at Mariveles on Bataan. Unlike most of the POWs on the *Arisan Maru*, he spent most of his time on Palawan Island. After his rescue, he remained on Formosa. (viii).

7 Michno, *Hellships*, 257 (Binder) and 257 and 266 (Hughes).

8 Major Paul Montgomery Jones, Class of 1935, *1989 USMA Register*, #10367, 396. There is an interesting entry that reported that he earned a Purple Heart for Merit, an unusual award in 1941 and 1942. Jones had been wounded in North Luzon. *ABMC Website*.

9 Most of the biographical information came from "Obituary for Paul Montgomery Jones," 19-20. For information about his assignment to North Luzon Force, see Chandler, "26th Cavalry," *ACJ*, Mar-Apr, 11-12.

10 *ABMC Website*.

11 http://www.mansell.com/pow_resources/camplists/philippines/Davao_prime_roster, 6 of 11 (2/26/2006).

12 The primary source for information about the sinking of the *Arisan Maru* came from Michno, *Hellships*, 249-258 and 332 (footnotes 74-77).

13 *Diary*, 164.

14 Michno, *Hellships*, 260. Kerr, *Surrender*, 218 gives slightly different figures: 1,035 officers, 500 enlisted men, 47 civilians, and 37 British soldiers. His total is the same: 1,619.

15 Michno, *Hellships*, 258-62 covers the *Oryoku Maru*. So does Kerr, *Surrender*, 217-30. There are many other useful accounts.

16 Michno, *Hellships*, 260.

17 Kerr, *Surrender*, 222.

18 General Order No 400, U. S. Army Forces, Pacific, 15 December 1945. Award of Bronze Star Medal to Trapnell. Copy in *Cullum File #8071*.

19 Kerr, *Surrender,* 255.

20 Colonel H. W. Tarkington, *There Were Others*, (Unpublished manuscript, n.d.), 299. Copy in possession of author.

21 Michno, *Hellships*, 258-62.

22 *ABMC Website;* http://www.mansell.com/pow_resources/camplists/philippines/Davao_/davao prime_roster (2/26/2006).

23 Michno, *Hellships*, 263-65 covers the *Enoura Maru*. Michno reported that the Japanese set the bodies on fire, 264. See also, Kerr, *Surrender*, 231-234.

24 Conversation with Lt. Colonel John B. Lewis, U. S. Army-Retired, Houston, TX, 28 February 2008. Lewis reported the burials in the Punchbowl Cemetery.

[25] *ABMC Website* and http://www.mansell.com/pow_resources/camplists/philippines/Davao/ davao_prime_roster (2/26/2006).

[26] Chester L. Johnson, "The Memorials at Cabanatuan and the Tragedy They Record,' *Assembly Magazine*, June 1986, 36.

[27] "Obituary for William Starr Van Nostrand," *Assembly Magazine*, September 1978, 135.

[28] Tarkington, *There Were Others*, 246 and 400-1. Also, see pages 16, 176, and 309 for other items.

[29] Colonel (posthumous) William Starr Van Nostrand, Class of 1934, *1989 USMA Register*, #10105, 391 was a classmate of Joe Cleary. Also see *ABMC Website* and *Assembly Magazine*, September 1978, 135.

[30] Roper, *Brothers of Paul*, 286.

[31] Lt. (later Captain) Mathias A. Zerfas. See Keith, *Anguish*, 166. Keith mentioned Zerphas (sic Zerfas) often in his book; see: 93-94, 98, 100, 110, 117, and 144-47. The book centers on Captain Robert Preston Taylor, Chaplain, 31st U. S. Infantry Regiment, who was captured on Bataan. Keith included many stories about other chaplains. Also see the *ABMC Website*.

[32] Orson, "Service in the Far East," 19-20.

[33] Tarkington, *There Were Others*, 373.

[34] Betty B. Jones, *The December Ship, A Story of Lt. Col. Arden R. Boellner's Capture in the Philippines, Imprisonment, and Death on a World War II Japanese Hellship* (London: McFarland & Company, 1992), 63.

[35] Jacobs, *Blood Brothers*, 100.

[36] Kerr, *Surrender*, 236-7; Michno, *Hellships*, 265.

[37] Major General Chester Johnson, "The Memorials at Cabanatuan and The Tragedies They Record, Part II-The Hell Ships," *Assembly Magazine*, March 1987, 33.

[38] Major James Chester Blanning, Class of 1931, *1989 USMA Register*, #9135, 373 and *ABMC Website*. Blanning graduated one file higher than Fleeger. Major Calvin Ellsworth Chunn, *Of Rice and Men, The Story of Americans Under the Rising Sun* (no data), 51.

[39] "Roster of men from the *Brazil Maru* taken to Fukuoka #3, Kokura," http://people.tamu.edu/ ~jwerickson /POW/BMKk-3roster.html (2/25/2006).

[40] "Roster of men from the *Brazil Maru* taken to Fukuoka #1, Fukuoka," http://people.tamu.edu / ~jwerickson/POW/BMFk-1roster.html. Mickelsen is not listed on the *ABMC Website* or in any of the *NARA Website* listings.

[41] Orson, "Service in the Far East," 21.

[42] "Roster of men from the *Brazil Maru* taken to Moji Hospital," (Kokura Military Hospital) Kokura, Japan," http://people.tamu.edu/~jwerickson/POW/BMKHroster.html, (2/25/2006), and the *ABMC Website*.

Nine

"Chaplain Houden
died on detail"

Tablets of the Missing, Manila Cemetery

The forty-nine officers and thirty-five soldiers from other units that Fleeger mentioned or wrote about in his diaries also suffered heavy losses. They included his *bahay* mates, shooting squad mates, West Point classmates, various West Pointers, officers and men who worked in his kitchen, and the new friends he made in camp. Some died before October 1944, but most perished on the POW ships. (See Appendix P)

Battle Deaths

Three of his friends from other units fell in battle: Captain (actually Major) Sam Edward Jones, Major Floyd Pell, and Major Dudley Strickler.

Sam Jones, Fleeger's classmate from Kentucky, died in action on 23 January at Agloloma on Bataan. The thirty-six-year-old infantryman had served in the headquarters of the Philippine Department. While Fleeger knew about Jones' death[1] – he wrote in his diary that he would write his widow, Irene, after the war - apparently USAFFE did not, or could not, confirm it because the Army carried Jones as missing in action on its rolls during the war. Mostly likely, that meant "presumed dead" because the Army listed captured officers as "prisoners of war."[2]

"Slugger" Pell from Ogden, UT died during an air mission near Darwin, Australia. A transfer from the Cavalry to the Air Corps, the twenty-eight-year-old flyer served in the 33rd Fighter Squadron of the U. S. Far East Air Forces and won a DSC. Pell graduated from West Point in the Class of 1937. Fleeger noted his friend's death in his diary: "Killed – Australia – Slugger Pell – Aircorps."[3] His obituary described his death.

> *Pell was assigned to Nichols Field, P. I. at the time of his death. The Australian field to which he was temporarily attached while on combat duty was fired upon during the morning of February 19, 1942 by* [approximately 110] *Japanese bombers and fighters. According to a report of a fellow officer, Major Pell took off from the ground* [leading his flight of ten planes] *despite enemy planes strafing him.*
>
> *Before he was in the air, three enemy fighters were firing on him. He had the plane off the ground and made a heroic effort to defend the air base before he was shot down.*[4]

The "tall, thin, and wiry" Strickler, West Point 1927, commanding the 3rd Battalion, 45th Infantry (PS), died in action on Bataan on 8 February 1942.[5] An infantryman who had been an impressive athlete in basketball and track in college[6], a graduate of the regular course at the Cavalry School before deploying to the Philippines, and a "fine polo player," the major had taken his battalion into the Battle of Quinauan Point on the west coast of Bataan. General Wainwright described the action there: "The 3d Battalion went into action with a major, four captains, a full complement of lieutenants and 600 men.

When it was withdrawn twelve days later, after driving the Japs into the China Sea, it was commanded by a second lieutenant and its forces had been hacked down to 212 men. Every other officer and man was accounted for as having been buried or evacuated wounded. There were no stragglers. Its gallant Major Strickler – a heroic leader in the close-quarter fighting – was found on the front line of the battalion, a bullet through his helmet."[7]

"STRICKLER WAS NEVER SEEN AGAIN..."

Contrary to Wainwright's report, former Captain John Olson, the S-1 of the 57th Infantry (PS), reported that Strickler had become impatient with the lack of success in cracking the Japanese position after he had "pushed his men relentlessly, spending most of the daylight hours with the front line elements. In spite of his example and pressure, progress was measured in feet as the men crawled from the shelter of one tree to another, only to be pinned down for hours by fire from invisible subterranean hiding places." He added, "The major, exhausted and harassed after days and nights of unsuccessful trying, became infuriated. He arbitrarily ordered the platoon leader [from a reinforcing company from the 57th Infantry] to get his men to their feet to close with the enemy ... His impetuosity caused the deaths of [two Filipino Scouts] and the severe wounding of [two other Scouts, one of whom was awarded a DSC for his actions]." Olson concluded, "Strickler was never seen again. The next day an extensive, but fruitless search was made for him. The conclusion was that in the gathering twilight he had lost his bearings and had blundered into another portion of the Japanese line. It was not until February 6th that his body was recovered some twenty yards forward of the right platoon of the Third Battalion. He was lying face down toward the Japanese positions."[8]

Louis Morton reported a different final scene. After the Japanese stopped his reinforced battalion again on 1 February, Morton wrote that "Major Strickler went forward to the front lines to make a personal reconnaissance. He was last seen in the vicinity of Company B, 5th Infantry." He added: "After an intensive search during the day battalion headquarters regretfully reported that its commander was missing, presumably killed in action." According to Morton, the Americans recovered Strickler's body on 7 February.[9]

Strickler may have fought under the direct command of Wainwright or under the direct command of Brigadier General Pierce, formerly of the 26th Cavalry (PS), whom USAFFE had placed in command of the area.[10]

The Hoosier, decorated with two DSCs and a possible Bronze Star, died at age thirty-nine. With two DSCs, Strickler joined Praeger as a rare battlefield hero. He certainly fulfilled the plea from his college drinking song, "May we find a soldier's resting place beneath a soldier's blow, with room enough beside our graves for Benny Haven's, Oh!" While reports said that the Americans recovered his body, no remains were buried after the war in Manila Cemetery.

Murders

Fleeger also reported that four other friends, all senior field grade officers, perished shortly after the surrender on Bataan. The Japanese murdered two of them, Colonel Ralph Hirsch and Lt. Colonel John Ward, and most likely shot the other two.

Colonel Hirsch died on 13 April 1942 after he arrived at Camp O'Donnell. The Japanese seized him and several other officers and soldiers, beat them savagely, marched them off to a guardhouse, and killed them because the Americans apparently possessed something of Japanese origin - a fan, Japanese money, or a souvenir of some sort. No one learned what Hirsch's transgression was; no one ever saw him again. The former field artilleryman from Arkansas had served as the Ordnance Officer in the Headquarters of Luzon Force and received a Legion of Merit.[11]

THE JAPANESE MURDERED TWO OF THEM: COLONEL RALPH HIRSCH AND LT. COLONEL JOHN WARD...

"Tubby" Ward, a Quartermaster officer, graduated from West Point with the Class of 1920. He was one of the older officers Fleeger knew. Ward had joined the Army to be a "Captain of Cavalry," and he gained that rank in 1935 after serving in many cavalry units including the 26th Cavalry (PS) in 1928. While with the regiment, he had "planned and built a model barrio [town] for Filipino Soldier's families." The town "turned out so well that the General [n.d.] named it Wardville." An expert horseman, Ward became a star polo player. At the request of the Quartermaster General of the Army, Ward had accepted a detail with the Quartermaster Corps and in 1941 the Quartermaster General picked him to go to the Philippines to fulfill a request from General MacArthur "for five officers of superior rating and outstanding ability who were young enough for field duty." Ward arrived in the Philippines sixteen days before Pearl Harbor. Assigned to Ft. Stotsenburg, he organized an advanced Quartermaster Depot for Luzon.

...WARD DECIDED TO GO ON THE DEATH MARCH RATHER THAN REMAIN WITH THE WOUNDED IN THE HOSPITAL, A FATAL MISTAKE.

Wounded in action on 7 February 1942 on Bataan, the lieutenant colonel recuperated from his serious wounds until 14 March. About that time, General MacArthur offered Ward – who apparently wore a plaster body cast - a chance to serve on Corregidor, but he chose to remain on Bataan with his troops. Although he was not physically fit, Ward decided to go on the Death March rather than remain with the wounded in the hospital, a fatal mistake. On the march, he had trouble keeping up. An eyewitness reported his death: "They were on a narrow bridge; and as a truck was coming, they were told to move against the railing. Colonel Ward staggered against the railing. It gave way, and he fell in the shallow creek below. The Japanese guard shot once, but missed. He went down, picked him up, and bayoneted him [to death on 11 April 1942]" near the town of Limay. Buried with six others near Orion, the Army carried Ward as missing in action for the duration of the war. The 42 year-old Mississippian received two Purple Hearts. One report said that he received two decorations for gallantry in action, but that information cannot be confirmed.[12]

The two other senior officers perished in April. Lt. Colonel Ralph Garver, West Point 1925, was killed on 14 April 1942 at Lubao during the Bataan Death March. Garver, born in Illinois, had entered West Point from the Army in San Antonio, TX, apparently deeply in love with a "lass way back home." "Tibbs" did well there, graduating "approximately within the first score [actually #21] in the class," and upon graduation he chose the cavalry as his branch of service. Before arriving in the Philippines, Garver had spent time with the ROTC unit at Millikan University in Illinois. An Adjutant General when war broke out, Garver was serving in the Headquarters of the Philippine Department or as an Adjutant General in the Philippine Army. The former cavalryman from Illinois died at age forty-one.[13] The War Department reported that the Japanese killed him in a POW camp. An unidentified American general reported that the Japanese killed him at Lubao on Bataan and that he was buried on Luzon. His wife, who tried to find out how and where he died, wrote in a letter in February 1946 that: "There are several conflicting stories, the two most likely are that he dropped out of the March because of fatigue and was shot and that he dropped out because of malaria and was bayoneted."[14]

TREASON

"THE MOST SERIOUS CHARGES AGAINST AN EX-POW AFTER WORLD WAR II WERE MADE AGAINST JOHN D. PROVOO.

IN OCTOBER 1952 THE U. S. GOVERNMENT ACCUSED HIM OF TREASONABLE ACTS WHICH INCLUDED OFFERING HIS SERVICES TO THE JAPANESE ARMY AFTER THE CAPTURE OF CORREGIDOR, HELPING TO CAUSE THE EXECUTION OF CAPTAIN THOMPSON ON THE ISLAND, AND PARTICIPATING IN WARTIME JAPANESE PROPAGANDA BROADCASTS."

JOHN A. GLUSMAN

Garver's son and grandson followed him to West Point and both joined the Corps of Engineers. Son, Ralph, Class of 1952, retired as a colonel in 1979; Grandson, Ralph, Class of 1977, retired as a lieutenant colonel in 1999.[15]

The Japanese reportedly shot Lt. Colonel Alf Uddenberg, Wainwright's I Corps Adjutant General, on 20 April 1942. The Californian received a Bronze Star.[16]

The Army Register carried Hirsch, Garver, and Ward as missing in action in 1943, but did not list Uddenberg as missing, as a POW, or as a serving officer.[17]

The Army awarded posthumous Purple Hearts to Jones, Pell, Strickler, and the four senior officers. The American Government buried the remains of Garver and Ward in the American Cemetery in Manila and memorialized the other officers on the *Tablets of the Missing* in the cemetery. Ward is also memorialized in Cullum Hall at West Point.[18]

POW Camp Deaths

The Japanese executed one of Fleeger's friends - Captain Burton Thomson, Veterinary Corps - just after they seized Corregidor. Thomson served as the Mess Officer in Malinta Tunnel. American Sergeant John David Provoo, an instant collaborator, caused his death. Thomson had been able to stockpile food for the wounded and a young private had "found several cases of peaches and brought them out of the tunnel." Provoo asked a navy corpsman if Thomson could get some dessert for the Japanese officers. Reportedly, "Thomson told the corpsman that Provoo could go to hell." Provoo reported the situation to the enemy. Japanese soldiers soon appeared and seized Thomson, tried and sentenced him, and then drove him down to Monkey Point where the Japanese shot him five times in the head. Thomson had been a Veterinarian for the 26th Cavalry. Fleeger noted him as "Missing Since Corregidor, Lt B. Thompson, Vet from Stots."[19] The Japanese sycophant, Provoo, got off Scot free for his betrayal of Thomson. After being convicted of four counts of treason in 1953, a U. S. District Judge ruled that Provoo had not received a speedy trial and ordered him released.[20] Had the Army charged Provoo with treason immediately after the war and tried him by general court-martial, there is little doubt that a court-martial would have found him guilty, and the Army in 1945 would have executed Provoo for his inexcusable actions.

ΩΩΩ

Three of Fleeger's friends died in Cabanatuan in 1942: Captain Kenneth Griffiths, Lt. Colonel Thomas Horton, and Major Evert "Pop" Thomas. Some deaths were inevitable because all the POWs in Cabanatuan were in terrible shape in 1942, especially those captured on Bataan and imprisoned in Camp O'Donnell. Lester Tenney, Company B, 192nd Tank Battalion, highlighted the terrible condition of the Bataan POWs when he arrived in the camp after being on a work detail: "The men we saw walking around camp were living zombies, with their eyes sunken, heads bowed down, and their backs curved in defeat. Most were skin and bones, after losing fifty and sixty pounds from their normal weight...the healthy men walking around were captives from Corregidor."[21]

"THE MEN WE SAW WALKING AROUND CAMP WERE LIVING ZOMBIES, WITH THEIR EYES SUNKEN, HEADS BOWED DOWN, AND THEIR BACKS CURVED IN DEFEAT. MOST WERE SKIN AND BONES, AFTER LOSING FIFTY AND SIXTY POUNDS FROM THEIR NORMAL WEIGHT..."

Griffiths died of cerebral malaria in Cabanatuan on 22 August 1942. He had served with the 24th Field Artillery Regiment (PS) on Bataan. During the war the Army carried Griffiths as missing in action, but after the war it recovered the twenty-four-year-old Kansan's remains, buried them in Manila Cemetery, and awarded him a Purple Heart.[22] Fleeger planned to write Anne Griffiths about her husband's death.[23] Horton, West Point 1926, died in Cabanatuan on 11 June 1943 at the age of thirty-nine. The Texan, commissioned an infantryman, had accepted a detail to the Quartermaster as Tubby Ward had done, and when war broke out he was serving as the Quartermaster of the Post of Manila. According to his obituary, "Tommy immediately volunteered for combat duty when war was declared. His request was granted and he and a group of officers from the headquarters formed a provisional cavalry squadron from the men and polo ponies at the stables near Nichols Field. He rode with Strickler and fought the Jap in the delaying action that ended, finally on Bataan." His memorialist added: "We do not know the details of Bataan...We know what Tommy would do in a game or in a war. Play it hard."[24]

There is more to Horton's story. Following the transfer of most of the American POWs from Camp O'Donnell to Cabanatuan, Camp O'Donnell became a "ghost camp" on 5 June 1942 and the bulk of the remaining POWs were sick. "As of the time of the departure of the last group there were 59 officers, 191 Non-Commissioned officers and 567 Privates First Class and Privates {in the hospital]. All were classified as patients. Many were on the verge of death."[25] Command of all these remaining 1,008 POWs[26] passed to Horton who "had been suffering from dysentery and malaria since before his arrival." His adjutant reported that he was so sick that he was unable to get "around the camp to observe what was going on." Moreover, "This handicap coupled with the adamant refusal of the Japanese Camp Commander to deal with him, forced Major Horton [he had been promoted to lieutenant colonel but did not know it] to rely on his staff to cope with the problems of the prisoners." The adjutant reported that after the transfer of Americans, the Japanese moved Filipinos into the American side of the camp, and this gave some of the Americans the chance to meet Filipino POWs and through them have "the chance to deal with the Filipino civilians on the outside...They had what was most needed, food and medicine."

...CAMP O'DONNELL BECAME A "GHOST CAMP" ON 5 JUNE 1942 AND THE BULK OF THE REMAINING POWs WERE SICK.

On 30 June, the advance party from General Hospital #1 on Bataan arrived in Camp. On 1 July, Horton met with the commander, and on 3 July the main body of the hospital staff arrived under the command of Colonel James Duckworth, MC.[27] On 5 July, all but 125 patients, some staff, and medical personnel departed for Cabanatuan. Tragically, two hundred and twenty-seven POWs had died during the short time Horton commanded the POWs in Camp O'Donnell.[28]

Years later, an angry enlisted POW who most probably knew nothing about Horton's wartime performance or his terrible health provided an ugly view of Horton. The soldier-turned-officer called Horton a "disgrace to West Point" because he reportedly had organized a Fourth of July meal in Camp O'Donnell and had used "powdered milk and sugar taken from the sick prisoners to the 'officer's mess' for the meal."[29]

As a quartermaster officer with purchasing connections to local merchants and as an officer with more funds than an enlisted soldier, Horton could have purchased the food on his own rather than using food taken from sick prisoners as charged. Trading went on in Camp O'Donnell as one officer reported: "I was entrusted with money collected from our barracks to buy canned food of any kind from the Filipinos...I would wade across the river, bargain with the Filipinos, throw the goodies back across the river where we carried them back into the barracks."[30] Moreover, the new hospital personnel in camp could have brought in additional rations since they had been well treated on Bataan. Perhaps Horton and his officers pooled their meager rations to celebrate their departure from Camp O'Donnell.

But perception can be reality, and obviously to the soldier, Horton had sinned mightily. And just as obviously, he either did not know more about Horton's background or he dismissed it as irrelevant or incorrect. We will never know Horton's side of the story.

"Pop" Thomas, Fleeger's "blood brother" and *bahay* mate, died of pellagra in November 1942. A friend, Thomas had provided *quan* to Fleeger on one occasion.[31] Thomas, a Coast Artillery Officer, had served as the Adjutant General for the Philippine Division.[32] Early in camp life, he had been the Details Officer of Group 1. His POW

> *...HOWDEN DID NOT HAVE TO DEPLOY WITH HIS REGIMENT, BUT CHOSE TO DO SO TO BE WITH HIS MEN...*

details cut weeds, dug latrines, moved houses, disposed of garbage, and performed other jobs such as driving trucks and operating pump houses. Harry Packard assisted Thomas until "Pop" stepped down because of his poor health. Major James Blanning, the Details Officer for Group 2, replaced Thomas.[33]

ΩΩΩ

Fleeger also noted that: "Chaplain Houden [sic] died on detail – Mindanao – Feb 43. Memorial service here." Chaplain Frederick Howden, Jr. actually died in the Davao Penal Colony on 22 November 1942 from pellagra and dysentery.[34] Twelve other POWs died in that POW camp. One of the "most respected" officers in the 200th Coast Artillery Regiment, the Chaplain, a son of the Episcopal Bishop of New Mexico, had graduated from Yale in 1925[35] and had returned to New Mexico to pursue his ministry. An older man, Howden did not have to deploy with his regiment, but chose to do so to be with his men, even though most of the soldiers were Roman Catholics. On Luzon, Howden became a friend of Fleeger's *bahay* mate, Father Braun, and asked Braun to celebrate Mass for the Catholics in the regiment. Like most of the chaplains, he moved among the troops during the fighting. Later on Bataan, the chaplain chose to stay with his unit after being offered a chance to leave for Australia. After the surrender, the chaplain wound up in Cabanatuan. In October 1942, the Japanese sent Howden to Davao Penal Colony with two friends, Father Braun and Father Herman Baumann, and during the trip Howden fell "gravely ill." Unbeknownst to his wife and family, he asked Braun and Baumann to baptize him into the Roman Catholic faith just before he died in Davao.[36]   After the war, his remains apparently were recovered and they were re-interred in Albuquerque, NM. Strangely, his marker shows just "1942" as the date of death.[37]

THE JAPANESE HAD IN FACT EXECUTED MAJOR HAROLD COYLE IN CEBU ON 17 APRIL 1942, A DAY AFTER THEY HAD CAPTURED THE FIELD ARTILLERYMEN.

These were four more needless deaths brought on by malnutrition and disease. Adequate food and medicine most likely would have prevented them. Horton, Thomas, and Howden received no known decorations.

The Army carried Horton on its rolls as missing in action but did not list Thomas and Howden.[38]

Fleeger also reported two early deaths on the island of Cebu, in the Central Philippines – the Visayas. He noted that "Ole" Olson died in Cebu. Olson cannot be positively identified in available records. On 30 November 1942, Fleeger noted that "Bud Coyle died – Cebu – write Paul Disney after the war."[39] The Japanese had in fact executed Major Harold Coyle in Cebu on 17 April 1942, a day after they had captured the field artillerymen. He had been born in New York and appointed to West Point from New Jersey just like his classmate, Tom Trapnell. Coyle was serving with Headquarters, U. S. Army Air Force Pacific at the time of his capture. Previously, he had commanded Battery F, 24th Field Artillery (PA) and had been with Cebu Force. Apparently, the Army did not confirm his death at the time because in 1943 it still carried Coyle as missing in action. The Americans never recovered his body and he is listed on the *Tablets of the Missing* in the Manila Cemetery. Coyle received a posthumous Purple Heart. He died at thirty-eight.[40]

Arisan Maru

Another of Fleeger's friends, Lt. Colonel Albert Svihra, died with him on the *Arisan Maru*. Fleeger had noted in December 1943 that he was a "blood brother" and noted his birthday and his address in Long Beach, California.[41] Svihra in his surviving diary talked about celebrating his daughter Betsy's birthday on December 1, (no year given) by hosting a coffee in the morning and "inviting Major Harry Fleeger, Major Gross, Major Blanning, and Captain "Pappy" Archer (64 years old, a veteran of the Spanish American and World War) to join me."[42] Svihra was an interesting man. His parents were from Czechoslovakia and immigrated to the United States in 1888 and 1890. His wife noted in a questionnaire that the Svihras "May be the first parents of Slovakian origin to have a son graduate of U.S.M.A."[43] After his graduation, Svihra served as a signal corps officer and then transferred to the Field Artillery. After serving as an Assistant Professor of Military Sciences at Yale and coaching the Yale Polo Team, he attended the University of Virginia and earned a law degree. Consequently the army assigned Svihra to the Judge Advocate General's Department in Washington and in 1940 sent him to the Philippines where he served as the Judge Advocate on General Wainwright's divisional staff at Fort McKinley. "On Bataan he had charge of security and sanitation, and of "trying" to secure food for his men. Captured on Corregidor, Svihra spent some time there and at Bilibid before he arrived in Cabanatuan.[44] In camp, he became the Camp Judge Advocate and from the tone of his diaries had a bit easier time of it than Fleeger. But one reflection in his diary was eerily reminiscent of Fleeger's self-evaluation of himself as a husband. The colonel wrote:

> *When I look back I see so many of my shortcomings that it makes me positively ashamed – the scolding, the nagging, fault-finding, the frowns and all the rest. What a fine example to set for the children! And when I was reminded of it, instead of doing something about it, what did I do? I wish I could forget but I can't – I flew into a rage – couldn't even exercise a little self control necessary to hold my tongue. But I only aggravated matters – all because I hated to admit I was wrong. Just wasn't big enough or grown up enough or maybe a mistaken sense of superiority – or perhaps inferiority is the better term. I just couldn't stand losing out for fear it would lessen your estimation and that of the children if I were to agree. I can see it much more clearly now. It just keeps getting worse and worse for me. And instead of raising your esteem and the children's it only lowered it. Well, I only hope I can be given the chance and can be spared to show you what I'm really like, and how different I can be – the kindness, the appreciation, the devotion of which you are deserving. I took no vows when we were married that can't be fulfilled the rest of my days and my vow on this anniversary is simply this – that henceforth, God willing, I'll be what a husband and father should be.[45]*

How many other POWs had similar reflections?

Svihra earned a posthumous Bronze Star for directing the movement of the rear echelon of the Philippine Division to Bataan and serving "as the Chairman of the Board of Review established to review convictions by general courts-martial." The Army, as with Fleeger, awarded him a posthumous Purple Heart, and promoted Svihra one grade to colonel.[46] He is memorialized on the *Tablets of the Missing* in the Manila Cemetery.

Fleeger's Soldiers

Nine of the young soldiers for whom Fleeger planned to write commendations to the Adjutant General of the Army died with Fleeger on the *Arisan Maru*: Private Arthur Bates, Technical Sergeant Charles Henderson, Private Jess House, Private First Class Billy Ka-

"FINE AMERICAN BOYS"

PVT ARTHUR BATES

TSG CHARLES HENDERSON

PVT JESS HOUSE

PFC BILLY KANALLY

PFC MANUEL MARQUEZ

CPL EMANUEL RADA

SGT JOHN REYNOLDS

PVT BERTRAM SANDOVAL

PVT WALTER STRUS

PVT REYNALDO TRUJILLO

nally, Private First Class Manuel Marquez, Corporal Emanuel Rada, Sergeant John Reynolds, Private Walter Strus, and Private Reynaldo Trujillo.[47] Besides these casualties, most of whom were coast artillerymen, another coast artillery soldier Fleeger planned to commend, Private Bertram (Bert) Sandoval, had died earlier when the Americans torpedoed the *Shinyo Maru* on 7 September 1944. Sandoval had served in Battery E of the 200th Coast Artillery.[48] Private Bates was the lone member of the U. S. Army Air Corps among the group. He had served with the 4th Chemical Company (Aviation), most probably as a ground crewman rather than as an air crewman. Bates had entered the service from Oklahoma.

Sergeant Henderson entered the Army from Ohio and had served with Headquarters Company, Philippine Department. Private House had served with Battery A of the 200th Coast Artillery Regiment. He entered the Army from New Mexico. Private Kanally also came from New Mexico. He had soldiered with the 515th Coast Artillery. Private First Class Marquez had served with House in Battery A, 200th Coast Artillery. He, too, entered the service from New Mexico. Corporal Rada, who entered the service from Wisconsin, had served in the Harbor Defense of Manila, in Battery C, 59th Coast Artillery. Rada, and as mentioned before, served as Fleeger's orderly. Fleeger noted that the corporal after getting new Red Cross shoes in December 1943 said, "it's O.K. – but "I want to go home." He also wrote Rada's name and address down so that he could send "messages or gifts" to him c/o Mrs. Mary Muzacko, Route 2, Box 72, Lodi, Wisconsin on his birthday, 22 August.[49] Sergeant Reynolds, who hailed from Clovis, NM, had served with Battery E, 200th Coast Artillery. Fleeger considered Reynolds to be a "good soldier friend," and he noted that Reynolds had been sent out on a Japanese detail on 12 December 1942. Fleeger reported "Sgt Reynolds felt badly about leaving us." As with Rada, Fleeger added

Reynolds to his birthday list and showed his birthday as 17 November.[50]

Private Strus came from Michigan and served with Battery C of the 515th Coast Artillery Regiment. Private First Class Trujillo deployed to the Philippines with the 515th Coast Artillery. Fleeger admired young Trujillo, who came from Taos, NM and he described him as "a slight, dark boy – very bashful – wood carver by trade – with some talent." He reported that Trujillo's father was a Spaniard and his mother was an Indian, and that the soldier had lost all trace of them. Trujillo said to Fleeger one day in the mess: "Major, before the war officers used to scare me so bad that I didn't even want one to speak to me, and now look at me – I even say - Hey major - butts." Fleeger obviously became very fond of the soldier because he concluded his anecdote with: "I plan to have 'Ray' make us several pieces of carved mahogany furniture when we are back in the states. We will also dine with him at the Hotel Hilton, Albuquerque (where he was once a bellhop)." Apparently after his mess detail ended, Trujillo joined Reynolds on a Japanese detail. Fleeger, who considered Trujillo to be another good soldier friend, wrote: "On leaving, Ray told me that he had never known anyone so swell (me!)." Fleeger, however, did not put Trujillo on his birthday list.[51] Fleeger noted that he should write to Reynolds and Trujillo "when we are home again." He added that they and a Private Turner were "All fine American boys."[52]

> *TRUJILLO SAID TO FLEEGER ONE DAY IN THE MESS: "MAJOR, BEFORE THE WAR OFFICERS USED TO SCARE ME SO BAD THAT I DIDN'T EVEN WANT ONE TO SPEAK TO ME, AND NOW LOOK AT ME – I EVEN SAY - HEY MAJOR - BUTTS."*

The Army awarded posthumous Purple Hearts to these "fine American boys" and memorialized them on the *Tablets of the Missing*.

Oryoku Maru & Enoura Maru

Many of Fleeger's friends who survived him died on two other POW ships. Two "blood brothers" who lived with Fleeger in *Bahay* #39, died on the *Oryoku Maru* on 15 December. They were Majors Karol Bauer and William Dunmyer.

Bauer, West Point 1936, born a Connecticut Yankee, had served as an enlisted soldier before entering West Point. He had soldiered with the 26th Infantry Regiment, Plattsburg Barracks, at Pine Camp, NY, and at Camp Perry, OH before being assigned as the Provost Marshal at Ft. Ord, CA. An infantryman "by instinct and choice," Bauer deployed to the Philippines in 1939 and joined the 45th Infantry (PS). Three sources reported that he fought with the 45th Infantry (PS) on Bataan. Captain Manny Lawton, a POW, however, reported that Bauer served as the Executive Officer with the 31st Infantry (PA). Lawton reported that during the fight on Luzon, as the Filipino and American forces were being pushed back and his unit was in danger of being isolated, Major Bauer led a convoy of buses into his position to rescue the troops. Later, Lawton described Bauer when he first saw him in Cabanatuan, highlighting the terrible impact of the war on the American POWs: "Bauer didn't resemble the short, wiry, neat officer with crew-cut black hair I remembered. Before me now stood a weak, gaunt, ghost of a West Pointer of only a few months earlier. His cheeks were sunken and his eyes set deep, but his warm smile was still with him." After they spoke, they concluded that they were two of the three surviving

...THEY CONCLUDED THAT THEY WERE TWO OF THE THREE SURVIVING AMERICAN OFFICERS OF THEIR REGIMENT.

American officers of their regiment. Lawton would survive, the other officer did not, and Bauer died on *Oryoku Maru.* Lawton reported that a bomb killed the thirty-one-year-old major. Bauer received a posthumous Bronze Star Medal.[53]

Dunmyer, like Bauer, had served as an enlisted soldier before he entered West Point on a Regular Army appointment. The infantry officer had graduated from Johnstown High School in Pennsylvania, served for "3 yrs, 3 days" as a "Reg. Army Cpl, Hq Btry, 51st [Coast Artillery]," and had attended the 3rd Coast Artillery Prep School at Ft. Monroe, VA for two years. The latter assignment may have "prepped" him to attend West Point. At Ft. Monroe, he played varsity basketball and played on the 3rd Coast Artillery championship team. On Bataan, he and Fleeger had written: "I pray that I may never be tired, hungry, dirty or lonely again." Neither Dunmyer nor Fleeger could have imagined how filthy, hungry, thirsty, and desperate they would become in the holds of the hot, crowded, and foul POW ships, and they could never have imagined their exits. At West Point, the Pennsylvania-born officer was noted for "the systematic, energetic and efficient manner" in which he attacked problems and for "his strong determination to be successful." He had been the First Sergeant and the Captain of his company and had played basketball and football as a plebe. Apparently, "Dunnie" served with the 45th Infantry Regiment (PS) before he served in Headquarters, II Philippine Corps on Luzon and Bataan. The last known report about the major came from Wilmington [DE] Journal on 26 July 1945. It read: "An officer who knew Major Dunmyer, who had been returned to this country after his release from Philippine prison camp, confirmed that the soldier was well and had been serving as supply officer at the prison camp, so he did not have to work in the fields....The released officer told Mrs. [Eleanor] Dunmyer that he knew the major had been scheduled to sail on the prison ship, but understood that he and some others had planned to escape during the excitement of loading on the beach." He did not escape. Another unidentified newspaper clipping announced that the Army had presented a posthumous Silver Star to his widow. One source reported that he received a Bronze Star. The major died at age thirty-two.[54] The Dunmyers, who had married in the Philippines, had one son who was born there in 1940. Eventually, James William Dunmyer graduated from West Point as an engineer and served a full career in the Army – including serving with the 1st Cavalry Division in Vietnam. He retired as a lieutenant colonel and earned two Bronze Stars for his war service.[55]

ΩΩΩ

Three other Fleeger comrades died on the *Oryoku Maru*. The first, Army Major Philip Lauman, Jr., had served with the Headquarters, I Philippine Corps and had survived the Death March and Camp O'Donnell. Lauman, a Navy Junior, had received a Presidential Appointment to West Point. In high school in Washington, D. C., Lauman had gained the position of cadet captain in the cadet corps. At West Point, he had fenced and earned a varsity "A" in *epee*. He was noted for "an amazing tolerance of others' shortcomings, and in the ability to find the pleasant side in most of the things distasteful to him." Commissioned in the field artillery in 1937, Lauman had been stationed at Ft. Bragg, NC before deploying to Ft. Stotsenburg in 1939. After the surrender on Bataan, the War Department announced his capture along with 196 other Army personnel that the Japanese identified in their first report of POWs. The Washington D. C. native received a Silver Star. One source reported him receiving the Legion of Merit, but not the Silver Star.[56] Fleeger noted that "I will always remember Phil Lauman's solo *Noel*" during Christmas services in 1942.[57]

"I WILL ALWAYS REMEMBER PHIL LAUMAN'S SOLO NOEL" DURING CHRISTMAS SERVICES IN 1942.

The second comrade, Major William Priestley, 57th Infantry Regiment (PS), came from Washington and earned a Legion of Merit and a Bronze Star.[58] Priestley had served for two years in the Coast Artillery of the Washington National Guard, attaining the rank of corporal, before he entered West Point. A friendly, accomplished, and militarily proficient cadet and an aggressive athlete in baseball and soccer – he earned six letters in the sports - Priestley sought a commission in the field artillery, but instead he gained a commission in the infantry. Before joining the 57th Infantry, where he was seconded as the Executive Officer, 1st Battalion, Priestley had served as the Aide-de-Camp to High Commissioner Francis Sayer, the senior American civilian governmental official in the

Philippine Islands. On Bataan, Priestley fought in many actions with his battalion, especially during the last few confused days when the American commanders tried to stem the Japanese onslaught.[59]

Many years later, 1st Lieutenant John Wright, Jr. – who eventually became a lieutenant general – reported that Priestley had been an excellent leader in Cabanatuan. Wright wrote: "The happiness or discontent of men in barracks depended greatly upon the way the barracks leaders ran their organization. Miller and Priestley were very considerate and always concerned themselves with the welfare of each individual. Nothing we did escaped their attention."[60] Major Frank Anders, formerly the S-2 of the 57th Infantry (PS), probably recorded the last snippets about his regimental comrade when he wrote in his diary in Bilibid Prison on 14 December 1944: "57th Infantry officers in draft: ...Major Wm. J. Priestley," and then on 31 December added "Major Wm. J. Priestley missing."[61] The Aide-de-Camp turned combat leader left behind notebooks in which he apparently summarized combat operations.[62]

Fleeger had planned to visit his third friend, Major John W. Turner, Jr., after the war. Turner, from the 515th Coast Artillery Regiment, came from Silver City, New Mexico.[63]

MOST LIKELY, DUNMYER, LAUMAN, PRIESTLEY, AND TURNER DIED IN THE AFT HOLD OF THE SHIP ON 15 DECEMBER ALONG WITH BAUER.

Most likely, Dunmyer, Lauman, Priestley, and Turner died in the aft hold of the ship on 15 December along with Bauer. None of their bodies were recovered, or if recovered, none were identified.

Another Fleeger "blood brother" and *bahay* mate, Major Charles Browne, Jr., West Point 1937, died on the *Enoura Maru* on 9 January 1945, most probably as a result of the bomb that exploded near the forward hold. Six years junior to Fleeger, the easygoing, well-dispositioned, chess-playing, infantry major had served with the American 31st Infantry of the Philippine Division and also with the 91st Division (PA) before his capture. The son of the late Major Charles Browne of the U. S. Army Air Corps, Texas-born "Brownie" died at age thirty on 9 January 1945.[64] Browne was fortunate to have survived the Death March as an officer with the 91st Division, Philippine Army. As mentioned earlier, the Japanese conducted a terrible reprisal on the Filipinos in that division.

Brazil Maru

Several other Fleeger associates who had survived Bataan, O'Donnell, and Cabanatuan and then the bombing of the *Oryoku Maru* and the *Enoura Maru* died on the *Brazil Maru* as it sailed to Japan in January 1945.

Lt. Colonel James Robert Lindsay, Jr. - the "Bob" Lindsey Fleeger mentioned in his pre-war letters - died of "exposure" on 20 January. Lindsay, the son of Brigadier General J. R. Lindsay, West Point, 1890, was born at Ft. Leavenworth and had lived in the Philippines before entering West Point. An apparent cut-up while he was a cadet, Lindsay made over a cadet uniform in the exact replica of a uniform that General MacArthur wore as the Superintendent and then had himself photographed in it. He and a classmate also "vied with each other in attaching nicknames to their classmates. Bob became "Plute" to his classmates. Lindsay graduated third from the bottom of his class -- thus avoiding being the "Class Goat" for the West Point Class of 1923 – most likely because of his extensive and time-consuming activities that included organizing and leading the Bugle Club and riding with the polo squad in his First Class year. The new lieutenant joined the 11th Infantry at Ft. Benjamin Harrison, IN after graduation and by 1927 had completed his first tour in the Philippines. Transferred to the artillery, Plute served with the 68th Field Artillery (Mechanized) at Ft. Knox and the following year, 1935, he received his promotion to captain. Four years later, Lindsay returned to the Philippines and joined the 24th Field Artillery (PS), and the next year, as a newly-promoted major, Lindsay assumed command of a battalion in the 23rd Field Artillery (PS). He fitted in well in the artillery units because he admired the Philippine Scouts: "They are worth their weight in gold." He was scheduled to return to the U. S. on 8 December 1941.

When war began, Lindsay led a battery of self-propelled guns in North Luzon, and after the withdrawal into Bataan became the Assistant to the Chief of Artillery and then became Chief of Artillery of I Philippine Corps. The Army awarded him a Legion of Merit for his war service. Shrapnel from Corregidor artillery wounded him on the Death March. In Cabanatuan and Bilibid, the nearly-crippled artilleryman entertained his friends with his ukulele and encouraged others with his "eternal optimism." Focusing on military matters, he "worked out complete plans for the reorganization of the Philippine Scouts and the Philippine Army. The plans were left with a fellow prisoner, who...forwarded

•••HE TRAPPED AND TRAINED MICE...

them to the proper authority [after the war]."[65] Fleeger wrote a puzzling entry about him in his diaries: "Ask me about Bob Lindsey – his wound – his cage of mice and rat tenko – and his delaga fit."[66] Lindsay's obituary explained the impact of the wound, and the role of the mice - he trapped and trained mice - but did not explain the delaga fit. The Kansas-born infantryman turned field artilleryman died en route to Japan from "extreme exposure and dehydration." He was forty-five.[67]

Air Corps Captain Jack Batchelor, formerly a "well-built man with broad shoulders, closely cropped hair, and a mustache,"[68] died on the same day as Lindsay. Fleeger did not write much about his Air Corps friend who had entered the service from Arkansas. Batchelor had served with the Philippine Air Depot on Bataan before his capture. According to one soldier, the Air Depot was "an outfit of technicians picked up to keep the few airplanes that we have left flying." The captain and his men performed yeoman service under terrible conditions. At first, some worked out of a windowless shack made out of wooden crates. Inside the shack, "Workbenches full of radio equipment and electrical compartments lined two walls." Batchelor used a crate for his desk. Other men worked at dispersed outdoor sites nearby. Later on, the captain moved the Air Depot south when the Japanese broke through line Filipino-American front lines. Soon after that, he announced the surrender of Bataan to his surprised men, and then he met and surrendered his command to a Japanese officer. After the Japanese soldiers searched the area and after some of them stole rings and watches from the new POWs, they moved Batchelor and his men out toward the main road where they joined other POWs marching north out of Bataan.[69] Fleeger noted Batchelor's birthday as 4 January.[70]

ΩΩΩ

Fleeger's boss in the Cabanatuan Library, Lt. Colonel David Babcock, died on 23 January as a result of wounds he received on the *Enoura Maru.* He was forty-five. The field artillery officer - a classmate of Bob Lindsay – had received a grievous wound in his left breast at Takao. With adequate medical treatment, he most likely would have survived. Babcock earned a Legion of Merit for his service on Luzon.

Babcock was born on Staten Island, NY and grew up in Bronxville and Mt. Vernon, NY where he attended public schools. In 1917, as World War I raged in Europe, he enlisted in the cavalry while a senior in high school and served at Ft. Myer, VA. After graduating from West Point in 1923, Babcock served tours at Ft. Sam Houston, TX, Schofield Barracks, TH,[71] Ft. Sill, OK, and Ft. Ethan Allen, VT. Following his assignment to the ROTC at Michigan State University, Babcock served with the 19th Artillery in Indiana and with the 5th Division at Ft. Knox, KY. Just before deploying to the Philippines on 1 November 1941, he commanded an experimental Tank Destroyer Group and "developed tactics in this field."

Babcock married in 1924 but then abandoned his first wife shortly after their marriage. She eventually sued for an annulment of her marriage because "her husband refused to have a religious service performed" following their civil ceremony before a Justice of the Peace.[72]

After war broke out, Babcock commanded the Southern Luzon 2nd Provisional Group, FA, a battalion of 75mm self-propelled guns. His corps chief of artillery wrote that "Bab served with distinction during the difficult withdrawal from Southern Luzon," and his battalion executive officer reported that "The battalion kept the town of Baliwag [Baliuag] under heavy fire, thus preventing the Japs from cutting off the withdrawal of Southern Luzon Force."[73]

Some authorities say that the colonel started the library at Cabanatuan.[74] According to one POW, Babcock served as the Morale Officer of Group 2 when the library began operations in November 1942. Before the organization of the central library, other small libraries formed and operated in the camp. The colonel helped to consolidate two in August 1942. About that time, Captain Leland Cramer of the 26th Cavalry joined the staff and another POW group contributed its books to the larger library. Eventually, Babcock assumed control and became the Camp Librarian and Assistant Camp Morale Officer. Cramer remained his assistant.[75]

SOME AUTHORITIES SAY THAT BABCOCK STARTED THE LIBRARY AT CABANATUAN.

In addition to running the library, Babcock surreptitiously "distributed Churchill's speeches and other anti-Nazi works among the American prisoners by inserting them in copies of *Alice in Wonderland* and similar books and so hoodwinking the Japanese censors into stamping these books *with approval*." On a more political note, "he also wrote a monograph on an international police force, one of the phases of world federation in which he was deeply interested." That seemed a strange fixation for an American officer at the time when the United States was coming out of a period of deep isolation. Also, Babcock reportedly instigated the start of a "medicine show" in the camp, and on one occasion presented a one-hour talk entitled, "Union Now With Great Britain." His comments did not sit too well with his audiences because many POWs believed that "we should have to do all of Britain's fighting if we joined them."[76] Babcock left behind a short diary of his service in the Philippines but he did not mention his strange marriage or his unusual ideas.[77] Fleeger did not say much about Babcock and never mentioned that Cramer worked in the Library. Presumably the two worked together at some time.

ΩΩΩ

On the 24 January 1945, another of Fleeger's classmates, Lt. Colonel Frederick Saint, Corps of Engineers,[78] died at age thirty-six from a minor wound received on the *Enoura Maru*. A survivor reported that Saint "was sitting with his left side pressed closely against the right side of a friend as the attack began. A small sliver of hot metal struck his left arm just above the elbow causing a wound which under normal circumstances would have been readily treated and soon forgotten."[79] Armand Hopkins described Saint's last hour on the *Brazil Maru*: "I was surprised to see several of the medicos hurrying towards a dark corner of the hold with some articles that had a surgical-ward appearance. They were going to try to give some blood plasma to Freddy Saint. Freddy had been wounded during the strafing in Takao harbor, and had bled considerably. A few friends had nursed him along, but under our impossible conditions, he had lost strength and was now unconscious. The doctors managed to scare up, whether among their prisoner colleagues or through [Interpreter Shunusuke] Wada,[80] the makeshift paraphernalia for a transfusion: plasma, tubes, needles, boiled water, or whatever. It was a noble effort, but in the dark of that unsanitary hold, it had little chance of saving Freddy's life. Unhappily it didn't succeed."[81] Saint had led the 14th Engineer Regiment (PS) on Bataan and had worked closely with the 26th Cavalry and the 57th Infantry (PS). John Olsen noted that "Just after dawn they encountered the remains of the 26th Cavalry (PS) under Colonel Vance and the 14th Engineers (PS) commanded by Lt. Col. Saint. The engineers were preparing ... anti-tank obstacles where the trail crossed the headwaters of the Alangan

...SAINT BUILT AN EXPERIMENTAL SEPTIC TANK OUT OF SCRAP LUMBER AND SALVAGED TIN. LATER, HIS GROUP BUILT AND INSTALLED ADDITIONAL SEPTIC TANKS AND SUBSEQUENTLY THE FLY POPULATION NEARLY VANISHED.

River." Later, he added that Saint "...was busy directing his men in creating an obstacle at the crossing [of the Lamao River] and preparing defensive works on the south bank."[82] In Cabanatuan, Saint continued his engineering work and with his men made a huge contribution to the health of the POWs.[83] As the Engineering Officer, he supervised the digging of drainage ditches to drain off water, prepared and cleaned latrines, and policed the camp. Eventually, Saint built an experimental septic tank out of scrap lumber and salvaged tin. Later, his group built and installed additional septic tanks and subsequently the fly population nearly vanished. The remaining flies in the POW Camp came from the Japanese side of the camp because the Japanese did not install similar septic tanks. The huge bluebottle flies were terrible insects: they "swarmed so thickly that one either had to eat his food beneath a mosquito bar or else continually fan flies away with one hand while trying to grab a bite of rice with the other."[84]

Once aboard the ill-fated *Oryoku Maru*, Saint found himself among screaming, hysterical, and irrational soldiers who had been crammed into his hold where the temperature was well above 100 degrees. One report said: "Some men would recall the soothing voice of Lt. Col. Frederick E. Saint, which helped to bring some order to the chaotic situation in the forward hold."[85] Hopkins recalled: "I could distinguish [the voice] of Freddy Saint… He and some of his engineer crew had apparently managed to stay together; and he was using them, now, as moving trouble shooters to help keep the touchy situation under control. His voice could be heard from time to time, calling them by name, and telling them to *get over there where that fellow is hollering and see what the trouble is.*"[86] Two sources reported that Saint was awarded a Bronze Star Medal with Oak Leaf Cluster; another source reported that Saint received a Silver Star.[87]

Saint left behind a tremendous example of leadership to his son who followed him to West Point, became an armor officer, fought in Vietnam, and rose to wear the four stars of a general and command the United States Army in Europe.[88]

ΩΩΩ

Three other officer friends perished. Harry Packard, who had lived with Fleeger and provided a special dinner on occasion, died of "malnutrition" aboard the *Brazil Maru* on 27 January 1945.[89] A former National Guardsmen from Maine, he entered West Point in 1926, captained the cadet soccer and wrestling teams and won five letters with the teams, captained his cadet company, and graduated in 1930. The young officer had deployed to the Philippines in 1939 from his position in the History, Economics, and Government Department at West Point. Like Fleeger, Packard had been looking forward to returning to the United States as tensions mounted in the Far East.

Major Packard had fought on Bataan with the 24th Field Artillery Regiment (PS), and was the Assistant G-3 of II Philippine Corps at the time of surrender. Fellow officers respected him. One reported: "I marveled at his cool and collected efficiency in combat when the fighting was critical and the

situation almost hopelessly confused. His logically organized approach to every danger and every demand was an inspiration to all."[90] On the Bataan Death March, Colonel Louis Dougherty recalled that Packard has shared his last can of fish with him and had helped many during the march. Another officer reported favorably on his service as a supervisor of six or seven messes in Cabanatuan. On the *Oryoku Maru*, Packard distinguished himself "by helping desperate men starving for oxygen find and share precious breaths of fresh air available through a small slit a bomb fragment had made in the ship's side."[91] He earned two Silver Stars (at least one was posthumous) and two Bronze Stars for his combat service.

Another casualty was Major Andrew Zwaska from Milwaukee, WI. Zwaska had been sent to the Davao Penal Colony and then had returned to Cabanatuan. He survived the sinking of three POW ships: the *Shinyo Maru* in September 1944, the *Oryoku Maru*, and the *Enoura Maru*. After all his trials and tribulations, Zwaska died with Packard on 27 January 1945 before reaching Japan.[92]

One of Fleeger's roommates and a blood brother, Lt. Colonel William W. Murphy (actually Murphey), died of "acute colitis" either on the *Brazil Maru* just before arriving in Japan, or in Moji Hospital in Japan on 31 January 1945, just after being taken off the ship. Fleeger's brief entry about him listed his name as "Col. W. W. Murphy" and his birthday as 29 April. Murphy served in the 24th Field Artillery (PS).[93]

Packard, Zwaska, and Murphy were the last of Fleeger's friends to die in captivity.

More Posthumous Purple Hearts

The Army awarded posthumous Purple Hearts to Fleeger's officer friends who were killed or died on the POW ships or drowned at sea.[94] No one recovered the bodies of those who died on the *Arisan Maru* and *Brazil Maru*. Consequently, the American Battle Monuments Commission memorialized all of the deceased prisoners of war whose bodies were not recovered - except Major Harry Packard - on the *Tablets of the Missing* in the Manila Cemetery. For unknown reasons, the Commission memorialized Packard on the *Tablets of the Missing* at the Honolulu Memorial in the Punchbowl Cemetery in Honolulu.[95]

Notes

[1] *Diary*, 59.

[2] Major Samuel Edward Jones, Class of 1931, *1989 USMA Register*, #9286, 375 and *ABMC Website*. See also *1943 Army Directory*, 273.

[3] Major Floyd Joaquin Pell, Class of 1937, *1989 USMA Register*, #10871, 407. *Diary*, 61.

[4] Obituary for Major Floyd Joaquin Pell, *Assembly Magazine*, July 1947, 19-20.

[5] Major Dudley George Strickler, Class of 1927, *1989 USMA Register,* #8187, 356 and *ABMC Website*. Killed on Bataan, age 39. He received two DSCs and a Purple Heart. Both sources listed his

date of death as 8 February 1942. So does his obituary in *Assembly Magazine,* April 1946, 7 and the War Department's "Statement of Military Service" found in Strickler's *Cullum File #8187.* His service information came from his obituary and the "Statement of Military Service." A description of his polo playing prowess is found in the newspaper clipping: "Husband Killed in the Philippines," in the *Meridian, Miss Star,* dated Feb 12, 1942, which is in his *Cullum File.*

6 Johnson, "The Memorials at Cabanatuan," 36. Strickler earned six letters in the sports.

7 Wainwright, *Wainwright's Story,* 56.

8 Olson, *Anywhere-Anytime,* wrote about Strickler: 124 (fought under Pierce), 124 (tall, thin, wiry), 125 (relentlessly), 126 (impatient), and 127 (exhausted and harassed and never seen alive again). Olson's book provides much fascinating information, but unfortunately, the author did not record his sources in footnotes.

9 Morton, *Fall of the Philippines,* 309-10. Footnote 50 gives the source of the death report as a "Memo from the QM HQ Philippine Department to the QM of USAFFE."

10 Morton, *Fall of the Philippines,* 305 and Olson, *Anywhere-Anytime,* 124.

11 Lt. Colonel Ralph Hirsch. See *ABMC Website* and Olson*, Andersonville of the Pacific,* 151 and 154. *1943 Army Directory,* 259 carried Hirsch as missing in action. A MIA listing at that time most probably meant "MIA-Presumed Dead."

12 Lt. Colonel John Taylor Ward, Class of 1920, *1989 USMA Register,* #6806, 332 and *AMBC Website.* See also his obituary in *Assembly Magazine,* Winter 1970, 122-23. *1943 Army Directory,* 390 carried Ward as missing in action.

13 Lt. Colonel Ralph Tibbs Garver, Class of 1925, *1989 USMA Register,* #7646, 347. *Register* lists him as killed at Lubao and as Adjutant General, Philippine *Army. ABMC Website* lists him as serving with the Philippine Department. *1943 Army Directory,* 235 carried Garver as missing in action. *Howtizer, Class of 1925,* 127, provided cadet information. Questionnaire in *Cullum File #7646* provides ROTC information.

14 Letter, Mrs. Ralph T. Garver, 19 February 1946, Martinsville, IL. No addressee. *Cullum File #7646.* Letter covers War Department death report and report of unidentified general officer.

15 *2002 USMA Register.* Ralph Tibbs Garver, Class of 1952, #18577, 577, and Ralph Tibbs Garver, III, Class of 1977, #34642, 628.

16 Lt. Colonel Alf E. Uddenberg. *Diary,* 61, *ABMC Website,* and Wainwright, *General Wainwright's Story,* 94.

17 *1943 Army Directory.* The Army did not list Uddenberg. Officials either knew about Uddenberg's death or he was not a regular officer.

18 For decorations and memorializations, see the *ABMC Website* listing for each officer. For Ward, see "Obituary for John Taylor Ward," *Assembly Magazine,* Winter 1970, 123.

19 *Diary,* 62.

Kenneth B. Thomson at http://www.west-point.org/family/adbc/Branches_files/army.htm lists his father's assignments as 26th Cavalry Regiment, Fort Stotsenburg, and Post Veterinarian, Fort Mills (Corregidor)" (Consulted 21 Jan 2008). The *1943 Army Directory* did not list Thomson. The Army either knew about his death or Thomson was a reserve officer.

20 Glusman, *Conduct Under Fire,* 210-11 and 481. "The most serious charges against an ex-POW after World War II were made against John D. Provoo. In October 1952 the U.S. Government accused him of treasonable acts which included offering his services to the Japanese Army after the capture of Corregidor, helping to cause the execution of Captain Thompson on the island, and participating in wartime Japanese propaganda broadcasts. In early 1953, after a lengthy trial at which a number of ex-POWs and some Japanese testified, a jury found Provoo guilty and a judge sentenced him to life imprisonment. However, in August 1954 the U. S. Circuit Court of Appeals in New York declared the trial invalid because of the introduction of irrelevant and prejudicial allegations pertaining to Provoo's homosexuality and, in addition, declared that the case was tried in the wrong court jurisdiction. While federal prosecutors were preparing to try the case again, a U. S. district judge ordered that all proceedings against Provoo cease on the grounds that he had been denied the right of a speedy trial within the meaning of the Sixth Amendment to the Constitution.

The U. S. Supreme Court subsequently upheld this ruling and in the fall of 1955 Provoo was a free man." See Kerr, *Surrender and Survival*, 73 and 298-99.

[21] Tenney, *My Hitch in Hell*, 108.

[22] Captain Kenneth Charles Griffiths, Class of 1939, *1989 USMA Register*, #11445, 418, *ABMC Website*, and *Diary* 60. The *Register* and the *ABMC Website* list his date of death as 22 August; Fleeger listed it as 20 August 1942. Griffiths graduated two files lower than Charles R. Bowers. *1943 Army Directory*, 243 listed Griffiths as missing in action.

[23] *Diary*, 60.

[24] Lt. Colonel Thomas Randall Horton, Class of 1926, *1989 USMA Register*, #8016, 353 and *ABMC Website*. No listed decorations. See also his obituary in *Assembly Magazine*, April 1944, 8. *1943 Army Directory*, 263 listed Horton as missing in action.

[25] Olson, *Andersonville of the Pacific, 68.*

[26] *Ibid*, 76. "during the scant thirty-one days of Phase II, the American population was reduced from 1,008 (90 officers, 271 NCOs; 637 EM and 10 Civilians) to 781 (89 officers; 199 NCOs; 441 EM and 7 Civilians)."

[27] There are many stories about Colonel (Doctor) James W. Duckworth in POW books. The well-respected doctor remained in Cabanatuan until the 6th Rangers liberated the prison camp.

[28] Olson, *Andersonville of the Pacific,* provides information about Horton. See 68-69 (illness), 69 (contact with Filipinos), 70 (advance party), 73 (Duckworth on Bataan), 74 (meeting, main body, and departure), 75 (5 July Strength Return), and 76 (127 deaths).

[29] Richard M. Gordon with the assistance of Benjamin S. Llamzon, Ph.D., *HORYO, Memoirs of an American POW* (St. Paul, MN: Paragon House, 1999), 116-117. Gordon provides no other source for his remarks than "I can swear to the event, possibly along with others who survived."

[30] Olson, *Andersonville of the Pacific*, 113. Comments by Captain Colman. See also comments by Captain Berg.

[31] *Diary*, 75.

[32] *NARA Website* lists Evert S. Thomas, O109097, as a casualty. He is not listed on the *ABMC Website* as a war casualty. There is no listing of Thomas in the *1943 Army Directory* so the Army must have learned of his death in 1942 or he was a reserve officer.

[33] Chunn, *Of Rice and Men*, 51.

[34] *Diary*, 12.

Chaplain Frederick B. Howden's death is recorded in a section entitled: "Known to have perished at Davao POW Camp" at the following website: http://www.mansell.com/pow_resources/camplists/philippines/Davao/davao_dead.html (2/26/2006).

[35] "old yale," *Yale Alumni Magazine*, May/June 2006 has information about Howden.

[36] For Howden, see Adrian R. Martin, *Brothers from Bataan, POWs 1942-1945* (Manhattan, KS: Sunflower University Press, 1992), 37 for comments about his respect and conversion. Also, see Roper, *Brothers of Paul*, 138-140, for the actions of Braun and Baumann.

[37] See the *"Names Project-NM."* Consulted 17 Dec 2007.

[38] The *1943 Army Directory* did not list Howden because he was a National Guard officer.

[39] *Diary*, 75 (Coyle). Disney was most likely Lt. Colonel Paul A. Disney, Cavalry, who was serving with the 82nd Armored Reconnaissance Battalion overseas in 1943. See *1943 Army Directory*, 213.

[40] Major Harold James Coyle, Class of 1927, *1989 USMA Register*, #8117, 355. He had been with Cebu Force. Executed 17 Apr 42 at age 38. Awarded Purple Heart. Also, see *ABMC Website* and *Diary*, 74. In the *1943 Army Directory*, 201, he is listed as "Coyle, Harold J., O16828, maj. (capt.) FA, missing in action." Apparently, no authority reported his death or confirmed his death by that time.

[41] *Diary*, 128.

[42] Svihra, Albert, *Diary of Colonel Albert Svihra, U.S.M.A Class 1922*, 87. Typewritten copy in the West Point Library.

[43] "Vital Statistics Questionnaire," prepared by Ila Whiteside Svihra and brother Peter P. Svihra, 8 March 1951, found in *Cullum File #6860*.

[44] "Obituary for Albert Svihra," *Assembly Magazine*, January 1947.

[45] *Svihra Diary*, 100-01.

[46] *ABMC Website*. See also "Svihra Obituary," "Questionnaire," and "Citation for the Bronze Star Medal" in *Cullum File #6860.*

[47] *Diary*, 77 and 78 listed the names of the men for whom Fleeger planned to write commendations to the Adjutant General of the Army. For details about the deaths of the nine soldiers - Bates, Henderson, House, Kanally, Marquez, Rada, Sandoval, Strus, and Trujillo - see *ABMC Website*. See also: *"Names Project–NM."*

[48] *Diary*, 132. Fleeger listed a "B" Sandoval in Battery E, 200th Coast Artillery. Bertram O. Sandoval is listed on the *"Names Project-NM."* No other "B" Sandoval is listed. The *ABMC Website* lists Sandoval's death on 7 September 1944. *NARA Website* records list Bertram O. Sandoval, Serial Number 38012213, as dying on *the Shinyo Maru.*

[49] *Diary*, 131-32. PFC Emanuel Rada.

[50] *Ibid*, 78 and 132. SGT John E. Reynolds, 6257084.

[51] *Ibid*, 11, 78, and 131-32. PFC Reynaldo Trujillo, 38012573.

[52] *Ibid*, 78.

[53] Major Karol Anthony [name changed from Carl A.] Bauer, Class of 1936, *1989 USMA Register*, #10652, 402. Also see: *ABMC Website,* "Obituary for Karol Anthony Bauer," *Assembly Magazine*, n.d., 110, and Manny Lawton, *Some Survived* (Chapel Hill, NC: Algonquin Books of Chapel Hill, 2004). For Bauer, see 33 (Cabanatuan), 171 (death), and 176 (Luzon).

[54] Major William J. Dunmyer. See "William James Dunmyer," *Howitzer*, U. S. Military Academy, 1937, 111. For regular army service, see *Cullum File #10845* for "Cadet Personal Record" and for the newspaper clippings. See also Chunn, *Of Rice and Men, 61.* Chunn listed Dunmyer as one of several supply officers.

[55] James William Dunmyer, *Class of 1962, 1989 USMA Register, #23853*, 665.

[56] "Philip Gatch Lauman, Jr." in *Howitzer*, 1937, 208. See "Cadet Personal Record," "Public Relations Office Questionnaire," and "Three From D.C. Listed as Japs' War Prisoners," Washington D.C. *Times Herald*, n.d., all in *Cullum File #10844.*

[57] *Diary*, 83. Italics added.

[58] Major William John Priestley, Class of 1936, *1989 USMA Register*, #10845, 402. See *AMBC Website* and *Howitzer*, Class of 1936, U. S. Military Academy, 187. See also "Cadet Personal Record," "Public Relations Office Questionnaire" and letter of Frank L. Anders to Secretary of Association of Graduates, USMA, 25 February 1945 in *Cullum File #10845.*

[59] Olson, *Anywhere-Anytime*, mentions Priestley several times and Olson indicated that he consulted Priestley's diary for some of his entries. See: 92, 173, 174, 177, and 186.

[60] John M. Wright, Jr., *Captured on Corregidor, Diary of an American P.O.W. in World War II* (Jefferson, NC: McFarland & Company, Inc., 1988), 55.

[61] Letter of Frank L. Anders, 25 February 1945. Anders was the father of Captain Frank O. Anders of the 57th Infantry (PS). He had served in the Philippines and had won a Medal of Honor during the Philippine Insurrection.

[62] Author has extracts from William Priestley's *Notebook #1* in which he recorded the history of the 71st Infantry (PA).

[63] *ABMC Website* and *Diary*, 17-18.

[64] Major Charles Janvrin Browne, Class of 1937, *1989 USMA Register*, #10896, 407, *Diary* 12, *ABMC Website*, and *Howitzer*, U. S. Military Academy 1937, 109. See also "Cadet Personal Record," Public Relations Office Questionnaire," and news clipping "Major Killed in Sinking of Jap Transport," San Antonio *Texas Light*, 10 August 1945 in *Cullum File #10896.*

[65] Lt. Col James Robert Lindsay, Jr., Class of 1923, *1989 USMA Register*, #7218, 339. Died on the *Brazil Maru*, 20 January 1945. Awarded a Legion of Merit. For the extensive biographical information, see "Obituary, James Robert Lindsay, Jr.," *Assembly Magazine*, July 1948, 15-16.

[66] *Diary*, 130.

[67] "Obituary, James Robert Lindsay, Jr."

[68] Tony [Anton F.] Bilek in collaboration with Gene O'Connell, *No Uncle Sam, the Forgotten of Bataan* (Kent, Ohio: The Kent University Press, 2003), 31.

[69] *Ibid*, 43, 45-47

[70] Captain Jack F. Batchelor, *ABMC Website*, and *Diary*, 74 and 132.

[71] Territory of Hawaii.

[72] Obituary for "David Sherman Babcock," *Assembly Magazine*, July 1946, 13, provided most of the biographical information. See also Lt. Colonel David Sherman Babcock, Class of 1923, *1989 USMA Register*, #7183, 339 and *ABMC Website*.

[73] Ibid.

[74] *1989 USMA Register*, 339. John A. Glusman, *Conduct Under Fire, Four American Doctors and Their Fight for Life as Prisoners of the Japanese, 1941-1945* (NY: Penguin Books, 2006), 266. Alexander, *Surviving Bataan*, 296 (fn 34).

[75] Captain Ralph Keeler, MI, "Take a Break," in Chunn, *Of Rice and Men*, 78-80. See also *Babcock Diary*, 11: "Nov 12, I am appointed Group II Morale Officer again by new regime (Col Parquette)."

[76] Chunn, *Of Rice and Men*, 63-64.

[77] *Cullum File, #7183* contains diary and newspaper clipping about Babcock's annulment.

[78] *Diary*, 149.

[79] Johnson, "The Memorials at Cabanatuan, Part II," 35.

[80] Wada and his commander were merciless tyrants. Both "were accused of mistreating and abusing, causing mental and physical suffering to, and, ultimately, causing the deaths of 1,039 Americans' on the three POW ships they served on." The War Crimes Tribunal sentenced Wada to life imprisonment. The Americans executed his commander. A later reviewer concluded that Wada rather than his commander should have been executed for his terrible actions. Michno, *Hellships*, 302.

[81] Armand Hopkins, *Prisoner of War, 1942-1945, Reminiscences of Armand Hopkins*, c. 1984, 100-01. Unpublished manuscript. Copy in Special Collections, West Point Library.

[82] Olson, *Anywhere-Anytime*, 180 and 185.

[83] Knox, *Death March*, 224 (footnote septic tanks). See also Chunn, *Of Rice and Men*, 59

[84] Chunn, *Of Rice and Men*, 59.

[85] Kerr, *Surrender*, 220.

[86] *Hopkins, Prisoner of War*, 77. Italics added.

[87] Lt. Colonel Frederick Gilman Saint, Class of 1931, *1989 USMA Register*, #9031, 371 and *ABMC Website*.

[88] General Crosbie E. "Butch" Saint, Class of 1958, USMA. Personal knowledge.

[89] Major Henry Brown Packard, Class of 1930. *1989 USMA Register*, #8856, 368. Died on *Brazil Maru*, 27 January 45, at age 38. Awarded 2 Silver Stars, 2 Bronze Star Medals, and a Purple Heart. See also "Obituary for Henry Brown Packard," in *Assembly Magazine*, April 1948, 19-20.

[90] "Packard Obituary," 20.

[91] Johnson, "The Memorials at Cabanatuan, Part II," 33.

[92] See *ABMC Website*. http://www.mansell.com/pow_resources/camplists/philippines/Davao prime roster...2/26/2006, 11 of 11.

[93] Fleeger listed Lt. Colonel W. W. Murphy. *Diary*, 62. *Oryoku Maru* Roster listed William W. Murphy, http://oryokumaruonline.org/m.html (1/28/2006), 4 of 4. Correct name, however, was "Murphey." The *1923 Army Directory*, 318 listed only Lt. Col. William W. Murphey, FA, as a POW. There is no "Murphy" listed as a POW. A William W. "Murphey" is listed on "Roster of men from the *Brazil Maru* taken to Moji Hospital," (Kokura Military Hospital) Kokura, Japan," at http://people.tamu.edu/jwerickson/POW/ BMKHroster.html (2/25/2006) with a date of death of 31 January 1945. *POW Research Network Japan*, "Fukuoka No. 22 Branch Camp...," 4 lists Lt. Col. "Murphey" as "died at Kokura" of "acute colitis" and gave a possible middle name, Wayne. (9 Aug 2010).

[94] *Diary*, 61-62 for names and details. Also, see *ABMC Website*.

[95] John Bradley photos of Punchbowl Memorial and Packard memorial.

Ten

*"At the request of
the President,
I write to inform
you that the
Purple Heart has
been awarded
posthumously to
your husband"*

Americans sustained high casualties on Luzon in 1941 and 1942. Initially, over 300 Americans died fighting, but those losses paled compared to those suffered by the American POWs. By the year's end, nearly 5,000 American POWs had died: 650 of about 10,000 POWs died during the Bataan Death March;[1] 1,500 of 9,300 perished in Camp O'Donnell;[2] and 1,318 out of the original 15,000 POWs died in the Cabanatuan Camps by the end of July and 1,196 more died there by the end of 1942.[3]

An estimated 13,250 remained in captivity after the Japanese had moved several hundred to other countries.[4] Thousands of those POWs died before the end of the war.

An Overwhelming Tragedy

During the war, the Japanese moved the POWs from Cabanatuan to and from work camps on Luzon and to the Davao Penal Colony on Mindanao. The kept some POWs in Bilibid Prison and Ft. McKinley in Manila and at a camp on Palawan Island. During the war, they also moved thousands to Japan, Korea, and Manchuria to work in war industries and in mines. Many perished at all locations. While many POWs died in the northern countries, their survival rates surpassed their comrades on Luzon and Mindanao and Palawan because hundreds of those left behind died on POW ships and the Japanese massacred nearly two hundred on Palawan in 1944 as the Americans approached the island.

By the end of the war, about one-third of all American POWs perished at the hands of the Japanese compared to one tenth of the Americans captured by the Germans.

26th Cavalry

The cavalry officers sustained a death rate that exceeded the death rate for all American POWs of the Japanese during World War II and exceeded the death rates for all the armies in World War I.

As noted, Fleeger reported that fourteen cavalry officers died in combat. Those who fell before 9 April 1942 died doing what they were trained to do – fight an enemy in combat, but, incredibly, most of the cavalry officers died after the surrender of all the American and Filipino troops in the Philippines.

All told, forty-two – forty American and two Filipino officers - or sixty-eight percent (68%) of the sixty-two officers Fleeger and others identified as members of the 26th Cavalry died in the war. They included:

☐ Thirty-eight of the original fifty-five cavalry officers Fleeger named as officers of the 26th Cavalry;

☐ Two of the five medical officers Fleeger named as officers serving with the 26th Cavalry (Mickelsen, an American, and Laragay, a Filipino);

☐ Two officers who joined Troop C after war began and Fleeger did not name (Bowen, an American, and Furagganan, a Filipino).

ΩΩΩ

The causes for the deaths of the forty-two cavalry officers are show in TABLE 1.

The fourteen battle deaths - twenty-three percent (23%) of all the cavalry officers - showed the intensity of the fighting. The one fatality on the Death March reflected either good luck or highlighted the toughness of the newly captured cavalry officers. The four executions of captured guerrilla officers highlighted the unusual savagery of the Japanese against Americans and Filipinos who opposed them following the surrender of the Philippines. The deaths in the POW camps – four after sick and weak POWs arrived in Japan in 1945 - reflected the Japanese indifference to feeding and caring for the POWs, and the sixteen deaths of cavalry officers on POW ships enhanced the overall POW tragedy.

The twenty-seven POW deaths nearly doubled the combat deaths; the sixteen POW ship deaths exceeded the combat deaths. The twenty-seven POW deaths totaled sixty percent (60%) of the forty-five American and Filipino officers from the 26th Cavalry who fell into Japanese hands, and they totaled forty-four percent (44%) of the sixty-two cavalry officers in the regiment. The forty-four percent death rate for the cavalry POWS exceeded the thirty-three percent death rate for all American POWs of the Japanese during the war and greatly exceeded the ten percent death rate for American POWs imprisoned by the Germans.

PHILIPPINE SCOUT LOSSES

RECORDS SHOW THAT AT LEAST 266 OR THIRTY-FOUR PERCENT (34%) OF THE 787 FILIPINO SCOUTS IN THE REGIMENT DIED DURING THE WAR. THERE IS NO WAY TO TELL IF ANY OF THE FILIPINOS WHOM PRAEGER HAD INDUCTED INTO HIS TROOP C — OR IF ANY OF THE 200 REPLACEMENTS BROUGHT INTO THE REGIMENT AFTER FIGHTING BEGAN — WERE INCLUDED IN THE CASUALTIES OR IN THE TOTAL ESTABLISHED STRENGTH OF THE REGIMENT AFTER 8 DECEMBER 1941.

TABLE 1 CAUSES OF ALL OFFICER DEATHS 26TH CAVALRY REGIMENT (PS) (42 OF 62) 68%					
COMBAT OPERATIONS (14 OF 62) 23%	GUERRILLA OPERATIONS (1 OF 62) 2%	POWs OR CAPTIVES (27 OF 62 OFFICERS OR 44%) (27 OF 45 POWs OR 60%)			
KIA LUZON	DIED AS GUERRILLA	KILLED ON BATAAN DEATH MARCH	CAPTIVES EXECUTED	DIED IN POW CAMPS	KIA OR DIED ON POW SHIPS
14	1	1	4	6	16

Looking only at the two deaths in the POW Camp in the Philippines, the cavalry loss was about four percent (4%), significantly smaller that the average loss in German Camps, and looking at the six losses in the POW Camps – about thirteen percent (13%) – the cavalry loss approximately the average loss in German POW camps.

World War I provides grim standards for casualty rates. Consider the death rates during the war – not the number of casualties: France lost sixteen percent of her soldiers killed (1,385,000 of 8,410,000 million) and had fifty-one percent of her soldiers wounded (4,266,000 of 8,410,000) and, thus, sustained a combined casualty rate of sixty-seven percent (67%) of her troops. As staggering as that rate was, the sixty-eight percent death rate for the officers of the small 26th Cavalry Regiment exceeded the combined dead and wounded casualty rate of the French in the first war. For another perspective, consider the United States in the same war. American troops sustained a death rate of three percent (126,000 of 4,355,000) and a wounded rate of five percent (234,000 of 4,355,000), which resulted in a combined casualty rate of eight percent (8%). The American casualty rates in very bloody World War I showed the significance of the cavalry losses in World War II.[5]

Fortunately, the Japanese did not ship out all the surviving cavalry POWs in the Philippines on the *Arisan Maru*. If they had, only the four officers whom the Japanese imprisoned on Formosa and Manchuria, Pierce, Vance, McLennan, and Nelson, and the two guerrilla officers who remained at large on Luzon, Merrill and Ramsey, and young Lieutenant Wills, who escaped to Mindanao, would have survived the war.

Friends

Fleeger's friends also died in appalling numbers, but their overall numbers were fewer than those for the 26th Cavalry officers. Thirty-nine or forty-six percent (46%) of Fleeger's eighty-four friends died in the war, including:

☐ Twenty-nine of the forty-nine officers he listed in his diaries; and

☐ Ten of the thirty-five soldiers he associated with in Cabanatuan.

TABLE 2 shows the causes of deaths.

TABLE 2				
CAUSES OF DEATHS				
FLEEGER'S FRIENDS				
(39 OF 84)				
46%				
COMBAT OPERATIONS (3 OF 84) 4%	POWs (36 OF 84 TOTAL OR 43%) (36 OF 81 POWs OR 44%)			
KIA LUZON	KILLED/EXECUTED ON BATAAN DEATH MARCH	EXECUTED	DIED IN POW CAMPS	KIA OR DIED ON POW SHIPS - 14 OFFICERS - 10 SOLDIERS
3	3	3	6	24

Three out of eighty-four of Fleeger's friends fell in combat, many fewer than the 26th Cavalry lost. The Japanese captured the remaining eighty-one, and apparently killed one just after capture and two shortly thereafter. They also killed or executed three of his older friends when they faltered on the Death March: two faltered, most likely, because they had served at high staff positions on Bataan and were not as strong as the battle-tested cavalry officers; and one faltered because he had not recovered from serious wounds. Tragically, the Japanese killed or executed the six officers for their own whims – there were no just causes - and exacerbated their reputation for unjustified punishments and unusual savagery (Appendix T).

The deaths in POW camps doubled the combat deaths among Fleeger's friends, and the twenty-four POW ship deaths exceeded all other categories for the group. Moreover, the POW ship deaths exceeded the cavalry losses on the POW ships: the fourteen officers killed at sea approximated the cavalry losses; but, the ten enlisted deaths increased the total ship loss significantly.

Thirty-six or forty-four percent (44%), of the eighty-one POWs among Fleeger's friends died under Japanese control. That percentage also exceeded the thirty-three percent death rate for all American POWs of the Japanese.

Eleven of the eight-one POWs, approximately fourteen percent (14%), perished before the POW ship disasters, about the same percentage as the cavalry officers who died before the POW ship disasters, and slightly more than the ten percent of the POWs who died in German camps. Again, the losses on the POW ships increased the death rates considerably.

ΩΩΩ

TABLE 3 summarizes the causes of death for all the officers whom Fleeger identified in his diaries plus the two additional cavalry officers and highlights various death rates.

TABLE 3 SUMMARY OF ALL CASUALTIES & CASUALTY RATES						
	ALL PERSONNEL			POWs		
GROUP	TOTAL NUMBER OF PERSONNEL	TOTAL NUMBER OF DEATHS	**TOTAL DEATH RATES**	TOTAL NUMBER OF POWs/ CAPTURED	TOTAL NUMBER POW DEATHS	**TOTAL POW DEATH RATES**
26TH CAVALRY OFFICERS	62	42	**68%**	45	27	**60%**
ALL OF FLEEGER'S FRIENDS	84	39	**46%**	81	36	**44%**
FLEEGER'S OFFICER FRIENDS	49	29	**59%**	46	26	**57%**
FLEEGER'S SOLDIER FRIENDS	35	10	**29%**	35	10	**29%**

Fleeger's friends – officer and enlisted - fered much lower death rates than the cavalry officers. His officer friends suffered a much lower death rate overall, and they also suffered a lower death rate as POWs. Fleeger's enlisted friends suffered the lowest death rates of any group. However, the non-cavalry officers and enlisted soldiers still exceeded the death rates for the French and Americans in World War I.

Some smaller POW groups, made up of cavalry officers and other officers, sustained lower death rates, but still suffered dreadful losses.

- Four of the eight officers assigned to Fleeger's *bahay* (listed on the sketch on page 154) or fifty percent (50%) died.
- Among his blood brothers and all of his *bahay* mates, seven of fourteen including Fleeger – also fifty percent (50%) – died.
- Among Fleeger's West Point classmates, eight of the thirteen including Fleeger, or sixty-two percent (62%) perished. (Appendix S)

These losses and loss rates stagger and they do so because of the deaths of so many men on the POW ships. And when you envision the men behind the numbers, and realize how and why they died, the numbers become horrific. Bad as they were, however, there were worse ones, but not among Americans. The death rates among Jews in German concentration camps exceeded those of the 26th Cavalry and Fleeger's friends, and the death rates of German POWs held by the Germans and of Russian POWs held by the Germans also exceeded them.

TABLE 4
POW SHIP SURVIVORS
OCTOBER 1944-AUGUST 1945

8

SURVIVED OF THE 1,783
EMBARKED ON THE *ARISAN MARU* IN
OCTOBER 1944

271

RECOVERED IN AUGUST 1945
FROM THE 1,619 EMBARKED ON THE
ORYOKU MARU, ENOURA MARU, AND
THE *BRAZIL MARU,*
DURING DECEMBER 1944-JANUARY
1945

3,123 DIED (1,783+1,619-279)
OF THE 3,402 EMBARKED

279

(8+271) SURVIVED

THE NUMBERS SHOW THAT THE POWS WERE ACTUALLY SAFER IN THE PHILIPPINES AND THAT FLEEGER AND HIS FRIENDS WERE JUSTIFIED IN FEARING A MOVE NORTH TO JAPAN IN 1944.

POW Ship Deaths

When considering all the POW ship casualties from October 1944 to January 1945, the numbers are even more appalling. Ninety-two percent (92%) of the 3,123 of the 3,402 POWs removed from Cabanatuan, Bilibid, and other places on Luzon in October and December 1944 perished on *Arisan Maru, Oryoku Maru, Enoura Maru,* and the *Brazil Maru* or as a result of their voyages. TABLE 4 summarizes the POW ship information.

The 828 POWs left behind in Bilibid Prison in Manila, and the sick and incorrigible 511 who remained in Cabanatuan in late January 1945 became the lucky ones.[6]

The ninety-two percent death rate dramatizes the horrors of the Death Ships and the criminal indifference of the Japanese to:

- ☐ Feeding the POWs;
- ☐ Providing adequate clothing for them especially during the winter voyage to Japan;
- ☐ Providing adequate medical care for the sick and wounded POWs;
- ☐ Transporting them in unmarked POW ships in a war zone; and
- ☐ Rescuing those adrift in the sea.

The numbers show that the POWs were actually safer in the Philippines and that Fleeger and his friends were justified in fearing a move north to Japan in 1944.

As Fleeger had written earlier, "It was rough." But by the end of January 1945 only a handful of his officer and soldier friends could say as he once said: "I was a survivor." The 1944 and 1945 POW ships had created an overwhelming tragedy.

Notes

[1] Exact casualty numbers are difficult to determine. T. Dodson Stamps and Vincent J. Esposito (eds.), *A Military History of World War II, Volume II, Operations in the Mediterranean and Pacific Theaters* (West Point, NY: AG Printing Officer, 1956), 263 stated that approximately 950 Americans perished in the last days of the fight on Bataan and on the Bataan Death March but give no casualty figures for North and South Luzon Forces or I and II Philippine Corps on Bataan before the last Japanese offensive. Morton, *Fall of the Philippines*, gave no summary of American casualties for the fight on Luzon. Most authors writing about the Bataan Death March reported that approximately 650 Americans died on the March. Falk, *Bataan*, 197 concluded that between 600 and 650 Americans died on the March. Knox, *Death March*, 155 stated between 600 and 700 Americans died on the Death March and later at page 199 stated that 650 men died on the Death March. Using these figures, I have concluded that over three hundred Americans died in combat before the Death March and I have used 650 for the number of Americans who died on the Death March. That would bring the Cabanatuan total to 2,801.

[2] Falk, *Bataan*, 197 and 199 reported that approximately 1,600 of 9,300 Americans died in Camp O'Donnell. Kerr, *Surrender*, 80 said that 1,500 Americans died in the camp. Knox reported that 1,500 of 9,300 Americans died in the camp, and William B. Breuer, *The Great Raid on Cabanatuan* (NY: John Wiley & Sons, 1994), 60 stated that 1,602 American soldiers and 49 American sailors died at O'Donnell. Olson, *Andersonville of the Pacific*, as mentioned earlier, reported 1,508 deaths by July 1942.

[3] Kerr, *Surrender*, 102 reported that in June and July 1942, 1,286 of 9,000 POWs had died at Camp 1 and 32 of 6,000 POWs had died at Camp 3, a total of 1,318. He added that 287 more died in August for a total of 1,605 by that time, but he gave no figures for the rest of the year. Knox, *Death March*, 199 reported that 740 POWs died in June in Camp 1 and nearly 2,000 more died in Camp 1 and at least 61 more died in Camp 3 (199) by the end of the year, a total of about 2,801. Using those figures, 1,196 POWs died (2,801-1,605) after the end of July, about 300 per month.

[4] Using Kerr's and Knox's numbers, the estimated total of American POWs captured in 1942 on Luzon was 18,650 - 650 estimated killed on the Death March, plus 9,300 who arrived at Camp O'Donnell, plus 8,700 who were captured on Corregidor (Kerr, *Surrender*, 61 and 71). With losses of 300 (KIA), 650 (Death March), 1,500 (Camp O'Donnell), 1,605 (Cabanatuan thru August 1941), and about 1,196 (September through December in Cabanatuan), approximately 5,251 died on Luzon by the end of 1942. Using these numbers (18,650-5,251), about 13,399 POWs remained on Luzon. The Japanese, however, had moved some Americans out of the Philippines by then, and they had captured more Americans than those on Bataan and Corregidor. Kerr, *Surrender*, 124 stated that 13,250 American POWs remained in the Philippines at the end of 1942. Because of the difficulty of reconciling varied POW totals, I have used Kerr's estimate of 13,250.

[5] James K. Martin, et. al. *America and Its Peoples*, Volume 2 from 1865, 5th Edition (NY: Pearson Longman, 2004), 616. France lost 1,385,000 dead out of 8,410,000 mobilized (16.5%) and Romania lost 336,000 dead out of 750,000 mobilized (45%).

[6] Breuer, *The Great Raid*, 201 reported that 511 were rescued at Cabanatuan. Two died after the rescue. Kerr, *Surrender*, 248 provided the number of POWs in Bilibid in January 1945. He wrote that the 828 survivors included 400 POWs transferred in from Ft. McKinley. There also were 500 internees in Bilibid in January 1945.

Tables

Table 1, Causes of Officer Deaths, 26th Cavalry Regiment
Appendices I, J, K, and T

Table 2, Causes of Deaths, Fleeger's Friends
Appendices P and T

Table 3, Summary of All Casualties
Appendices I, J, K, P, and T

Table 4 POW Ship Survivors
Arisan Maru reporters agreed on survivors but not on numbers embarked. I have used **1,783** as the number of POWs embarked on the *Arisan Maru* found in Gladwin, "American POWs on Japanese Ships," (see fn 6 above). Other sources list varied numbers. Daws, *Prisoners of the Japanese*, 293 listed 1,802 embarked POWs with 8 survivors. Kerr, *Surrender*, 208-9 did not list the total embarked but listed 9 initial survivors of the ship. He noted one died later. Michno, *Hellships*, 249 listed 1,782 POWs embarked and listed 9 survivors of the sinking, 258. Later, he listed 1,800 embarked on the *Arisan Maru* with, 1,792 deaths, leaving 8 survivors, 316. The *1989 USMA Register*, 30 listed 1,790 embarked with 9 survivors on the October ship. All agreed on the survivors, but not on the numbers embarked.

Oryoku Maru reporters agreed on the number embarked but not on survivors. Charles M. Brown. The *Oryoku Maru* Story http://www.oryokumaruonline.org/oryoku_maru_story.html, Part 1, 2 of 3 reported 1,619 embarked and Part 2, 3 of 3 with 271 survivors. Daws, *Prisoners of the Japanese*, 295 listed 1,619 embarked and fewer than 400 survivors by February 1945. Kerr, *Surrender*, 217 listed 1,619 embarked and said less than 300 survived from the original group, 237. Michno, *Hellships*, 258 reported 1,619 embarked. The *1989 USMA Register*, 30, listed 1,800 embarked on the ship but gives no number for total survivors of the December ship. I have chosen to use Brown's numbers of **1,619 and 271.**

Sidebar Note

Philippine Scout Casualties
ABMC Website, Casualties for 26th Cavalry (PS). There were 301 soldiers listed, thirty-five of whom were officers. Several other cavalry officers were not listed.

Eleven

"Will it ever end?"

Survivor - Trapnell

There was some good news. Several 26th Cavalry officers, some of Fleeger's officer friends, and a few of his enlisted friends returned home, and many of the officers returned to active duty and had successful careers.

Two of Fleeger's friends, Alva Fitch and Thomas Trapnell, became lieutenant generals, but only Trapnell had survived the Bataan Death March. Only one POW rose to higher rank after the war: Lt. Colonel Harold K. Johnson of the 57th Infantry (PS), a Death March survivor who was not in Fleeger's immediate circle of friends but whom POWs respected for his fair dealing, became the Chief of Staff of the U. S. Army during the Vietnam War. He was one of two Pacific War veterans to gain that high position in a post-war Army dominated by European veterans.

A Handful

SURVIVORS
26TH CAVALRY

COL (BG)	1
COL	4
MAJ (LTC)	1
MAJ	2
MAJ (MD)	1
CPT	4
CPT (MD)	1
CPT (VC)	1
1LT	5

Twenty of Fleeger's sixty American cavalry comrades survived the war, but neither of the two Filipino officers – Furagganan of Troop C and Dental Officer Laragay - survived. Seventeen of the line cavalry officers and three of the medical officers returned to the United States.

The two senior officers serving with the regiment when war began and three colonels on detached service made it home. They did so in great part because the Japanese eventually imprisoned the generals and full colonels on Formosa and then moved them to the north safely. Additionally, only two - Brigadier General Pierce and Colonel Vance - completed the Death March.

Pierce had earned an excellent reputation for his handling of the 26th Cavalry. After leaving the regiment, he had relieved another general, been promoted to brigadier general, and given command of the West Sector on Bataan. In his new job, he controlled operations against the Japanese forces that landed on the west coast of the peninsula.[1] Pierce earned an early headline for being the first general wounded in World War II. After his release from the Mukden (Hoten) POW Camp in Manchuria, he continued active service in the Philippines, Germany, and the United States. Pierce donated his collection of photographs to the Military History Research Institute in Carlisle Barracks, PA. He died in 1966.[2]

Colonel Vance, Pierce's replacement as the Regimental Commander, gained his release from Mukden (Hoten) POW Camp in Manchuria in August 1945, as did the two cavalry colonels on detached service: Carter McLennan, Chynoweth's "Dour Scot," and

Frank Nelson, Wainwright's G-3. The Japanese had imprisoned the three earlier on Formosa.[3] The third colonel, tough Gyles Merrill, the frustrated guerrilla leader, made it through the war. One of the few guerrilla officers to do so, Merrill reported with his command for duty with the U. S. Army when American troops moved south toward Manila in January 1945.[4]

Two other cavalrymen who had survived the Death March, Camp O'Donnell, Cabanatuan, and the sinking of two POW ships also gained their freedom in Mukden: Trapnell and Fowler. So did Chandler.

Trapnell, the dedicated polo player who had commanded the 2nd Squadron of the 26th Cavalry before becoming the Regimental Executive Officer and the Regimental Commander, returned to active duty following his repatriation to the United States. He became a paratrooper, deployed to Korea where his paratroopers helped clean out and pacify rioting Communist POWs in the camps on Koje-do Island, served in French Indochina where he barely missed being captured with the French forces at Dien Bien Phu, and then commanded the 4th Armored Division and the 82nd Airborne Division in the United States. As a lieutenant general, he commanded I Corps (Group) in Korea and XVIII Airborne Corps and the Strategic Army Corps (STRAC) at Ft. Bragg, served as the Deputy Commander of the U. S. Army, Pacific, in Hawaii, and commanded Third Army before retiring from the Army in 1962. As the STRAC Commander, he visited Indochina to evaluate the military situation there at the request of President John Kennedy. On his return he briefed the President and his advisors aboard Air Force One on his findings. According to some reports, Trapnell recommended that the United States not become involved in the pending war in the peninsula.

Trapnell never talked much about World War II or his time as a POW and never wrote

HE DID SAY, HOWEVER, THAT THE BATAAN DEATH MARCH WAS LIKE "AN ENGLISH TEA PARTY" COMPARED TO THE POW SHIPS.

any memoirs. He did say, however, that the Bataan Death March was like "an English tea party" compared to the POW ships. But the war stayed with him, albeit quietly, because his family members reported after his death that he had nightmares about the war throughout his life. General Trapnell died in 2002 at age ninety-nine and three months. His family buried his ashes at West Point with his wife's ashes. At the time of his death, he was the senior surviving officer of the Bataan Death March and the oldest survivor of the Death March. One of the general's proudest possessions was a photo of the 3rd Cavalry at Ft. Meyer in the 1930s when Jonathan Wainwright commanded the regiment.

"Trap" thought the world of Wainwright. Another was the photo of his brother and himself taken when they captained their college lacrosse teams.[5]

Captain John Fowler traveled the same route to Manchuria as Trapnell did, and he left Mukden in August 1945.[6] According to one reporter, Fowler distinguished himself on two occasions aboard the battered POW ships. Following the bombing of the *Oryoku Maru*, Fowler and other survivors tried to take care of the dead by putting two bodies in a rice sack on the deck. Then, after the bombing of the *Enoura Maru* in Takao harbor, he and nine other officers moved the dead to shore because the Japanese did absolutely nothing to help the wounded or to remove the dead. After placing bodies aboard a small vessel the officers "... reached a breakwater, tied up, but found that they were too weak to carry the bodies ashore one by one. They attached ropes to the naked feet, dragged them to the point where the breakwater met the sand, and laid them out in rows. It was a coal dumping yard, and there were black mountains of bituminous coal, thousands of tons nearby. They left the bodies on the beach the first night, beside the coal." The officers returned the following day with more bodies, and then on the third day "they took all the bodies back to a Japanese crematorium near a shrine, and rendered them into ashes."[7] It had to be heart rending work for Fowler and his starved comrades.

Chandler, the regimental operations officer in the 26th Cavalry, returned to active duty. Wounded on the last day of the fighting on Bataan, he did not make the Death March or stay in Camp O'Donnell. Fleeger noted that he arrived in Cabanatuan from Bilibid in 26 June 1942. Chandler survived the voyages of the three POW ships to Japan and transshipment to Hoten. The veteran cavalry officer earned a Silver Star, Legion of Merit, and a Purple Heart for his service on Luzon, and retired from the Army in 1961 as a colonel.[8] After the war he wrote a valuable summary of the 26th Cavalry's operations on Luzon and Bataan. He died in 2006, at age ninety-eight.

JONES, WHO HAD BEEN DEATHLY ILL AND WHO THE JAPANESE EXPECTED TO DIE IN 1944, REMAINED EXTREMELY SICK IN EARLY 1945.

Captain Jones and Captain Minton of Troop C survived. Jones, who had been deathly ill and who the Japanese expected to die in 1944, remained extremely sick in early 1945. Because of his grave condition - he had lost seventy pounds of weight and weighed only seventy pounds in July 1944 - the Japanese had not executed him as they had his commander, Praeger. After his release from Bilibid, Jones wrote a valuable summary of Troop C's operations. He also continued his army career as an armor (tank) officer, rising to be a colonel, and retiring in 1962. Jones served in French Indochina in the 1950s (perhaps while Trapnell was there) and later spent seven years in South Vietnam (1966-1973) as a pacification advisor.[9] Minton, released from a POW Camp in Japan, returned with a tarnished reputation because he had served with the unreliable, alcoholic, and inept Major Everett Warner after he left Troop C in the mountains of Luzon. Warner, called "Major Bottle" by the Filipinos, with information and most likely help from Minton, had submitted the falsified report to USAFFE about the Tuguegarao Raid conducted by Troop C, the report which resulted in MacArthur promoting Warner and decorating him with a DSC for doing absolutely nothing. Warner's report, not Praeger's, had triggered the award of the DSC to Minton as well as his promotion to captain. Following the war, Minton further tarnished his reputation as noted by guerrilla historian Bernard Norling who wrote, "Minton claims all sorts of important achievements for Lieutenant Warner and himself...Nobody has ever been able to discover either the accomplishments or grand designs of Warner and Minton." Apparently, Minton did not measure up to his boss, Praeger or his comrade, Thomas Jones.[10]

Fun-loving Lieutenant Ramsey barely survived the war as a guerrilla. He collapsed shortly after he returned to American lines. General MacArthur awarded Ramsey a Distinguished Service Cross for his efforts on Luzon after the surrender of the Filipino-American forces in 1942 and then sent him home. When Ramsey checked into a military hospital in Topeka, Kansas, he weighed ninety-three pounds and "was diagnosed with malaria, amoebic dysentery, anemia, acute malnutri-

... RAMSEY BARELY SURVIVED...HE WEIGHED NINETY-THREE POUNDS AND "WAS DIAGNOSED WITH MALARIA, AMOEBIC DYSENTERY, ANEMIA, ACUTE MALNUTRITION, AND GENERAL NERVOUS COLLAPSE."

tion, and general nervous collapse." It took him eleven months to regain his health. Ramsey also earned two Silver Stars, a Bronze Star Medal, and a Purple Heart. Subsequently, he wrote about his experiences, went back to the Philippines in business, and lectured widely about his wartime exploits. Currently there is a dated webpage that highlights his accomplishments.[11]

Lieutenant Arthur Whitehead survived and wrote a number of articles for the Cavalry Journal in 1944. He seemed to have been with the 26th until 22 December 1941 and then served on Panay.

Another cavalry officer, First Lieutenant Donald Wills, the Regiment's Transportation Officer, made it home and wrote a book about his remarkable experiences. Captured on Bataan, he wound up in Cabanatuan. But later when the Japanese called a draft of

POWs to move to a plantation-type camp in the south that was several hundred miles closer to American forces, Wills volunteered to go. On the trip, the Japanese surprisingly fed the 1,000 POWs better than expected and allowed them to stay on deck during the sea voyage. In one case, however, life aboard the ship turned out to be less than pleasant for Wills: on a rainy day he slept in a coal bunker where giant flying cockroaches which infested the bunker crawled all over him. When the POWs landed in Davao in November 1942, the Japanese marched them about fifteen miles to the Davao Penal Colony where the Japanese commandant greeted them with a message that they were there to work. Regardless of what he faced in his new camp, Wills thought anything would be better than Cabanatuan. The Japanese commandant, however, was unhappy because he got "walking corpses" not able-bodied workers.

In 1944, while being transported back to Luzon on the *Yashu Maru*, a resourceful Wills escaped. After Fleeger's classmate, Lt. Colonel John McGee, had jumped off the ship and successfully escaped, the Japanese guards cracked down on the remaining POWs. Subsequently, Wills decided that he also would jump ship and devised an ingenious plan to do so. On a rainy night when the guards were "bundled up and didn't appear alert," Wills asked

...HE RAN QUICKLY TO THE SIDE OF THE SHIP AND JUMPED INTO THE SEA. AFTER SURVIVING SOME EXCITING MINUTES IN THE WATER, THE YOUNG OFFICER SWAM FOR ABOUT FIVE HOURS BEFORE REACHING LAND.

permission to go to the deck-side toilet. After gaining permission, he ran quickly to the side of the ship and jumped into the sea. After surviving some exciting minutes in the water, the young officer swam for about five hours before reaching land. He must have gained some weight and strength in Davao because he most likely would have been unable to survive if he had just come out of Cabanatuan. Fortunately, friendly Filipinos found him. Wills eventually joined the local guerrillas and later he claimed to have "led the liberation of Western Mindanao." The cavalry officer rejoined American forces on Leyte in April 1945.[12]

Four other cavalry officers imprisoned in Japan survived. Major Houston Farris gained his freedom from the Shinjuki POW Camp, Captains Fred Evans, Jr. and Joseph Siciliano gained theirs from the Osaka POW Camp, and First Lieutenant Clinton Seymour, who was also claimed by the New Mexico Anti-Aircraft regiment, left the Zentsuji POW Camp a free man.

American troops liberated three of the five medical officers who remained in the Philippines. The 6th Ranger task force rescued Major Emil Reed, the Regimental Surgeon and the Surgeon for the 1st Squadron, from Cabanatuan on 30 January 1945. Reed, the only 26th Cavalry officer left in Cabanatuan, had a thankless job in the camp: at his Group 1 Dispensary he had to determine which sick POWs could not work and which "sick" POWs might be goldbricking to avoid work.[13] Reed, other doctors, and the camp leaders had to provide sufficient numbers of POWs to meet each day's work quota. One POW reported that "...no one in camp was sufficiently strong to be doing the necessary work, and it was generally conceded one had to be just about dead to rate a day off (star quarters). The POWs nicknamed the hardworking Reed "Rigor Mortis" because many POWs "thought they were about to die when he said they were well enough to go back on the work detail."[14] A few days later, troops of the 37th Infantry Division freed Captain Vaughn Shaw, the 2nd Squadron's Surgeon, and Captain William Gochenour, the Regimental Veterinarian, from Bilibid Prison in Manila. Shaw had served as a Ward Officer in Cabanatuan. Gochenour at one time served as an officer supervisor in one of the American guard companies that patrolled inside the fence to prevent escapes. His non-combatant peers in the guard force included two medical doctors and a chaplain.[15]

...ONLY FOUR OF FLEEGER'S CLASSMATES WHO FOUGHT IN THE PHILIPPINES IN 1941-1942 LIVED.

Another Handful

Besides Chandler, only four of Fleeger's classmates who fought in the Philippines in 1941-1942 lived. Fleeger mentioned two in his diaries: Houston Parks Houser and Charles Howard.

Parks Houser from Perry, Georgia gained a reputation for having a hot temper while a cadet at West Point along with "plenty of what it takes to stand behind one." He had a lot of friends and he "never failed to stand behind one of them either." His friend wrote also that "he knows all about Georgia peaches... and worries about the peach market on days when the mail man gives him a cold shoulder." The same friend reported that Houser had a pleasing personality and was "one of the best mixers we know," and then summed him up, saying, "He owes no man, barring Lt. Smyser, who taught him his arm swing." Commissioned into the infantry in 1931, Houser served with the 29th Infantry at Ft. Benning, GA, and then commanded a company in the 33rd Infantry in the Panama Canal Zone while a second lieutenant. As a first lieutenant, he commanded a company in the 66th Infantry at Ft. Meade, MD and a platoon of the 45th Infantry (PS) in the Philippines. Just before war broke out, the experienced Captain Houser took command of the 2nd Battalion of the 45th Infantry (PS) at Ft. McKinley, and in January 1942, after being promoted to major, he became the G-1 in I Philippine Corps. Following surrender, he survived the Death March, Camp O'Donnell, and Cabanatuan.[16] Houser distinguished himself during imprisonment. A young officer wrote in Cabanatuan: "Major Houser was one of the most outstanding officers under whom I served. He had unlimited initiative and resourcefulness, and accepted responsibilities along with the privileges of his position. Many commanders issued orders and regulations to govern every man under them, excluding themselves from compliance. Major Houser won the confidence of all his men when he showed his convictions in the fairness and reasonableness of his regulations by complying with them himself." He gained more laurels for his actions on the *Oryoku Maru.* The night after the Americans had bombed and strafed the POW ship and many deranged roamed about, Houser "took on the job of security officer," and with "the help of four strong enlisted men selected by him, [confined] the troublemakers to one section in a corner and guarded them." Then on the *Brazil Maru,* he "organized a military police detail of eight officers" to "maintain order around the ladder, and to allow only five men on deck at any one time to use the latrine." And later, in Jinsen POW Camp in Korea, the POWs apparently placed him in command of a hut when another officer had proved less than fair and honest. Moreover, POWs judged Houser's integrity as impeachable because "he exercised his command in the best interest of the group." Released from Jinsen POW Camp in Korea in 1945, he found that he had earned a Soldier's Medal and a Legion of Merit for his wartime service.[17] Erroneously, a war correspondent shortly after the end of the war reported Houser dead and wrote the following for his paper, the *Chicago Daily News*:

> *Major Houston B. Houser, an outstandingly capable figure who had organized M.P.s of a sort to keep order in the darkness, who busied himself running up the ladder to keep order in the darkness, was felled with exhaustion and later took the short way home. He had been Wainwright's adjutant during the part of the battle for Bataan.[18]*

Fortunately, he was wrong.

Houston Parks Houser III followed his father to West Point and into the army. An infantry officer and a paratrooper, he distinguished himself in Vietnam with the 101st Airborne Division, winning a Silver Star, three Bronze Star Medals, and seven Air Medals.

"BUDGE" HOWARD GAINED A REPUTATION AT WEST POINT FOR STEALING HEARTS

He retired from the Army as a brigadier general after thirty-one years of service. Houser ended his career as the Chief of Staff and Deputy Commander of Third U.S. Army.[19]

An original Fleeger *bahay* mate, "Budge" Howard, gained a reputation at West Point for stealing hearts, being modest, and being a dreamer. Appointed a second lieutenant in the field artillery, he served with the 83rd Field Artillery at Ft. Benning, probably at the same time as Houser. Later, he worked with the Civilian Conservation Corps in Louisiana and South Carolina, and in 1934 became the aide-de-camp to the Commanding General of IV Corps Area, headquartered in San Antonio. After attending the Field Artillery School, Howard selected Ft. Bragg for his next assignment. Following that, he deployed to the Philippines and moved to Ft. Stotsenburg with his family. During the ensuing fight on Bataan - and until surrender - the artilleryman commanded the 2nd Battalion, 88th Field Artillery (Philippine Scouts). "Budge" Howard survived the Death March, O'Donnell, and Cabanatuan, and earned a Silver Star, Legion of Merit, and two Purple Hearts during the war.[20]

The citation for the Legion of Merit gives an exceptional evaluation of the officer. It commended him for developing his inexperienced force "into a successful combat unit," and then recounted that he demonstrated "outstanding courage during a damaging air raid on positions of Battery D in Abucay, [when] he deliberately exposed himself to Japanese aircraft fire, as he moved about his forces, encouraging them to their greatest effort." The citation continued, "Ever solicitous for the welfare of his troops and striving to increase their maximum efficiency, he made repeated tours of battery positions with complete disregard for his own safety."[21]

The Japanese moved Howard to Japan where he "served out the war as a Japanese Prisoner-of-War Camp Commander" in one or more camps at Osaka, Zentsuji, Sholahu, or Roca Rochi (Honshu). Howard returned to active duty, but he never fully recovered his health. While on active duty, he graduated from the U. S. Army Command & General Staff College at Ft. Leavenworth, KS, and from the Naval War College at Newport, RI, and served as an intelligence officer in assignments in the Pentagon, V Corps in Germany, and Second Army in the United States. He also became the Executive Officer, Division Artillery, 1st Infantry Division in Germany and the Senior Advisor to Korea's V Corps. He retired as a colonel in 1961 after thirty years of service and died after a long illness in 1977. In the post-war years, Howard became a member of the historic Society of Cincinnati which dated from the American Revolution.[22]

ΩΩΩ

Half of Fleeger's other *bahay* mates survived. Chaplain Albert Braun returned home. Born in Los Angeles in 1889, educated in California and in St. Louis, Missouri, Braun had been ordained a Catholic priest in St. Louis in 1915. After working briefly as a

HALF OF FLEEGER'S OTHER BAHAY MATES SURVIVED.

CHAPLAIN BRAUN

"...CHRIST TOLD HIS DISCIPLES TO GO OUT INTO THE WORLD, NOT SIT AT A DESK AND MOVE PAPER AROUND."

missionary with the Mescalaro Apache Indians in New Mexico, he became an Army chaplain and served with the 6th Infantry Regiment in France during World War I. Wounded while tending other wounded and the dying, he was recommended for, but did not receive, a Distinguished Service Cross. After the war, he returned to mission work among the Apaches and in the 1930s worked for the Civilian Conservation Corps in New Mexico. Recalled to active duty in 1941, then assigned to recruit chaplains for the Philippines, Braun deployed there himself along with Father Zerfas in 1941. One source said that he was assigned to the 45th Infantry (PS) upon his arrival, but in a more substantial work he is carried as a member of the 200th Coast Artillery Regiment. Captured on Corregidor, he initially pressured the Japanese to permit the Americans to bury their dead, later cared for the sick during the diphtheria epidemic at Cabanatuan, and got smuggled vaccine into camp to help some of the infected POWs. Transferred to Davao, he continued his smuggling efforts there. Braun drew a lucky straw – unlike Fleeger - when the Japanese shipped him to Japan in August 1944 aboard the *Noto Maru* which the Americans did not attack. Imprisoned for the remainder of the war at Omori POW Camp near Tokyo, he gained his release on 29 August 1945. After returning to the United States, he went back to his missionary work, was recalled to active duty in 1947, and retired to the Phoenix area in 1949. The Church authorities gave Braun an unchallenging office job, so he requested a transfer to a poor Hispanic community in South Phoenix – stating that "Christ told his disciples to go out into the world, not sit at a desk and move paper around." The Franciscan priest continued to work until age seventy-three. He lived until he was ninety-four. Braun earned a Silver Star and a Legion of Merit for his service in World War II.[23] Fleeger called Braun "Padre" but never wrote about any of his activities in Cabanatuan.

Two West Pointer majors whom Fleeger identified as *bahay* mates survived: Clarence Bidgood and Alva Fitch. Bidgood, four years junior in service to Fleeger, had commanded the 71st Engineer Battalion (PA) on Bataan. Like so many others, he had survived the Death March and imprisonment in Camp O'Donnell, Cabanatuan, and Japan. In Cabanatuan, Bidgood had been the Details Officer for Group 2 before Major Blanning took over the job.[24] In camp, he also "taught sanitation, engineering and mathematics to his fellow prisoners." The Army decorated the major with a Legion of Merit and two Commendation Ribbons for his wartime service.

Bidgood had enlisted in the Army in 1929 and the Army assigned him to the Philippines. After two years as a private, facing little chance of promotion, he decided to become an officer. Shortly thereafter, he attended the U. S. Army Prep School at Ft. McKinley and the following year entered West Point. While there, he earned a reputation that he performed every duty – military, academic, or social - with the greatest care and that he was a man "who has pushed away all obstacles and gone steadily upward." Commissioned into the infantry and assigned first to Ft. Benning, he secured a transfer to the Corps of Engineers and performed normal duties of a junior engineer officer. In 1938-1939, Bidgood earned a Master of Science in Civil Engineering at Cornell University, and in September 1941 with members of the 803rd Engineer Battalion Aviation he departed New York by rail for San Francisco and then the Philippines, arriving most likely in early November. After being repatriated from the Osaka Main POW Camp in 1945, he found that he had a four-year old daughter and he returned to active duty. Reportedly a tough taskmaster, Bidgood "was not always a popular superior, for he had little patience and compassion for those who performed below their capabilities, or for those who did not possess complete integrity." Intense and enthusiastic, honest and fair, he gave "the full measure of himself in everything he did" and consequently became highly respected. In his last assignment in the Army, he worked with NASA on the construction of the Vertical Assembly Building and the launch complex where the first flight to the moon began. After he retired as a colonel in 1963, he continued to work with NASA on the Saturn Project. Shortly after retiring from business, Bidgood died at Ft. Belvoir, VA, in February 1970, at age sixty.[25] For a legacy, he left behind a son, Ferdinand, who followed him to West Point and into the Army, served in engineer construction groups in

INTENSE AND ENTHUSIASTIC, HONEST AND FAIR, HE GAVE "THE FULL MEASURE OF HIMSELF IN EVERYTHING HE DID" AND CONSEQUENTLY BECAME HIGHLY RESPECTED.

"BEST DAMNED GUNNER ON BATAAN"

Vietnam, completed twenty-six years as a Corps of Engineer officer, and retired as a much decorated colonel.[26]

Fitch graduated a year ahead of Fleeger from West Point. An artilleryman, Fitch had commanded the 9th Battalion, 91st Artillery (PA) & Battery A, 23rd Field Artillery (PS) on Luzon. Thomas Dooley commented on 24 February 1942 that Fitch was the "real ramrod" in the battalion and the "best damned gunner on Bataan."[27] Fitch earned three awards for bravery – a DSC, Silver Star, Bronze Star Medal - and a Purple Heart. He survived the Death March, O'Donnell, Cabanatuan, the sinking of the *Oryoku Maru* and *Enoura Maru*, transportation to Japan, and imprisonment in Japan and in Jinsen, Korea. Fitch returned to active duty following his repatriation, reached the rank of lieutenant general, and retired from the Army in 1966.[28]

Gardner Gross also survived.[29] The only available records show that he survived at Jinsen POW Camp in Korea.[30]

ΩΩΩ

A few of Fleeger's other friends survived: Major Roy Doran, Major Winnifred Dorris, Major Harry Fischer, Major Chester Johnson, Lt. Colonel (Doctor) William North, Major Royal Reynolds, Jr., Lieutenant Prior Thwaits, and Lt. Colonel Ovid Wilson.

Not much is known about Doran and Dorris. The Japanese had shipped Doran to Japan and then to Mukden where the Russians liberated him. Dorris served in the 200th Coast Artillery. He survived in the Philippines, but no record shows where.[31]

Fischer, from the 803rd Engineers, had been transferred from Cabanatuan to Davao, and in 1944, the Japanese embarked him on the *Shinyo Maru* to sail to Japan. After the USS *Paddle* torpedoed the POW ship on 7 September, Fischer escaped along with eighty-two others and made it to shore. Friendly Filipinos on Mindanao rescued them, and, reportedly, guerrillas led by Colonel John McGee secured them and then notified MacArthur's headquarters of their presence.[32] On 27 October, the USS *Narwhal* evacuated Fischer and eighty-one other POWs to American lines.

He was fortunate because the Japanese had practiced killing all the POWs aboard in case of a submarine attack, and the Japanese began to do so when they spotted the first torpedo wakes heading toward the *Shinyo Maru.* Following the first strikes which blew the ship up, about 500 died instantly or drowned inside the ship, and most of the initial survivors died when the Japanese shot at them from other ships, directed an aircraft to strafe them in the water, sent motor boats to find and kill them, and shelled and machine-gunned the beach. Many of the survivors died from Japanese fire or from their resultant wounds and others drowned trying to reach shore. The Japanese executed about thirty survivors after rescuing them; they "tied the men up by their wrists, hung them up, and shot them one by one."[33] Fischer, whose pre-war residence was Texas, died in 1973.

"Johnnie" Johnson, West Point 1937, one of the younger officers, had served with the 24th Artillery (PS) on Bataan where he won a Silver Star and two Bronze Stars. He survived the Death March and three Hell Ships. Two years after the war ended he earned a Master's Degree in Political Science from Harvard and taught in the Department of Social Sciences at his alma mater. Johnson served as an assistant division commander, division commander, a corps commander, and as the commander of Army Southern Command, before retiring as a major general in 1973.[34]

Doctor North, whom Fleeger mentioned operating on him, returned to private practice. North, summoned by the Japanese Interpreter Wada, had gone topside with other doctors and medics to tend to hundreds of wounded Jap-

SHINYO MARU

FOLLOWING THE FIRST STRIKES WHICH BLEW THE SHIP UP, ABOUT 500 DIED INSTANTLY OR DROWNED INSIDE THE SHIP, AND MOST OF THE INITIAL SURVIVORS DIED WHEN THE JAPANESE SHOT AT THEM FROM OTHER SHIPS, DIRECTED AN AIRCRAFT TO STRAFE THEM IN THE WATER, SENT MOTOR BOATS TO FIND AND KILL THEM, AND SHELLED AND MACHINE-GUNNED THE BEACH.

anese on the *Oryoku Maru*. North and his associates saw hundreds of Japanese dead and
wounded civilians and soldiers on 14 December 1944.[35]

Reynolds, who had served as the S-3 of
the 57th Infantry (PS),[36] had escaped from Bataan and spent the war holed up with the

guerrillas. He never became an active guerrilla leader as Barker, Lapham, and Ramsey
did. He spent most of the war as an "evader," but at the end of the war he worked under
Colonel Gyles Merrill. Reynolds earned a Bronze Star and a Combat Infantryman's
Badge during the war. The West Pointer had a distinguished career: he earned a Silver
Star, Legion of Merit, Bronze Star Medal for Valor, and a second Combat Infantryman's
Badge in Korea, served as an Assistant Division commander, and retired in 1963 as a
Brigadier General.[37]

Prior Thwaits survived. No other information was found about him.[38]

"Zero" Wilson survived the Death March and the December and January POW ships.
Liberated at Mukden, the former aide-de-camp of General Wainwright and the G-1 of II
Philippine Corps, Wilson was noted for "his deep, deep sense of humor." It was his "most
dominant characteristic."[39] One commentator said that "through his leadership and inspiration he influenced many others [to survive]." During his time in Cabanatuan, Wilson
became the show impresario of the camp. Reflecting on his shows, he said, "The men
were down so low that they would listen to anything." The shows continued for about two
years because the POWs demanded the cheerful diversions from their daily grind. Wilson
himself put on the most celebrated performance of the Cabanatuan Mighty Art Players
when he starred in *Our Town* and described his
own home town, Normangee, Texas. Calvin
Chunn described the impact: "Colonel "Zero"
impersonated each character he described.
Tears welled up. There was home right before
our eyes, almost within our grasp...yet, dear,
inaccessible home was really 8,000 miles
beyond those hills where that lazy moon lin-
gered...we could see it through the crystal ball

of tears...8000 miles away." Wilson repeated his performance three or four times. The
Mighty Art Players eventually put on fifty-four "works."[40] Upon his release Wilson returned to active duty and retired in as a Colonel in 1954. He served for a time as the

Professor of Military Science & Tactics at the New Mexico Military Institute and then in the Headquarters of the U. S. Army Pacific in Honolulu. The Texan returned to his native state after he retired and went into business in Houston, eventually becoming the President of the Board of his marine insurance brokerage company. He died there in 1982 at age 80 after five trying years in a nursing home, years which must have challenged his wonderful sense of humor. Wilson received a Legion of Merit, two Bronze Stars, and a Purple Heart for his service on Luzon.[41]

Major Paul Wing survived. The Signal Corps officer along with Lt. Colonel Babcock and "Zero" Wilson had contributed to the entertainment of the POWs. On one occasion, Wing kept his audience more than the scheduled hour by talking about the movie industry. He and his daughter, Toby, an actress, had worked in Hollywood.[42] One soldier reported that Wing spoke to about two hundred POWs about how his daughter got into pictures. Wing, a patient on the "Malaria Side" of the camp at the time, "looked a bit fatigued" as he sat on a stool with "his hands folded in front of him" and talked to the men who were seated on the ground around him.[43]

In addition to the Army officers, Marine Lt. Colonel Curtis T. Beecher, the senior officer in Cabanatuan after the Japanese transferred the full colonels to Formosa, survived all the movements to Japan and lived to be evacuated from Jinsen POW Camp, his last prison camp. Fleeger wrote about him once in 1943: "Colonel Beecher's *bahay* has hatched a litter of small ducks – also chicks."[44] Beecher ran a relatively taut ship in Cabanatuan, complying with the Japanese as needed and demanding that the POWs be as clean and orderly as possible. Many POWs, particularly many junior officers did not like him or his methods. Several young officers resented that lieutenant colonels and majors and the enlisted soldiers working for them did not have to work on the farm. Beecher worked out a compromise. One of the several veterinary officers did not like the marine colonel. He wrote, "...Beecher was the ranking officer in camp and was carrying on like he had a command stateside – a special mess for him and his staff (cronies). They cooperated with the Japanese and used their position for special privileges. That was the talk of the camp. As you can imagine, he was almost universally hated." He went on to say that Beecher retaliated against one medical officer by sending him out on the draft that embarked on the *Arisan Maru* after the doctor refused to provide the desired number of POWs for a work detail because too many of his group were sick.[45] If true, Beecher gave the doctor an inadver-

BEECHER RAN A RELATIVELY TAUT SHIP IN CABANATUAN, COMPLYING WITH THE JAPANESE AS NEEDED AND DEMANDING THAT THE POWS BE AS CLEAN AND ORDERLY AS POSSIBLE.

SURVIVORS FLEEGER PLANNED TO COMMEND

200TH COAST ARTILLERY

A BATTERY
PFC AARON DRAKE
PFC ADRIAN OLDHAM
PFC SYD HUDGENS

B BATTERY
PFC CARL PLEMMONS

D BATTERY
SGT JAMES ARGENAS

G BATTERY
PFC LUCIANO MARTINEZ

H BATTERY
PFC ELOY CARDENAS
PFC PHILIP RIVERA
SGT JOSEPH SEGURA

tent death sentence. Given the conditions, however, Beecher faced an impossible situation, trying to work with the Japanese, on one hand, and please the prisoners on the other. Leaders in Santo Tomas Internment Camp in Manila faced similar situations.[46] Moreover, Beecher, a marine officer with some marine staff, probably did not fit in well with the hundreds of Army officers in the camp. But Beecher paid a price on the POW ships. Manny Lawton described his landing in Japan: "Lieutenant Colonel Beecher, with a month's growth of matted beard and hair, dressed in filthy pants and shirt with a dirty towel wrapped around his head to protect a wound, climbed out and gave a feeble salute. That done, he leaned back against the bulkhead, as if exhausted by the effort."[47]

ΩΩΩ

Ten soldiers Fleeger planned to commend for their work in the mess halls - all from the 200th Coast Artillery Regiment - survived: Sergeant James Argeanas (D Battery), Private Eloy Cardenas (H Battery), Private First Class Aaron Drake (A Battery), Private First Class Eugene Hamrick (F Battery), Private First Class Sidney (Syd) Hudgens (A Battery), Private First Class Luciano Martinez (G Battery), Private First Class Adrian Oldham (A Battery), Private First Class Carl Plemmons (B Battery), Private First Class Philip Rivera (H Battery), and Sergeant Joseph Segura (H Battery).[48]

The Japanese had moved all the soldiers except Hudgens to Japan; they had moved Hudgens to Manchuria. No additional information was found about these soldiers.

In addition, four soldiers from the 515th Coast Artillery returned home safely from their camps in Japan. Private Jack Cater (E Battery), Sergeant Robert Davis (D Battery) from Gallup, Private First Class Ceofas Garcia (D Battery), and Private Herschel Gardner (F Battery).[49]

One of the survivors, Sergeant Robert Davis, reported many interesting stories about his service. He recalled the following about the 200th Coast Artillery Regiment:

> *The Army swallowed us up and mixed us with its own throwing of enlisted men, officers, and Selective Service draftees. Bunching us with others did not spell harmony. Draftees resented enlisted men, enlisted men resented the Guard, guardsmen resented cadets, cadets and officers looked down on the rest of us, creating one big unhappy family.*[50]

During the fight on Bataan, Davis reported that a piece of shrapnel wounded him slightly when a 37mm artillery round from G Battery hit his position. Fortunately, his wound did not affect him on the subsequent Death March. Davis said that he marched with only one friend during the march, but he estimated that thirty-six battery mates survived it. At Camp O'Donnell, "Davis managed to stay healthy. Farm and restaurant work had made him a stickler on sanitation. He never ate a questionable food."[51] And, he got lucky because the Japanese assigned him to a work party a few days after he arrived at the camp. He added to his luck because during the six weeks in the camp he worked as a cook and did not go out on work details. In June, the Japanese moved him into Cabanatuan. There, according to his biographer, "Davis' kitchen duty did not last. Politics rules, even in prison camp. Without his buddies he was a loner and his coveted position was usurped by somebody else's friend." He never mentioned Fleeger and his kitchen. During these grim days, he lost friends murdered by the Japanese, searched for friends in Zero Wards, saw comrades die from disease, and helped bury the dead. Davis apparently had remained reasonably healthy, but he did not remain dimpled and baby-faced and one-hundred and forty pounds. Only five feet seven inches tall, about Fleeger's size, his small body may have been a blessing in disguise with starvation facing him. The Japanese shipped him north with seventeen hundred other POWs – only two were buddies from Battery D - in November 1942 aboard an early filthy POW ship, *Nagato Maru*.[52]

DURING THESE GRIM DAYS, HE LOST FRIENDS IN ZERO WARDS, SAW COMRADES DIED FROM DISEASE, AND HELPED BURY THE DEAD.

In Japan, Sergeant Davis reported that, "We worked at the railroad yard moving gunny sacks and heavy crates of food fertilizer, chopsticks, rice, and a myriad of other goods, even Japanese money. We loaded from warehouse to train, train to truck, truck to ship, and back to the warehouse again; whatever our overseers ordered." He recalled that the POWs stole as much food as they could to survive and that on one occasion he stole a large pickle and on another found a full Japanese lunch box that he ate immediately. His worst incident came when a Japanese guard hit him twenty-six times with a bayonet and he collapsed. Davis got up and nearly retaliated. "My only thought was to kill the devil with his own weapon,"[53] he said, but the guard stopped the beating. Hard work and virtual starvation continued, but Davis survived. After the war, he went back to Bataan to try to recover some gambling winnings that a buddy had hidden there before the surrender, but someone else had found the $18,000. Later, he returned to Japan to testify at the War Crimes trials. Davis continued to serve in the Army in the Philippines and Korea until he retired in 1961. Following his military service he taught school in California until 1981.[54]

Fleeger had planned to commend Ceofas Garcia for his work in the mess halls. Garcia lived until 1994 and died in Albuquerque.[55]

No other information is available about Herschel Gardner.

ΩΩΩ

Five other soldiers Fleeger listed with the coast artillerymen survived. Three from the Ordnance Corps had served with the 454th Ordnance Aviation Bomb Group: Private First Class (later Staff Sergeant) Frederick Lappin from Tennessee, Private First Class (later Staff Sergeant) John Lewis from North Carolina, and Private First Class Wilson Thompson also from North Carolina.

FIVE OTHER SOLDIERS FLEEGER LISTED WITH THE COAST ARTILLERYMEN SURVIVED.

Two others from the Air Corps had served with Headquarters & Headquarters Squadron, 27th Bomb Group – Sergeant (later Technical Sergeant) Arthur Stear from Ohio, and Private First Class Robert Smythe from Mississippi.

Sergeant Clarence Bramley from the 21st Pursuit Squadron and Private First Class William Van Orden of the 803rd Engineers, Major Harry Fischer's unit, survived. So did Technical Sergeants James E. Delanty from a finance unit and Jay C. Tracer of the Air Corps. [56] Bramley, Delanty, and Tracer went home from Japan.

Philip Travera is listed as a survivor because no information can be found about his possible death.

The lone marine among Fleeger's friends, Corporal Kenneth Rice, made it home. Rice recalled his early World War II experiences: "I was with the 4th Marine Regiment in Shanghai when we were transferred to the Philippines about a week before the Pearl Harbor attack. [We] were attacked about the same time as Pearl Harbor. Next we were sent to Corregidor where we set up defense on the beaches." Then, he recounted his prisoner of war experiences.

"IN JAPAN I WORKED IN A COAL MINE FOR THE MITSUI COMPANY AS A SLAVE LABORER."

> *With the fall of the Philippines I was marched as a P.O.W. from Manila to Camp Cabanatuan. I was sent on a work detail under the Japanese officer called the "White Angel" (dressed completely in white and very mean). We were extending an airfield. I was sent back to Cabanatuan Camp where later I was put on a freighter to Japan. Many of the men in the ship's hold died on the way to Japan. Those that died were dropped into the sea. I can still remember that.*

> *In Japan I worked in a coal mine for the Mitsui Company as a slave laborer.*

Rice regained his health after he returned to the United States and, consequently, remained on active duty in the Marine Corps. He fought in Korea, and later retired as the Sergeant Major of the Marine Corps Base at Camp Lejeune, NC. After leaving active duty, Rice joined the Saginaw County Sheriff's Department in Michigan and retired as a Detective Lieutenant.[57]

All told, twenty-five of Fleeger's soldier friends survived the war. Did any of them ever think about the major who thought so much of many of them?

ALL TOLD, TWENTY-FIVE OF FLEEGER'S SOLDIER FRIENDS SURVIVED THE WAR. DID ANY OF THEM EVER THINK ABOUT THE MAJOR WHO THOUGHT SO MUCH OF MANY OF THEM?

Return

Considering what Fleeger, his cavalry comrades, and his POW friends and associates had gone through, it is amazing that any survived the war, and especially the move north in POW ships. More amazing, most seemed to have successfully transitioned back into "normal life," in contrast to many other officers and men who found the transition traumatic. And most amazing, most seemed to have led productive lives, and a few hale and hearty ones lived into their nineties.

In May 2009, seventy-three Army and Air Corps survivors of the Bataan Death March gathered for the final scheduled reunion of the American Defenders of Bataan and Corregidor in San Antonio, Texas. The Japanese Ambassador to the United States attended and apologized for the Japanese Government:

> *We extend our heartfelt apologies for our country having caused tremendous damage and suffering to many people, including prisoners of war, those who have undergone tragic experiences in the Bataan Peninsula, in Corregidor Island in the Philippines and other places.*[58]

Many welcomed the first public apology to POWs from a representative of the Japanese Government; some criticized it. When the Ambassador finished his short speech, he received "a standing ovation from half or so of the 400 to 500 attendees."[59]

For many of the last handful, however, the war has never ended.

Notes

[1] Morton, *Fall of the Philippines*, 304-05, 310, and 314-17.

[2] See *Army Research Collection Online Research Catalog* at the U. S. Army War College website.

[3] For POWs on Formosa, see the *"Never Forgotten" Website*. For places of release see individual POW listings and the Mukden Rescue and Evacuation rosters available from the *NARA Website*.

[4] Schaefer, *Bataan Diary*, 328

[5] Personal knowledge.

[6] See http://people.tamu.edu/~jwerickson/POW/BMFk-1roster.html.

[7] George Weller, *First Into Nagasaki, The Censored Eyewitness Dispatches on Post-Atomic Japan and Its Prisoners of War* (NY: Crown Book, 2006), 199 (*Oryoku Maru*) and 219-20 (*Enoura Maru*).

[8] *1989 USMA Register*, 373.

[9] Norling, *Intrepid Guerrillas*, 234-35.

[10] Norling, *Intrepid Guerrillas*, 63-64, 72, 94-95, and 254 (fn 4).

[11] Lieutenant Edwin Ramsey. See Ramsey and Rivele, *Ramsey's War*, 323-33 and http:// www.militarymuseum.org/Ramsey.html.

[12] Michno, *Hellships,* 73-75 and 174-5. Information from Donald H. Wills, *The Sea Was My Last Chance: Memoir of an American Captured on Bataan in 1942 Who escaped in 1944 and Led the Liberation of Western Mindanao* (Jefferson, NC: McFarland, 1992), 2-12.

[13] Chunn, *Of Rice and Men*, 62. Dr. (Lt.) Musselman served in this dispensary.

[14] Stanley W. Smith, *Prisoner of the Emperor* (Boulder, CO: University Press of Colorado, 1991), 69.

[15] Chunn, *Of Rice and Men*, 58-59.

[16] Major Houston Parks Houser, Jr., Class of 1931, *1989 USMA Register*, #9309, 376. See *1931 Howitzer*, 195 for cadet information and the "Summary of Service" found in *Cullum File #9309* for Army assignments.

[17] Manny Lawton, *Some Survived* (Chapel Hill, NC: Algonquin Books of Chapel Hill, 1984), 163 told the story about Houser on the *Oryoku Maru*. 1st Lieutenant John M. Wright, Jr. wrote favorably about Houser in his book, *Captured on Corregidor*, 62, 128-29, and 166.

[18] Weller, *First Into Nagasaki*, 185.

19 Brigadier General Houston Parks Houser, Class of 1957, *1989 USMA Register*, #21392, 614. Houser also earned a Distinguished Service Medal, a Defense Superior Service Medal, two Meritorious Service Medals, and a Commendation Medal.

20 Major Charles Edward Nason Howard, Jr., Class of 1931. *1989 USMA Register*, #9215, 374. His entry does not mention being on a POW ship. He retired as a colonel in 1961. See "Obituary for Charles Edward Nason Howard, Jr.," *Assembly Magazine*, March 1978, 123 for details about his cadet and military service.

21 Citation in *Cullum File #9215.*

22"Howard Obituary," *Assembly Magazine*, March 1978, 123.

23 Roper, *Brothers of Paul*, 33-39. See Chapter Five, "Lieutenant Colonel Albert W. Braun, 'Friend, Warrior, Apostle, Soldier.'"

24 Chunn, *Of Rice and Men*, 51.

25 Major Clarence Bidgood, Class of 1935, *1989 USMA Register*, #10250, 394. See "Obituary for Clarence Bidgood," *Assembly Magazine*, September 1975, 129-30, and *Cullum File #10250.*

26 Colonel Ferdinand Clarence Bidgood, Class of 1960, *1989 USMA Register*, #23214, 652. Bidgood earned three Legions of Merit, a Bronze Star and an Air Medal in Vietnam, two Meritorious Service Medals, and a Commendation Medal.

27 Dooley, *Journal*, 95.

28 *1989 USMA Register*, 368.

29 *Diary*, 165.

30 *Ibid*, 61. See http://people.tamu.edu/~jwerickson/POW/BMFk-1roster.html.

31 *NARA Website*. See also *"Names Project-NM."*

32 Eugene A. Mazza, "The American Prisoners of War Rescued after the sinking of the Japanese transport Shinyo Maru, by the USS Paddle, SS 263, on 7 September 1944," at *Submarine Sailor.com* (2/25/2006), listed 83 survivors, with one dying on the beach, (3 of 13). On 27 October, the USS *Narwhal* evacuated 81 survivors. One remained behind to fight as a guerrilla. One listed survivor was Harry O. Fisher (sic), 803rd Engineers. Mazza listed his death on 29 June 1973 (4 of 13).

33 Michno, *Hellships*, 226-230. Paraphrase from 230.

34 Major Chester Lee Johnson, Class of 1937, *1989 USMA Register*, #10851, 406. During his later career Johnson earned two Distinguished Service Medals and two Legions of Merit.

35 *Diary*, 91 and Lawton, *Some Survived*, 162.

36 Olson, *Anywhere-Anytime*, 155.

37 Major Royal Reynolds, Jr., Class of 1933, *1989 USMA Register*, #9869, 386.

38 *"Names Project-NM."*

39 Joseph J. Wilson, "Obituary for Ovid Oscar Wilson," *Assembly Magazine*, June 1983, 133.

40 Chunn, *Of Rice and Men*, 64-66 and 70-72 provided useful information about O. O. Wilson.

41 Lt. Colonel Ovid Oscar Wilson, Class of 1925, *1989 USMA Register*, #7617, 346.

42 Chunn, *Of Rice and Men*, 64-65.

43 Bilek and O'Connell, *No Uncle Sam*, 110.

44 *Diary,* 113.

45 Orson, "Service in the Far East," 12-13.

46 Kerr, *Surrender*, 154-5 discussed Beecher's role and pointed out the difficulty of pleasing the Japanese and the POWs. I remember that my parents never said anything positive about the camp leaders in Santo Tomas.

47 Lawton, *Some Survived*, 211.

48 Survival for the ten confirmed on the New Mexico website – *"Names Project-NM."* Camps confirmed on the *NARA Website*.

49 *Ibid.* Survival for the three confirmed on the New Mexico website. Camps confirmed on the *NARA Website*.

50 Boisclaire, *Shadow*, 37.

51 *Ibid*, 80.

52 *Ibid,* 38 (size) and 89 (politics).

[53] *Ibid*, 123 (beatings), 198-200 (money), and 218 (army and teacher).

[54] *Ibid,* 208.

[55] *Ibid*, 208.

[56] Survival confirmed from *NARA Website, World War II Prisoners of War Data File.* http://aad. archives.gov/aad/record-detail.

[57] "Biography of Kenneth Rice," http://west-point-org/fam/abdc/autobios_files/Rice.html (15 Aug 2008).

[58] Guillermo Contreras, "Bataan survivors given an apology," Houston *Chronicle*, Monday, June 1, 2009, B4.

[59] *Ibid.*

Twelve

*"I have high hopes
for return home to
you three"*

Jap Radio Broadcast Declares
Maj. Fleeger Is Well in Camp

The war department today noti-fied Mrs. Louisa M. Fleeger, 401 East Twenty-fourth street, that an enemy propaganda broadcast from Japan has been intercepted, in which her husband, Maj. Harry J. Fleeger, assured her he is in good health and is in high hopes of re-turning home soon. The telegram included the complete message from her husband.

This is the first direct word from Maj. Fleeger in his 31 months as a prisoner in the Philippines, and supplements all previous re-ports from the war department. Four form cards had been received previously by the family. Maj. Fleeger, who was serving in the 26th Cavalry, was taken prisoner when Bataan fell.

Mrs. Fleeger was evacuated from the Philippines in May of 1941, and is teaching at Scottsbluff high school. She has lived here ap-proximately four years. The mes-sage reads, in part:

"My dearest Louise: Here is to assure you that I am well. My health is good and I have high hopes for return home to you three.

"I received the box of goods in good shape. It was my most prized article. I will never forget this favor. I also received 20 letters from you. I got three letters and eight pictures from mother. I al-ways think of her. Please tell dad I enjoyed his picture.

"Hello brother Sam and sister Frances. My constant love to you all. Tell Jim and Larry (Maj. Fleeger's young sons) I will be home some day to give them all the good times they have missed. Hello Jacky (his nephew). I am extending my love to you all."

The message concluded with Maj. Fleeger's name, middle initial and serial number.

Lack of information proved a distressing aspect of the POW situation. Fleeger mentioned how he longed for information from his family. But just as important, and possibly more critical, the families lacked information about the POWs – especially accurate and current information. The POWs could not report true information because the Japanese would never have permitted them to write derogatory comments on the cards and letters they sent to their families. Some people, as noted, often provided excessively hopeful news and sometimes they provided wildly inaccurate information to POW families. In doing so, the erstwhile reporters of good news added to the tragedy of the POWs.

False Hope

Fleeger wrote an apparently cheerful letter – obviously with the Japanese censors in mind – on 2 March 1944. It is not clear to whom he addressed it. He started it with

...THE ERSTWHILE REPORTERS OF GOOD NEWS ADDED TO THE TRAGEDY OF THE POWs.

"What a Washington's Birthday! 21 letters – my first during captivity...All probably on the Gripsholm, the grand mercy ship! No package yet but hoping soon." Then he wrote: "Am still well and hopeful. My life not dull. Much good reading, healthy amount of work and some writing. Much verse – expect to have a book...Keep busy and cheerful and believe in me. Time passes. It can't be so much longer now. We'll make up for this in happiness later."

His message must have created false hope. Except for being "hopeful," he did not provide an accurate picture of his life. He was not in good health at this time. Fleeger reported in his diary, as mentioned earlier, that he was suffering from *beri-beri*, and he added, "Don't mind the pain but don't want to come out of it with a weak heart." He was reading letters he had received earlier and the book, *Dildo Cay,* at the time, and he had read many books earlier. Fleeger did work. But his work at the airport could not be described as a "healthy amount" considering the long work hours in the sun, the lack of rest, and the brutal supervision. As for writing, Fleeger must have meant his diaries, but his entries tapered off in 1944. His comment about being cheerful seemed deceptive because his morale rose and fell constantly and by 1944 it was deteriorating steadily. Fleeger's analysis of himself as a husband and his proposed actions after he returned to the United States did not reflect a great belief in his own worthiness. Time indeed had passed, but it would be many months before the Americans returned to the Philippines. Moreover, no POW ever reported that time passed quickly."[1]

Unknown to Fleeger and the other POWs, the Japanese War Ministry issued an order to all POW Camp Commanders to kill the POWs before the Allies could recover them. The order directed the methods:

Whether they are destroyed individually or in groups, or, however it is done, with mass bombing, poisonous smoke, poisons, drowning, decapitation, or what, dispose of them as the situation dictates.

In any case it is the aim not to allow the escape of a single one, to annihilate them all, and not to leave any traces.[2]

So much for hope.

ΩΩΩ

Just after the November elections in 1944, the War Department notified Mrs. Fleeger that Americans had intercepted a message from her husband. It was the first "direct word from Maj. Fleeger in his 31 months as a prisoner in the Philippines." The information appeared in a newspaper article.

Jap Radio Broadcast Declares Maj. Fleeger Is Well in Camp.

The article quoted Fleeger's message:

My Dearest Louise:

Here is to assure you I am well. My health is good and I have high hopes for return home to you three.

I received the box of goods in good shape. It was my most prized article. I will never forget this favor. I also received 20 letters from you. I got three letters and eight pictures from mother. I always think of her. Please tell dad I enjoyed his picture...Tell Jim and Larry (Maj. Fleeger's young sons) I will be home some day to give

HOPE 1944

FEBRUARY
MACARTHUR INVADED THE ADMIRALTY ISLANDS. OPENED ADVANCE TO THE PHILIPPINES.

MAY
U. S. INVADED HOLLANDIA, NEW GUINEA.

JUNE
NIMITZ INVADED SAIPAN, GUAM, AND TINIAN IN THE MARINAS.

AUGUST
JAPANESE WAR MINISTRY ISSUED ORDER TO DESTROY ALL POWS.

SEPTEMBER
MACARTHUR INVADED MOROTAI PREPARATORY TO INVADING MINDANAO.

OCTOBER
FLEEGER BOARDED THE *ARISAN MARU*.

20 OCTOBER
MACARTHUR INVADED LEYTE.

24 OCTOBER
U. S. SUBMARINE SUNK THE *ARISAN MARU*.

NOVEMBER
JAPANESE RADIO BROADCAST DECLARED MAJOR FLEEGER WAS WELL.

them all the good times they have missed...I
am extending my love to you all.[3]

It was great news, but there would be no good times. Fleeger had died two weeks earlier. The Japanese high command had to have known this. Why then did the Japanese release the messages from those POWs who had died aboard the *Arisan Maru*?

Probably about the same time, another undated, unidentified newspaper article reported:

MAJ. FLEEGER SENDS MESSAGE FROM JAPAN

The Provost Marshal's office in the war department in Washington, D. C., has advised the family of Judge L. L. Fleeger of Parker, S. D. of a short wave message picked up last week purported to be sent from Japan from their son Maj. Harry J. Fleeger, who has been a prisoner in the Philippines for more than three years.

The authenticity of the radiogram is certain for Maj. Fleeger not only sent the message to his wife and two small children in Nebraska, but mentioned his mother by her pet name, "Cliffie," also told of receiving pictures from his father, Judge Fleeger, and expressed thanks for a box of medicine sent to him by a doctor from the states.

In the three years that hundreds of letters have been sent him, he mentions receiving only 20. He stated he was well and hoping for the time to come when he might be home again.

Judge Fleeger concluded from the message, that "his son has been moved with prisoners from the Philippines to Japan.[4] Unfortunately, he drew the wrong conclusion.

Another undated and unidentified newspaper article announced that Mrs. Fleeger had better news about her husband.

Mrs. Fleeger Hears Reports on Husband

Through a war correspondent liberated from internment in the Philippines, Mrs. Harry J.

> *Fleeger, Scottsbluff school teacher, has received word concerning her husband, Maj. Fleeger, who was captured on Bataan.*
>
> *Monday, Mrs. Fleeger received a wire from Franz Weissblatt, United Press correspondent, who informed her that he had seen Maj. Fleeger last October, that he was well and not to worry. The wire ended with the words "Harry Japan," possibly a garbled statement that Maj. Fleeger has been taken to a war prisoner camp in the Jap home islands.*

Weissblatt, a civilian employee in the Adjutant General's Corps, had been with the 26th Cavalry during the fight on Bataan. He had accompanied Lt. Leisenring and his scout cars when the Americans found that the Japanese had cut off their small group from the 26th Cavalry Regiment and, in turn, had cut off the regiment from other units on Bataan. Weissblatt had left the area with the scout cars as the cavalrymen tried to rejoin the regiment. Unfortunately, the Japanese ambushed the group at Culis, destroyed three of the four scout cars and severely wounded and captured Weissblatt. Most likely, from the tone of his letter, he knew Fleeger and the other officers of the regiment before he was captured.[5] Fleeger, however, never mentioned his being in Cabanatuan, so Weissblatt must have spent the war in Bilibid Prison in Manila. After being released from Bilibid in February 1945 he returned to the United States where he contacted POW families.[6]

On 10 March 1945, Weissblatt typed a detailed letter to Mrs. Fleeger on United Press Associations' letterhead (Appendix Y). He reported:

> *As I told you in my wire, Harry was okay when I saw him just before he went to Japan. He was with Paul Jones of the 26th and <u>that ship arrived in Japan alright</u>, all other rumors not withstanding. I am sure of that as I saw the list that the Japs in Nippon sent back to Bilibid.*
>
> *Harry's <u>morale was high</u> when I saw him and he was about <u>135-140 in weight</u>. He and Paul had a chance to pick up lots of corn meal before they left and we had lots of parties during their stay in Bilibid.*
>
> *Do not worry about him as I am sure that he will come thru this alright. We have heard from reliable sources that the <u>prisoners in Japan are being well treated</u>. The chances are that Harry and the other field officers have been taken to Wainwright's camp in Manchuria. They all had heavy clothing issued to them when they left Manila. They were Jap uniforms but that doesn't matter so long as the men are able to keep warm.*
>
> *I just reread your letter. About the broadcast. Harry did not make one while in Bilibid so <u>I guess that it was made in Japan</u>. <u>The October boat WAS NOT sunk</u>. The survivors that arrived in the States were on a ship that left Lansang, Mindanao*

with 800 aboard and was torpedoed in September. There are a series of articles running in COLLIERS magazine right now written by three other survivors of that same boat. So you see the whole darn story has been misquoted or the men have forgotten dates. I have been trying to get permission from the War Department to write a corrected story on the matter.[7]

ΩΩΩ

But remember Fleeger's final notes on 8 October 1944. "Very hungry. Weigh 119 – want to recall these days when I have food again – ... We wait and hope ... we fear a trip north now with real reason. The month will tell – 2½ years a prisoner tomorrow – will it ever end -----" [8]

Weissblatt's letter must have thrilled Mrs. Fleeger and Fleeger's family. Shortly thereafter, Mrs. Fleeger reported to other POW wives that "Alas, Harry was not in Camp No 1 [Cabanatuan] on their Liberation Day. However, I have heard from a very reliable source that he arrived safely in Japan. They were issued heavy clothing before sailing. It is also wonderful to know that he was at a normal weight last Fall. It looks like some of us still have a long wait ahead of us, but we can take it if it doesn't last forever. Carry on."[9]

Weissblatt was criminally wrong (note the underlined passages above). Fleeger did not weigh 135-140 pounds. What parties in Bilibid? Fleeger's morale had dropped into the tank again, the Japanese did not treat the POWs well in Japan, and the Japanese had sunk the October boat. And Weissblatt wanted to correct the story about the *Shinyo Maru*?

The reporter wrote a similar letter to the widow of Lieutenant William Bowen, Troop C, 26th Cavalry, who had perished with Fleeger on the *Arisan Maru*, but he wrote a second one to Mrs. Bowen and qualified his earlier report. Apparently, he did not write a follow-up letter to Mrs. Fleeger.[10]

Weissblatt's hopeful message, much like Mrs. O. O. Wilson's earlier one, was fiction. By 10 March 1945, Fleeger and his comrades had been dead for over four months. And by that time, American Rangers, Alamo Scouts, and Filipino guerrillas had rescued the 511 POWs who were still in Cabanatuan. Those survivors had already contacted their families. Mrs. Fleeger, seeking information about her husband, in turn, contacted one of them: Captain Merle Musselman, U. S. Army Medical Corps. On 2 May 1945, Dr. Musselman, wrote Mrs. Fleeger. He was in a position to bring real news to her, but he wrote; "I just can't place your brother but feel that I must know him." While that must have been terribly disappointing, the doctor did explain the radio messages. He reported: "Some few men & officers chosen by lot were allowed to prepare 300 word messages to be radioed home while we were in Cabanatuan in the summer and early fall of '44. We never thought any of them had been sent however. Yours is the first suggestion that any were received." So at least the radio intercepts were real!

Musselman ended his short, handwritten letter with "I certainly appreciate the hours of suspense and the disappointment that you have suffered and I know how difficult it is to go on about the every day duties under such circumstances. I am so sorry. I join you in every hope for the future.[11]

Truth

Around 23 June 1945 while the war against Japanese forces continued in the mountains of Luzon, Mrs. Fleeger learned the truth: her husband had been killed. Another newspaper article announced:

Major Fleeger Dead on Jap Prisoner Vessel Sunk by Sub Attack

In part, it reported:

> *The name of Maj. Fleeger is on an official list of prisoners lost on Oct. 24 last year, obtained from the Jap government by International Red Cross after long delay. Maj. Fleeger will be carried on war department records as killed in action.[12]*

Young Jim Fleeger was at summer camp in Minnesota. When he returned, his uncle, Sam Fleeger, met his bus and told him about his father's death.[13] Reality came nearly eight months to the day after the *Arisan Maru* sank into the cold waters of the East China Sea. There would be no more false hope.

On 9 July 1945, Secretary of War Henry L. Stimson hand wrote a letter to Mrs. Fleeger. He said: "little that we can do or say will console you for the death of your loved one. We profoundly appreciate the greatness of your loss for in a very real sense the loss suffered by any of us in the battle for our country is a loss shared by all of us. When the medal, which you will shortly receive, reaches you, I want you to know that with it goes my sincerest sympathy and the hope that time and the victory of our cause will finally lighten the burden of your grief."[14]

"WE PROFOUNDLY APPRECIATE THE GREATNESS OF YOUR LOSS...AND...HOPE THAT TIME AND THE VICTORY OF OUR CAUSE WILL FINALLY LIGHTEN THE BURDEN OF YOUR GRIEF."

SECRETARY OF WAR HENRY STIMSON

Soon the three notebooks Harry Fleeger had left behind in Cabanatuan would reach his wife. Those along with his pre-war letters and photographs, the telegram, letters, and cards received during the war, the Purple Heart, and a charcoal rubbing[15] of his name on the *Tablets of the Missing and Buried at Sea* in the Manila Cemetery would become his physical legacy to his family.

Reutel

In his book *Prisoners of the Japanese*, Gavan Daws wrote that among POWs there were questions about "the overall performance or non-performance of POW officers in the camps," and he added that "officer privilege was a running sore[16] He obviously implied that American officers failed to provide strong leadership to the enlisted men in the camps. In modern parlance, they failed to eat last.[17] Captain John Wright also criticized brother officers, writing that "...in many cases, West Pointers failed to accept leadership responsibility." He said they should have been outstanding leaders. He reported that some were, but "many were doubly conspicuous because they failed to perform in a manner expected of them by the people who believed West Point should produce the leaders." He added, however, that "the integrity of West Pointers never faltered, at a time when animalism tended to disregard honor, and dishonesty was not uncommon," and that their "devotion to their country never wavered." [18]

Fleeger said nothing about the camp leaders or brother officers that would shed any light on Daws' comments or on Wright's comments. He did not mention any actions of Marine Lt. Colonel Curtis Beecher, the senior line officer in Cabanatuan. How would he have evaluated him? Would he have supported Captain Oliver Orson's negative view or said that Beecher did a good job under adverse circumstances? He said nothing about the official actions of his cavalry comrade, Trapnell, who commanded Group II in the camp, although he did note that he would contact Trapnell for commendations that he planned to write after the war.[19] But how would he have evaluated Trapnell's performance in the camp? He never mentioned Lt. Colonel Harold Johnson, a future Army Chief of Staff, who did a great job in managing food in the camp.

Fleeger also did not touch on another subject that Daws highlighted: "the lengths to which POW officers would go to maintain their privileges of rank at the expense of their own enlisted men."[20] Daws did not clarify whether he was talking about the general officers only, the field grade officers, or all officers. Would Fleeger have agreed with Daws? Fleeger mentioned that he had an orderly. Was he an example of what Daws was talking about? Having an orderly seemed a bit incongruous for Americans in a POW camp, unless the orderly volunteered for the job and gained an exemption from required labor, or unless Fleeger hired his POW orderly and paid him in some fashion. Also, he said nothing about Americans who failed to meet proper ethical and soldierly standards: the men who turned in the three officers whom the Japanese brutalized and then savagely killed, and the collaborators who helped the Japanese for their own personal gain. His insights and comments would have been priceless.

WHAT WERE GOING TO BE FLEEGER'S REUTEL STORIES?

There were many holes in the diary that his family and historians would like to know more about. What were going to be Fleeger's Reutel stories? Would he flesh out his own experiences during the campaign on Luzon and on Bataan? Obviously, from Chandler's comments, Fleeger had to have been privy to some "inside dope" from the senior commanders when he brought back their operating instructions to the 26th Cavalry. He probably could have added some interesting "inside information" to the history of the campaign. How did he measure the various commanders: which ones impressed him, and which ones did not? Was he present when Wainwright visited the regiment, if so, what were his impressions of the cavalry warrior? Would the major recall his actions on Luzon and Bataan and would he tell his family about them and about his brief time as a squadron commander? There is no full record of his staff actions or his command actions so his comments would have been invaluable. What would Fleeger tell his wife and children about his horse or horses and his reactions to the slaughtering of the horses? It must have been a bad moment for him on Bataan. Would he be able to tell the families of the fallen – especially those he planned to write to when he returned home - anything more than he had written in his diaries. Perhaps all he could add were his personal con-

HOW WOULD FLEEGER REMEMBER THE DEATH MARCH AND WOULD HE BE ABLE TO TELL ANYBODY ABOUT IT...?

AT CAMP O'DONNELL, WHAT DID HE HEAR AND SEE?

dolences unless some died in his presence. What did he know about the deaths of the scout car lieutenants, Lieutenant Marks, and Lieutenant Colonel Ketchum that Chandler did not know and how much first-hand information did he have about Captain Wheeler's and Lieutenant Ramsey's actions on Bataan? As the Adjutant for so long, he should have gathered up all the available information about them to prepare their various citations for decorations. Would he concur that Ramsey and his men made the last cavalry charge in U. S. military operations at Moron? Because he fought nearby, he might have been able to verify that information.

How would Fleeger remember the Death March and would he be able to tell anybody about it, or like so many survivors would he have just kept everything inside for decades? Was he lucky to march in a group with "good guards" or was he in a group with brutal guards? With whom did he walk on the march? Did he march with 26th Cavalrymen or with strangers? Was he near Captain Miller when the Japanese killed him? Did he begin the March with his cavalry boots on as Miller had, or had he discarded them, or had they worn out? Was he in Trapnell's group? Whom did he see on the March? Did he see the Japanese kill anyone? Did he see any American officer stand up to the Japanese? Did he know about the atrocity against the Filipinos of the 91st Division? If so how did he learn about it? Why didn't he try to escape? Why did others not try to escape? How did he manage to survive the March? What drove him on? Did he need help; if so, who helped him? In turn, who did he help?

At Camp O'Donnell, what did he hear and see? Did he work on any burial parties? Why was he sick? Did he get placed in the Zero Ward and survive, or did he just get minimal attention in a primitive medical building? Did he know anything about the murder of Colonel Hirsch or the death of Lt. Colonel Uddenberg whom he mentioned in his diary? Did he know anything about Lt. Colonel Horton's activities in the camp? If so, how did he evaluate Horton? Was there more to the story that Horton's severe critic reported? What was said at Horton's funeral? Who stood out as heroes in the dismal environment and who were not heroes? Did people cooperate in O'Donnell, or was it "everyman for himself?"

There are many questions about Cabanatuan. Why did Fleeger almost die there? Was he ill with malaria or dysentery? He talked about diphtheria, but he did not say if he contracted the disease. What did he mean when

> **THERE ARE MANY QUESTIONS ABOUT CABANATUAN. WHY DID FLEEGER ALMOST DIE THERE?**

he wrote, "I will write the agonies of 'Boot Hill' – as part of my post war notes"?[21] Why did he include Siegfried Sassoon's Poem, "The Troops," in his diary? How did Sassoon's words affect him?

> *Death will stand grieving in the field of war*
> *Since your unvanquished hardihood is spent.*
> *And thru some mooned Valhalla there will pass*
> *Battalions and Battalions, scarred from hell;*
> *The unrelenting army that was youth –*
> *The legions who have suffered and are dust.*[22]

Fleeger made several references to several of his "blood brothers" - Bauer, Bidgood, Browne, Dunmyer, Murphey, Svihra, and Zwaska – members of his "shooting squad." Almost immediately, the Japanese had organized the POWs into groups of ten "blood brothers" and told each group if one or more escaped they would execute the remainder of the group. But he did not say whether the organization of "blood brothers" undermined any overt resistance in the camp or put escape "off limits" for most prisoners. In one early episode involving a work party, the Japanese did execute a shooting squad in front of other POWs. In that incident, an older brother witnessed the killing of his younger brother. Executing a soldier for trying to escape or escaping – unless he killed in the process - violated the Geneva Conventions that the Japanese said they would honor and violated the general laws of war.[23] Fleeger did not mention this or any similar action. And he did not mention the brutalization and execution of Lt. Colonel Howard Breitung and his two companions. Did the POWs who stopped them fear for their lives if the three escaped? What did the other POWs do to those who caused the brutal deaths? His insights would have been priceless.

These were some big holes in his story, but there were smaller holes created by several Reutel stories. What was he going to tell Louise after he wrote about meeting a soldier named Cater who knew his brother Sam? Why did he write Reutel and follow it with "rewrite enroute." He gave no clue. What did he mean when he wrote: "Buggery in the bahay" – The book I will write of all of this." Was homosexuality rife in the camp or did buggery have another meaning? And why did he write Reutel next to his "P-J idea" and "the altar."[24] How about his "What achievement" written on 29 July 1943 with Reutel attached? What were the million dreams of better ways to do things for Louise that he mentioned on New Year's Day 1944?

And who were the heroes in Cabanatuan and who were the slugs? How did his brother 26th Cavalry officers perform? What did he think of Minton? Did he know about his self-serving actions? What about the treasonous Provoo who caused the Japanese to execute his friend Burton Thomson? Did Fleeger know about Provoo? If the traitor, Provoo, lived in Cabanatuan or anywhere near American POWs, why didn't the POWs kill him? Were there any POWs prepared to do that?

...AND WHO WERE THE HEROES IN CABANATUAN AND WHO WERE THE SLUGS?

Finally, who would Fleeger have blamed for his capture and imprisonment? He could have blamed President Franklin Roosevelt for basically ignoring the situation in the Far East while concentrating on saving England, and then have blamed him for backing the United States into war because he wanted Japan to fire the first shot. Would he have blamed Roosevelt for the disaster at Pearl Harbor rather than the local commanders, Admiral Husband Kimmel and Lt. General Walter Short? Sailors could have done so because the President, against the advice of the U. S. Fleet Commander, Admiral J. O. Richardson, ordered the fleet from the West Coast to the small, restricted anchorage at Pearl Harbor that became a death trap. Or would he have blamed General George Marshall, the Army Chief of Staff, for not doing enough for the Philippine garrison? He could have done so because Marshall focused on the situation in Europe and many on the Army Staff, including Brigadier General Dwight Eisenhower who had just returned from the Philippines, had concluded that the Philippines could not be defended, or would he have blamed the navy commanders who had no intention of driving across the Pacific to reinforce the Philippines as originally planned under War Plan Orange and who withdrew the Asiatic Fleet so quickly from Philippine waters? He could have done that and scorched Admiral Thomas Hart who led his Asiatic Fleet to the relative safety of the Netherlands

...WHO WOULD FLEEGER HAVE BLAMED FOR HIS CAPTURE AND IMPRISONMENT?

East Indies? Or would he have blamed all the key <u>na</u>tional leaders for his predicament? Obviously, they had ignored the situation too long and then did too little too late to help the Philippine garrison defeat the Japanese or at least to survive until they sent real help to the isolated garrison.

In the Philippines, would he have blamed General George Grunert, the Commander of the Philippine Department, for not developing the existing American forces (including the Philippine Scouts) into more well trained and prepared units? Some would have blamed the disaster on MacArthur who took over in July 1941, barely five months before Pearl Harbor or some would have concluded that Roosevelt gave MacArthur an impossible task but still have blasted MacArthur for not doing enough with what he had. Would he have criticized MacArthur for focusing on March 1942 as the date of the war beginning against Japan, as he had done, and for failing to take actions that would have been more useful in December 1941? He could have concluded that MacArthur made a catastrophic decision by being too aggressive by trying to defend at the beaches with raw troops and by doing so added to the tactical dilemma by moving critical supplies of ammunition, food, and medicine out of Bataan. However, he could have reasoned that MacArthur took a needed, calculated risk to try to stop the projected Japanese landings before the Japanese could gain footholds on Luzon. Would Fleeger have considered MacArthur's faith in the Filipino soldier unjustified considering the collapse of so many of the newly recruited, untrained, and ill equipped Philippine Divisions? Perhaps so, but he could have supported MacArthur's faith because of the stout fighting of the Philippine Scouts and many other Filipinos, including Filipino airmen, by the immediate development of a Filipino guerrilla movement that focused on MacArthur's return, and by the loyalty of the vast number of Filipinos during the war. Finally, would he have blamed Generals Wainwright, Parker, Jones, et. al. for not doing enough to prepare their troops for war and consequently being overwhelmed? He might

... WOULD FLEEGER HAVE BLAMED HIMSELF AND HIS COMRADES FOR THEIR SURRENDER AND IMPRISONMENT OR CONSIDERED THAT HE AND HIS FRIENDS HAD NOT BEEN PREPARED TO FIGHT?

have echoed General Chynoweth's concerns or he might have just concluded that the Japanese had been too strong and too good to have been stopped in 1941 and 1942.

And, what about Fleeger and his friends - would Fleeger have blamed himself and his comrades for their surrender and imprisonment or considered that he and his friends had not been prepared to fight? From his pre-war comments, if brutally honest with himself, he might have drawn that conclusion. Would he have supported Chandler's assertion that the 26th Cavalry was superbly trained or would he have reported that his regiment and too many other formations were running around pretending to get trained? After the Army and Navy issued war warnings, would Fleeger have considered that polo was a good substitute for hard field training for the cavalry? Probably, he would not have drawn such a conclusion. How would he explain that no units were deployed into beach positions or how would he explain that the air commanders did not have air patrols up during all daylight hours before war began? Perhaps, the issues did not concern him, but they should have. Was Fleeger blinded to the criticality of the situation on Luzon in late 1941 by his expectation to rotate home, and were many of his friends also blinded by their desire to rotate back to the United States? Again, if he were brutally honest with himself as he had been with his evaluation of himself as a husband, he might have concluded that he and many others did not lean forward in their saddles or foxholes when war was ominously close. Or did the Americans Fleeger knew underestimate the Japanese and consider that Japan would not dare to strike the United States in the Philippines? The majority of the soldiers, sailors, air men, and marines in the Philippines could not have been as confident as the Americans in the United States that the U. S. Navy could handle Japan as, *Life* Magazine stated on 8 December 1941? Would Fleeger have agreed with Roy Doolan's anonymous critic who said – "If the situation in the Far East was so critical, the Americans out there had better pack and come home"? Nothing he wrote before the war would suggest that he would have reached that conclusion if he had survived.

Finally, would Fleeger have ignored the American problems – as well as the British ones – and just blamed Japan for being an acquisitive and war mongering power determined to eradicate white influence from East Asia and the Pacific and bring the vital areas under Japanese suzerainty under the banner of "Asia for Asiatics." Most likely, he would not have because he would have concluded that American leaders at all levels made too many poor decisions with respect to war with Japan, and consequently they set up the fall of the Philippines and the loss of so many American and Filipino lives.

FLEEGER'S ANSWERS WOULD HAVE AFFECTED HIS LIFE AFTER THE WAR. WOULD THEY HAVE MADE HIM A BITTER SURVIVOR OR A REFLECTIVE ONE...?

These were key questions for thinking professionals who fought and lost in the Philippines. Fleeger's answers would have affected his life after the war. Would they have made him a bitter survivor or a reflective one who could have pushed on to a continued army career and a rich and productive life? One can only guess, but if he had continued to serve until 1950, he most likely would have been shocked to see a new and aggressive

North Korean Army strike without warning and overrun poorly prepared South Korean troops and their American advisors in days and then overrun poorly prepared American troops who deployed to stop the enemy onslaught just as the Japanese had done to the Filipinos and Americans on Luzon nine years earlier. And, most likely, he also would have been appalled to learn about new death marches that one Philippine veteran said were worse than the Bataan Death March.

Legacy

Fleeger's letters and diaries revealed that he was a good and decent man, a dedicated Army officer who may have been so dedicated before war began that he had put his family below his professional duty, a POW who faced challenges that he could never have expected to face in war, and a man who had to dig down deep inside himself to survive.

Fleeger went through all sorts of exercises to hang on mentally when the physical condition of camp life was terrible and he was beaten down. Whether he was extracting ideas from books to strengthen his will, or reviewing religious themes to enhance his spirit, or constructing his own new rules for living in Cabanatuan, or designing his post-war life, Fleeger tried desperately to survive mentally. His many forays into the camp chapel and his attendance at religious services seemed to be a change from his pre-war life and seemed to bolster his morale and will to survive. So much evidence from POW survivors of newer wars indicates that the ability to survive mentally is the key to surviving physically. And Fleeger, despite many low points, survived mentally and emotionally until he left Cabanatuan, but just barely as his final question – "Will it ever end?" – indicated.

In great part he survived emotionally because of his wife. His story revealed that he was desperately attached

FLEEGER'S LETTERS AND DIARIES REVEALED THAT HE WAS A GOOD AND DECENT MAN...

IN GREAT PART HE SURVIVED EMOTIONALLY BECAUSE OF HIS WIFE... WITHOUT HER HE SEEMED LOST.

to Louise. Without her, he seemed lost. Even before war started, Fleeger suffered from her absence. His emotional dependence on her seemed to be the central story in his diaries, highlighted by getting her letters and hoping that she said she loved him. In the future, Fleeger seemed to have decided that he would place his wife before his career, so much so that at one time he wrote that he would never leave her. And more critically, he, as noted, feared that he would return a changed man and that his wife might not care for what he had become. Fleeger's story illustrated how separation, loneliness, and isolation took a terrible toll on him, and probably did the same to all the POWs.

ΩΩΩ

On the humorous side, reading Fleeger's plans for his sons, it appeared that he was well on the way to becoming an overwhelming parent who would move heaven and earth for his boys to give them more than he had, probably to their dismay. The major appeared to be a "soccer dad" in the making.

THE MAJOR APPEARED TO BE A "SOCCER DAD" IN THE MAKING.

On the historical side, there is little that anyone can take away historically from the diaries because Fleeger obviously chose not to write anything of intelligence or military value or anything critical of the Japanese because the Japanese could have confiscated his diaries and used his comments against him or other POWs. The Japanese certainly would have been brutal if they found that Fleeger had written about their sadistic treatment and punishment of the POWs on the Death March, at Camp O'Donnell, and at Cabanatuan. As the war neared its end, and before Fleeger boarded the *Arisan Maru*, the Japanese High Command had ordered all subordinate commanders to destroy POW records so that the Allies could not capture them. With such a mind set, they would have gone apoplectic if they found that POWs had secretly kept personal records about their atrocious handling of allied POWs. The interesting indiscretion in the diaries is that Fleeger identified POWs such as Thomas Trapnell and John Wheeler who had won DSCs in combat against the Japanese. The Japanese would not have been pleased to learn that highly decorated Americans were among their POWs. On Bataan, they massacred Filipino soldiers whom they knew had caused Japanese casualties. Of course, they could have read *Life* Magazine of that time and discovered the information.[25]

Fleeger's writings covered the lack of food and the lack of medicine in Cabanatuan, but not nearly as thoroughly as an historian would desire. The lack of sufficient food devastated the POWs and it triggered other problems: vulnerability to disease, inability to fight off infections and insect borne diseases such as malaria and dengue fever, and the needless rise of scurvy, pellagra, and *beri-beri*. Additionally, the general physical disability of the POWs prevented them from working productively. What showed up plainly was that when Fleeger and the POWs received food parcels with vitamins, they recovered some health quickly and maintained their improved health while the food and vitamins lasted. And even more revealing was that after the Cabanatuan survivors found and consumed the food stocks they found in the camp when the guards left for a few days in January 1945, they quickly regained some strength.[26]

Fleeger covered the lack of medicine periodically, noting, of course, his own health problems. Through friends, he got medicines to help him through some tough spots. The lack of proper medicine produced terrible results. People died when they could have recovered. Dysentery should not have been fatal, but hundreds died from it in captivity. Malaria should not have been fatal in most cases, but hundreds more died from it in captivity. In the early days of Cabanatuan, hundreds of POWs died each month, mostly from illnesses. To make matters worse, the U. S. Government and Red Cross had shipped over medicines for the POWs and the Japanese withheld them from the prisoners. This deprivation of medicine by the Japanese was criminal. Fleeger did not directly comment on the epidemic deaths in the camp in 1942.

The Japanese used POWs for laborers, but by starving them, failed to get any useful productivity from them. With modern slaves, the Japanese failed to protect their investment. Fleeger mentioned working on labor details, but he did not talk much about what he did. Underfed and always tired, the POWs were hardly productive workers. Fleeger did not explain how the Japanese had forced officers to work as laborers – in violation of the Rules of War and the Geneva Conventions. If the officers did not work, the Japanese would not feed them. And he did not write about the brutal treatment the Japanese handed out to weak or poor workers in the field, although he did talk about being disciplined: "quanned off" on one occasion and subjected to the "sun treatment" in others. But, he provided no details. Fortunately in the Philippines, the Japanese did not make the POWs work in their war industries as they did in Japan, Korea, and Manchuria. Luckily, Fleeger worked in the camp library for several months. That may have saved his life after he got over his initial bouts of sickness in 1942.

AND IN ALL THE WRITING, FLEEGER NEVER COMMENTED ABOUT THE JAPANESE OFFICERS AND MEN HE DEALT WITH EXCEPT TO WRITE DOWN A FEW NICKNAMES AND TO REFER TO "CHARLES."

And in all the writing, Fleeger never commented about the Japanese officers and men he dealt with except to write down a few

*ONE FEAR BURIED IN THE
DIARY TURNED OUT TO BE
FATAL: THE FEAR OF BEING
MOVED TO JAPAN.*

nicknames and to refer to "Charles." I am sure with his eye to people and his recording of the actions of his 26th Cavalry officers on Bataan, Fleeger had prepared a useful mental *dossier* about the brutal Japanese soldiers. The recorded "nicknames" most likely were reminders about the really nasty guards. If he had survived, he probably would have made an exceptional expert witness before the war crimes tribunals.

Fleeger also never mentioned how the loss of his friends and comrades and his troops in combat, during the Death March, at Camp O'Donnell, and in Cabanatuan affected him. But these deaths – "Pop" Thomas for instance - must have touched him deeply. To survive, and he said he was a survivor, he must have shut them out.

ΩΩΩ

One fear buried in the diary turned out to be fatal: the fear of being moved to Japan. On 12 April 1943, Fleeger wrote: "Bill is on a detail of 1,000 to leave soon for Japan – we may all go later – news very meager."[27] In September 1943, he mentioned "800 leave for Japan – 800 for detail here – our group stays on.[28] In early August 1944, he noted that a "big detail went to Japan – we hear ill news of them."[29] In his last entry Fleeger on 8 October 1944 wrote: "...we fear a trip north now with real reason. This month will tell."[30] It was his fourth to last comment.

In his entry before that, Fleeger summed up his life and looked at his future:

Meanwhile we hope – Grow Thinner – And I dream of you each hour that passes – my love for you is so great Louise – A sweet kiss – as the first on your front porch at home – You've ever been just that adorable – my wife – My notebooks are almost full – I plan to put them away soon – and will have to tell you the rest of my countless thoughts of you and our boys. God how I ache to be with you again – and to begin as a real dad to Jim and Larry.

But even without all the missing parts, the diaries provide a useful insight into life in a Japanese POW camp and a great insight into what defeat, disaster, and imprisonment did to one good and decent American soldier – Major Harry J. Fleeger, 26th Cavalry (PS) - who died in the service of his country so that, as President Harry Truman proclaimed to many war widows:

> "FREEDOM LIVES AND THROUGH IT HE LIVES,
> IN A WAY THAT HUMBLES THE UNDERTAKINGS OF MOST MEN."[31]

REUTEL.

Notes

[1] Original typed letter. (James Fleeger's Papers).

[2] Homes, *Unjust Enrichment*, 116,and 124.

[3] Original, undated, and unidentified newspaper clipping. Date taken from article on back of clipping. (James Fleeger's Papers).

[4] Original, undated, an unidentified newspaper clipping. (James Fleeger's Papers).

[5] Chandler, "26th Cavalry," *ACJ*, May-Jun 1947, 14.

[6] *NARA Website*, 13 March 2008. See "Frank" Weissblatt.

[7] Original typed and signed letter (James Fleeger's Papers).

[8] *Diary*, 164.

[9] Mary Grimes and Pat Diller (eds.), *Philippine Postcripts*, June 1945 (Charlotte, NC), 4.

[10] Weissblatt sent a similar letter to the widow of 2nd Lieutenant William E. Bowen, who had joined Praeger's Troop C in the northern mountains and who had perished on the *Arisan Maru* with Fleeger. Norling reported that Franz Weissblatt wrote "confidently with the news that Bowen's ship had arrived safely in Japan." According to Norling, in another letter dated 2 July 1945, Weissblatt "backpedals, reminding her that the U.S. War Department gets all its information about American POWs from the Japanese so nobody will really learn the fate of prisoners until the war ends." Norling, *Intrepid Guerrillas*, footnote 26, 267-268. There is no record of such a follow-up letter from Weissblatt to Mrs. Fleeger.

[11] Original handwritten letter sent to Mrs. Fleeger at 2503 – 3rd Ave, Scottsbluff, NE and mailed in St. Louis, MO. (James Fleeger's Papers). March 2006. The doctor had been with a provisional Philippine Scout field artillery unit before his capture. He was living at 404 South 13 Street, Nebraska City, NE when he wrote Mrs. Fleeger.

[12] Original, undated, unidentified newspaper clipping. Date taken from another entry. (James Fleeger's papers). March 2006.

[13] Comment to author, 17 March 2006.

[14] Letter from Henry L. Stimson, 9 July 1945. (James Fleeger's Papers).

[15] Rubbing made by Susan Bradley, January 2005.

[16] *Daws, Prisoners*, 2 (performance) and 110 (running sore).

[17] In my day, Army officers were advised always to eat last after they had ensured that their troops had all been fed. Good officers did that; good company commanders ensured that their junior officers observed the protocol.

[18] Wright, *Captured on Corregidor*, 150-51.

[19] *Diary*, 168.

[20] *Daws, Prisoners*, 405.

[21] *Diary*, 52.

[22] *Ibid*, 58.

[23] *Ibid*, 67. See also Knox, *Death March,* 182-84.

[24] Reutel entries, *Diary,* 110 and 111,

[25] Trapnell was written up in *Life* Magazine, March 1942

[26] Breuer, *The Great Raid*, 153 and 157-58.

[27] *Diary*, 91.

[28] *Ibid*, 117 (13 September).

[29] *Ibid*, 158.

[30] *Ibid*, 164.

[31] Words from an accolade presented by President Harry S. Truman to the next of kin of some Americans who perished in the war.

Epilogue

Master Sergeant Calvin Robert Graef,
1st Sergeant, Headquarters Battery,
515th Coast Artillery Regiment (AAA),
one of the five survivors of the Arisan
Maru picked up by Chinese, reported:

A red-headed major, who had been
desperately ill three-fourths of the
journey, mounted the steps and said:
'Boys, we're in a hulluva jam – but
we've been in jams before.
Remember just one thing: We're
American soldiers. Let's play it that
way to the very end of the script.'

Graef added that the men on the
sinking Arisan Maru cheered
the major.

Special Note

The quotation on 305 came from an undated, unidentified newspaper clipping. It may have been from Mason City, IA. (James Fleeger's papers).

The quotation originated in Calvin Graef's article, "We prayed to die," in *Cosmopolitan Magazine.* Since there were two "red-headed" majors on the *Arisan Maru,* it is not clear whether this report identified Fleeger or his comrade, Paul Jones. Jones' obituary in 1946 stated that Jones had been positively identified as the officer in question, but it gave no source of verification. Glusman, *Conduct Under Fire,* 359-60 and note on 539, identified Jones as the "red headed" officer. I have not examined Glusman's source so cannot verify the information.

The Fleeger family has always assumed that the "red-headed" major was Harry Fleeger.

ON 7 JUNE 1955,

NEARLY TEN YEARS AFTER HE LEARNED OF HIS FATHER'S

DEATH,

JAMES E. FLEEGER GRADUATED FROM WEST POINT

AND

JOINED THE ARMY

AS A

SECOND LIEUTENANT OF FIELD ARTILLERY.

Appendices

Special Symbols Used in the Appendices

♠ Memorialized on Tablets of the Missing/Buried at Sea at the American Military Cemetery in Manila, Philippines, an American Battle Monument Commission facility.

♠♠ Memorialized at Punchbowl Cemetery in Honolulu, Hawaii.

† Buried at the American Military Cemetery in Manila.

†† Buried at West Point.

▶ West Point Graduate.

Special Note

The names of the officers and men who did not survive the war are italicized in the Appendices, End Notes, and Index.

Appendix A

ABBREVIATIONS & SYMBOLS

Terms

ABMC	American Battle Monuments Commission
AGC	Adjutant General's Corps
CAC	Coast Artillery Corps
CAP	Captured – Not POW
CAV	Cavalry
CE	Corps of Engineers
CH (CHAP)	Chaplain's Corps or Chaplain
CIB	Combat Infantryman's Badge
DOW	Died of Wounds
DO	Dental Officer
DS	Detached Service (i.e., not serving with 26th Cavalry)
EX	Executed by the Japanese
FA	Field Artillery
HQ	Headquarters
INF	Infantry
KIA	Killed in Action
MD	Medical Officer
MG	Machine Gun
MIA	Missing in Action
NARA	National Archives
NC	Not captured; not POW
ND	No data or no other data
POW	Prisoner of War
PA	Philippine Army
PS	Philippine Scouts (US Army Units)
QM/QMC	Quartermaster Corps
TC	Transportation Corps
UNK	Unknown status
USA	U. S. Army
USAFFE	U. S. Army Forces Far East
USFEAF	U. S. Far Eastern Air Forces
USMC	U. S. Marine Corps
USN	U. S. Navy
VC	Veterinary Corps, Veterinary Officer
WIA	Wounded in Action

Ranks

PVT	Private
PFC	Private First Class
CPL	Corporal
SGT	Sergeant
SSG	Staff Sergeant
TSG	Technical Sergeant
MSG	Master Sergeant
1SG	First Sergeant
2LT	Second Lieutenant
1LT	First Lieutenant
CPT	Captain, all services
MAJ	Major
LTC	Lieutenant Colonel
COL	Colonel

BG	Brigadier General
MG	Major General
LTG	Lieutenant General
GEN	General
RADM	Rear Admiral
VADM	Vice Admiral
ADM	Admiral

Positions

CG	Commanding General
CO	Commanding Officer

G-1	General Staff Officer, Personnel at a division or higher headquarters
G-2	General Staff Officer, Intelligence at a division or higher headquarters
G-3	General Staff Officer, Operations (also Plans, Training, and Organization) at a division or higher headquarters
G-4	General Staff Officer, Supply & Logistics at a division or higher headquarters

S-1	Special Staff Officer, Personnel (Adjutant) at a battalion or regiment
S-2	Special Staff Officer, Intelligence at a battalion or regiment
S-3	Special Staff Officer, Operations (also Plans, Training, and Organization) at a battalion or regiment
S-4	Special Staff Officer, Supply & Logistics at a battalion or regiment

Selected Decorations

		Decoration	Reasons for Awards
	PH	Purple Heart	Wounds or death in or as a result of combat Previously for merit
	CM	Commendation Ribbon	Commendable service; generally not in combat
	AM	Air Medal	Commendable actions in the air or in air combat
	BSM	Bronze Star Medal	Commendable service in combat zone or actions in combat
	SM	Soldier's Medal	Heroic or life-saving actions, normally in peacetime
	LM	Legion of Merit	Exceptional service; generally not in combat
	SS	Silver Star Medal	Gallantry in Action
	DSC	Distinguished Service Cross	"Extraordinary heroism" in combat

The Army awarded a Bronze Oak Leaf Cluster for each additional award of a decoration or a Silver Oak Leaf Cluster for five additional awards of a decoration. It also awarded a "V" device with a Commendation Ribbon, Air Medal, or Bronze Star Medal if the award was made for valor.

Appendix B

SELECTED JAPANESE POW SHIPS

7 September 1944 - *Shinyo Maru*[1]

The Japanese embarked 750 POWs on this ship.
POWs were from the Davao POW Camp, many of whom had first been in Cabanatuan.
An American submarine torpedoed this unmarked POW ship off of Mindanao.
There were 82 survivors.

No 26th Cavalry Officers died on this ship.

24 October 1944 - *Arisan Maru* [2]

The Japanese embarked 1,783 POWs on this ship.
An American submarine sunk the unmarked POW ship in East China Sea.
There were 9 survivors of the sinking. Only 8 survived the war.

Four 26th Cavalry officers died on this ship.

15 December 1944 - *Oryoku Maru* [3]

The Japanese embarked 1,619 POWs – mostly officers - on this ship.
American naval pilots bombed and strafed the unmarked POW ship at sea and then in Subic Bay, north of Manila.
About 276 POWs died, died of wounds, or drowned. Others were killed ashore. Survivors were transferred to the *Brazil Maru* and the *Enoura Maru* and shipped to Formosa.

Two 26th Cavalry officers died on this ship.

9 January 1945 - *Enoura Maru* [4]

American naval pilots strafed and bombed the unmarked POW ship in Takao Harbor, Formosa.
The ship carried the survivors of the *Oryoku Maru* and those transferred from the *Brazil Maru* on 6 Jan 1945 (about 1,300 in all).
Nearly 300 POWs were killed or died of wounds as a result of the US attacks.

Five 26th Cavalry Officers died on this ship.

12-29 January 1945 - *Brazil Maru* [5]

The POW ship with about 900-1,000 of the original POWs embarked on the *Oryoku Maru* reached Japan on 30 Jan 1945.
Hundreds of POWs died of disease, malnutrition, or exposure while en route from Takao.
Between 400 and 500 arrived in Japan.

Three 26th Cavalry Officers died on this ship.

NOTE

Only 271 of the original 1,619 POWs embarked on the *Oryoku Maru* survived the war.[6]

Appendix C

ORGANIZATION
26th Cavalry Regiment (PS)[7]

At outbreak of the war – 8 December 1941

Officer Breakdown, 26th Cavalry	
Total Officers Assigned (Fleeger Diary)	60
Cavalry officers on duty with regiment	38
Medical Officers on duty with regiment	5
Chaplain on duty with regiment	1
Officers on Detached Service	16

Regimental Commander & Staff (8)				
		Commander COL C Pierce		
		Executive Officer LTC L Vance		
S1 Officer (Adjutant/Personnel)	**S2 Officer** (Intelligence)	**S3 Officer** (Operations)	**S4 Officer** (Supply)	**Chaplain**
CPT J Fleeger	*CPT P Jones* (Also Communications Officer)	CPT W Chandler	*CPT W Buboltz*	*CPT M Zerfas*
			Asst S4 *1LT S Chamberlin*	

Regimental Medical & Veterinary Staff (5)				
Regimental & 1st Squadron Surgeon	**2nd Squadron Surgeon**	**Regimental Dental Officer**	**Regimental & 1st Squadron *Veterinarian***	**2nd Squadron Veterinarian**
MAJ E Reed	CPT V Shaw	*CPT E Laragay*	CPT W Gochenour	*1LT C Mickelsen*

Squadron and Support Troop Commanders (4)			
CO, Headquarters & Service Troop	**CO, 1ˢᵗ Squadron**	**CO, 2ⁿᵈ Squadron**	**CO, Machine Gun Troop**
CPT F Richards (CPT J Fowler)	*MAJ H Ketchum*	MAJ T Trapnell	*CPT J Ford*
	A, B & C Troops	**E, F & G Troops**	

Headquarters & Service Troop (6)					
CPT F Richards, Commanding (Replaced by CPT J Fowler)					
Transportation Platoon Ldr	**Scout Car Platoon Ldr**	**Scout Car Platoon Ldr**	**Scout Car Platoon Ldr**	**Scout Car Platoon Ldr**	**Scout Car Platoon Ldr**
1LT D Wills	*1LT E Bowers*	*1LT C Cahoon*	*1LT E Cunningham*	*1LT J George*	*1LT S Graves*

Machine Gun Troop (4)		
CPT J Ford, Commanding		
Platoon Leader	**Platoon Leader**	**Platoon Leader**
1LT P Allen	1LT J Siciliano	*1LT D Truglia*

A Troop (3)	
CPT L Cramer, Commanding	
Platoon Leader	**Platoon Leader**
1LT F Evans	*1LT W Leisenring*

B Troop (3)	
CPT H Farris, Commanding *(CPT J Spies, Commanding)*	
Platoon Leader	**Platoon Leader**
1LT H Mark	1LT C Seymour

C Troop (3)

CPT R Praeger, Commanding

Platoon Leader   **Platoon Leader**

1LT T Jones   1LT W Minton

E Troop (4)

LT J Wheeler, Commanding

Platoon Leader   **Platoon Leader**   **Platoon Leader**

1LT A Hendricks   *1LT W Ward*   1LT A Whitehead

F Troop (1)

CPT P Wrinkle, Commanding

Platoon Leader   **Platoon Leader**   **Platoon Leader**

none   *none*   *none*

G Troop (3)

CPT J Barker, Commanding

Platoon Leader   **Platoon Leader**

1LT D Hardwicke   1LT E Ramsey

Appendix D

ORGANIZATION
26th Cavalry Regiment (PS)[8]

On Bataan after initial fighting stopped - 23 February 1942

Officer Breakdown, 26th Cavalry	
Original Officers Assigned (Fleeger Diary)	**60**
Added Officers - Troop C (Praeger)	2
Total Officers Assigned (All Sources)	**62**
Promoted and transferred to another command	(1)
Killed in Action (KIA)	(11)
Remaining Officers Assigned	**50**
Cavalry Officers on duty	26
Medical Officers on duty	5
Chaplain on duty	1
Officers on Detached Service	16
Added Officers - Troop C (Praeger)	2

Hereafter, the officer strength of the regiment will be 62.

Regimental Commander & Staff (7)

Commander
COL L Vance

Executive Officer
LTC T Trapnell

S1 Officer	**S2/S3 Officer**	**S4 Officer**	**Chaplain**
MAJ P Jones	MAJ W Chandler	*CPT W Buboltz*	*CPT M Zerfas*

Asst S4
1LT S Chamberlin

Regimental Medical & Veterinary Staff (5)				
Regimental & 1st Squadron Surgeon	**2nd Squadron Surgeon**	**Regimental Dental Officer**	**Regimental & 1st Squadron *Veterinarian***	**2nd Squadron Veterinarian**
MAJ E Reed	CPT V Shaw	*CPT E Laragay*	CPT W Gochenour	*CPT C Mickelsen*

Squadron and Special Troop Commanders (4)			
CO, Headquarters & Service Troop	**CO, 1st Squadron**	**CO, 2nd Squadron**	**CO, Machine Gun Troop**
CPT J Fowler	*MAJ J Fleeger*	*MAJ J Blanning*	*CPT J Ford*
	Remnants A & B Troops	**Remnants E-F & G Troops**	

Headquarters & Service Troop (2)					
CPT J Fowler, Commanding					
Transportation Platoon Leader	**Scout Car Platoon Leader**	**Scout Car Platoon Leader**	**Scout Car Platoon Leader**	**Scout Car Platoon Leader**	**Scout Car Platoon Leader**
1LT D Wills	*KIA*	*KIA*	*KIA*	*KIA*	*KIA*

Machine Gun Troop (2)		
CPT J Ford, Commanding		
Platoon Leader	**Platoon Leader**	**Platoon Leader**
KIA	1LT J Siciliano	*KIA*

A Troop (3)	
CPT L Cramer, Commanding	
Platoon Leader	**Platoon Leader**
1LT F Evans	*1LT W Leisenring*

B Troop (2)

CPT J Spies, Commanding

Platoon Leader   **Platoon Leader**

KIA   1LT C Seymour

E-F Troop (3)

CO, KIA

Platoon Leader   **Platoon Leader**   **Platoon Leader**

1LT A Hendricks   *1LT W Ward*   1LT A Whitehead*

G Troop (2)

CPT J Barker, Commanding

Platoon Leader   **Platoon Leader**

KIA   1LT Ramsey

Fighting in Northern Luzon

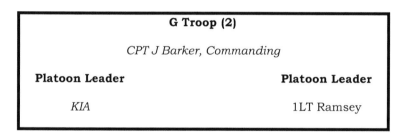

C Troop (Detached) (All Missing at Surrender) (5)

MAJ R Praeger, Commanding*

Platoon Leader   **Added Officers**   **Platoon Leader**
         (Commissioned by Praeger)

CPT T Jones*   *2LT W Bowen**   CPT W Minton*
         *1LT A Furagganan**

CHART NOTES
*Missing at Surrender on Bataan

ORGANIZATIONAL NOTES

Reorganization[9]
On or about 30 December 1941, the regiment reorganized.
- Decimated Troops E and F were combined into Troop E-F and placed under the command of Captain John Z. Wheeler.
- Then a new command, made up of Troop A, Troop E-F, and Troop G, was placed under the command of Major Thomas J. H. Trapnell, the surviving 2nd Squadron Commander.

☐ Troop B and the Machine Gun Troop were dismounted, motorized, and placed under the command of Captain Joseph R. Barker.

Troop C remained on detached service in the North under Captain Ralph B. Praeger.

Basically by the end of December, the regiment approximated one operational squadron of three troops.

In late January, the regiment reorganized again.
☐ Lt. Colonel Lee C. Vance became the regimental commander and Major Trapnell became the Executive Officer. Both were promoted.
☐ Major Fleeger took command of the 1st Squadron with two troops: A and B.
☐ Major James C. Blanning took command of the 2nd Squadron with two troops: E-F and G.

Obviously there was not much left of the original regiment. The second organization charts reflect these changes.

Then, just before the surrender, Brigadier General Clifford Bluemel incorporated Colonel Vance and his staff into his Philippine Army Division and appointed Vance as his deputy. Subsequently, newly promoted Lt. Colonel Trapnell took command of the 26th Cavalry.

Early Detached Service (DS)

On 8 December, the regiment sent Captain Paul Jones to be the Headquarters Commandant of General Jonathan Wainwright's North Luzon Force. After organizing the headquarters' enlisted personnel, Jones returned to the regiment (about 13 December) and Lt. William Leisenring replaced him. But, because a more senior officer was needed the regiment detached Captain James Blanning to be the Headquarters Commandant and Leisenring returned to troop duty. Blanning did not return to the regiment until late January 1942 at which time he became the commander of the 2nd Squadron. When Blanning returned, Major Houston Farris took over as Headquarters Commandant of I Philippine Corps (formerly North Luzon Force).

26th Cavalry Officers on Detached Service at the End of the Bataan Campaigns (16)

Fleeger listed the following officers as being on detached service.

COL Frank Nelson	G3 Officer (Operations), I Philippine Corps
COL Gyles Merrill	G4 Officer (Supply), I Philippine Corps
COL Carter R. McLennan	Visayan Command, Negros
LTC Claude A. Thorp	*Provost Marshal, I Philippine Corps*
MAJ Joseph A. Cleary	*Philippine Army, Luzon*
MAJ Houston S. Farris	Headquarters Commandant, I Philippine Corps (formerly CO, Troop B)
CPT David A. Miller	*Assistant Provost Marshal, I Philippine Corps*
CPT Forrest C. Richards	*Liaison Officer (LNO), 11th Philippine Division (formerly CO, HQ Troop)*
CPT William S. Van Nostrand	*61st Infantry Regiment, 61st Philippine Division, Negros & Mindanao*
1LT James C. Bickerton	*Philippine Army, Negros*
1LT Robert C. Burlando	*Philippine Army, Mindanao*
1LT Robert L. Carusso	*Provost Marshal Section, I Philippine Corps (808th MP Company)*
1LT David L. Coale, III	*Philippine Army, Mindanao*
1LT William M. Cummings	*53rd Infantry Regiment, 51st Philippine Division*
1LT James A. Seay	*Philippine Army, Mindanao*
1LT Frederick F. Thomas	*Philippine Army, Luzon*

NOTES

1. CLEARY - Cleary died in action on 16 January 1942 at Abucay on Bataan. Fleeger did not indicate whether he knew this at the time he listed these officers as missing.

2. MCLENNAN - Fleeger listed him as a lieutenant colonel but added "probably full colonel."

3. THOMAS - Thomas also died in action on Bataan on 8 April 1942. Fleeger did not report this.

Appendix E

Rosters of
ALL OFFICERS
26th Cavalry Regiment (PS)

May 1942

Officer Breakdown, 26th Cavalry, All Sources	
Original Officers Assigned (Fleeger Diary)	**60**
Cavalry officers with regiment	38
Medical Officers with regiment	5
Chaplain with regiment	1
Officers on Detached Service	16
Added officers, Troop C (Praeger)	**2**
Total Officers (All Sources)	**62**

Officer Status, All Sources	
Killed in Action (KIA)	14
Not Captured (NC)	9
Prisoners of War (POW)	39
Total Officers	**62**

26th CAVALRY OFFICERS LISTED IN A FLEEGER DIARY

Alphabetical

	Name	Rank	Duty Status	Status May 42
1	Allen, Paul K.	1LT	Machine Gun Platoon Leader	KIA
2	Barker, Joseph R., II ▶	CPT	Troop Commander	NC
3	Bickerton, James E.	1LT	DS - Philippine Army	POW
4	Blanning, James C. ▶	MAJ	DS - North Luzon Force - then Squadron CO	POW
5	Bowers, Charles R. ▶	1LT	Scout Car Platoon Leader	KIA
6	Buboltz, Walter J.	CPT	Regimental S-4 Officer	POW
7	Burlando, Robert C.	1LT	DS - Philippine Army	POW
8	Cahoon, Carol I.	1LT	Scout Car Platoon Leader	KIA
9	Carusso, Robert L.	1LT	DS - 808th Military Police Company	POW
10	Chamberlin, Stephen S.	1LT	Assistant Regimental S-4 Officer	POW
11	Chandler, William E. ▶	MAJ	Regimental S-3 - then S-2/S-3 Officer	POW
12	Cleary, Joseph A. ▶	MAJ	DS – Philippine Army	KIA

13	*Coale, David L., III*	*1LT*	*DS – Philippine Army*	*POW*
14	*Cramer, Leland W.*	*CPT*	*Troop Commander*	*POW*
15	Cummings, William M.	CPT	DS – Philippine Army	POW
16	*Cunningham, Ethan R.*	*1LT*	*Scout Car Platoon Leader*	*KIA*
17	Evans, Fred B.	1LT	Platoon Leader	POW
18	Farris, Houston S.	MAJ	DS – I Philippine Corps	POW
19	*Fleeger, Harry J.* ▶	*MAJ*	*Regimental S-1 Officer - then Squadron CO*	*POW*
20	*Ford, Jack A.*	*CPT*	*Machine Gun Troop Commander*	*POW*
21	Fowler, John M.	CPT	Troop Commander	POW
22	*George, John A.*	*1LT*	*Scout Car Platoon Leader*	*KIA*
23	Gochenour, William S.	CPT (VC)	Regimental & 1st Squadron Veterinarian	POW
24	*Graves, Steven S.*	*1LT*	*Scout Car Platoon Leader*	*KIA*
25	*Hardwicke, Clifford, Jr.*	*1LT*	*Platoon Leader*	*KIA*
26	*Hendricks, Archie M., Jr.*	*1LT*	*Platoon Leader*	*KIA*
27	*Jones, Paul M.* ▶	*MAJ*	*Regimental S-2 Officer - then Regimental S-1 Officer*	*POW*
28	Jones, Thomas S.	CPT	Platoon Leader - then Guerrilla	NC
29	*Ketchum, Hubert W.* ▶	*LTC*	*Squadron CO*	*KIA*
30	*Laragay, Edwin J.*	*CPT(DO)*	*Regimental Dental Officer*	*POW*
31	*Leisenring, William P.*	*1LT*	*Platoon Leader*	*POW*
32	*Mark, Henry D.*	*1LT*	*Platoon Leader*	*KIA*
33	McLennan, Carter R.	COL	DS – Visayan Command (Negros)	POW
34	Merrill, Gyles	COL	G-4 Officer, I Philippine Corps - then Guerrilla	NC
35	*Mickelsen, Clayton H.*	*CPT (VC)*	*2nd Squadron Veterinarian*	*POW*
36	*Miller, David A.*	*CPT*	*DS - Assistant Provost Marshal, I Philippine Corps*	*POW*
37	Minton, Warren A.	CPT	Platoon Leader - then Guerrilla	POW
38	Nelson, Frank	COL	DS – G-3 Officer, I Philippine Corps	POW
39	Pierce, Clinton A.	COL	Regimental CO - Promoted and transferred	POW
40	*Praeger, Ralph B.* ▶	*CPT*	*Troop Commander - then Guerrilla*	*NC*
41	Ramsey, Edwin P.	1LT	Platoon Leader - then Guerrilla	NC
42	Reed, Emil P.	MAJ (MD)	Regimental & 1st Squadron Surgeon	POW
43	*Richards, Forrest C.*	*CPT*	*DS - 11th Division, Philippine Army*	*POW*
44	*Seay, James C.*	*CPT*	*DS – 71st Infantry, Philippine Army*	*POW*
45	Seymour, Clinton C.	1LT	Platoon Leader	POW
46	Shaw, Vaughn	CPT (MD)	2nd Squadron Surgeon	POW
47	Siciliano, Joseph M.	1LT	Machine Gun Platoon Leader	POW
48	*Spies, George J. (Jack)*	*CPT*	*Troop Commander - then Guerrilla*	*NC*
49	*Thomas, Frederick F.*	*1LT*	*Platoon Leader*	*KIA*
50	*Thorp, Claude A.*	*LTC*	*DS – PM, I Philippine Corps - then Guerrilla*	*NC*
51	Trapnell, Thomas J. H. ▶	MAJ	Squadron CO, Executive Officer - then Regt CO	POW
52	*Truglia, Dominick*	*1LT*	*Machine Gun Platoon Leader*	*KIA*
53	Vance, Lee C.	LTC	Executive Officer - then Regimental CO	POW
54	*Van Nostrand, Wm S.* ▶	*CPT*	*DS – 61st Infantry Regiment, Mindanao*	*POW*
55	*Ward, William H.*	*1LT*	*Platoon Leader*	*POW*
56	*Wheeler, John Z.*	*CPT*	*Troop Commander*	*POW*
57	Whitehead, Arthur	1LT	Platoon Leader	POW
58	Wills, Donald H.	1LT	Transportation Platoon Leader	POW
59	*Wrinkle, Paul H.*	*CPT*	*Troop Commander*	*KIA*
60	Zerfas, Mathias E.	CPT (CH)	Chaplain	POW

ADDED CAVALRY OFFICERS, TROOP C (2)

The *ABMC Website* and Other Sources reported that 2nd Lieutenant William A. Bowen and 1st Lieutenant Arthur P. Furagganan were members of the 26th Cavalry. They are included in the list of "All Cavalry Officers" below. Fleeger did not list them.

ALL 26th CAVALRY OFFICERS

By Rank

	Rank and Name	Duty Status	Status May 42
	Brigadier General (1)		
1	Pierce, Clinton A.	Regimental CO - Promoted and transferred	POW
	Colonels (3)		
2	Nelson, Frank	DS – G-3 Officer, I Philippine Corps	POW
3	Merrill, Gyles	DS – G-4 Officer, I Philippine Corps - then Guerrilla	NC
4	McLennan, Carter R.	DS – Visayan Command (Negros)	POW
	Lt Colonels (4)		
5	*Ketchum, Hubert W.* ▶	*Squadron CO*	*KIA*
6	Thorp, Claude A.	*DS – PM, I Philippine Corps - then Guerrilla*	NC
8	*Trapnell, Thomas J. H.* ▶	Squadron CO, Executive Officer - then Regimental CO	POW
7	Vance, Lee C.	Executive Officer - then Regimental CO	POW
	Majors (9)		
9	*Blanning, James C.* ▶	*DS – North Luzon Force - then Squadron CO*	POW
10	*Chandler, William E.* ▶	Regimental S-3 - then Regimental S-2/S-3 Officer	POW
11	*Cleary, Joseph A.* ▶	*DS – Philippine Army*	*KIA*
12	Farris, Houston S.	DS – I Philippine Corps	POW
13	*Fleeger, Harry J.* ▶	*Regimental S-1 Officer - then Squadron CO*	*POW*
14	*Jones, Paul M.* ▶	*Regimental S-2 Officer - then Regimental S-1 Officer*	*POW*
15	*Praeger, Ralph B.* ▶	*Troop Commander - then Guerrilla*	*NC*
16	Reed, Emil P. (MD)	Regimental & 1st Squadron Surgeon	POW
17	*Van Nostrand, William S.* ▶	*DS - 61st Infantry Regiment, Mindanao*	*POW*
	Captains (20)		
18	*Barker, Joseph R., II* ▶	*Troop Commander*	*NC*
19	*Buboltz, Walter J.*	*Regimental S-4 Officer*	*POW*
20	*Burlando, Robert C.*	*DS – Philippine Army*	*POW*
21	*Cramer, Leland W.*	*Troop Commander*	*POW*
22	*Cummings, William M.*	*DS – Philippine Army*	*POW*
23	*Ford, Jack A.*	*Machine Gun Troop Commander*	*POW*
24	Fowler, John M.	Troop Commander	POW
25	Gochenour, William S. (VC)	Regimental & 1st Squadron Veterinarian	POW
26	Jones, Thomas S.	Platoon Leader - then Guerrilla	NC
27	*Laragay, Edwin J. (DO)*	*Regimental Dental Officer*	*POW*
28	*Mickelsen, Clayton H. (VC)*	*2nd Squadron Veterinarian*	*POW*
29	*Miller, David A.*	*DS - Assistant Provost Marshal, I Philippine Corps*	*POW*
30	Minton, Warren A	Platoon Leader - then Guerrilla	POW
31	*Richards, Forrest C.*	*DS - 11th Division, Philippine Army*	*POW*
32	*Seay, James C.*	*DS – 71st Infantry, Philippine Army*	*POW*
33	Shaw, Vaughn (MD)	2nd Squadron Surgeon	POW
34	*Spies, George J. (Jack)*	*Troop Commander - then Guerrilla*	*NC*
35	*Wheeler, John Z.*	*Troop Commander*	*POW*
36	*Wrinkle, Paul H.*	*Troop Commander*	*KIA*
37	*Zerfas, Mathias E. (CH)*	*Chaplain*	*POW*
	1st Lieutenants (24)		
38	*Allen, Paul K.*	*Machine Gun Platoon Leader*	*KIA*
39	*Bickerton, James E.*	*DS - Philippine Army*	*POW*
40	*Bowers, Charles R.* ▶	*Scout Car Platoon Leader*	*KIA*
41	*Cahoon, Carol I.*	*Scout Car Platoon Leader*	*KIA*
42	*Carusso, Robert L.*	*DS - 808th Military Police Company*	*POW*

43	*Chamberlin, Stephen S.*	*Assistant Regimental S-4 Officer*	*POW*
44	*Coale, David L., III*	*DS – Philippine Army*	*POW*
45	*Cunningham, Ethan R.*	*Scout Car Platoon Leader*	*KIA*
46	Evans, Fred B.	Platoon Leader	POW
47	*Furagganan, Arthur P.*	*Guerrilla, Troop C*	*NC*
48	*George, John A.*	*Scout Car Platoon Leader*	*KIA*
49	*Graves, Steven S.*	*Scout Car Platoon Leader*	*KIA*
50	*Hardwicke, Clifford, Jr.*	*Platoon Leader*	*KIA*
51	*Hendricks, Archie M., Jr.*	*Platoon Leader*	*KIA*
52	*Leisenring, William P.*	*Platoon Leader*	*POW*
53	*Mark, Henry D.*	*Platoon Leader*	*KIA*
54	Ramsey, Edwin P.	Platoon Leader - then Guerrilla	NC
55	Seymour, Clinton C.	Platoon Leader	POW
56	Siciliano, Joseph M.	Machine Gun Platoon Leader	POW
57	*Thomas, Frederick F.*	*Platoon Leader*	*KIA*
58	*Truglia, Dominick*	*Machine Gun Platoon Leader*	*KIA*
59	*Ward, William H.*	*Platoon Leader*	*POW*
60	Whitehead, Arthur	Platoon Leader	POW
61	Wills, Donald H.	Transportation Platoon Leader	POW

2nd Lieutenant (1)

| 62 | *Bowen, William E.* | *Guerrilla, Troop C* | *NC* |

NOTES

1. BOWEN - Bowen, an American enlisted soldier, joined Troop C from Camp John Hay near Baguio He became a valuable member of the unit. Praeger commissioned him a second lieutenant.

2. BURLANDO - Burlando was reported to be a captain during the last fights on Mindanao.

3. FURAGGANAN - The Filipino civilian joined Troop C in North Luzon as a communications specialist and fought on after the surrender. Praeger first promoted him to sergeant and then commissioned him a first lieutenant.

4. KETCHUM - Ketchum was promoted to lieutenant colonel about the time of his death. He may not have known about his promotion.

5. MICKELSEN - Fleeger listed Mickelsen as a lieutenant in the early fight when he won a DSC and later as a captain. He did the same with Wheeler.

6. PRAEGER - Praeger had been promoted to major by May 1942.

7. SEYMOUR - Seymour is also listed as an officer in the 200th/515th Coast Artillery Regiment on the New Mexico website. Most likely Seymour deployed with the NM unit and transferred to the 26th Cavalry in the Philippines. The NM units had formerly been cavalry units. Fleeger listed Seymour twice in his diary (18 and 56).

8. SHAW - Fleeger listed Shaw as "W" Shaw in his original diary.

9. VAN NOSTRAND - Van Nostrand was reported to be a major during the last fights on Mindanao, but may have been advanced to the rank of lieutenant colonel by that time. When he surrendered, Van Nostrand commanded the 81st Infantry Regiment, having been transferred to it from the 61st Infantry Regiment.

Appendix F

Rosters of
OFFICERS MISSING AFTER SURRENDER
26th Cavalry Regiment (PS)

Status of the Missing	
Surrendered on Luzon	4
Surrendered Visayas or Mindanao	3
Continued Combat Operations, Troop C	4
Killed in Action Before Surrender	2
Evaded/Captured	2
Escaped/Evaded/Never Captured	2
Total	**17 of 62 (27%)**

Fleeger identified thirteen regimental officers as "missing since surrender" and one as "Missing in Action."[10] He did not mention Merrill, and he did not include the two new officers with Troop C.

CAVALRY OFFICERS MISSING AFTER SURRENDER

Alphabetical

	Name	Rank	Status Apr-May 42	Status Jun 42
1	*Barker, Joseph R., II* ▶	*CPT*	*Troop Commander - Evaded*	*Guerrilla*
2	*Bickerton, James E.*	*1LT*	*DS - Philippine Army - Surrendered on Iloilo*	POW
3	*Bowen, William E.*	*2LT*	*Troop C – Continued Operations*	*Guerrilla*
4	*Burlando, Robert C.*	*1LT*	*DS – Philippine Army - Surrendered on Mindanao*	POW
5	*Cahoon, Carol I.*	*1LT*	*Scout Car Platoon Leader - KIA before surrender*	*KIA*
6	*Coale, David L., III*	*1LT*	*DS – Philippine Army – Surrendered on Mindanao*	POW
7	*Furagganan, Arthur P.*	*1LT*	*Troop C – Continued Operations*	*Guerrilla*
8	Jones, Thomas S.	CPT	Platoon Leader, Troop C - Continued operations	Guerrilla
9	McLennan, Carter R.	COL	DS – Visayan Command (Negros) - Surrendered on Cebu	POW
10	Merrill, Gyles	COL	G-4 Officer, I Philippine Corps - Escaped	Guerrilla
11	*Praeger, Ralph B.* ▶	*MAJ*	*Troop C Commander - Continued operations*	*Guerrilla*
12	Ramsey, Edwin P.	1LT	Platoon Leader – Evaded	Guerrilla
13	*Spies, George J. (Jack)*	*CPT*	*Troop Commander - Evaded*	*Guerrilla*
14	*Thomas, Frederick F.*	*1LT*	*Platoon Leader - KIA before surrender*	*KIA*
15	*Thorp, Claude A.*	*LTC*	*DS – PM, I Philippine Corps - Evaded*	*Guerrilla*
16	*Van Nostrand, Wm S.* ▶	*MAJ*	*DS - 61st Infantry Regiment - Surrendered on Mindanao*	POW
17	Whitehead, Arthur	1LT	Platoon Leader – Surrendered (ND)	POW

CAVALRY OFFICERS MISSING AFTER SURRENDER

By Rank

	Rank and Name	Status Apr-May 42	Status Jun 42
	Colonels (2)		
1	McLennan, Carter R.	DS – Visayan Command (Negros) - Surrendered on Cebu	POW
2	Merrill, Gyles	G-4 Officer, I Philippine Corps - Escaped	Guerrilla
	Lt Colonel (1)		
3	*Thorp, Claude A.*	*DS – PM, I Philippine Corp - Evaded*	Guerrilla
	Majors (2)		
4	*Praeger, Ralph B.* ▶	*Troop C Commander - Continued operations*	*Guerrilla*
5	*Van Nostrand, William S.* ▶	*DS -61ˢᵗ Infantry Regiment - Surrendered on Mindanao*	*POW*
	Captains (4)		
6	*Barker, Joseph R., II* ▶	*Troop Commander - Evaded*	*Guerrilla*
7	Burlando, Robert C.	*DS – Philippine Army - Surrendered on Mindanao*	*POW*
8	Jones, Thomas S.	Platoon Leader, Troop C - Continued operations	Guerrilla
9	*Spies, George J. (Jack)*	*Troop Commander - Evaded*	*Guerrilla*
	1ˢᵗ Lieutenants (7)		
10	*Bickerton, James E*	*DS - Philippine Army - Surrendered on Iloilo*	POW
11	*Furagganan, Arthur P.*	*Troop C – Continued Operations*	*Guerrilla*
12	*Cahoon, Carol I.*	*Scout Car Platoon Leader - KIA before surrender*	*Dead*
13	*Coale, David L., III*	*DS – Philippine Army – Surrendered on Mindanao*	*POW*
14	Ramsey, Edwin P.	Platoon Leader - Evaded	Guerrilla
15	*Thomas, Frederick F.*	*Platoon Leader - KIA before surrender*	*Dead*
16	Whitehead, Arthur	Platoon Leader - Surrendered (ND)	POW
	2ⁿᵈ Lieutenants (1)		
17	*Bowen, William E.*	*Troop C - Continued Operations*	*Guerrilla*

NOTES

1. BOWEN - Eventually surrendered to protect his family.

2. CAHOON - Fleeger listed him as MIA rather than "missing since surrender." Cahoon had been killed in the early days on Luzon, but apparently Fleeger did not know that and listed the officer as MIA.

3. FURAGGANAN, JONES & PRAEGER - The Japanese eventually captured them.

4. MERRILL - Fleeger listed him as the G-4, I Corps with no indication that he was missing. Merrill had surrendered, but he escaped immediately. The Japanese never captured Merrill.

5. RAMSEY - The Japanese never captured Ramsey.

Appendix G

Rosters of
OFFICERS WHO SURRENDERED OR WERE CAPTURED*
26th Cavalry Regiment (PS)

POWs & Captured Officers	
Surrendered & Prisoners of War	40
Captured as Guerrillas*	5
Total	**45 of 62 (73%)**

CAVALRY OFFICERS WHO SURRENDERED OR WERE CAPTURED

Alphabetical

	Name	Rank	Duty Status	War Status
1	*Barker, Joseph R., II* ▶	*CPT*	*Troop Commander*	*CAP*
2	Bickerton, James E.	1LT	DS - Philippine Army	POW
3	*Blanning, James C.* ▶	*MAJ*	*DS – North Luzon Force - then Squadron CO*	POW
4	Bowen, William E.	2LT	Guerrilla, Troop C	*POW*
5	Buboltz, Walter J.	CPT	Regimental S-4 Officer	*POW*
6	Burlando, Robert C.	1LT	DS – Philippine Army	*POW*
7	Carusso, Robert L.	1LT	DS - 808th Military Police Company	*POW*
8	Chamberlin, Stephen S.	1LT	Assistant Regimental S-4 Officer	*POW*
9	Chandler, William E. ▶	MAJ	Regimental S-3 – then Regimental S-2/S-3 Officer	POW
10	Coale, David L., III	1LT	DS – Philippine Army	*POW*
11	Cramer, Leland W.	CPT	Troop Commander	*POW*
12	Cummings, William M.	CPT	DS – Philippine Army	*POW*
13	Evans, Fred B.	1LT	Platoon Leader	POW
14	Farris, Houston S.	MAJ	DS – I Philippine Corps	POW
15	*Fleeger, Harry J.* ▶	*MAJ*	*Regimental S-1 Officer - then Squadron CO*	*POW*
16	*Ford, Jack A.*	*CPT*	*Machine Gun Troop Commander*	*POW*
17	Fowler, John M.	CPT	Troop Commander	POW
18	*Furagganan, Arthur P.*	*1LT*	*Guerrilla, Troop C*	*CAP*
19	Gochenour, William S.	CPT VC)	Regimental & 1st Squadron Veterinarian	POW
20	*Jones, Paul M.* ▶	*MAJ*	*Regimental S-2 Officer - then Regimental S-1 Officer*	*POW*
21	Jones, Thomas S.	CPT	Platoon Leader - then Guerrilla	CAP
22	*Laragay, Edwin J.*	*CPT(DO)*	*Regimental Dental Officer*	*POW*
23	*Leisenring, William P.*	*1LT*	*Platoon Leader*	*POW*
24	McLennan, Carter R.	COL	DS – Visayan Command (Negros)	POW
25	*Mickelsen, Clayton H.*	*CPT (VC)*	*2nd Squadron Veterinarian*	*POW*
26	Miller, David A.	CPT	DS - Assistant Provost Marshal, I Philippine Corps	*POW*
27	Minton, Warren A.	CPT	Platoon Leader - then Guerrilla	POW
28	Nelson, Frank	COL	DS – G-3 Officer, I Philippine Corps	POW
29	Pierce, Clinton A.	COL	Regimental Commander - Promoted and transferred	POW
30	*Praeger, Ralph B.* ▶	*CPT*	*Troop C Commander - then Guerrilla*	*CAP*
31	Reed, Emil P.	MAJ (MD)	Regimental & 1st Squadron Surgeon	POW
32	*Richards, Forrest C.*	*CPT*	*DS - 11th Division, Philippine Army*	*POW*
33	Seay, James C.	CPT	*DS – 71st Infantry, Philippine Army*	POW

34	Seymour, Clinton C.	1LT	Platoon Leader	POW
35	Shaw, Vaughn	CPT (MD)	2nd Squadron Surgeon	POW
36	Siciliano, Joseph M.	1LT	Machine Gun Platoon Leader	POW
37	*Thorp, Claude A.*	*LTC*	*DS – PM, I Philippine Corps, Guerrilla*	*CAP*
38	Trapnell, Thomas J. H. ▶	MAJ	Squadron CO, Executive Officer - then Regimental CO	POW
39	Vance, Lee C.	LTC	Executive Officer - then Regimental CO	POW
40	*Van Nostrand, William S.* ▶	*CPT*	*DS - 61st Infantry Regiment, Mindanao*	*POW*
41	*Ward, William H.*	*1LT*	*Platoon Leader*	*POW*
42	*Wheeler, John Z.*	*CPT*	*Troop Commander*	*POW*
43	Whitehead, Arthur	1LT	Platoon Leader	POW
44	Wills, Donald H.	1LT	Transportation Platoon Leader	POW
45	*Zerfas, Mathias E.*	*CPT (CH)*	*Chaplain*	*POW*

CAVALRY OFFICERS WHO SURRENDERED OR WERE CAPTURED

By Rank

	Rank and Name	Duty Status	War Status
	<u>Brigadier General</u> (1)		
1	Pierce, Clinton A.	Regimental CO – Promoted and transferred	POW
	<u>Colonels</u> (2)		
2	Nelson, Frank	DS – G-3 Officer, I Philippine Corps	POW
3	McLennan, Carter R.	DS – Visayan Command (Negros)	POW
	<u>Lt Colonels</u> (3)		
4	*Thorp, Claude A.*	*DS – PM, I Philippine Corps - then Guerrilla*	*CAP*
5	Trapnell, Thomas J. H. ▶	Squadron CO, Executive Officer - then Regimental CO	POW
6	Vance, Lee C.	Executive Officer - then Regimental CO	POW
	<u>Majors</u> (8)		
7	*Blanning, James C.* ▶	*DS – North Luzon Force - Squadron CO*	*POW*
8	*Chandler, William E.* ▶	*Regimental S-3 – then S-2/S-3 Officer*	*POW*
9	Farris, Houston S.	DS – I Philippine Corps	POW
10	*Fleeger, Harry J.* ▶	*Regimental S-1 Officer – then Squadron CO*	*POW*
11	*Jones, Paul M.* ▶	*Regimental S-2 Officer - then Regimental S-1 Officer*	*POW*
12	*Praeger, Ralph B.* ▶	*Troop Commander - then Guerrilla*	*CAP*
13	Reed, Emil P. (MD)	Regimental & 1st Squadron Surgeon	POW
14	*Van Nostrand, William S.* ▶	*DS - 61st Infantry Regiment, Mindanao*	*POW*
	<u>Captain</u> (18)		
15	*Barker, Joseph R., II* ▶	*Troop Commander*	*CAP*
16	*Buboltz, Walter J.*	*Regimental S-4 Officer*	*POW*
17	*Burlando, Robert C.*	*DS – Philippine Army*	*POW*
18	*Cramer, Leland W.*	*Troop Commander*	*POW*
19	*Cummings, William M.*	*DS – Philippine Army*	*POW*
20	*Ford, Jack A.*	*Machine Gun Troop Commander*	*POW*
21	Fowler, John M.	Troop Commander	POW
22	Gochenour, William S. (VC)	Regimental & 1st Squadron Veterinarian	POW
23	Jones, Thomas S.	Platoon Leader - then Guerrilla	CAP
24	*Laragay, Edwin J. (DO)*	*Regimental Dental Officer*	*POW*
25	*Mickelsen, Clayton H. (VC)*	*2nd Squadron Veterinarian*	*POW*
26	*Miller, David A.*	*DS - Assistant Provost Marshal, I Philippine Corps*	*POW*
27	Minton, Warren A.	Platoon Leader - then Guerrilla	POW
28	*Richards, Forrest C.*	*DS - 11th Division, Philippine Army*	*POW*
29	*Seay, James C.*	*DS – 71st Infantry, Philippine Army*	*POW*
30	Shaw, Vaughn (MD)	2nd Squadron Surgeon	POW

| 31 | Wheeler, John Z. | Troop Commander | POW |
| 32 | Zerfas, Mathias E. (CH) | Chaplain | POW |

1ˢᵗ Lieutenants (12)

33	Bickerton, James E	DS - Philippine Army	POW
34	Carusso, Robert L.	DS - 808ᵗʰ Military Police Company	POW
35	Chamberlin, Stephen S.	Assistant Regimental S-4 Officer	POW
36	Coale, David L., III	DS – Philippine Army	POW
37	Evans, Fred B.	Platoon Leader	POW
38	Furagganan, Arthur P.	Guerrilla, Troop C	CAP
39	Leisenring, William P.	Platoon Leader	POW
40	Seymour, Clinton C.	Platoon Leader	POW
41	Siciliano, Joseph M.	Machine Gun Platoon Leader	POW
42	Ward, William H.	Platoon Leader	POW
43	Whitehead, Arthur	Platoon Leader	POW
44	Wills, Donald H.	Transportation Platoon Leader	POW

2ⁿᵈ Lieutenant (1)

| 45 | Bowen, William E. | Guerrilla, Troop C | POW |

NOTE

CAP – Indicates that the Japanese captured these officers after the U. S. forces surrendered throughout the Philippines and did not treat them as POWs.

Appendix H

Rosters of
OFFICERS WHO DID NOT SURRENDER
26th Cavalry Regiment (PS)

Total Cavalry Officers	62
Escaped from Bataan	5
At Large with Troop C, April 1942	5
At large, April 1942	**10 of 62 (16%)**
Surrendered after surrender on Corregidor	-2
Captured in 1942-1943	-5
Died after escape	-1
Escaped in 1944	1
At Large in 1945	**3 of 62 (5%)**

ALL CAVALRY ESCAPEES

	Name	Rank	Unit	Status
1	Merrill, Gyles	COL	DS – G-4 Officer, I Philippine Corps	Became Guerrilla leader, Luzon
2	*Thorp, Claude A.*	*LTC*	*DS - PM, I Philippine Corps*	*Became Guerrilla leader, Luzon*
3	*Barker, Joseph R., II* ▶	*CPT*	*Troop G*	*Became Guerrilla leader, Luzon*
4	Ramsey, Edwin P.	CPT	Troop G	*Became Guerrilla leader, Luzon*
5	*Spies, George J. (Jack)*	*CPT*	*Machine Gun Troop*	*Became Guerrilla leader, Luzon*
6	Wills, Donald H.	1LT	Transportation Platoon	Became Guerrilla leader, Mindanao

Troop C Officers – Surrendered in 1942

	Name	Rank	Unit	Status
1	Minton, Warren A.	CPT	1st Provisional Guerrilla Regiment	Chose to surrender
2	*Bowen, William E.*	*2LT*	*Troop C*	*Surrendered to protect family*

Troop C Officers - Captured in 1943
Became Cagayan-Apayao Force (CAF)

	Name	Rank	Unit	Status
1	*Praeger, Ralph B.* ▶	*MAJ*	*Troop C/CAF*	*Japanese captured*
2	Jones, Thomas S.	CPT	Troop C/CAF	*Japanese captured*
3	*Furagganan, Arthur P.*	*1LT*	*Troop C/CAF*	*Japanese captured*

Other Officers - Captured in 1942
Luzon Guerrilla Force

	Name	Rank	Unit	Status
1	*Thorp, Claude A.*	*LTC*	*Luzon Guerrilla Force*	*Japanese captured*
2	*Barker, Joseph R., II* ▶	*CPT*	*Luzon Guerrilla Force*	*Japanese captured*

Died in field in 1942
Luzon Guerrilla Force

	Name	Rank	Unit	Status
1	*Spies, George J. (Jack)*	*CPT*	*Luzon Guerrilla Force*	*Guerrilla leader, Luzon*

At Large in 1945 (3)

	Name	Rank	Unit	Status
1	Merrill, Gyles	COL	Luzon Guerrilla – no unit	Guerrilla leader, Luzon
2	Ramsey, Edwin P.	1LT	Luzon Guerrilla Force	Guerrilla leader, Luzon
3	Wills, Donald H.	1LT	Mindanao Guerrilla Force	Guerrilla leader, Mindanao

NOTES

1. BARKER, SPIES & THORP - Evaded capture after the surrender on Bataan.

2. MERRILL - Escaped after becoming a POW on Bataan.

3. WILLS – Escaped from a POW ship off Mindanao in 1944.

Appendix I

Rosters of
ALL OFFICER DEAD
26th Cavalry Regiment (PS)

From the Fleeger Diaries, ABMC Website, and NARA Website

All Officer Deaths	
Battle Deaths (14)	
Battle Deaths, Luzon and Bataan	14
POW Deaths (11)	
Killed on Death March	1
Executed	4
Died in POW Camps Luzon	2
Died in POW Camps Japan, Korea, and Manchuria	4
POW Ship Deaths (16)	
KIA Arisan Maru	5
KIA Oryoku Maru	2
KIA Enoura Maru	5
Died on Brazil Maru	4
Other Death (1)	
Died as Guerrilla	1
Total	**42 of 62 (68%)**

ALL CAVALRY DEAD

Alphabetical

	Name	Rank	Date of Death	Cause of Death
1	*Allen, Paul K.*	*1LT*	*22 Dec 41 †*	*KIA, Luzon*
2	*Barker, Joseph R., II*	*CPT*	*01 Nov 43 ♠*	*Executed, Luzon*
3	*Bickerton, James E.*	*1LT*	*15 Dec 44 ♠*	*KIA, Oryoku Maru*
4	*Blanning, James C.* ▶	*MAJ*	*25 Jan 45 ♠*	*Died, Brazil Maru*
5	*Bowen, William E.*	*2 LT*	*24 Oct 44 ♠*	*KIA, Arisan Maru*
6	*Bowers, Charles R.* ▶	*1LT*	*24 Dec 41 †*	*KIA, Luzon*
7	*Buboltz, Walter J.*	*CPT*	*15 Dec 44 ♠*	*KIA, Oryoku Maru*

8	Burlando, Robert C.	1LT	12 Jan 45 ♠	Died, Enoura Maru
9	Cahoon, Carol I.	1LT	05 Jan 42 ♠	KIA, Luzon
10	Carusso, Robert L.	1LT	05 Feb 45 †	Died, Moji Hospital, Japan
11	Chamberlin, Stephen S.	1LT	14 Jun 42 ♠	Died, Cabanatuan
12	Cleary, Joseph A. ▶	MAJ	16 Jan 42 ♠	KIA, Luzon
13	Coale, David L., III	1LT	09 Jan 45 ♠	KIA, Enoura Maru
14	Cramer, Leland W.	CPT	03 Feb 45	Died, Kokura POW Camp, Japan
15	Cummings, William M.	CPT	21 Jan 45 ♠	Died, Brazil Maru
16	Cunningham, Ethan R.	1LT	23 Jan 42 ♠	KIA, Bataan
17	Fleeger, Harry J. ▶	MAJ	24 Oct 44 ♠	KIA, Arisan Maru
18	Ford, Jack A.	CPT	09 Jan 45 ♠	KIA, Enoura Maru
19	Furagganan, Arthur P.	1LT	04 Feb 45 †	Executed, Luzon
20	George, John A.	1LT	22 Dec 41 ♠	KIA, Luzon
21	Graves, Steven S.	1LT	16 Jan 42 ♠	KIA, Bataan
22	Hardwicke, Clifford, Jr.	1LT	17 Jan 42 ♠	KIA, Bataan
23	Hendricks, Archie M., Jr.	1LT	06 May 42 ♠	KIA, Luzon
24	Jones, Paul M. ▶	MAJ	24 Oct 44 ♠	KIA, Arisan Maru
25	Ketchum, Hubert W. ▶	LTC	24 Dec 41 ♠	KIA. Luzon
26	Laragay, Edwin J.	CPT (DO)	23 Jan 45 ♠	Died, Brazil Maru
27	Leisenring, William P.	1LT	24 Oct 44 ♠	KIA, Arisan Maru
28	Mark, Henry D.	1LT	24 Dec 41 †	KIA, Luzon
29	Mickelsen, Clayton H.	CPT (VC)	04 Feb 45	Died, Fukuoka POW Camp 1, Japan
30	Miller, David A.	CPT	16 Apr 42 ♠	KIA, Bataan Death March
31	Praeger, Ralph B. ▶	CPT	31 Dec 44 ♠	Executed, Luzon
32	Richards, Forrest C.	CPT	30 Jan 45	Died, Moji Hospital, Japan
33	Seay, James C.	CPT	24 Oct 44 ♠	KIA, Arisan Maru
34	Spies, George J. (Jack)	CPT	21 Oct 42 †	KIA or Died, Luzon
35	Thomas, Frederick F.	1LT	08 Apr 42 ♠	KIA, Bataan
36	Thorp, Claude A.	LTC	01 Nov 43 ♠	Executed, Luzon
37	Truglia, Dominick	1LT	19 Jan 42	KIA, Bataan
38	Van Nostrand, William S. ▶	CPT	09 Jan 45 ♠	KIA, Enoura Maru
39	Ward, William H.	1LT	20 Jul 42 †	Died, Cabanatuan
40	Wheeler, John Z.	CPT	26 Jan 45 ♠	Died, Brazil Maru
41	Wrinkle, Paul H.	CPT	17 Feb 42 ♠	KIA, Bataan
42	Zerfas, Mathias E.	CPT (CH)	09 Jan 45 ♠	KIA, Enoura Maru

ALL CAVALRY DEAD

By Rank

	Name	Date of Death	Cause of Death
	Lt Colonels (3)		
1	Ketchum, Hubert W. ▶	24 Dec 41 ♠	KIA. Luzon
2	Thorp, Claude A.	01 Nov 43 ♠	Executed, Luzon
3	Van Nostrand, William S. ▶	09 Jan 45 ♠	KIA, Enoura Maru
	Majors (6)		
4	Bickerton, James E.	15 Dec 44 ♠	KIA, Oryoku Maru
5	Blanning, James C. ▶	25 Jan 45 ♠	Died, Brazil Maru
6	Fleeger, Harry J. ▶	24 Oct 44 ♠	KIA, Arisan Maru
7	Cleary, Joseph A. ▶	16 Jan 42 ♠	KIA, Luzon
8	Jones, Paul M. ▶	24 Oct 44 ♠	KIA, Arisan Maru
9	Praeger, Ralph B. ▶	31 Dec 44 ♠	Executed, Luzon
	Captains (16)		
10	Barker, Joseph R., II	01 Nov 43 ♠	Executed, Luzon
11	Buboltz, Walter J.	15 Dec 44 ♠	KIA, Oryoku Maru

12	*Burlando, Robert C.*	*12 Jan 45* ♠	*Died, Enoura Maru*
13	*Coale, David L., III*	*09 Jan 45* ♠	*KIA, Enoura Maru*
14	*Cramer, Leland W.*	*03 Feb 45*	*Died, Kokura POW Camp*
15	*Cummings, William M.*	*21 Jan 45* ♠	*Died, Brazil Maru*
16	*Ford, Jack A.*	*09 Jan 45* ♠	*KIA, Enoura Maru*
17	*Laragay, Edwin J. (DO)*	*23 Jan 45* ♠	*Died, Brazil Maru*
18	*Mickelsen, Clayton H.(VC)*	*04 Feb 45*	*Died, Fukuoka POW Camp 1, Japan*
19	*Miller, David A.*	*16 Apr 42* ♠	*KIA, BDM*
20	*Richards, Forrest C.*	*30 Jan 45*	*Died, Moji Hospital*
21	*Seay, James C.*	*24 Oct 44* ♠	*KIA, Arisan Maru*
22	*Spies, George J. (Jack)*	*21 Oct 42* †	*KIA or Died, Luzon*
23	*Wheeler, John Z.*	*26 Jan 45* ♠	*Died, Brazil Maru*
24	*Wrinkle, Paul H.*	*17 Feb 42* ♠	*KIA, Bataan*
25	*Zerfas, Mathias E.*	*09 Jan 45* ♠	*KIA, Enoura Maru*

1st Lieutenants (16)

26	*Allen, Paul K.*	*22 Dec 41* †	*KIA, Luzon*
27	*Bowers, Charles R.* ▶	*24 Dec 41* †	*KIA, Luzon*
28	*Cahoon, Carol I.*	*05 Jan 42* ♠	*KIA, Luzon*
29	*Carusso, Robert L.*	*05 Feb 45* †	*Died, Moji Hospital, Japan*
30	*Chamberlin, Stephen S.*	*14 Jun 42* ♠	*Died, Cabanatuan*
31	*Cunningham, Ethan R.*	*23 Jan 42* ♠	*KIA, Bataan*
32	*Furagganan, Arthur P.*	*04 Feb 45* †	*Executed, Luzon*
33	*George, John A.*	*22 Dec 41* ♠	*KIA, Luzon*
34	*Graves, Steven S.*	*16 Jan 42* ♠	*KIA, Bataan*
35	*Hardwicke, Clifford, Jr.*	*17 Jan 42* ♠	*KIA, Bataan*
36	*Hendricks, Archie M., Jr.*	*06 May 42* ♠	*KIA, Luzon*
37	*Leisenring, William P.*	*24 Oct 44* ♠	*KIA, Arisan Maru*
38	*Mark, Henry D.*	*24 Dec 41* †	*KIA, Luzon*
39	*Thomas, Frederick F.*	*08 Apr 42* ♠	*KIA, Bataan*
40	*Truglia, Dominick*	*19 Jan 42*	*KIA, Bataan*
41	*Ward, William H.*	*20 Jul 42* †	*Died, Cabanatuan*

2nd Lieutenant (1)

| 42 | *Bowen, William E.* | *24 Oct 44* ♠ | *KIA, Arisan Maru* |

NOTES

1. BICKERTON – *ABMC Website* lists him as a major.

2. BULBOLZ – *ABMC Website* lists him as captain.

3. BURLANDO – *ABMC Website* lists him as a captain. One source, Captain Oliver Orson (VC) identified him as a major in his memoir.

4. COALE – *ABMC Website* lists him as a captain at his death.

5. VAN NOSTRAND - Fleeger listed Van Nostrand as a captain. According to his obituary in *Assembly Magazine* in September 1978, Van Nostrand was a lieutenant colonel at his death. According to the 1989 *USMA Register*, the Army promoted Van Nostrand to colonel posthumously. *ABMC Website* lists him as a colonel.

6. Most deaths in POW camps attributed to starvation (nice word is malnutrition), illness, disease, lack of medicine, or despondency or two or more of the causes. For some who reached Japan in January 1945, add "exposure to cold" as a cause for death.

Appendix J

Rosters of
OFFICER BATTLE DEAD
26th Cavalry Regiment (PS)

Battle Deaths in 1941 and 1942 Non-Ship Deaths	
KIA Luzon (Before Bataan)	**6**
KIA Bataan	**8**
Total	**14 of 62 (23%)**

CAVALRY BATTLE DEATHS

Alphabetical

	Name	Rank	Date of Death	Cause of Death
1	*Allen, Paul K.*	*1LT*	*22 Dec 41 †*	*KIA, Luzon*
2	*Bowers, Charles R.* ▶	*1LT*	*24 Dec 41 †*	*KIA, Luzon*
3	*Cahoon, Carol I.*	*1LT*	*05 Jan 42 ♠*	*KIA, Luzon*
4	*Cleary, Joseph A.* ▶	*MAJ*	*16 Jan 42 ♠*	*KIA, Luzon*
5	*Cunningham, Ethan R.*	*1LT*	*23 Jan 42 ♠*	*KIA, Bataan*
6	*George, John A.*	*1LT*	*22 Dec 41 ♠*	*KIA, Luzon*
7	*Graves, Steven S.*	*1LT*	*16 Jan 42 ♠*	*KIA, Bataan*
8	*Hardwicke, Clifford, Jr.*	*1LT*	*17 Jan 42 ♠*	*KIA, Bataan*
9	*Hendricks, Archie M., Jr.*	*1LT*	*06 May 42 ♠*	*KIA, Luzon*
10	*Ketchum, Hubert W.* ▶	*LTC*	*24 Dec 41 ♠*	*KIA. Luzon*
11	*Mark, Henry D.*	*1LT*	*24 Dec 41 †*	*KIA, Luzon*
12	*Thomas, Frederick F.*	*1LT*	*08 Apr 42 ♠*	*KIA, Bataan*
13	*Truglia, Dominick*	*1LT*	*19 Jan 42*	*KIA, Bataan*
14	*Wrinkle, Paul H.*	*CPT*	*17 Feb 42 ♠*	*KIA, Bataan*

CAVALRY BATTLE DEATHS

By Rank at Date of Death

	Name	Date of Death	Cause of Death
	Lt Colonel (1)		
1	*Ketchum, Hubert W.* ▶	*24 Dec 41 ♠*	*KIA, Luzon*
	Major (1)		
2	*Cleary, Joseph A.* ▶	*16 Jan 42 ♠*	*KIA, Luzon*
	Captain (1)		
3	*Wrinkle, Paul H.*	*17 Feb 42 ♠*	*KIA, Bataan*
	1st Lieutenants (11)		
4	*Allen, Paul K.*	*22 Dec 41 †*	*KIA, Luzon*
5	*Bowers, Charles R.* ▶	*24 Dec 41 †*	*KIA, Luzon*

6	*Cahoon, Carol I.*	*05 Jan 42* ♠	*KIA, Luzon*
7	*Cunningham, Ethan R.*	*23 Jan 42* ♠	*KIA, Bataan*
8	*George, John A.*	*22 Dec 41* ♠	*KIA, Luzon*
9	*Graves, Steven S.*	*16 Jan 42* ♠	*KIA, Bataan*
10	*Hardwicke, Clifford, Jr.*	*17 Jan 42* ♠	*KIA, Bataan*
11	*Hendricks, Archie M., Jr.*	*06 May 42* ♠	*KIA, Luzon*
12	*Mark, Henry D.*	*24 Dec 41* †	*KIA, Luzon*
13	*Thomas, Frederick F.*	*08 Apr 42* ♠	*KIA, Bataan*
14	*Truglia, Dominick*	*19 Jan 42*	*KIA, Bataan*

NOTES

1. SPIES - Captain Jack Spies died after he evaded capture on Bataan and became a guerrilla leader. Fleeger reported a rumor that he had died (10 May 1943). Lt. Edwin Ramsey, a fellow guerrilla leader, reported that the Japanese had killed Spies. Another guerrilla leader, Major Robert Lapham, also reported that the Japanese had killed Spies. However, a Jesuit priest, Forbes J. Monahan reported in detail that Spies had died from a severe illness. Consequently, I have not listed Spies as KIA.

2. TRUGLIA – Fleeger reported that a bomb killed Truglia. No other source provided any information about the officer's death. His name is not listed on the *ABMC Website*, *NARA Website*, or on the Tablets of the Missing in Manila Cemetery. Truglia is included as dead in casualty numbers. Remains may have been recovered and returned for burial in the US after the end of the war.

Appendix K

Rosters of
OFFICER POW & CAPTIVE DEAD
26th Cavalry Regiment (PS)

All Cavalry POW & Captive Officer Dead
From the Fleeger Diaries, ABMC Website, and National Archives

POW & Captive Deaths	
Killed on Death March	1
Executed	4
Died in POW Camps	6
Died on POW Ships	16
Total	**27 of 62 (44%)**

CAVALRY POW & CAPTIVE DEAD

Alphabetical

	Name	Rank	Date of Death	Cause of Death
1	Barker, Joseph R., II	CPT	01 Nov 43 ♠	Executed, Luzon
2	Bickerton, James E.	1LT	15 Dec 44 ♠	KIA, Oryoku Maru
3	Blanning, James C. ▶	MAJ	25 Jan 45 ♠	Died, Brazil Maru
4	Bowen, William E.	2LT	24 Oct 44 ♠	KIA, Arisan Maru
5	Buboltz, Walter J.	CPT	15 Dec 44 ♠	KIA, Oryoku Maru
6	Burlando, Robert C.	1LT	12 Jan 45 ♠	Died, Enoura Maru
7	Carusso, Robert L.	1LT	05 Feb 45 †	Died, Moji Hospital, Japan
8	Chamberlin, Stephen S.	1LT	14 Jun 42 ♠	Died, Cabanatuan
9	Coale, David L., III	1LT	09 Jan 45 ♠	KIA, Enoura Maru
10	Cramer, Leland W.	CPT	03 Feb 45	Died, Kokura POW Camp, Japan
11	Cummings, William M.	CPT	21 Jan 45 ♠	Died, Brazil Maru
12	Fleeger, Harry J. ▶	MAJ	24 Oct 44 ♠	KIA, Arisan Maru
13	Ford, Jack A.	CPT	09 Jan 45 ♠	KIA, Enoura Maru
14	Furagganan, Arthur P.	1LT	04 Feb 45 †	Executed, Luzon
15	Jones, Paul M. ▶	MAJ	24 Oct 44 ♠	KIA, Arisan Maru
16	Laragay, Edwin J.	CPT(DO)	23 Jan 45 ♠	Died, Brazil Maru
17	Leisenring, William P.	1LT	24 Oct 44 ♠	KIA, Arisan Maru
18	Mickelsen, Clayton H.	CPT (VC)	04 Feb 45	Died, Fukuoka POW Camp 1, Japan
19	Miller, David A.	CPT	16 Apr 42 ♠	KIA, Bataan Death March
20	Praeger, Ralph B. ▶	CPT	31 Dec 44 ♠	Executed, Luzon
21	Richards, Forrest C.	CPT	30 Jan 45	Died, Moji Hospital, Japan
22	Seay, James C.	CPT	24 Oct 44 ♠	KIA, Arisan Maru
23	Thorp, Claude A.	LTC	01 Nov 43 ♠	Executed, Luzon
24	Van Nostrand, William S. ▶	CPT	09 Jan 45 ♠	KIA, Enoura Maru
25	Ward, William H.	1LT	20 Jul 42 †	Died, Cabanatuan
26	Wheeler, John Z.	CPT	26 Jan 45 ♠	Died, Brazil Maru
27	Zerfas, Mathias E.	CPT (CH)	09 Jan 45 ♠	KIA, Enoura Maru

CAVALRY POW & CAPTIVE DEAD

By Rank at Date of Death

	Name	Date of Death	Cause of Death
	Lieutenant Colonels (2)		
1	*Thorp, Claude A.*	*01 Nov 43* ♠	*Executed, Luzon*
2	*Van Nostrand, William S.* ▶	*09 Jan 45* ♠	*KIA, Enoura Maru*
	Majors (5)		
3	*Bickerton, James E.*	*15 Dec 44* ♠	*KIA, Oryoku Maru*
4	*Blanning, James C.* ▶	*25 Jan 45* ♠	*Died, Brazil Maru*
5	*Fleeger, Harry J.* ▶	*24 Oct 44* ♠	*KIA, Arisan Maru*
6	*Jones, Paul M.* ▶	*24 Oct 44* ♠	*KIA, Arisan Maru*
7	*Praeger, Ralph B.* ▶	*31 Dec 44* ♠	*Executed, Luzon*
	Captains (14)		
8	*Barker, Joseph R., II*	*01 Nov 43* ♠	*Executed, Luzon*
9	*Buboltz, Walter J.*	*15 Dec 44* ♠	*KIA, Oryoku Maru*
10	*Burlando, Robert C.*	*12 Jan 45* ♠	*Died, Enoura Maru*
11	*Coale, David L., III*	*09 Jan 45* ♠	*KIA, Enoura Maru*
12	*Cramer, Leland W.*	*03 Feb 45*	*Died, Kokura POW Camp, Japan*
13	*Cummings, William M.*	*21 Jan 45* ♠	*Died, Brazil Maru*
14	*Ford, Jack A.*	*09 Jan 45* ♠	*KIA, Enoura Maru*
15	*Laragay, Edwin J. (DO)*	*23 Jan 45* ♠	*Died, Brazil Maru*
16	*Mickelsen, Clayton H. (VC)*	*04 Feb 45*	*Died, Fukuoka POW Camp 1, Japan*
17	*Miller, David A.*	*16 Apr 42* ♠	*KIA, Bataan Death March*
18	*Richards, Forrest C.*	*30 Jan 45*	*Died, Moji Hospital, Japan*
19	*Seay, James C.*	*24 Oct 44* ♠	*KIA, Arisan Maru*
20	*Wheeler, John Z.*	*26 Jan 45* ♠	*Died, Brazil Maru*
21	*Zerfas, Mathias E. (CH)*	*09 Jan 45* ♠	*KIA, Enoura Maru*
	1ˢᵗ Lieutenants (5)		
22	*Carusso, Robert L.*	*05 Feb 45* #	*Died, Moji Hospital, Japan*
23	*Chamberlin, Stephen S.*	*14 Jun 42* ♠	*Died, Cabanatuan*
24	*Furagganan, Arthur P.*	*04 Feb 45* †	*Executed, Luzon*
25	*Leisenring, William P.*	*24 Oct 44* ♠	*KIA, Arisan Maru*
26	*Ward, William H.*	*20 Jul 42* †	*Died, Cabanatuan*
	2ⁿᵈ Lieutenant (1)		
27	*Bowen, William E.*	*24 Oct 44* ♠	*KIA, Arisan Maru*

CAVALRY POW & CAPTIVE DEAD

By Classification

Killed on Bataan Death March (1 of 62) (2%)

	Rank and Name	Date of Death	Cause of Death
	Captain (1)		
1	*Miller, David A.*	*16 Apr 42* ♠	*Bayoneted on march*

Executed (4 of 62) (6%)

	Rank and Name	Date of Death	Cause of Death
	Lt Colonel (1)		
1	Thorp, Claude A.	*01 Nov 43* ♠	*Executed, Luzon*
	Major (1)		
2	Praeger, Ralph B. ▶	*31 Dec 44* ♠	*Executed, Luzon*
	Captain (1)		
3	Barker, Joseph R., II ▶	*01 Nov 43* ♠	*Executed, Luzon*
	1ˢᵗ Lieutenant (1)		
4	Furagganan, Arthur P.	*04 Feb 45* †	*Executed, Luzon*

Died in POW Camps (6 of 62) (10%)

	Rank and Name	Date of Death	Place of Death
	Captains (3)		
1	Cramer, Leland W.	*03 Feb 45*	*Kokura POW Camp, Japan*
2	Mickelsen, Clayton H. (VC)	*04 Feb 45*	*Fukuoka POW Camp 1, Japan*
3	Richards, Forrest C.	*30 Jan 45*	*Moji Hospital, Japan*
	1ˢᵗ Lieutenants (3)		
4	Carusso, Robert L.	*05 Feb 45* †	*Moji Hospital, Japan*
5	Chamberlin, Stephen S.	*14 Jun 42* ♠	*Cabanatuan POW Camp*
6	Ward, William H.	*20 Jul 42* †	*Cabanatuan POW Camp*

Died or Killed on POW Ships (16 of 62) (26%)

Arisan Maru (5)

	Rank and Name	Date of Death	Cause of Death
	Majors (2)		
1	Fleeger, Harry J. ▶	*24 Oct 44* ♠	*KIA, US Torpedo Attack or drowned*
2	Jones, Paul M. ▶	*24 Oct 44* ♠	*KIA, US Torpedo Attack or drowned*
	Captain (1)		
3	Seay, James C.	*24 Oct 44* ♠	*KIA, US Torpedo Attack or drowned*
	1ˢᵗ Lieutenants (1)		
4	Leisenring, William P.	*24 Oct 44* ♠	*KIA, US Torpedo Attack or drowned*
5	**2ⁿᵈ Lieutenant** (1)		
	Bowen, William E.	*24 Oct 44* ♠	*KIA, US Torpedo Attack or drowned*

Oryoku Maru (2)

	Rank and Name	Date of Death	Cause of Death
	Majors (2)		
1	Bickerton, James E.	*15 Dec 44* ♠	*KIA, US Air attack*
	Captain (1)		
2	Buboltz, Walter J.	*15 Dec 44* ♠	*KIA, US Air attack*

Enoura Maru (5)

	Rank and Name	Date of Death	Cause of Death
	Lt Colonel (1)		
1	*Van Nostrand, William S.* ▶	*09 Jan 45* ♠	*KIA, US Air attack*
	Captain (4)		
2	*Burlando, Robert C.*	*12 Jan 45* ♠	*DOW, US Air Attack*
3	*Coale, David L., III*	*09 Jan 45* ♠	*KIA, US Air Attack*
4	*Ford, Jack A.*	*09 Jan 45* ♠	*KIA, US Air Attack*
5	*Zerfas, Mathias E.(CH)*	*09 Jan 45* ♠	*DOW, US Air Attack*

Brazil Maru (4)

	Rank and Name	Date of Death	Cause of Death
	Majors (1)		
1	*Blanning, James C.* ▶	*25 Jan 45* ♠	*Died, Starvation/Illness/Exposure*
	Captain (3)		
2	*Cummings, William M.*	*21 Jan 45* ♠	*Died, Starvation/Illness/Exposure*
3	*Laragay, Edwin J. (DO)*	*23 Jan 45* ♠	*Died, Starvation/Illness/Exposure*
4	*Wheeler, John Z.*	*26 Jan 45* ♠	*Died, Starvation/Illness/Exposure*

NOTES

1. All deaths confirmed on *ABMC Website* except two.

2. CRAMER - Cramer's death is reported from Kokura POW Camp in Mukden and is recorded in the National Archives. *ABMC Website* does not list him.

3. MICKELSEN - Mickelsen's death is reported from Fukuoka POW Camp #1 in Japan and is recorded in the National Archives. *ABMC Website* does not list him. Captain Oliver Orson, DVM, confirmed it in person.

4. Deaths in POW camps attributed to one or more of the following: starvation (nice word is malnutrition), illness, disease, lack of medicine, or despondency. For those who reached Japan in January 1945, add "exposure to cold" as an additional cause for death.

OTHER SOURCES

1. http://people.tamu.edu/~jwerickson/POW/BMFk-1roster.html (Jinsen).
2. Moji Military Hospital Camp Roster, Buried in Charnel (ashes combined).
3. Orson, Oliver W., DVM, "U. S. Army Veterinary Corps Services in the Far East, September 1, 1940-August 1945." Paper in possession of author.

Appendix L

Rosters of
OFFICER SURVIVORS
26th Cavalry Regiment (PS)

Total Officers Fleeger Diaries	60
Survived	20 (33%)
Total Officers All Sources	62
Survived	**20 (32%)**

CAVALRY SURVIVORS

Alphabetical

	Name	Rank	Status
1	Chandler, William E. ▶	MAJ	Released, Mukden POW Camp, Manchuria
2	Evans, Fred B.	1LT	Released, Osaka Main POW Camp, Japan
3	Farris, Houston S.	MAJ	Released, Shinjuku POW Camp, Japan
4	Fowler, John M.	CPT	Released, Mukden POW Camp, Manchuria
5	Gochenour, William S., Jr.	CPT (VC)	Liberated, Bilibid Prison, Manila
6	Jones, Thomas S.	CPT	Liberated, Bilibid Prison, Manila
7	McLennan, Carter	COL	Released, Mukden POW Camp, Manchuria
8	Merrill, Gyles	COL	Recovered, MIA/Escaped (Luzon)/Guerrilla
9	Minton, Warren	CPT	Released, Tsumori-Osaka-Oeyama POW Camp, Japan
10	Nelson, Frank	COL	Released, Mukden POW Camp, Manchuria
11	Pierce, Clinton A.	BG	Released, Mukden POW Camp, Manchuria
12	Ramsey, Edwin P.	1LT	Recovered, MIA/Escaped (Luzon)/Guerrilla
13	Reed, Emil P.	MAJ (MD)	Liberated, Cabanatuan POW Camp
14	Seymour, Clinton C.	1LT	Released, Zentsuji POW Camp, Japan
15	Shaw, Vaughn	CPT (MD)	Liberated, Bilibid Prison, Manila
16	Siciliano, Joseph M.	CPT	Released, Osaka Main POW Camp, Japan
17	Trapnell, Thomas J. H. ▶	LTC	Released, Mukden POW Camp, Manchuria
18	Vance, Lee C.	COL	Released, Mukden POW Camp, Manchuria
19	Whitehead, Arthur	1LT	Survived, no other details
20	Wills, Donald H.	1LT	Recovered, POW/Escaped Mindanao/Guerrilla

CAVALRY SURVIVORS

By Rank

	Rank and Name	Rank	Status
	Brigadier General (1)		
1	Pierce, Clinton A.	BG	Released, Mukden POW Camp, Manchuria
	Colonels (4)		
2	McLennan, Carter R.	COL	Released, Mukden POW Camp, Manchuria
3	Merrill, Gyles	COL	Recovered, MIA/Escaped (Luzon)/Guerrilla

| 4 | Nelson, Frank | COL | Released, Mukden POW Camp, Manchuria |
| 5 | Vance, Lee C. | COL | Released, Mukden POW Camp, Manchuria |

Lt Colonel (1)

| 6 | Trapnell, Thomas J. H. ▶ | LTC | Released, Mukden POW Camp, Manchuria |

Majors (3)

7	Chandler, William E. ▶	MAJ	Released, Mukden POW Camp, Manchuria
8	Farris, Houston S.	MAJ	Released, Shinjuku POW Camp, Japan
9	Reed, Emil P.	MAJ (MD)	Liberated, Cabanatuan POW Camp

Captains (6)

10	Fowler, John M.	CPT	Released, Mukden POW Camp, Manchuria
11	Gochenour, William S., Jr.	CPT (VC)	Liberated, Bilibid Prison, Manila
12	Jones, Thomas S.	CPT	Liberated, Bilibid Prison, Manila
13	Minton, Warren	CPT	Released, Tsumori-Osaka-Oeyama POW Camp, Japan
14	Shaw, Vaughn	CPT (MD)	Liberated, Bilibid Prison, Manila
15	Siciliano, Joseph M.	CPT	Released, Osaka Main POW Camp, Japan

1st Lieutenants (5)

16	Evans, Fred B.	1LT	Released, Osaka Main POW Camp, Japan
17	Ramsey, Edwin P.	1LT	Recovered, MIA/Escaped (Luzon)/Guerrilla
18	Seymour, Clinton C.	1LT	Released, Zentsuji POW Camp, Japan
19	Whitehead, Arthur	1LT	Survived, no other details
20	Wills, Donald H.	1LT	Recovered, POW/Escaped Mindanao/Guerrilla

NOTES

1. FORMOSA POWs - The Japanese imprisoned BG Pierce and COLs McLennan, Nelson, and Vance on Formosa before moving them to Manchuria.

2. MUKDEN POWs - The other Mukden POWs – Trapnell, Chandler, and Fowler – survived the *Oryoku Maru*, the *Enoura Maru,* and the *Brazil Maru* before the Japanese moved them to Manchuria.

3. RAMSEY – Used his initial rank. Could not determine his actual rank as a guerrilla during the war because most of the American officers promoted themselves unofficially to enhance their status among the Filipino guerillas. Eventually, Ramsey became a lieutenant colonel.

Appendix M

Summary of
KNOWN DECORATIONS
Officers, 26ᵗʰ Cavalry Regiment (PS)

Number of Decorations	
Total Officers	**62**
Distinguished Service Cross (DSC)	11
Silver Star (SS)	22
Legion of Merit (LM)	6
Bronze Star Medal (BSM)	12
Purple Heart (PH)	42

The Distinguished Service Cross

Recipients, 26ᵗʰ Cavalry

Joseph R. Barker, II, EX
William E. Bowen, KIA POW Ship
Henry D. Mark, KIA
Clayton H. Mickelsen, VC, Died POW
Warren Minton
Ralph B. Praeger (2 awards), EX
Edwin Ramsey
Claude A. Thorp, EX
Thomas J. H. Trapnell
John Z. Wheeler, Died POW

"may be awarded to a person who, while serving in any capacity with the Army, distinguishes himself by extraordinary heroism not justifying the award of a Medal of Honor. This extraordinary heroism must take place while the individual is engaged in an action against an enemy of the United States; or while he is engaged in military operations involving conflict with an opposing foreign force; or while he is serving with friendly foreign forces that are engaged in an armed conflict against an opposing armed force in which the United States is not a belligerent party. The act or acts of heroism must be so notable and involve risk of life so extraordinary as to set the individual apart from his comrades."

KNOWN AWARDS

26th Cavalry Officers

	Name	Rank	Decorations				
			DSC	SS	LM	BSM	PH
			11	*22*	*6*	*12*	*42*
1	*Allen, Paul K.*	*1LT*					*PH*
2	*Barker, Joseph R., II* ▶	*CPT*	*DSC*	*SS*	*LM*		*PH*
3	*Bickerton, James E.*	*MAJ*					*PH*
4	*Blanning, James C.* ▶	*MAJ*			*LM*	*BSM*	*PH*
5	*Bowen, William E.*	*2LT*	*DSC*			*BSM*	*PH*
6	*Bowers, Charles R.* ▶	*1LT*					*PH*
7	*Buboltz, Walter J.*	*CPT*		*2 SS*			*PH*
8	*Burlando, Robert C.*	*CPT*					*PH*
9	*Cahoon, Carol I.*	*1LT*					*PH*
10	*Carusso, Robert L.*	*1LT*					
11	*Chamberlin, Stephen S.*	*1LT*		*SS*			*PH*
12	*Chandler, William E.* ▶	*MAJ*		*SS*	*LM*	*BSM*	*PH*
13	*Cleary, Joseph A.* ▶	*MAJ*		*SS*		*BSM*	*PH*
14	*Coale, David L., III*	*CPT*				*BSM*	*PH*
15	*Cramer, Leland W.*	*CPT*					
16	*Cummings, William M.*	*CPT*				*BSM*	*PH*
17	*Cunningham, Ethan R.*	*1LT*		*SS*			*PH*
18	Evans, Fred B.	1LT					
19	Farris, Houston S.	MAJ					
20	*Fleeger, Harry J.* ▶	*MAJ*					*PH*
21	*Ford, Jack A.*	*CPT*					*PH*
22	Fowler, John M.	CPT					
23	*Furagganan, Arthur P.*	*1LT*				*BSM*	*PH*
24	*George, John A.*	*1LT*					*PH*
25	Gochenour, William S.	CPT (VC)					
26	*Graves, Steven S.*	*1LT*		*SS*			*PH*
27	*Hardwicke, Clifford, Jr.*	*1LT*		*SS*			*PH*
28	*Hendricks, Archie M., Jr.*	*1LT*					*PH*
29	*Jones, Paul M.* ▶	*MAJ*		*SS*		*BSM*	*2 PH*
30	Jones, Thomas S.	CPT					
31	*Ketchum, Hubert W.* ▶	*LTC*		*SS*	*LM*		*PH*
32	*Laragay, Edwin J.*	*CPT (DO)*		*SS*			
33	*Leisenring, William P.*	*1LT*		*SS*			*PH*
34	*Mark, Henry D.*	*1LT*	*DSC*	*SS*			*PH*
35	McLennan, Carter R.	COL					
36	Merrill, Gyles	COL					
37	*Mickelsen, Clayton H.*	*CPT (VC)*	*DSC*				
38	*Miller, David A.*	*CPT*					*PH*
39	Minton, Warren A.	CPT	DSC				
40	Nelson, Frank	COL					
41	Pierce, Clinton A.	COL					PH
42	*Praeger, Ralph B.* ▶	*CPT*	*2 DSC*		*LM*		*PH*

43	Ramsey, Edwin P.	1LT	DSC	2 SS	LM		PH
44	Reed, Emil P.	MAJ (MD)					
45	*Richards, Forrest C.*	*CPT*					
46	*Seay, James C.*	*CPT*					*PH*
47	Seymour, Clinton C.	1LT					
48	Shaw, Vaughn	CPT (MD)					
49	Siciliano, Joseph M.	1LT					
50	*Spies, George J. (Jack)*	*CPT*					*PH*
51	*Thomas, Frederick F.*	*1LT*		*SS*			*PH*
52	*Thorp, Claude A.*	*LTC*	*DSC*				*2 PH*
53	Trapnell, Thomas J. H. ▶	MAJ	DSC	SS		BSM	PH
54	*Truglia, Dominick*	*1LT*					
55	Vance, Lee C.	COL					
56	*Van Nostrand, William S.* ▶	*LTC*		*SS*		*2 BSM*	*PH*
57	*Ward, William H.*	*1LT*		*SS*			
58	*Wheeler, John Z.*	*CPT*	*DSC*	*SS*		*BSM*	*2 PH*
59	Whitehead, Arthur	1LT					
60	Wills, Donald H.	1LT					
61	*Wrinkle, Paul H.*	*CPT*		*SS*			*PH*
62	*Zerfas, Mathias E.*	*CPT (CH)*					*PH*

SOURCES

1. *ABMC Web*site provided most of the information about decorations for the deceased non-West Pointers. No central information source was found for decorations for surviving non-West Point officers.

2. *Cullum Files* and *1989* USMA *Register* provided most of the information about decorations for West Point officers.

3. PURPLE HEARTS – Most of these awards were posthumous awards for the deaths of officers resulting from enemy action. No known posthumous awards were made to those officers who died of illness, disease, malnutrition, or exposure in the POW camps or on POW ships.

Appendix N

OTHER OFFICERS ASSOCIATED WITH THE 26th CAVALRY (PS)

Varied sources list five officers as being assigned to the 26th Cavalry (PS). Fleeger did not mention them in his diaries; his friend, Bill Chandler, did not mention them in his regimental history; and associated reports on the regiment do not mention them. For historical purposes they are listed below rather than in the narrative. I did not list any of the officers as being active officers in the 26th Cavalry.

The *ABMC Website* lists the following Filipino officers as assigned to the 26th Cavalry (PS):

- *Baclig, Eustaquio S., Lt. Colonel, O012186, Died 30 Nov 1944, Memorialized Manila Cemetery* ▶
- *Layog, Basilio C., 1st Lieutenant, 2031907, Died 14 Feb 1945, Memorialized Manila Cemetery*
- *Moran, Juan S., Colonel, O-014791, Died 7 Jan 1945, Memorialized Manila Cemetery*

The *NARA Website* lists the following American and Filipino officers as assigned to the 26th Cavalry (PS):

- *Moran, Juan S., O01479, Died 7 Jan 1945, Memorialized Manila Cemetery*
- Russell, Andrew G., Jr., O278235
- *Youmans. Joseph M., O294147, Died 9 Jan 1945, Memorialized Manila Cemetery*
- Wohlfeld, Mark M., O314054

Only Russell and Wohlfeld survived.

PERSONAL SUMMARIES

<u>Baclig, Eustaquio S.</u> *11* ▶♠

Baclig was a Philippine Scout officer in the Regular Army.

The Filipino officer graduated from West Point with the Class of 1918 as Eustaquio Baclig y Sabio and was commissioned into the Philippine Scouts.

He was born in Cabugao, Ilocos Sur, Luzon on 20 September 1895. His mother was Leoncia Baclig. He attended grammar school and high school in Vigan, Ilocos Sur. Baclig wrote in a questionnaire that "My mother sent me to school up to 1st Yr. high school then my uncle Crispin Serrano sent me till graduation." Awarded a scholarship to the Silliman Institute, Dumaguate, Oriental Negros, he studied there for five months before the Governor General of the Philippines appointed him to the Military Academy. After graduation, he married Juana Ferinas in 1921. The couple had two sons.

In 1921, Baclig served at Camp Eldridge in Laguna Province where his first son was born. Two years later, he formally changed his name to the one listed. In 1930, he was at Ft. Stotsenburg as a first lieutenant with the 26th Cavalry (PS). In 1942, he served with the Visayan-Mindanao Force, but, unfortunately, neither Brig. General Bradford Chynoweth nor Colonel H. W. Tarkington mentioned him in their memoirs. One record reported that he survived the Bataan Death March, but he would have had to have returned to Bataan to make that march. The *1943 Army Register* listed him as a lieutenant colonel, Philippine Scouts, a cavalry officer, and as "missing in action."

After his surrender or capture, he became a POW, but the Japanese released him in 1943. He then worked with the underground. The Japanese re-captured him in on 2 November 1944, and they executed him on 30 November 1944 at Ft. Santiago in Manila. Baclig is memorialized in the Tablets of the Missing in the Manila Cemetery.

He was a colonel at his death and received a posthumous Purple Heart.[12]

Layog, Basilio C. ♠ [13]

Layog is listed as a regimental officer in one source, but that cannot be confirmed. He was not a regular officer in the U. S. Army.

Nothing is known about his military service.

Layog died on 14 February 1945 after the American troops returned to Manila. No source reported the cause or place of death. *Ancestry.com* (Layog) reports that his body was not recovered. He is memorialized on the Tablets of the Missing in the Manila Cemetery.

Because the Japanese released most of the captured Filipino officers early in the war, it is most likely that the Japanese paroled Layog. Subsequently, they may have re-captured Layog for working with or in some way helping the guerrillas and then executed him. The Japanese executed a number of Americans and Filipinos in January 1945 for working with the guerrillas. Or, they may have killed him during their murder spree in Manila as the American troops fought to recapture the city.

He was a first lieutenant at his death.

Moran, Juan ♠ [14]

Moran was a Philippine Scout officer in the Regular Army of the United States.

The *1943 Army Register,* 315 listed Moran as a colonel of cavalry (major, PS) and as "missing in action." No available report about the 26th Cavalry identifies him as a regimental officer and no information was found about his service or his death. The *ABMC Website* and the *NARA Website* show him to have been assigned the 26th Cavalry. No other available record confirmed this.

The Japanese may have released him and then re-captured him or he may have fought as a guerrilla and been captured. Because of his 1945 date of death, a strong presumption can be made that he was captured and held prior to that date.

Moran died on 7 January 1945 just before the Americans returned to Luzon. If held by the Japanese, they probably executed him on that day. As mentioned, the Japanese executed a number of Americans and Filipinos about that time. He was a U. S. Army colonel at his death.

Moran earned a Silver Star, Legion of Merit, and Purple Heart.

Russell, Andrew G., Jr.[15]

Russell was a captain of cavalry from Texas.

No information was found about his military service. Russell probably surrendered on Bataan and survived Camp O'Donnell.

The Japanese imprisoned him in Cabanatuan. Later, they moved him to Japan – but not on the *Oryoku Maru* – and then imprisoned him at Fukuoka 17 POW Camp. Finally, the Japanese transferred him to the Hoten POW Camp (Mukden) in Manchuria. He was released on 10 September 1945.

The Mukden Evacuation Roster for group TFR2-56 listed Russell as a returnee, along with Major William Chandler, Colonel Carter R. McLennan, Lt. Colonel T. J. H. Trapnell, and Colonel Lee Vance of the 26th Cavalry, and Lt. Colonel Ovid O. Wilson.

Wohlfeld, Mark M.[16]

Wohlfeld was a Reserve Cavalry Officer from New York.

Called to active duty in July 1941 as 1st Lieutenant of Cavalry, the Army assigned Wohlfeld to be a Supply Officer in the 48th Material Squadron at Savannah Air Base in Georgia. Promoted to Captain, Cavalry Reserve in August, he participated in the Louisiana Maneuvers. Assigned to the Philippines, Wohlfeld moved to San Francisco, embarked on the SS *President Coolidge* and arrived in Manila in November where he joined to the 27th Bombardment Squadron (Light) at Ft. McKinley. After war broke out, his squadron was re-designated the 2nd Battalion, Infantry, Provisional (Air Corps) and Wohlfeld became the Executive Officer. In December, the battalion deployed to Bataan where it soon found itself in the line against the Japanese.

After the surrender, Wohlfeld began the Death March. One morning the Japanese loaded him onto a truck and drove him and others to Capas where he and his comrades marched into Camp O'Donnell. Early on, he got out of O'Donnell and led a "Bataan Salvage Detail" until October 1942 when the Japanese sent him to Cabanatuan.

In November 1942, the Japanese sent Wohlfeld to the Davao Penal Colony where he worked in the rice fields and on road gangs. On 27 March 1944, he noted: "Assigned to fence-post hole digging detail 2 miles from main prison compound, with 10 Americans. Attacked and overpowered 5 man Japanese Guard complement. Effected escape into Jungle." He joined the guerrillas on Mindanao in April and became the Guerrilla Chief of Staff of the 100th Division.

In October 1944, Wohlfeld made his way to Leyte after U. S. forces had landed and "Volunteered for return to duty with Rifle Company." Assigned to the 7th Cavalry Regiment of the 1st Cavalry Division, he joined the unit as it was fighting in the Ormoc Valley. Wohlfeld landed with his regiment at Lingayen Gulf in January 1945 and led his company in clearing the "Manila water supply reservoir area" and in neutralizing "hold-out areas."

The captain rotated back to the United States in March and returned to New York. After some quiet months, he volunteered for reassignment to the 1st Cavalry Division in Japan and upon arrival became the Executive Officer of the 2nd Squadron, 12th Cavalry in August 1946. In 1947, the Army transferred Major Wohlfeld to Korea and assigned him to the reconstituted 31st Infantry Regiment (part of the destroyed Philippine Division) as the Executive Officer of the 2nd Battalion.

In November, back in the United States, he rejoined the Active Reserve in New York as a lieutenant colonel of armor. From 1955 to 1957, Wohlfeld commanded the 325th Heavy Tank Battalion, U. S. Army Reserve on Long Island. After twenty-seven years of active and reserve service, he retired in June 1960.

Wohlfeld remained active in military affairs. He served with a ceremonial pack howitzer battery – The Veteran Corps of Artillery Military Society of the War of 1812 - that fired a 21-gun salute during the celebration of the 200th Birthday of the U. S. Army at West Point on 14 June 1976.[17]

Youmans, Joseph M. ♠

Youmans was a Second Lieutenant of Cavalry from Pennsylvania.

No information was found about his military service. No unit is given on the *ABMC Website.* He is merely listed as "Cavalry." Most likely, he fought on Bataan and survived the Death March and Camp O'Donnell. He survived imprisonment in Cabanatuan.

The Japanese moved him north on the *Oryoku Maru* in December 1944. He died on 9 January 1945, the day the naval aircraft bombed the *Enoura Maru* in Takao Harbor.

Youmans is memorialized on the Tablets of the Missing in the Manila Cemetery. He received a posthumous Purple Heart.

Appendix O

Rosters of
FLEEGER'S FRIENDS

Fleeger's Friends	
Total Officers	49
Total Soldiers	35
Total	84

Fleeger mentioned many officers and soldiers – called Fleeger's Friends - who did not serve in the 26th Cavalry. They are listed below.[18]

FLEEGER'S OFFICER FRIENDS

Alphabetical

	Name	Rank	Position if Known
1	Archer, Herman N. (Pappy)	CPT	Headquarters, II Philippine Corps
2	*Babcock, David S.* ▶	*LTC*	*CO, Field Artillery Battalion*
3	Batchelor, Jack F.	CPT	*Philippine Air Depot*
4	*Bauer, Karol A.* ▶	*MAJ*	*45th Infantry Regiment (PS)*
5	Beecher, Curtis T.	LTC, USMC	CO, 4th Marine Regiment
6	*Bidgood, Clarence* ▶	*MAJ*	*CO, 71st Engineer Battalion (PA)*
7	Braun, Albert W.	MAJ (CH)	200th or 515th Coast Artillery
8	Brinkmeyer, John E.	CPT/MAJ	Finance Department
9	*Browne, Charles J.* ▶	*MAJ*	*91st Infantry Division (PA)*
10	Clemons, Carl C.	2LT	*75th Bomber Squadron, 42nd Bomber Group, Medium*
11	*Coyle, Harold J.* ▶	*MAJ*	*24th Field Artillery Regiment (PS); Cebu Force (42)*
12	Cox, Thomas C.	LT	200th or 515th Coast Artillery Regiment
13	Doran, Roy E.	MAJ	71st Artillery Regiment
14	Dorris, Winnifred O.	LTC	200th Coast Artillery
15	*Dunmyer, William* ▶	*MAJ*	*Headquarters, II Philippine Corps*
16	Fischer, Harry O.	MAJ	803rd Engineer Battalion (PS)
17	Fitch, Alva R.	MAJ	CO, 9th Battalion, 91st FA (PA) & 23rd Field Artillery (PS)
18	*Garver, Ralph T.* ▶	*LTC*	*Headquarters, Philippine Department*
19	*Griffiths, Kenneth C.* ▶	*CPT*	*24th Field Artillery Regiment (PS)*
20	Gross, Gardner B.	MAJ	No data
21	*Herrick, Leroy M.*	*MAJ*	*Signal Corps – no unit data*
22	Hirsch, Ralph	COL	Headquarters, Luzon Force
23	*Horton, Thomas R.* ▶	*LTC*	*Office of the Quartermaster, Manila*
24	*Houser, H. Parks, Jr.* ▶	*MAJ*	I Philippine Corps
25	*Howard, C. E. N., Jr.* ▶	*MAJ*	CO, 2nd Battalion, 88th Field Artillery (PS)
26	*Howden, Frederick B.*	*CPT (CH)*	*200th or 515th Coast Artillery Regiment*
27	Johnson, Chester L. ▶	MAJ	24th Field Artillery Regiment (PS)
28	*Jones, Samuel Edward* ▶	*MAJ*	*Headquarters, Philippine Department*
29	Koenig, Fred W.	LT	*No data*
30	*Lauman, Philip G., Jr.* ▶	*MAJ*	Headquarters, I Philippine Corps
31	*Lindsay, James R.., Jr.* ▶	*LTC*	*Artillery Officer, I Philippine Corps*
32	*Murphey, William W.*	*LTC*	*24th Field Artillery Regiment (PS)*
33	North, William D.	LTC (MD)	*No data*
34	*Packard, Harry B.* ▶	*MAJ*	*24th Field Artillery Regiment (PS)*
35	*Pell, Floyd J. (Slugger)* ▶	*MAJ*	*33rd Fighter Squadron, FEAF*

36	*Priestley, William J.* ▶	*MAJ*	*57th Infantry Regiment (PS)*
37	*Reynolds, Royal, Jr.* ▶	MAJ	57th Infantry Regiment (PS)
38	*Saint, Frederick. G.* ▶	LTC	CO, 14th Engineer Regiment (PS)
39	*Strickler, Dudley G.* ▶	MAJ	45th Infantry Regiment (PS)
40	*Svihra, Albert G.* ▶	LTC	Headquarters, Philippine Division
41	*Thomas, Evert S. (Pop)*	MAJ	Adjutant General, Philippine Division
42	*Thomson, Burton C.*	CPT (VC)	Post Veterinarian, Ft. Mills, Corregidor
43	*Thwaits, Pryor [Prior]*	2LT	200th or 515th Coast Artillery Regiment
44	*Turner, John W., Jr.*	MAJ	200th or 515th Coast Artillery Regiment
45	*Uddenberg, Alf E.*	LTC	Headquarters, North Luzon Force
46	*Ward, John T.* ▶	LTC	Quartermaster Corps, Bataan
47	*Wilson, Ovid Oscar* ▶	LTC	G-1 Officer, South Luzon Force, G-1, I Philippine Corps
48	*Wing, Paul R.*	MAJ/LTC	No data
49	*Zwaska, Andrew B.*	MAJ	45th Infantry Regiment (PS)

FLEEGER'S SOLDIER FRIENDS

Alphabetical

	Name	**Rank**	**Unit if Known**
1	Argeanas, James	SGT	D Battery, 200th Coast Artillery Regiment
2	*Bates, Arthur E.*	*PVT*	*4th Chemical Company, Aviation*
3	Bramley, Clarence H.	SGT	21st Pursuit Squadron
4	Cardenas, Eloy P.	PVT (PFC)	H Battery, 200th Coast Artillery Regiment (SPM)
5	Cater, Jack A.	*PVT*	E Battery, 515th Coast Artillery Regiment
6	Davis, Robert	SGT	E Battery, 515th Coast Artillery Regiment
7	Delanty, James E.	TSGT	Finance – no unit data
8	Drake, Aaron C.	PFC (CPL)	A Battery, 200th Coast Artillery Regiment
9	Garcia, Cleofas	PFC	D Battery, 200th Coast Artillery Regiment
10	Gardner, Herschel R	PVT	H Battery, 200th Coast Artillery Regiment (SPM)
11	Hamrick, Eugene E.	PFC (CPL)	H Battery, 200th Coast Artillery Regiment (SPM)
12	*Henderson, Charles W.*	*TSGT*	*Headquarters Company, Philippine Department*
13	*House, Jess C.*	*PVT*	*A Battery, 200th Coast Artillery Regiment*
14	Hudgens, S. R. (Syd)	PFC (CPL)	A Battery, 200th Coast Artillery Regiment
15	*Kanally, Billy B.*	*PFC*	*H Battery, 515th Coast Artillery Regiment*
16	Lappin, Frederick B.	PFC	454th Ordnance Aviation Bomb Group
17	Lewis, John E.	PVT	454th Ordnance Aviation Bomb Group
18	*Marquez, Manuel O.*	*PFC*	*A Battery, 200th Coast Artillery Regiment*
19	Martinez, Luciano	PFC (CPL)	G Battery, 200th Coast Artillery Regiment
20	Oldham, Adrian E.	PVT	A Battery, 200th Coast Artillery Regiment
21	Plemmons, Carl K.	PFC	B Battery, 200th Coast Artillery Regiment
22	*Rada, Emanuel*	*CPL*	*Harbor Defense of Manila*
23	*Reynolds, John E.*	*SGT*	*Detached enlisted group*
24	Rice, Kenneth V.	CPL	USMC – Probably 4th Battalion
25	Rivera, Philip F.	PFC	H Battery, 200th Coast Artillery Regiment (SPM)
26	*Sandoval, Bertram (Bert)*	*PFC*	*E Battery, 200th Coast Artillery Regiment*
27	Segura, Joseph A. (Jose)	SGT (TSGT)	H Battery, 200th Coast Artillery Regiment (SPM)
28	Smythe, Robert W.	PFC	HQ & HQ Squadron, 27th Bomb Group
29	Stear, Arthur W.	SGT	HQ & HQ Squadron, 27th Bomb Group
30	*Strus, Walter P.*	*PVT*	*C Battery, 515th Coast Artillery Regiment*
31	Thompson, Wilson S.	PFC	454th Ordnance Aviation Bomb Group
32	Tracer, Jay C.	TSGT	Air Corps – no unit data
33	Travera, Philip	PVT	No data
34	*Trujillo, Reynaldo(Ray)*	*PFC*	*H Battery, 515th Coast Artillery Regiment*
35	Van Orden, William N.	PFC	803rd Engineers

NOTE

200th or 515th Coast Artillery Regiment personnel confirmed in *NM Names Project* at http://www.angelfire.com/nm/bcmfofnm/names/a.html

Appendix P

Rosters of
DEAD AMONG FLEEGER'S FRIENDS

Officers & Soldiers Mentioned in Fleeger's Diaries

Confirmed Deaths	
Total Officers	49
Officer Deaths	29 (59%)
Total Soldiers	35
Soldier Deaths	10(29%)
All Deaths	**39 of 84 (46%)**

OFFICER DEAD

Alphabetical

	Name	Rank	Date of Death	Cause of Death
1	Babcock, David S. ▶	LTC	23 Jan 45♠	DOW, Brazil Maru
2	Batchelor, Jack F.	CPT	20 Jan 45♠	Died, Brazil Maru
3	Bauer, Karol A. ▶	MAJ	15 Dec 44♠	KIA, Oryoku Maru
4	Browne, Charles J. ▶	MAJ	09 Jan 45♠	KIA, Enoura Maru
5	Clemons, Carl C.	2LT	12 Apr 44♠	Died, Cabanatuan POW Camp
6	Coyle, Harold J. ▶	MAJ	17 Apr 42 ♠	EX, Cebu
7	Dunmyer, William ▶	MAJ	15 Dec 44 ♠	KIA, Oryoku Maru
8	Garver, Ralph T. ▶	LTC	14 Apr 42 †	EX, Bataan Death March
9	Griffiths, Kenneth C. ▶	CPT	22 Aug 42 †	Died, Cabanatuan POW Camp
10	Herrick, Leroy M.	MAJ	15 Dec 44 ♠	KIA, Oryoku Maru
11	Hirsch, Ralph	COL	13 Apr 42 ♠	EX, Camp O'Donnell
12	Horton, Thomas R. ▶	LTC	06 Sep 42	Died, Cabanatuan POW Camp
13	Howden, Frederick B.	CPT (CH)	1942	Died, Davao Penal Colony
14	Jones, Samuel Edward ▶	MAJ	23 Jan 42	KIA, Bataan
15	Lauman, Philip G., Jr. ▶	MAJ	15 Dec 44 ♠	KIA, Oryoku Maru
16	Lindsay, James R.., Jr. ▶	LTC	20 Jan 1945	Died, Brazil Maru
17	Murphey, William W.	LTC	31 Jan 1945	Died, Moji Hospital, Japan
18	Packard, Harry B. ▶	MAJ	27 Jan 45 ♠♠	Died, Brazil Maru
19	Pell, Floyd J. (Slugger) ▶	MAJ	19 Jan 42 ††	KIA Air Operations, Darwin
20	Priestley, William J. ▶	MAJ	15 Dec 44♠	KIA, Oryoku Maru
21	Saint, Frederick. G. ▶	LTC	24 Jan 45 ♠	DOW, Brazil Maru
22	Strickler, Dudley G. ▶	MAJ	8 Feb 42 ♠	KIA, Bataan
23	Svihra, Albert G. ▶	LTC	24 Oct 44 ♠	KIA, Arisan Maru
24	Thomas, Evert S. (Pop)	MAJ		Died, Cabanatuan POW Camp
25	Thomson, Burton C.	CPT (VC)	May 1942	Executed, Corregidor
26	Turner, John W., Jr.	MAJ	15 Dec 44 ♠	KIA, Oryoku Maru
27	Uddenberg, Alf E.	LTC	20 Apr 42 ♠	EX, Bataan POW
28	Ward, John T. ▶	LTC	11 Apr 42 ♠	EX, Bataan POW
29	Zwaska, Andrew B.	MAJ	27 Jan 45 ♠	Died, Brazil Maru

SOLDIER DEAD

Alphabetical

	Name	Rank	Date of Death	Cause of Death
1	Bates, Arthur E.	PVT	24 Oct 44 ♠	KIA, Arisan Maru
2	Henderson, Charles W.	TSGT	24 Oct 44 ♠	KIA, Arisan Maru
3	House, Jess C.	PVT	24 Oct 44 ♠	KIA, Arisan Maru
4	Kanally, Billy B.	PFC	24 Oct 44 ♠	KIA, Arisan Maru
5	Marquez, Manuel O.	PFC	24 Oct 44 ♠	KIA, Arisan Maru
6	Rada, Emanuel	CPL	24 Oct 44 ♠	KIA, Arisan Maru
7	Reynolds, John E.	SGT	24 Oct 44 ♠	KIA, Arisan Maru
8	Sandoval, Bertram (Bert)	PFC	07 Sep 44 ♠	KIA, Shinyo Maru
9	Strus, Walter P.	PVT	24 Oct 44 ♠	KIA, Arisan Maru
10	Trujillo, Reynaldo(Ray)	PFC	24 Oct 44 ♠	KIA, Arisan Maru

NOTES

Deaths confirmed on the *ABMC Website* or on *200th Coast Artillery, NM Website* or on *NARA POW Data Base.*

JONES – Remains Interred in Santa Fe, NM.

Appendix Q

Rosters of
SURVIVORS AMONG FLEEGER'S FRIENDS

Officers & Soldiers Mentioned in Fleeger's Diaries

Survivors	
Total Officers	49
Officer Survivors	20 (41%)
Total Enlisted Soldiers	35
Soldier Survivors	25 (71%)
Total Survivors	**45 of 86 (52%)**

OFFICER SURVIVORS

Alphabetical

	Name	Rank	POW Camp
1	Archer, Herman N. (Pappy)	CPT	Liberated, Bilibid POW Camp, Manila
2	Beecher, Curtis T.	LTC, USMC	Released, Jinsen POW Camp, Korea
3	Bidgood, Clarence ▶	MAJ	Released, Osaka Main POW Camp, Japan
4	Braun, Albert W.	MAJ (CH)	Released, Shinjuku POW Camp, Japan
5	Brinkmeyer, John E.	CPT/MAJ	Liberated, Cabanatuan POW Camp
6	Cox, Thomas C.	2LT	Released, Jinsen POW Camp, Korea
7	Doran, Roy E.	MAJ	Released, Mukden POW Camp, Manchuria
8	Dorris, Winnifred O.	LTC	Recovered, Undetermined, Luzon
9	Fischer, Harry O.	MAJ	Escaped, *Shinyo Maru, Repatriated*
10	Fitch, Alva R.	MAJ	Released, Jinsen POW Camp, Korea
11	Gross, Gardner B.	MAJ	Released, Jinsen POW Camp, Korea
12	Houser, H. Parks, Jr. ▶	MAJ	Released, Jinsen POW Camp, Korea
13	Howard, C. E. N., Jr. ▶	MAJ	Released, Osaka Main POW Camp, Japan
14	Johnson, Chester L. ▶	MAJ	Released, Jinsen POW Camp, Korea
15	Koenig, Fred W.	LT	Released, Osaka Main POW Camp, Japan
16	North, William D.	LTC (MD)	Liberated, Cabanatuan POW Camp
17	Reynolds, Royal, Jr. ▶	MAJ	Recovered, Escaped/Evaded/Guerrilla, Luzon
18	Thwaits, Pryor [Prior]	2LT	Released, TAI 1-Taihoku POW Camp, Japan
19	Wilson, Ovid O. ▶	LTC	Released, Mukden POW Camp, Manchuria
20	Wing, Paul R.	MAJ/LTC	Liberated, Cabanatuan POW Camp

SOLDIER SURVIVORS

Alphabetical

	Name	Rank	POW Camp
1	Argeanas, James	SGT	Released, Tokyo #2 POW Camp, Japan
2	Bramley, Clarence H.	SGT	Released, Shinjuku POW Camp, Japan
3	Cardenas Eloy P.	PVT (PFC)	Released, Shinjuku POW Camp, Japan

4	Cater, Jack A.	*PVT*	Released, Tokyo Sectional Camp #3, Japan
5	Davis, Robert	SGT	Released, Osaka 5 POW Camp, Japan
6	Delanty, James E.	TSGT	Released, Osaka Main POW Camp, Japan
7	Drake, Aaron C.	PFC (CPL)	Released, Shinjuku POW Camp, Japan
8	Garcia, Cleofas	PFC	Released, Fukuoka 1 POW Camp, Japan
9	Gardner, Herschel R	PVT	Released, Osaka-Main POW Camp, Japan
10	Hamrick, Eugene E.	PFC (CPL)	Released, Shinjuku POW Camp, Japan
11	Hudgens, S. R. (Syd)	PFC (CPL)	Released, Mukden POW Camp, Manchuria
12	Lappin, Frederick B.	PFC	Released, Fukuoka 1 POW Camp, Japan
13	Lewis, John E.	PVT/SSG	Released, Fukuoka 1 POW Camp, Japan
14	Martinez, Luciano	PFC/CPL	Released, Fukuoka 1 POW Camp, Japan
15	Oldham, Adrian E.	PVT/PFC	NM listing. No other data.
16	Plemmons, Carl K.	PFC	Released, Fukuoka 1 POW Camp, Japan
17	Rice, Kenneth V.	CPL	Released, Japan, (ND)
18	Rivera, Philip F.	PFC	Released, Osaka-Main POW Camp, Japan
19	Segura, Joseph A. (Jose)	SGT/TSGT	Released, Fukuoka 1 POW Camp, Japan
20	Smythe, Robert W.	PFC	Released, Osaka-Main POW Camp, Japan
21	Stear, Arthur W.	SGT	Released, Shinjuku POW Camp, Japan
22	Thompson, Wilson S.	PFC	Released, Fukuoka 1 POW Camp, Japan
23	Tracer, Jay C.	TSGT	Released, Yodogawa Bunsho Osaka, Japan
24	Travera, Philip	PVT	No data
25	Van Orden, William N.	PFC	Recovered, no data.

NOTES

BRINKMEYER - One record shows Brinkmeyer released from Cabanatuan, but he is not listed on the rescue roster for the camp.

Confirmed on *NARA POW Data Base* or *NM Names Project* - http://www.angelfire.com/nm/bcmfofnm/names/a.html, the site for the 200th and 515th Coast Artillery Regiments.

Appendix R

Summary of
KNOWN DECORATIONS
Fleeger's Friends

Officers & Soldiers Mentioned in Fleeger's Diaries

Number of Known Decorations	
Distinguished Service Cross (DSC)	4
Silver Star (SS)	14
Legion of Merit (LM)	8
Bronze Star Medal (BSM)	17
Air Medal (AM)	2
Commendation Ribbon (CR)	2
Purple Heart (PH)	38

The Distinguished Service Cross

Recipients, Fleeger's Friends

Alva Fitch
Floyd J. Pell, KIA, Darwin, Australia
Dudley G. Strickler (2 awards), KIA, Bataan

KNOWN AWARDS to OFFICERS

Name	Rank	DSC 4	SS 14	LM 8	BSM 17	AM 2	CR 2	PH 28
Archer, Herman N. (Pappy)	CPT							
Babcock, David S. ▶	*LTC*			*LM*				*PH*
Batchelor, Jack F.	*CPT*							*PH*
Bauer, Karol A. ▶	*MAJ*							*PH*
Beecher, Curtis T.	LTC, USMC							
Bidgood, Clarence ▶	MAJ				BSM		2 CR	PH
Braun, Albert W.	MAJ (CH)		SS	LM				
Brinkmeyer, John E.	CPT/MAJ							
Browne, Charles J. ▶	*MAJ*		*SS*		*BSM*			*PH*
Clemons, Carl C.	*2LT, USAAF*					*2 AM*		*PH*
Coyle, Harold J. ▶	*MAJ*							*PH*
Cox, Thomas C.	2LT							
Doran, Roy E.	MAJ							
Dorris, Winnifred O.	LTC							
Dunmyer, William ▶	*MAJ*		*SS*		*BSM*			*PH*
Fischer, Harry O.	MAJ							
Fitch, Alva R.	MAJ	DSC	SS		BSM			PH
Garver, Ralph T. ▶	*LTC*							*PH*
Griffiths, Kenneth C. ▶	*CPT*							*PH*
Gross, Gardner B.	MAJ							
Herrick, Leroy M.	*MAJ*		*SS*					*PH*
Hirsch, Ralph	*COL*		*SS*					*PH*
Horton, Thomas R. ▶	*LTC*							
Houser, Houston P., Jr. ▶	MAJ		SS	LM				
Howard, C. E. N., Jr. ▶	MAJ		SS	LM				2 PH
Howden, Frederick B.	*CPT (CH)*							
Johnson, Chester L. ▶	MAJ		SS		2 BSM			
Jones, Samuel Edward ▶	*MAJ*							
Koenig, Fred W.	LT							
Lauman, Philip G., Jr. ▶	*MAJ*		*SS*	*LM*				*PH*
Lindsay, James R., Jr. ▶	*LTC*			*LM*				
Murphey, William W.	*LTC*							
North, William D.	LTC (MD)							
Packard, Harry B. ▶	*MAJ*		*2SS*		*2 BSM*			*PH*
Pell, Floyd J. (Slugger) ▶	*MAJ*	*DSC*						*PH*
Priestley, William J. ▶	*MAJ*			*LM*	*BSM*			*PH*
Reynolds, Royal, Jr. ▶	MAJ							
Saint, Frederick. G. ▶	*LTC*		*SS*		*2BSM*			*PH*
Strickler, Dudley G. ▶	*MAJ*	*2 DSC*			*BSM*			*PH*
Svihra, Albert G. ▶	*LTC*				*BSM*			*PH*
Thomas, Evert S. (Pop)	*MAJ*							
Thomson, Burton C.	*CPT (VC)*							
Thwaits, Pryor [Prior]	2LT							
Turner, John W., Jr.	*MAJ*							*PH*
Uddenberg, Alf E.	*LTC*				*BSM*			*PH*
Ward, John T. ▶	*LTC*							*2 PH*
Wilson, Ovid O. ▶	*LTC*			*LM*	*BSM*			*PH*
Wing, Paul R.	MAJ/LTC							
Zwaska, Andrew B.	*MAJ*		*SS*		*2 BSM*			*PH*

KNOWN AWARDS to SOLDIERS

Name	Rank	Decorations						
		DSC	SS	LM	BSM	AM	CR	PH 10
Argeanas, James	SGT							
Bates, Arthur E.	*PVT*							*PH*
Bramley, Clarence H.	SGT							
Cardenas Eloy P.	PVT (PFC)							
Cater, Jack A.	*PVT*							
Davis, Robert	SGT							
Delanty, James E.	TSGT							
Drake, Aaron C.	PFC (CPL)							
Garcia, Cleofas	PFC							
Gardner, Herschel R.	PVT							
Hamrick, Eugene E.	PFC (CPL)							
Henderson, Charles	*TSGT*							*PH*
House, Jess C.	*PVT*							*PH*
Hudgens, S. R. (Syd)	PFC (CPL)							
Kanally, Billy B.	*PFC*							*PH*
Lappin, Frederick B.	PFC							
Lewis, John E.	PVT							
Marquez, Manuel O.	*PFC*							*PH*
Martinez, Luciano	PFC (CPL)							
Oldham, Adrian E.	PVT							
Plemmons, Carl K.	PFC							
Rada, Emanuel	*CPL*							*PH*
Reynolds, John E.	*SGT*							*PH*
Rice, Kenneth V.	CPL							
Rivera, Philip F.	PFC							
Sandoval, Bertram	*PFC*							*PH*
Segura, Joseph A.	SGT (TSGT)							
Smythe, Robert W.	PFC							
Stear, Arthur W.	SGT							
Strus, Walter P.	*PVT*							*PH*
Thompson, Wilson S.	PFC							
Tracer, Jay C.	TSGT							
Travera, Philip	PVT							
Trujillo, Reynaldo(Ray)	*PFC*							
Van Orden, William	PFC							PH

NOTE
Where there are differences in awards between sources, all listed awards are shown.

SOURCES

1. *ABMC Web*site provided most of the information about decorations for the deceased non-West Pointer officers and the soldiers. No central information source was found for decorations for surviving non-West Point officers or the soldiers.

2. *Cullum Files* and *1989 USMA Register* provided most of the information about decorations for West Point officers.

3. PURPLE HEARTS – Most of these awards were posthumous awards for the deaths of officers and soldiers resulting from enemy action. No known posthumous awards were made to those officers who died of illness, disease, malnutrition, or exposure in the POW camps or on POW ships.

Appendix S

Roster of
FLEEGER'S CLASSMATES (Class of 1931) IN THE PHILIPPINES, 1941-1942[19]

5 of 13 Survived (38%)

	Name	Rank	Died/Survived	Decorations
1	*Blanning, James Chester*	*MAJ*	*Died 25 Jan 45 – Brazil Maru*	*LM, PH*
2	Chandler, William Eaton	MAJ	Released, Mukden	SS, LM, BSM, PH
3	*Fleeger, Harry James*	*MAJ*	*KIA 24 Oct 44 - Arisan Maru*	*PH*
4	Houser, Houston Parks, Jr.	MAJ	Released, Jinsen, Korea	SS, SM
5	Howard, Charles Edward Nason, Jr.	MAJ	*No information*	SS, LM, PH
6	*Humber, Charles Ingram, Jr.*	*LTC*	*Died 22 Jan 45 - Brazil Maru*	*LM*
7	Johnston, Robert Daniel	MAJ	Liberated, Cabanatuan	LM, BSM
8	*Jones, Samuel Edward*	*MAJ*	*KIA 23 Jan 42 - Bataan*	*PH*
9	*McClellan, James Thomas*	*MAJ*	*DOW 27 Jan 45 - Brazil Maru*	*PH*
10	McGee, John Hugh	MAJ	Escaped POW Ship, Guerrilla, Mindanao	SS, LM, CIB
11	*Pahl, Howard Max*	*MAJ*	*KIA 15 Dec 45 - Oryoku Maru*	*BSM, PH*
12	*Raker, John Newlin*	*MAJ*	*KIA 24 Oct 44 - Arisan Maru*	*PH*
13	*Saint, Frederick Gilman*	*LTC*	*Died 25 Jan 45 - Brazil Maru*	*SS, 2 BSM, PH*

NOTES

1. CHANDLER, HOUSER, HOWARD & JOHNSTON returned to active service and retired as colonels.

2. MCGEE - Retired as a Brigadier General.

   He escaped from the *Yashu Maru* near the coast of Mindanao in June 1944.

   > "Shortly after midnight on the fifteenth, the prisoners topside heard a splash and then rifle shots. Lt. Col. John H. McGee had arranged for a friend to throw his barracks bag over the side. When the guards rushed to the spot and began shooting at the bag, McGee dove off the other side. He swam to shore and eventually joined the guerrillas."[20]

Appendix T

Rosters of
ALL OFFICERS EXECUTED

26th Cavalry (PS)

	Name	Rank	Date of Death	Place of Death	Reason
1	Barker, Joseph R., II ▶	CPT	01 Nov 43 ♠	Luzon	Guerrilla
2	Furagganan, Arthur P	1LT	04 Feb 45 †	Luzon	Guerrilla
3	Praeger, Ralph B. ▶	MAJ	31 Dec 44 ♠	Luzon	Guerrilla
4	Thorp, Claude A.	LTC	01 Nov 43 ♠	Luzon	Guerrilla

Fleeger's Friends

	Name	Rank	Date of Death	Place of Death	Reason
1	Coyle, Harold J. ▶	MAJ	17 Apr 42	Cebu Island	Not determined
2	Garver, Ralph T. ▶	LTC	14 Apr 42 †	Bataan	Not determined
3	Hirsch, Ralph	COL	13 Apr 42 ♠	Camp O'Donnell	Possessing some Japanese item
4	Tomson, Burton C.	CPT (VC)	May 1942	Corregidor	Not giving peaches to an American collaborator for the Japanese
5	Uddenberg, Alf E.	LTC	20 Apr 42 ♠	Bataan	Not determined
6	Ward, John T. ▶	LTC	11 Apr 42 ♠	Bataan	Falling out of ranks

NOTES

1. The executions of Fleeger's friends were totally unjustified. They reflected the atrocious behavior of Japanese to all their POWS at this time of the war.

2. COYLE – Japanese may have killed/executed Major Coyle just after they captured him. The Japanese executed more than one American soldier in the Visayas just after they captured them for flimsy charges such as resisting too long or destroying military supplies.

Appendix U

War Illness Record, Harry Fleeger

Bataan 1942

Date	Illness	Comments	Page
Jan-Feb	Piles	Operated on in March 1943	92
1-15 Mar	Dysentery	#1 Hospital	91

Prologue
"Pellagra and Beri Beri started to appear within 2 weeks – continued to grow in severity – eyes – joints – muscles –early affected by protein shortages and vitamin deficiencies. Scurvy appeared after about 5 months."

Camp O'Donnell 1942

Date	Illness	Comments	Page
10 Apr-1May	Piles	No details	91
1 May	Malaria	No treatment	91

Cabanatuan 1942

Date	Illness	Comments	Page
May-Jul	Diarrhea	No treatment	
27 Jun	Dying	"I was very weak and ill, a two month illness following the move June 1 from O'Donnell prison camp. Damned near died in fact." "last June [1942] I was dying – almost – as it later developed"	6 107
7 Sep	Common cold		92
10 Sep	Scurvy	"Usually in mouth – cleared somewhat with use of limes"	92
Sep	Dry *beri-beri*,	"aching feet and ankles"	92
30 Sep	Diarrhea		63
22 Nov	*Dry beri-beri*	"intense pain and ache in feet, legs, arms, hands" Received 16 Betaxain pills. "May save me – Can't sleep"	73
30 Nov	*Dry beri-beri*	"feet and legs in bad shape"	74
12 Dec	*Eye ulcers Scurvy*	"I need eggs, (Vitamin A for eye ulcers," fruit for scurvy	79

| 17 Dec | *Beri-beri* | "has my feet and ankles badly crippled" | 79 |

| 25 Dec | *Beri-beri* | "My health good but from dry beri beri in my feet. I'm marked quarters and still work in the camp library" | 83 |

Cabanatuan 1943

Date	Illness	Comments	Page
10 Jan	Hemorrhoids *Beri-beri*	"good food but much pain" "Severe case of hemorrhoids" "Feet are better"	86
8 Feb	*Beri-beri* Hemorrhoids	Feet almost normal "Hemorrhoids almost normal after three weeks of trouble"	88
12 Apr	Surgery for hemorrhoids	"Just back…after 4 weeks in the hospital area" "Colonel North operated on me" "Recovered without infection"	91
18 May	*Beri-beri*	"I am well except for beri beri and it is not so painful"	94
18 May	*Weigh 130*	Up from 95 pounds	94
27 Jun	*Dry Beri-beri*	Still weighed 130 "old weight"	107
29 Jul	*Beri-beri*	"feet sore with beri beri	112
25 Aug	"Cholera in Manila"	"Taking Jap shots – cholera, dysentery, typhoid, bubonic"	115
15 Oct	*Beri-beri*	Treatment: 20 more shots - BI-hydrochloride	125
3 Nov	*Beri-beri*	No comments	126
3 Nov	Possible sterility	"Most of us are possibly sterile from this racket"	126

Cabanatuan 1944

Date	Illness	Comments	Page
25 Feb	*Beri-beri*	"on a course of Thiamin" "don't mind the pain but don't want to come out of it with a weak heart"	143
23 Mar	Bad infection left hand and arm.	"Pretty sick" Hot packs and sulpha thiasol	147
	Beri-beri	Finished 30 days of thiamin "beri beri feet are better – best since '42"	147
7 May	Pellagra *Beri-beri*	"have pellagra blisters"	153
27 Jun	Pellagra Scurvy (3d time)		156

10 July	Sore feet and mouth		158
8 Aug	*Beri-beri* some edema sore eyes	"beri beri again"	158
15 Aug	*Weigh 115 pounds*	"no energy – no mental ability"	159
15 Aug	*Hunger headaches Beri-beri*	"no malaria or amoebic at present"	159
20 Aug	*Sore and cut feet*	"bare feet – cuts – sores—misery"	162
30 Sep	*Beri-beri* Pellagra worse Constant sunburn Burnt testicles	"beri beri so so" "pellagra worse"	163
8 Oct	*Weigh 119 pounds*		164

Fleeger also mentioned having "constant sunburn" and also "burnt testicles" caused by vitamin deficiencies.

Causations
Poor food, lack of protein, lack of Vitamin C, extreme sun exposure because of inadequate clothing, insect bites.

Note

Pages listed refer to the typed *Fleeger Diary*.

Appendix V

Fleeger Telegram, Christmas 1941

"No news."

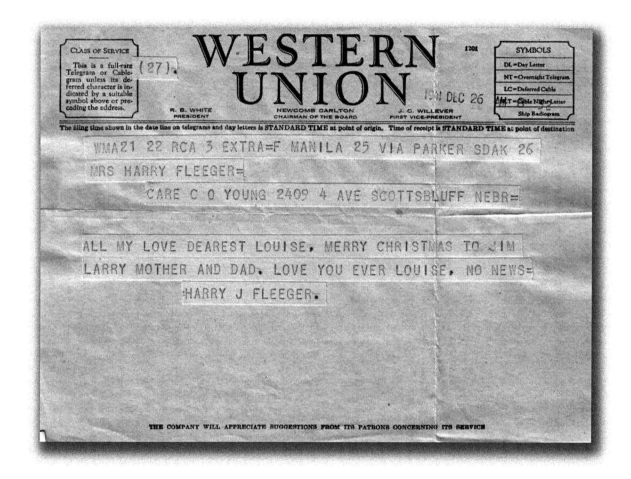

Appendix W

Extract Fleeger Letter, Bataan, 27 Feb 1942

"Not much news..."

Friday - Feb. 27 — '42 -

My Dearest Louise — I wrote to you about 10 days ago but will repeat in this letter — with the hope that at least one — will reach you eventually. We hear that some mail is going thru — I wrote a few notes in Dec. — not very well written — and alarming no doubt — for which I am very sorry. I know now that your concern should never have been added to by any remarks of mine. —

Not much news I can give you since it has to be censored. — I was promoted to Major Dec. 19 — and at once increased your allotment to 300 effective Jan 1. If it isn't increased to that, inquire by wire to Finance Officer — Wash. D.C. Jim & Bill also promoted. As you can imagine I will need everything new when I come home so will let my share accumulate to help with that. I have thought so often of

Appendix X

Fleeger Letter, Cabanatuan, 2 March 1944

"Am still well and hopeful..."

March 2, 1944

My Darling s:

What a Washington's Birthday! 21 letters--my first
during captivity. Six Frances, two Doris, two Betty,
three Dolly, one each Annie, Mary, Cliff, Aunt Bessie,
Marian Ennis, Lucy, the Nichols, Steve McDonough. I
was among the luckiest in number and variety. All probably on Gripsholm, the grand mercy ship! No package yet
but hoping soon. Much interest in your comments on conten
tents. My wife wise woman to put in pipe and sewing kit.
And how I have changed as prisoner! Wait until you see
patches on my pants and other sewing! You don't know
your Daddy! Grand news re Betty, Bugs, Dolly and Chris,
your home in Decatur, and activities. How hungry I was
for it! My soul feasted! How I'd love to see Dougie
and Patty! I loved Doris letters. Only pictures Dolly
on horse--lovely! Please send others, I lost all mine.
So glad you are enjoying joint interests with other "prison widows." Have been able to pass on some your comments
re friends. Am still well and hopeful. My life not dull.
Much good reading, healthy amount of work and some
writing. Much verse--expect to have book. Here is small
bit: "When twilight falls and silence calls To evening
prayer, Fair forms appear and hover near About my chair;
Soft hands entwine themselves in mine, Lips touch my face;
Then miles are not, and times forgot, As souls embrace."
Type in eight lines as indicated--title: "Love Wins."
Please answer all letters listed and thank writers.
Marian's letter beautiful. So happy we anticipated Betty's grad. present. Only sad news Puddles and Steve.
My love to Mother, Father, all dear friends. Keep busy
and cheerful and believe in me. Time passes. It can't
be so much longer now. We'll make up for this in happines
later. Love,

Daddy.

This is the last letter received from Harry Fleeger that remains in the family files.

Appendix Y

Weissblatt Letter, 10 March 1945

United Press Associations
INCORPORATED IN NEW YORK
GENERAL OFFICES
NEWS BUILDING NEW YORK CITY

Written From
PHILADELPHIA BUREAU
705 INQUIRER BUILDING
PHILADELPHIA 30, PA.

March 10th, 1945

DEAR Mrs. FLEEGER:

PLEASE EXCUSE my tardiness but I hAVE been trying to get into A hospital in New York And its tAking time. Gosh! Its Almost As hArd trying to break into A bone-setting joint in this pArt of the world As it is trying to break out of jAil in the Philippines.

As I told you in my wire, Harry wAs okay when I sAw him just before hE went to JApAn. HE wAs with PAul Jones of the 26th And that ship ArrivEd in JApAn Alright, all other rumors notwithstAnding. I Am surE of that As I sAw the list that the JAps in Nippon sEnt back to Bilibid.

Harry's morAle wAs high when I sAw him And he wAs About 135-140 in weight. HE And PAul had A chAnce to pick up lots of cornmeal before they left And wE had lots of pArties during their stAy in Bilibid.

Do not worry About him as I Am sure that he will come thru this Alright. We hAve heard from reliAble sources that the prisoners in JApAn ArE bEing well treAted. The chAnces ArE that Harry And the other field officers hAve been tAken to WAinwright's cAmp in MAnchuriA. They all hAd hEAvy clothing issued to them when they left ManilA. They wEre JAp uniforms but that does'nt mAtter so long as they men ArE Able to keEp wArm.

PLEASE cAll on me At anytime for xxxx anything that you xxx wish. I Am going bAck to the PAcific ArEa After my operation---thAt will bE in About four months. The Dr. sAys that I will bE in the hospital About three months. In Any cAsE, mE for the FAr EAst As soon as possible. I wAnt to go into JApAn with the forces And look up some friends. One in pArticulAr has A vEry good wAtch that used to belông to mE And I wAnt to get it back. My vEry best regArds to you And Harry's Mother ↓ Dad.

Sincerely
Franz Weissblatt
FrAnz Weissblatt

I just rerEAd your lEtter. About the broAdcast. Harry did not mAke onE while in Bilibid so I guess that it wAs mAde in JApAn. The October boAt WAS NOT sunk. The survivors that Arrived in the StAtes werE on A ship that left LasAng, MindAnao with 800 aboArd And wAs torpedoEd in SeptEmber. There ArE a series of Articles running in COLLIERS mAgazine right now written by three other survivors of thAt sAmE boAt. So you see---the whole darn story has been misquoted or the men hAve forgotten dAtes. I hAve bEen trying to get permission from the WAr DepArtment to xxx write A corrected story on this mAtter. Am going to WAshington MondAy to follow up this Angle.

FW

Notes

[1] *Shinyo Maru* statistics generally agree. Kerr, *Surrender*, 198-200 gave the figures of 750 embarked and 82 survivors. Michno, *Hellships*, 226 and 230, reported that "about 750" POWs were on the ship, 82 survived, and one died on the beach. Mazza, "The American Prisoners of War Rescued" (2/25/2006), listed 83 survivors, with one dying on the beach, (3 of 13). On 27 October, the USS *Narwhal* evacuated 81 survivors. One remained behind to fight as a guerrilla.

[2] See footnote 7 in Chapter Ten for more *Arisan Maru* information. *See also* Bill Bowen's *Arisan Maru* Roster (www.west-point-org/family/japanese-pow/Bowen_AM.htm).

[3] See footnote 8 in Chapter Ten for more *Oryoku Maru* information.

[4] *Enoura Maru* statistics vary. Kerr, *Surrender*, 231 listed 450 POWs in the upper hold and 900 in the lower hold for a total of 1,350 on the ship in the harbor of Takao when the Americans struck the ship. He reported that 200 men died instantly in the forward hold where about 600 from the lower hold had been moved, 232-3. Eventually, nearly 300 dead were removed from the ship, 234. Michno, *Hellships*, 317 listed 316 deaths out of 1,070 who left the Philippines on the ship. Another 250 were transferred to the ship from the *Brazil Maru* before the Americans hit the ship, 316.

[5] *Brazil Maru* statistics vary. Kerr, *Surrender*, 234 reported that 1,000 of the original 1,619 from the *Oryoku Maru* departed on the *Brazil Maru*. He added that about 500 of the 1,619 arrived in Japan on 29 January and over 100 died within the next weeks, 237. He reported that fewer than 300 survived the war, 237. Michno, *Hellships*, 265 said that "no more than 900 prisoners" (another entry said 925 POWs, 317) embarked on the *Brazil Maru* and that 450 POWs landed in Japan.

[6] Brown, *Oryoku Maru Story*, listed 271 survivors.

[7] Organization derived from *Fleeger Diary* and from Chandler, "26th Cavalry", *ACJ*, Mar-Apr 1947, Number 1, 10-11.

[8] Organization derived from *Fleeger Diary* and from Chandler, "26th Cavalry," *ACJ*, Mar-Apr 1947, Number 1, 10-11.

[9] Chandler, "26th Cavalry," *ACJ*, May-Jun, 12-13 and Jul-Aug, 16-17 and 21.

[10] *Diary*, 53-55.

[11] *ABMC Website*. Search results for 26 CAV REGT/PS. Listing of casualties from the 26th Cavalry.

[12] Colonel Eustaquio S. Baclig, *1989 USMA Register*, Class of November 1918, #6195, 322, *1943 Army Register*, 160, *ABMC Website*, and *NARA Website*. Personal information found in Cullum File #6195.

[13] *ABMC Website*. Search results for 26 CAV REGT/PS. Listing of casualties from the 26th Cavalry.

[14] *1943 Army Directory*, 315 listed Juan S. Moran, O14791, as a "colonel (major, PS), Cav), missing in action." *AMBC Website* lists his date of death, assignment to the 26th Cavalry, and decorations.

[15] "Mukden Train Evacuation Rosters," http://www.mansell.com/pow_resources/camplists/china hk/mukden, accessed 1/21/2008. See also *NARA Website* for overall details.

[16] Career details found in Mark M. Wohlfeld, "Chronological Record of Military Service," 4 typed pages, copy in possession of author. See also Knox, *Death March*, 99, 110, 112, 127, 132, fn 461, and Kerr, *Surrender & Survival*, 85, fn 195.

[17] "Letter Lt Colonel Mark M. Wohlfeld, AUS-Retired to 1st Cavalry Division Association, 16 June 1975," possession of author. Wohlfeld wrote: "I belong to THE VETERAN CORPS OF ARTILLERY MILITARY SOCIETY OF THE WAR OF 1812. This is a quasi-military ceremonial unit of the State of New York Guard. I am a Captain, Headquarters Battery Commandant. On June 14th, LTC BRADLEY invited a detachment of our Unit up to West Point to do some ceremonial cannon firing. We wore our 1812 uniforms. We fired 13 rounds (Blank) from each mountain pack Howitzer following which we were personally greeted by the Commanding General...."

[18] 200th or 515th Coast Artillery Regiment personnel confirmed in NM Names Project at http://www angelfire.com/nm/bcmfofnm/names/a.html.

[19] *1989 USMA Register*, 371-76, *ABMC Website*. For Jinsen and Mukden survivors, see http://people.tamu.edu/~jwerickson/POW/BMFk-1roster.html and http://people.tamu.edu / ~jwerickson /POW/BMFk-3roster.html (2/25/2006).

[20] Michno, *Hellships*, 174.

Selected Bibliography

Primary Sources

Association of Graduates, U. S. Military Academy. *Cullum Files.*

> *Provides additional information about several West Point officers. Some files include personal data sheets prepared by the graduates and personal notes and letters Generally includes entries from class yearbooks (Howitzers), press clippings, biographical information, and obituaries.*

Babcock, Lt. Colonel David S. *Diary of Lieut. Colonel D. S. Babcock. U. S. Army, American Prisoner of War Camp Cabanatuan, Phil. Islands*

> *Short, useful diary of a non-survivor - Fleeger's boss in the Cabanatuan Library.*

Bradley, Amelia M. and John H. Bradley. *MacArthur Moon*, unpublished manuscript.

> *Provides an account of internment in the University of Santo Tomas in Manila.*

Chandler, Lt. Colonel William E. "26th Cavalry (PS) Battles to Glory," *Armored Cavalry Journal*, March-April, May-June, and July-August 1947.

> *The former Regimental Operations Officer – and Fleeger's friend and classmate - reported the regiment's actions on Luzon and Bataan, 1941-1942.*

Fleeger, Major Harry J. *Diaries of Major Harry Fleeger* (3)

> *The three diaries used for this story.*

_____ Papers of Harry Fleeger

> *Valuable pre-war information as well as some war information.*

Fleeger Family Papers

> *Newspaper clippings, photographs, and other useful information.*

Hopkins, Armand. *Prisoner of War, 1942-1945, Reminiscences of Armand Hopkins*, c. 1984, 100-101. Unpublished manuscript. Copy in Special Collections, West Point Library.

> *Surviving POW's manuscript. Useful complement to Fleeger's diary.*

Knox, Donald. *Death March, The Survivors of Bataan* (NY: Harcourt Brace Jovanovich, Publishers, 1981)

> *Provides POW comments about the Death March, POW camps, Hellships, and their returns home. Provides information about 26th Cavalry officers and some of Fleeger's friends.*

Lapham, Robert and Bernard Norling. *Lapham's Raiders, Guerrillas in the Philippines, 1942-1945* (Lexington, KY: The University Press of Kentucky, 1996)

> *Tells the story of an important guerrilla leader on Luzon who was associated with many of the officers mentioned in Fleeger's diary.*

Olson, Colonel John E. *O'Donnell. Andersonville of the Pacific* (John Olson, 1985)

> *A POW survivor presents a gripping history of the atrocious Japanese POW Camp. Also, provides valuable personnel statistics.*

Ramsey, Edwin Price and Stephen J. Rivele. *Lieutenant Ramsey's War, From Horse Soldier to Guerrilla Commander* (Washington: Brassey's, 1996)

> *Ramsey recalls his service with the 26th Cavalry Regiment (PS) on Bataan and as a guerrilla.*

Svihra, Albert. *Diary of Albert Svihra, U.S.M.A. Class of 1922.* Unpublished manuscript. Copy in Special Collections, West Point Library.

> *One of Fleeger's POW friends, a non-survivor. Useful complement to Fleeger's Diary.*

Tarkington, Colonel H. W. *There Were Others.* Unpublished manuscript in possession of author.

> *Provides useful information about the officers of the 26th Cavalry Regiment (PS) detailed to service in the Visayas and on Mindanao.*

Whitcomb, Edgar R. *Escape from Corregidor (NY: Regnery, 1958)*

> *Tells the story of Whitcomb's escape from Corregidor and return to the Philippines in 1945.*

Special Directories

American Battle Monuments Commission Website (ABMC Website)

> *Provides information about American and Filipino casualties buried or memorialized in American cemeteries administered by the American Battle Monuments Commission.*

Army Directory, April 20, 1943 (Washington: War Department, 1943) (*1943 Army Directory*)

> *Lists information about all U. S. Army regular officers who were known to be alive at the time. Identifies the officers who were known POWs.*

Association of Graduates, U. S. Military Academy. *Register of Graduates and Former Cadets, U. S. Military Academy, 1802-1989 and other editions.* (*1989 USMA Register*)

> *Provides basic biographical and genealogical information about graduates.*

National Archives Website for World War II POWs (*NARA Website*)

> *Provides information about nearly all the American POWs, about POWs from different units, and about POWs in various camps. Invaluable for finding out information about POWs in smaller camps.*

Secondary Sources

Chang, Iris. *The Rape of Nanking,* (NY: Basic Books, 1997)

> *Tells the story about Japanese operations in China and their terrible treatment of the Chinese.*

Daws, Gavan. *Prisoners of the Japanese (NY: William Morrow, 1994)*

    Provides a comprehensive history of the allied POWs of the Japanese.

Kerr, E. Bartlett. *Surrender and Survival, The Experience of American POWs in the Pacific 1941-1945* (NY: William Morrow and Company, Inc., 1985)

    POW son tells the story about American POWs of the Japanese.

Falk, Stanley L. *Bataan. The March of Death* (NY: W. W. Norton & Company, Inc., 1962)

    U. S. Army Historian tells a graphic story about the Bataan Death March and provides cogent analyses about the causes of the march.

Michno, Gregory F. *Death on the Hellships, Prisoners at Sea in the Pacific War* (Annapolis, MD; Naval Institute Press, 2001)

    Provides detailed information about the POW ships and many of the survivors.

Morton, Louis. *The Fall of the Philippines*, (Washington: GPO, 1953)

    U. S. Army Historian provides the best history about the American defeat in the Philippines.

Norling, Bernard. *The Intrepid Guerrillas of North Luzon* (Lexington, KY: The University Press of Kentucky, 1999)

    Reports the unusual history of Troop C, 26th Cavalry Regiment (PS) which never surrendered and became a guerrilla unit.

Roper, Richard S. *Brothers of Paul, Activities of Prisoner of War Chaplains In the Philippines during WW II* (Odenton, MD: Revere Printing, 2003)

    Provides valuable information about the many chaplains covered in the story.

Photo & Map Credits

Photos

- Fleeger Family Photographs from the James Fleeger Collection.

- Photographs of the Manila Cemetery, Tablets of the Missing, and Graves and photos of the Punchbowl Cemetery and Tablets of the Missing in Honolulu from the John H. Bradley Photo Collection.

- Photo/Illustration on 263, *The Sunday Star*, Washington, DC, February 20, 1944, Gravure Section, 1.

Maps

- Maps 1-6
  Base Map of Luzon (Army Map Service, AMS-2, Northern Luzon, Series 5306), John H. Bradley Map Collection.

  Graphics and annotations by John H. Bradley

People Index

About the Author

John Bradley was born and raised in the Philippines. He and his parents became civilian POWs of the Japanese and spent thirty-seven months in Santo Tomas Internment Camp in Manila until rescued by the 1st Cavalry Division in February 1945. His father did not survive.

He graduated from the U. S. Military Academy and was commissioned an infantry officer in the U. S. Army. A parachutist and a Ranger, he served with the 1st Cavalry Division in Korea, the 82nd and 101st Airborne Divisions, XVIII Airborne Corps, and the Airborne Department of the Infantry School in the United States, and as a military field advisor in Vietnam. After retiring from the Army, he worked for corporations in Texas and California. In 1996, he opened a business in Houston.

After earning a MA in History from Rice University, Bradley returned to West Point where taught military history, wrote *The Second World War, Asia and the Pacific,* developed and presented a special lecture about General Douglas MacArthur, and spent four years managing projects associated with the Bicentennial of the American Revolution. Since 2001, he has taught courses in U. S. History and World War II at the University of Houston-Downtown. He also has taught courses about World War II and the Cold War for the Center for the American Idea and at the Glasscock School of Continuing Education at Rice University.

He continues to research and write military history.

Benny Havens

From Nevada's hoary ridges, from stormy coasts of Maine,
From Lava Beds and Yellow Stone the Story never waned;
Wherever duty called, they went, their steps were never slow,
With "Alma Mater," on their lips and "Benny Havens, Oh."

When this life's troubled sea is o'er and our last battle's through,
If God permits us mortals there his blest domain to view,
Then we shall see in glory crowned, in proud celestial row,
The friends we've known and loved so well at Benny Havens, Oh!

Bugle Notes
United States Military Academy
1928-1929